MORE TAILS OF
THE FIFTIES

ANOTHER ANTHOLOGY OF
AVIATION MEMORIES

PUBLISHED BY:
Cirrus Associates (S.W.),
Kington Magna,
Gillingham,
Dorset,
SP8 5EW, UK.

ISBN 0 951 5598 4 2

PRINTED IN ENGLAND BY:
The Book Factory,
35-37 Queensland Road,
London N7 7AH.

PHOTO SCANNING BY:
Castle Graphics Ltd.,
Nunney,
Nr. Frome,
Somerset,
BA11 4LW.

SOLE DISTRIBUTORS:
Cirrus Associates (S.W.),
Kington Magna,
Gillingham,
Dorset,
SP8 5EW.

COVER PHOTOS:
Four aircraft tails (Nos. 1, 3, 5 & 6): Peter Amos
Two aircraft tails (Nos. 2 & 4) & cloud background: Peter Campbell

EDITOR'S ACKNOWLEDGEMENTS

I would like to acknowledge with grateful thanks the help of the following persons, in purely alphabetical order, without whom this book could not have been completed (again, I hope I've not forgotten anyone!):

Peter Amos, Ambrose Barber, Jane Bellamy, Vivian Bellamy, Lewis Benjamin, Dennis Bird, John Blake, Chris Button, Honor Campbell, James Campbell, John Cooper, Jack Da-Costa, Chris Dearden, Clive Elton, Tony Farrell, Tim Foster, Ted Gould, Alan Hartfield, Mike Hooks, A.J. Jackson (via Air-Britain), Olive Marmol, Bernard Martin, Rex Nicholls, Arthur Ord-Hume, Christopher Paul, Ranald Porteous, John Pothecary, Anthony Preston, Richard Riding, Mike Stroud, John de Uphaugh, Tim Webb.

DEDICATIONS

It is very sad to have to report that two of the prospective authors for this book are no longer with us, which serves to emphasise one of the main reasons for compiling this book in the first place – my feeling that one should record these personal memories about flying while it is still possible.

Both the men who have passed on were real 'characters,' 'legends' even, in the world of aviation over many decades, and indeed they had been heroes of mine ever since my schooldays, but I had never met either of them personally until 1997.

The first, "Ladi" Marmol, died at the beginning of November 1997, before he had an opportunity to commit to paper any more of his varied aviation experiences. His widow Olive has very kindly agreed to allow me to include a few words about him below.

The second, Vivian Bellamy, passed away at the end of February 1998; he had had a stroke during the autumn of 1997, but seemed sprightly enough when I chatted with him about the book in November, a few weeks later. His contribution is included by kind permission of his widow Jane.

"LADI" MARMOL

"Ladi" was a well-known and respected figure in aviation (both in this country and overseas) for some five decades; gliders were undoubtedly his first love, but he is also remembered for his air racing skills and his many exploits, especially with Miles Aerovans, in the fifties. However it should not go unrecorded that he had many ongoing business interests in aviation right up to the end of his life – he never tired of flying.

Finding a letter from him in an aviation magazine early in 1997, I had written to him to ask if he would consider contributing to a chapter about Aerovans in our forthcoming book, which he agreed to do with a enthusiasm which pleasantly surprised me as he didn't know me from Adam! However I am sure that such enthusiasm was customary for him, as was evidenced by the fact that he and his wife Olive took the trouble to come all the way from Essex to our Vintage Flying Weekend at Old Sarum for the launch of the book. He seemed to thoroughly enjoy himself regaling us all with stories, and I could not resist asking him if he would like to contribute some more of these to *this* book which, without hesitation, he agreed to do. Sadly, it was not to be.

VIVIAN BELLAMY

Ted Gould, who was a friend of Vivian's over many years, offers this tribute:

"I got to know Vivian during the fifties at Eastleigh and Christchurch. Because of our mutual interest in flying we quickly formed a close and lasting friendship; he was always ready to share, and my wife and I enjoyed several flights abroad with him and other Club members. He was an excellent and (dare I say) adventurous pilot; life was certainly never dull in his company! Being ex-Navy he also retained an interest in boats and had a small cabin cruiser, whose facilities he was most happy to share with his many friends.

But he was really single-minded about building aeroplanes. The projects he started over the years (most of which were also finished!) were so numerous that they now seem hard to believe; but many still exist, either flying or in museums, and will remain witnesses to his passion for anything that flew.

I feel a great loss in his passing. Like everyone else who knew him, I was deeply affected by his encouragement, his boundless enthusiasm and his generosity. He was truly one of the 'greats' of his time."

*   *   *

"Ladi" and Vivian, both of you are sadly missed: mainly by your families, of course, with whom we deeply sympathise, but also by all those who were fortunate enough to have come into contact with you during your long and productive careers.

CONTENTS

PREFACE

by

Peter Campbell

During the winter of 1996-7, when I began to put together *"Tails of the Fifties,"* I had little idea of what the appeal of such a book might be. I was working on the hunch that there must be some people apart from myself who might appreciate an aviation book that was not about World War II, and that was fairly light and enjoyable to dip into rather than being just a collection of factual material; in other words, a "good read," the sort of book that you manage a chapter of before you go to sleep (cause and effect?), take on holiday with you, or give to your real friends!

My hunch must have been fairly accurate, as we have had a number of encouraging reviews in the aeronautical press, and also some very kind personal comments about the book; indeed, so much so that a number of the contributing authors have agreed to come up with a further supply of experiences for this sequel. Also, having established some sort of track record, it was not too difficult to persuade some other worthy and well-known names to contribute.

And so now we have "More Tails of the Fifties," by no means an imaginative title, but nevertheless still an appropriate one, I feel. The general formula is much as before; I have again stretched the decade of the fifties to include any time post-war up to the early sixties, and although the emphasis is still mainly on light aircraft there are several chapters on service flying and associated experiences from around the world.

At a time when there are moves from all sorts of directions, official and otherwise, to curtail the use of, or even close, a number of our civil airfields and private strips, it seems that the activities of recreational flying and general aviation need all the support they can get, not just from those who fly, but from all the genuine enthusiasts who give support from ground-level by attending displays, rallies, fly-ins and so on.

And yet it has been reported in the media that attending Flying Displays is one of the most popular leisure activities in this country; in numbers, apparently even more people attend than go to football matches. So large-scale support for flying in its broadest sense *does* exist, although many people who are happy to travel to events at Duxford,

9

Fairford, Farnborough, Biggin Hill and Cranfield would doubtless not approve at all if they happened to live close by – it's probably the NIMBY effect rearing its head once again. Also I find it difficult to understand why people *choose* to come and live in an area near an established airfield, and *then* complain once they are there. Some old-established airfields were in existence even before the concept of planning permission had been thought of.

So if we are among those who enjoy the freedom of the skies in one way or another, let us therefore do all we can to support private flying and general aviation as rewarding, challenging and yet safe leisure and business activities.

I'll now come off my soap-box and let you enjoy this latest collection of personal aviation memories from those who were 'there at the time.'

FOREWORD

by

Air Commodore Christopher Paul

It is a privilege to be invited to write a foreword to this book. Its galaxy of contributors, all distinguished in various ways in our sort of flying, ensures that it will comprise a unique record of the times. Its dedications to "Ladi" Marmol and to Vivian Bellamy are fitting tributes to two enthusiasts whose great love was flying.

It was at Hucknall in 1927 that the Grainger brothers, lace-makers in Nottingham, introduced me to their first home-built. A tiny biplane, its inverted Vee-twin ABC motor-bike engine lacked the power to get it airborne. This problem we solved with a car-powered launch, towing with a rope tied to the undercarriage. Thus exciting hops under auxiliary power became possible, and from that moment I was 'hooked.'

Since then I have flown many kinds of aeroplane: big and small, seaplanes and sailplanes, some very fast, some just hang-gliders. All have been interesting and most enjoyable. But happiest of all have been those able to float one up into a sky shared with the quiet graceful flight of birds: such as the graceful German Weihe sailplane, which I first flew after the end of the war, and my Druine Turbulent, so carefully fitted to me by Norman Jones, in which I escaped hours of tedious travel on dusty roads.

Today we have airlines carrying millions of uncaring passengers worldwide. We have air forces able to deliver all sorts of devastating weapons and, supporting them, great industries. Their importance and publicity dominates aviation news.

It seems to me, therefore, that a book of this kind has a special importance. It reminds us of where it all began: a desire to fly and a love of flying for flying's sake. This, I am sure, is what our kind of flying is all about. It is why many save and scrape to be able to afford to fly, and why many spend months and years building their own small aeroplane.

I hope that this book, telling the stories of those who have got into flying and love it, will both entertain and instruct. But, more importantly, I hope it will prove an encouragement and an inspiration to the next generation upon whom so much depends.

CHAPTER 1

SOME TIGER CLUB MEMORIES

by

John Blake

Apart from an all-too-brief love affair in 1944 with the first of the three aircraft I have owned (which is another and highly improbable story), I first became seriously involved with aircraft at Croydon, where, in October 1957, I joined the Tiger Club as a passenger member – almost the only one in those days. I joined at the same time as Wing Commander "Titch" Holmes, who became a pillar of the club, and through his connections with Lloyd's and others was the first person really to convince the insurance world that you did not have to be insane or have a death wish to insure light aircraft.

Titch was a most extraordinary man. He was very small and very quiet and never talked about himself, but brought to the club an unspoken but solid influence, through the Committee, on how we behaved ourselves.

Before the war he had flown Dragon Rapides for the Hon. Mrs Victor Bruce. She kept a fleet of them – I think at Hanworth – and apart from charter work Titch and others used to fly them into Paris just before dawn, landing in the twilight on the straight at Longchamps race course and delivering that morning's London papers for the big hotels and embassies.

When the war started, Titch, in the Reserve of Officers at that time, was impressed into the RAF along with a silver and black Olley Air Services Rapide from Croydon and found himself flying it to, from and around France as personal pilot to Air Marshal "Ugly" Barrett, AOC Advanced Air Sriking Force. After Dunkirk, when the bulk of remaining British Forces, Army and RAF, were falling back to the west and eventual evacuation from Cherbourg and other ports, he found himself employed, with his faithful Rapide (which in the stress of the times was still in its pre-war silver: indeed it was some time before Titch's new RAF uniforms caught up with him) on various odd tasks. On one occasion the seats were removed and the cabin filled with large quantities of highly-sensitive proximity fuses, packed between wet blankets, to supply to the ack-ack guns, Titch having to land, without previous acquaintance, on any field that presented itself at his destination with his touchy cargo.

Profiting by his pre-war experience he also used the Rapide, after the evacuation, to land on Longchamps racecourse at night and collect or deposit various people, the 'runway' nicely defined by the white rails. When he told me the story in his office in the City in 1958 – and I don't know that it has ever been told anywhere else – he made it sound terribly simple. With long extensions to the exhaust pipes the Rapide rumbled in very quietly and "any Germans a couple of fields away would have taken it for a belated motorcycle."

He was scathing about the later operations: "people rushing about all over the place flashing torches and making enough noise to wake the dead."

He considered the Lysander quite the wrong aircraft for that sort of thing, although recently I came across a pre-war flight test report by Titch on the Lysander after the annual Hendon display, and he was quite enthusiastic about it.

Titch served the Tiger Club well, becoming a senior check pilot and incidentally doing a lot of valuable work advising on and test-flying John Taylor's Monoplane and its successor – curiously enough called the Taylor Titch.

Flying at Croydon in those days was enormous fun. The Tiger Club was based in the Rollason hangar – Norman Jones, who had founded the club after the 1956 Air Racing Dinner, was involved with Rollasons – and we shared the area at the end of the hangar line with the compass platform, the Surrey Flying Club (run by Peter Chinn, "Tiny" Marshall – an ex-London bus driver – and a charming man called Pete Langton, who flew around deserts for oil companies) and the Airways Aero Club, very up-market with their Chipmunks.

Most of the early pilots in the Tiger Club were recently ex-RAF with a considerable number of hours per head or senior airline captains and such-like grandees, and the club ran with military precision. Each morning the Tigers, some seven or eight of them, were lined up outside the Rollason hangar, wheels aligned with the edge of the tarmac, cowlings opened ready for the DI. All the pilots wore white overalls and helmets, and the aircraft taxied out, took off, flew, landed and taxied in, in formation. Would you believe we had to stop this eventually? Other clubs were getting inferiority complexes and accused us of deliberately upsetting them.

One piece of aggression from another club had quite different origins. A.J. Jackson, who produced the monumental Putnam books on civil aircraft in Britain, was sitting in his "Tigger," engine running, waiting the statutory five minutes for the oil to wake up, when the aircraft began to vibrate. It got steadily worse and "Jacko" shut down in rather a hurry. However, the shaking continued somewhere behind him and he discovered an Airways Chipmunk chewing its way steadily up his fuselage, the pupil pilot too overcome to switch off.

One could go on for ever about the Tiger Club, but I promise I won't. Once we had started the displays, of course, the most extraordinary things began to happen as members' imaginations gathered speed. The first display I remember was on the Isle of Wight, and it was in the course of a joyride with Tony Oldham that I was shown how to spin a Tiger's wheels on the water . . .

The Tiger Club home-from-home on the island was then, and for many years to come, Bembridge Airport at the eastern end, where a modest private firm operated which in time became world-famous as Britten-Norman, creators of the Islander. Des Norman himself and Tony Oldham, with others, were in the early days flying Tigers all over the place for Crop Culture (Aerial) Ltd (Britten-Norman's spraying firm). They also flew Meteors at weekends in a celebrated Auxiliary squadron and nobody knew more about aggressive low-level flying in Tigers than they did. One of their display specialities was balloon-bursting; the balloons were inflated in the Tiger Club's Land Rover beside the runway and "Fitz" Fitzmaurice, who looked after a lot of the admin for us and during the week, as far as I recall, made corsets, would collect one in each hand and walk out onto the runway to release them. Des and Tony would lurk about behind the hill at one end and pounce on him from behind. It was very spectacular and has never been done better since. So much so that when Des enquired cheerfully how it had gone on one occasion, Fitz replied, rather tartly: "You're supposed to wait until I let go!"

Shortly after this episode I recall overhearing Des and Tony discussing quite seriously whether they could get their Meteors into Bembridge. As Bembridge was a short grass field sloping downhill towards the sea it is probably a good thing that the subsequent disbanding of the Royal Auxiliary Air Force prevented them from trying.

Virtually all the routines in the celebrated Tiger Club displays were worked out in those early days. Formation flying soon led to tied-together formation routines with the Tigers, quickly copied by the Turbulents as they began to accumulate. Any new events that were not actively dangerous were encouraged by Norman Jones, founder and Chairman, and if they involved a stand-up fight with the Ministry so much the better. It was after such a battle that we got approval for 'SOW' – Standing on the Wing (later referred to by some as "Girl on the Wing," as if 'SOW' was a dirty word).

In actual fact, we got permission to use the routine (which was originally proposed and flown by "Benjy" (see the end of this book for comment by him) because the girl was not standing on the *wing* (which was illegal) but on the centre-section fuel tank of the Tiger (which apparently was not so illegal), so both sides thought they'd won.

Inevitably, two routines merged and for several seasons the spectators could watch a young lady on the top wing/centre-section of a Tiger holding in each hand a beflagged cord, to the end of which was attached a Turbulent. There was another early SOW item that with careful help from the commentator (which was usually myself) could rouse strong emotions in the crowd. It involved a large parachutist called George Bottomer ("Colonel Crackshot") on top of the Tiger, taking pot-shots at tethered balloons set up between him and the crowd with a massive ·45 Webley revolver. Blanks in the gun and detonators in the balloons produced excellent results and if you mentioned that he was really using live ammunition . . .

One of the most spectacular routines was a crazy-flying sequence in which, at the top of a loop, the pilot apparently fell out, descending by parachute, while the "empty" aircraft flew off. This was only possible with Mike Reilly, the top British parachutist, who was small enough to crouch down in the rear cockpit and tough enough to stay there through Neil Williams' aerobatics. It was especially effective at Rochester where Neil disappeared into the the valley over the M2 and snuck away. Sadly, it ceased with the death of Mike when filming *The War Lover.*

There were a lot of items that never reached display presentation, largely because they frightened the participants or were just too difficult. Many involved SOW. I can remember Benjy standing on top of 'CDC holding a plastic bucket into which we attempted to lower a brick on a string from the Super Cub; *that* we never did get right. Barry Griffiths, one of the great characters from the early days at Redhill, where we fled when the Minister closed Croydon, was an early enthusiast for standing on top of aeroplanes, and thought up a routine of controlling a radio model from this position in close formation. That was abandoned, too, after he'd nearly brained himself with the thing. It was Barry who became, I think, the first person to fly across the Channel with a girl on top of the aircraft: an original start to a weekend in Le Touquet.

We tried bursting balloons set up on the ground like coconuts at a fair with Turb wingtips; on one occasion Ian Trethewey and I stood on the grass holding a very short pole (I thought) with one of those big car-wash Spontex sponges on top, while James Baring tried to remove that with *his* wingtip and Robin d'Erlanger tried picking up a handkerchief off the ground with *his.* Neither of those were repeated, but I think the only downright veto was when a gentleman from Brock's Fireworks turned up to fit electrically-fired rockets to James Baring's Turbulent.

Robin, incidentally, was the only person who has ever tried – very successfully – to ditch a Turbulent. An edict had come out grounding VW aircraft engines for quite a simple improvement in the oil supply. Robin's Turb had been in France when this had been announced and he was returning, escorted by Michael Jones in a radio-equipped Jodel, when the

16

engine failed in mid-Channel from lack of oil. As Robin said gleefully afterwards: "We were coming back to have it done, but I was too quick for them."

Summoned by Michael, a helicopter lifted him off the floating Turbulent, with literally only his feet wet, and dropped him at Manston, from where Michael collected him. The aircraft was rescued by a German tanker en route to Hamburg, which promptly put in a large claim for salvage. Fortunately the insurance company had been informed even more promptly.

"We've written it off; why don't you keep it?"

And that was the last we heard of that.

In those more relaxed days, when the whole Tiger Club used to fly off to France once a year to the Berck lunch (you could get Customs at Berck in them days, five kilometres south of Le Touquet), it was normal to cross the Channel at wave-top height – I have actually looked *up* at the Varne lightship – and continue at sand-dune-top height past Le Touquet to be out of the way of Silver City car ferries on finals. It worked very well.

The Turbulent team, which rapidly became something between an elite unit on its own and the "Bring-on-the-Clowns" bit in a circus is one part of the Tiger Club that has never changed to this day. Basically a four-ship formation that indulges in flour-bombing, streamer-cutting and flying under a ribbon between two quite short poles, it may have got more formal in recent years but I doubt it. Early highlights included a unique performance when the pilot of the Fleet Air Arm's Sea Fury, Lt. Cdr. Pete Sheppard, was persuaded late one evening in the hotel that the next day it would be possible for him to lead the Turb formation in the Fury. And that worked, too: the Fury with its nose in the air and pretty well full flap and what passed for nothing on the clock, the Turbs flat out and beyond. It was a really close formation, too; I remember John Taylor, then team leader, recalling that during the single pass at the show he was conscious of nothing but the appalling, deafening roar of the Centaurus exhaust in his ears.

In those days, I had two duties at displays; I was responsible for providing lunch for the pilots and ground crew, and I did the commentating. Lunch for thirty-odd people was no real problem, but the tins and boxes had to be distributed in the aircraft lockers for transport. Even with a primitive form of combat loading, there was always the dread that some essential items would be either stuck at Redhill or precautionary-landed en route, but I don't think they ever were.

Commentating was very laid-back and relaxed. Occasionally, of course, things went wrong or threatened to, but not often. Usually you just ignored it and talked about something else. Peter Phillips once had the embarrassment of stopping the prop in *"Ballerina,"* our Cosmic Wind racer, during an aerobatic sequence (Tiger Club aircraft *worked* for their living) at Fair Oaks. Following an exceptionally neat dead-stick landing on the runway, he subsequently thanked me for diverting the crowd from the incident by "directing their attention to some cows at the opposite end and starting a lecture on dairy farming."

It was at Fair Oaks, where the commentating position was on top of a thoroughly dangerous two-storey erection of scaffolding, that I discovered that with an off-crowd wind the Turbs were quiet enough for pilots to hear the commentary as they flew past. I had been rather letting myself go on the ancestry and personal habits of the pilots and after they had landed they came and took a pole each and tried to shake me off the tower. John "Harpo" Harper was leading that year. We had to empty our coffee flasks over them to make them go away. I say "we" as the other half of the commentary team, Stratton Richey, had just joined. I think he found commentating bewildering in those days but when I handed over Farnborough to him in 1996 he was beginning to get the hang of it.

It was at Farnborough, on one of the public days, either in 1960 or '61, I think, that I was commentating on a guest display by the Turb team when, halfway into the sequence, all four landed dead-stick in the middle of the airfield during the streamer-cutting. It turned out that Margo McKellar, who looked after the stores side of displays, and supplied the flour-bombing bags and the toilet rolls that were (and still are) used as streamers, had inadvertently bought some double-spliced super-fluffy special brand, and all four engines had their intakes completely choked. I can't remember what I said on that occasion, but I hope it was tactful.

One incident still remains a slight mystery to me; Neil Williams had perfected in his spare time – he was still in the RAF at Farnborough – an aerobatic display sequence that seemed to demand rather more than the average well-brought-up Stampe might be prepared to give, especially in the concluding one-and-a-half-flicks-from-inverted manoeuvre. It was at Biggin Hill that this bit went pear-shaped and the commentary concluded:

"Hello, he's taking it behind the hangar – and, by Jove, he's left it there!"

Or so I am informed by reliable witnesses; I have no recollection of saying it at all. Fortunately, unlike the Stampe, Neil emerged without injury.

It all seems a long time ago now, and of course it was, thirty-five years and more, but the spirit of the Club has not changed, thank goodness, even if some of the more ancient members don't get to Headcorn as often as we should. Must try and do better this year.

CHAPTER 2

HIGH-D-HIGH

by

Chris Dearden

PRELUDE

Just so's you know . . . Me first solo was in the Hawk Trainer G–AIYD at Redhill. It was 1440 hrs on the 14th November 1947 when I said to me instructor, I said: "I realise you may not think much of the situation as it stands at this present moment in time, what with the wings being sheared off short on account of I've just driven it through the hedge, like. But you will learn to thank me when you find 'ow it 'as increased the rate of roll at low altitude or, as we technical gentlemen say, 'decreased the moment of inertia about the rolling axis'."

"I'll decrease your moment of inertia about the toe of my boot when you get out of that aeroplane, my son," he riposted rudely.

"Be of good cheer," I smiled back, 'anding 'im a fragment of the fuselidge, what was also just the tiniest little bit broken. "See! It can all be stuck back together."

"Oh, I will stick it, my son," he said in a most unchristian manner. "Believe me, if it's the last thing I do I will stick it."

It was then that 'ee flung 'imself from the machine, beating upon the ground with 'is clenched fists and crying out in a loud voice: "I cannot take no more of this. I am off to become a nun."

Which I believe 'ee did do, an' I 'eard as 'ee was very 'appy with the arrangement.

An' that's 'ow I came to fly me first solo . . .

Well, that's how I imagined it might work out. That's what was swirling through my addled head as I sat at the end of the runway that bleak afternoon.

But all good trances come to an end. Fantasy had to give way to reality. This was the longed-for moment! Budge had disembarked and sauntered off with an experienced nonchalance. The moment hit me again: 'Nanny' was no longer there to hold my hand. I was on my own and wondering why the hell I'd ever said I wanted to fly in the first place.

Yet fly I did, though I bounced my first attempted landing almost to the Pearly Gates and back.

"If you get into trouble," Budge had said in parting, "remember, you've got a throttle. *Use it!*" . . . I used it. I *needed* it!

My second attempt was just a shade less grotesque, no doubt to the amazement of the worthy and watchful Budge. I'd done it! And that's the true story, folks. I know. I was there!

*　　*　　*

How high is high? As tall as from here to there I suppose. Depends on your viewpoint. From twenty-eight thousand feet, for example, a mere fourteen seems puny, a half-measure not worth mentioning. Pathetic, really.

I found myself brooding over this useless piece of homespun philosophy while I was on one of those excursion flights to Berlin when 'The Wall' was being opened. Our Tristar was way, way up in the wide blue yonder, sliding along at some phenomenal rate. Inside the cabin there was barely a whisper from the engines, not a tremor in the airframe. I was comfortable, warm, relaxed, a cup of coffee on the little table in front of me. Just too easy! A stewardess even nearly smiled at me in passing – I think. How easy could it get?

Maybe it was inevitable that I should have fallen prey to making an idle comparison. Memory drifted back to the late afternoon of 19th February 1949 when I was sitting up at fourteen thousand feet in a Magister – G-AIYC, from Redhill. Then I was frozen, shaken and distinctly stirred.

Although I'd secured my 'A' Licence in April '48, I'd flown as P1 on only two occasions since then, finances being what they were. So it wasn't surprising that Budge, my instructor, still regarded me as an unreliable entity, to put it kindly. Indeed, the very day the precious licence had arrived by post I'd bicycled out to the 'drome, feeling about ten feet tall. At last a cherished, childhood ambition had been realized; I was a *real* pilot!

"My licence has come," I'd said to Budge, a bit breathlessly, "I've got it here!"

He'd cut me down to about two inches tall with a single glance.

"Oh, good," he'd said, returning to the magazine he was reading. "Maybe now you can start learning to fly."

They didn't nurture over-confidence in the Redhill Flying Club. If the Min. of Civ. Av. in their unreasoning stupidity chose to call me a 'pilot' on the strength of three hours solo experience, that was their affair. As far as the Club was concerned I was . . . well, not very good.

But I was enthusiastic. And my 'A' (No.28241) grandly informed me that I was licensed to fly 'private flying machines . . . All types of landplanes.' *All* types. Wow! And what made a flying machine different from any other sort of machine? Why, that it could fly, of course! It could go up in the air. So the higher it went up in the air the more it was exploiting its unique quality. Logical? Well, it made sense to me at the time.

Besides, low flying was not smiled upon either by the population in general or the Club in particular. But who could grouse about high flying? The idea had been niggling at me for some time and I'd been putting a few shillings a week by for it. Three pounds an hour may sound Utopian now but it was over half a week's wages then – and living expenses devoured very nearly a whole week's wages at a time. Never mind, I'd give it a go.

Sure, the published figures gave "Maggie" a service ceiling of eighteen thousand feet. A brand spanking machine in experienced hands, probably. But what of a semi-clapped one in the hands of a sprog? That was what lured me on to find out.

As always, there was the weather to wait for. Merely to have a 'fine' day wouldn't do. To comply with VFR one had to stay at least two thousand feet vertically from all cloud. A clear sky was essential. 19th February 1949 came about as near as I reckoned I was going to get at that time of year. Horizontally, visibility wasn't brilliant, but it was good enough – the guideline was that if you could see Outwood windmill from the 'drome it was OK. Vertically there was a pretty uniform overcast, though obviously way above anywhere *I'd* be going. It was a dull, grey and cold day. But, for me, this had got to be it. And 'mum' was the word!

I presented myself to Budge, who was also Club Secretary, and asked if I could have a "Maggie."

"When did you last fly solo?" he enquired knowingly. The dreaded question!

"Just on two months ago."

He didn't hesitate. "I'll have to give you a check circuit first, then."

No doubt at all he was absolutely right. But here was the all-too-familiar poverty trap. The less often you could afford to fly, the more they insisted on a check circuit each time before they'd let you go off solo, licence or no licence. So the more the effective cost of your solo time, so the less often you could afford to fly. Brutally simple. A rich and loving widow would have been the only solution, but none ever came my way.

My log shows that I was twenty minutes with Budge that afternoon, suggesting that I'd had to do at least *two* check circuits. Clearly he was still not very impressed!

But at last he let me go with his usual, parting words of wisdom: "Have fun but don't make a nuisance of yourself to other people." The story of my life, except for the bit about having fun.

Paradoxically, the next forty-five minutes of my life were both boring and fascinating at the same time. Boring because the climb was a tedious affair, taken in stages with regular periods of level flight to rest the engine. Step by step we went. Bor-ing!

The fascination was of a technical nature (but not all *that* technical!). As someone who'd been interested in the theory of it I'd variously worked numerical examples and drawn graphs of – among other things – 'Horsepower Required' and 'Horsepower Available' . . .

"The student will note how, with increasing altitude, the 'power available' curves move downward and to the right, thus shortening the intercept on the 'power required' curve. This represents the reduction in speed range and the margin of power." . . . Duly noted (and I *did* once know what it all meant, honest!).

Eventually one could plot a 'power available' curve which just made a tangent to the underside of the 'power required' curve. That was it. Everything had converged to a single point; maximum speed, minimum speed, cruising speed and climbing speed were one and the same. Just enough power at full belt to hang in the air, and no more.

It'd been interesting enough to see it in theory on paper, but to have my backside in the driving seat, my frozen little mit on the stick and to feel it all happening for real was something else. No textbook could ever tell you this much.

Earlier in the climb the engine had protested a little and I reckoned this was just the onset of 'rich-cut.' The mixture needed to be leaned-off. 'IYC breathed a polite "Thank you" and showed a renewed willingness to climb.

But at around thirteen thousand feet she began to shudder. Maybe she was feeling as cold as I was. Maybe! In truth it was simply the recognised power-on stall warning (we'd been shown this as part of our tuition, though at a lesser altitude!). So this was about it. There was nothing I could do except check and re-check that I was flying the aeroplane as 'cleanly' as possible – no clumsy misalignment of the control surfaces causing extra drag, as was my common failing.

We were still climbing, slowly and painfully for both of us . . . Thirteen and a half . . . Fourteen . . . The shuddering had now become so uncomfortably marked that I felt it irresponsible to press on. My sneaking ambition to make fifteen thousand was not to be fulfilled. 'IYC had given her all, no matter what the published figure said. We seemed to be balancing right on that tangent point. Enough!

Here the Technician gave way to the Romantic. Never in a million years could I be a mountaineer yet here I could understand the feeling of being at a pinnacle, of savouring the moment, of facing the truth that there was nowhere to go but down.

I let the nose drop into the glide and hauled off the power. Beautiful; open to the elements and utterly alone in near-silence. The sky seemed immeasurably big, the ground – now just hazing-out – immeasurably far away. Not another living thing in sight. In spite of the cold and the slight pain in my ears I felt I was as near heaven as I was ever likely to get. A cynic might point out that the first symptom of oxygen starvation is a feeling of euphoria. At 14,000 ft? I think not. It just was glorious being up there.

Then, in a brief fit of idiotic bravado, I let the nose go on down and down and down until 'IYC was hanging vertically: a giant model on a sky-hook. After about 0.1 micro-seconds of it I suffered the pangs of severe apprehension and started a very, very cautious pull-out.

But I doubt if any eagle ever swooped with greater verve and joy than I did just then. Now just a touch of left-hand-down to keep the 'drome in sight. And so we went on in wide circles, round and down, now and then levelling off and giving the engine 1,900 revs to keep it warm and clear.

In those days (mercifully) we carried no radio, so there was a set pattern to be followed on return to the field – two thousand feet at the downwind end of the 'dead leg,' let down to one thousand at the upwind end, turn onto the first crosswind and join the circuit, if it were clear to do so. Eyes and common sense were the instruments to be used.

And I think even Budge might have approved of my eventual touch-down . . . For Gawd's sake keep it straight! I pumped at the rudder and only then realized that my feet were still attached to my legs. I thought they'd frozen solid and dropped off some way back. But, oh my knees! They'd set into a bent shape and seemed as if they intended to stay that way for the rest of my natural.

When I reported in, at 1705 hrs, Budge was not his usual, jovial self. No, sir! He met me with a stony glare and: "Where the hell have *you* been? We thought you'd got yourself lost. The CFI has gone off in the Auster looking for you."

"No," I said, quite honestly though maybe rather too cheerfully, "I was never out of sight of the field. I was straight over the top, here."

"Well, we couldn't see you."

"I was at fourteen thousand feet." I had no option but to confess.

Still I hoped the stony glare would soften into a moderately friendly scowl. It didn't. Instead, Budge winced like he'd just been set upon by an alien insect.

"Christ!" he exploded. "Don't tell me *that*. And don't ever do that again with one of our aeroplanes."

Well, I never did.

But as for the notion that I might one day be sitting in armchair comfort, in company with some three hundred other people, warm and relaxed, sipping coffee at around thirty thousand feet and five hundred knots and get almost smiled at by a stewardess . . . Ridiculous!

Pure science fiction, of course. Flying would never be like that – would it?

23

CHAPTER 3

AIR SERVICE TRAINING:

(HAMBLE IN THE FIFTIES)

by

Tony Farrell

I often think (with enormous nostalgia) about my many very happy flying days. Log books are wonderful for refreshing memories and even my pre-war experiences are as sharp and happy in my mind as the more recent ones.

The pre-war types I flew included the Drone G-AEEN; in 1936 I did seven hours in it! One flight from Hanworth to Ramsgate (60 miles) took me an hour and 55 minutes and I was passed by a Southern Railways train on the long straight from Reigate to Ashford! Other types which I enjoyed flying were the Spartan Arrow G-ABOB and the Miles Hawk Trainer G-AFEU in which I managed a climb to no less than 21,000 feet! I still have a graph of the climb in my log book. Mind you, the aeroplane was almost new at the time. I also had three short flights in the most delightful Miles (as we called it) Martlet G-AAYX, and over 22 hours on the graceful and easy Cirrus-engined BA Swallow G-AERK; 123 hours in 14 pre-war types in total.

I learned to fly at Ramsgate Airport in 1936, on Hornet Moth G-ADMM. The cost was £2 per hour dual and 30/- (£1.50) solo – a lot in those days. An overshoot cost half a crown (12½p), which I sometimes couldn't afford! My first flying instructor, Charles Eckersley-Maslin, was a tremendous character. He has recently died at the ripe old age of 95; so at least one of my many instructors wasn't frightened to death! My last flight as pilot in charge was on the 8th July 1984; total hours 16,400, total types flown solo 70.

AST was part of the Hawker-Siddeley Group. I believe that it began in the early thirties. During the war AST ran No.1 Beam Approach School at Watchfield (near Swindon) and No.3 EFTS (Elementary Flying Training School) at Shellingford, not far away. After the war AST moved back to Hamble to continue its main work, that of training commercial pilots and navigators.

I left Marshalls of Cambridge and joined AST in October 1949. At that time their fleet consisted of two Avro Anson Is (G-AHNS & 'HNT), five Airspeed Oxfords (G-AIAT, 'ITB, 'ITF, 'LTP & 'LTR), two Proctors (G-AHTV & 'KZN), one Miles Whitney Straight (G-AEVG), two Lycoming-engined Auster Vs (G-AKXP & 'KXR) and twelve Tiger Moths, the oldest being G-ACDI. In 1953 these were replaced by six DHC.1 Chipmunks (G-AMUC-'H) and two Auster Aiglet Trainers (G-AMUI & 'J). I remember collecting the first Chipmunk ('MUC) from the factory at Hawarden on the 30th October 1952.

Our students came from all over the world. The worst were the Persians (hopeless!); it's difficult to say who were the best, but the Burmese stood out. Israelis and Jordanians were good, and I forged a particularly strong friendship with an Indian who went on to have a very distinguished career in Indian and Canadian aviation. He ended up as a high official in ICAO at Montreal, from where he still travels round the world on trouble-shooting missions – and he still keeps in touch with me!

Memories come flooding back as I browse through my log books: retrieving a lost student in a Tiger Moth from a field in Wiltshire (who later became C. in C. of the Saudi Arabian Air Force): going up to Newbury on a night cross-country in a Chipmunk with a Nigerian, taking over and slow-rolling it to topple the artificial horizon to see how he coped with it! Earlier, when we did night cross-countries in Tiger Moths I remember seeing one ahead of me (we were both en route to Christchurch), switching off my navigation lights, opening up the throttle and coming alongside him and flashing my torch at him!

Night flying in those days was primitive – there was no radio, of course – and back at the airfield an old fashioned flarepath of paraffin flares just as in the earliest days. But we did have an angle of approach indicator to help (amber – too high, green – correct, red – too low). One final memory of night flying in Chipmunks is of an ex-Luftwaffe German pilot on a solo flight exercise who missed the airfield and went on westwards; fortunately by now we did have radio, and as his calls got fainter I took off in another Chipmunk and called him up from the air. I eventually got him to turn round and caught sight of him. I got him back safely – a happy ending.

We had an RAFVR unit at Hamble, operating Chipmunks, and we could combine our annual training with work. I remember one day sending a rather unreliable Iraqi on a solo cross-country to Blandford, getting into an RAF Chipmunk and following out behind him in line astern (he never saw me, naturally!). He went in the general direction of Blandford but never got there. I broke off pursuit in time to get back first and greet him on his return.

"Did you get there all right?" I asked.

"Oh! Yes, Sir," he replied.

Flight time limitations were not known in those early post-war days. On the 25th August 1954 I logged 8 hours and 25 minutes. We started work at 08.30 and it was about midnight when I got home. I found myself squeezing shaving cream on my toothbrush; how accident prone can you get?

We trained navigators as well as pilots, and one of my most pleasant memories was in April 1951 when I flew Anson G-AHNT from Hamble to Eastleigh (for Customs) – Lyons (overnight stop) – Rome (overnight stop) – Malta (day off!) – Sardinia (refuelling stop) – Lyons (overnight stop) – Eastleigh (for Customs) – Hamble. Coming back over the Channel the haze was very thick and in spite of three navigators (and the pilot!) I had a helluva job to find Eastleigh. Johnny Plowman was the staff navigator, and the two Burmese trainees were Kyaw and Wiltshire – how he got that name as a Burmese we never knew.

Then two Dakotas were brought in to complete a contract for training a large number of Indonesian pilots. They were splendid young men. I was quite glad I didn't fly the Dakotas myself. Hamble was a very small, awkwardly shaped grass airfield for such aircraft, and our longest run was about 1,100 metres (1,200 yards) north-south, very much a limit field for Daks.

Before the RAFVR changed their Tiger Moths for Chipmunks, we occasionally used to fly with a fellow instructor to practise instrument flight 'under the hood.' I remember doing quite a successful loop under it, and then my colleague Bob Whitehead did so when we changed over.

It was nice to be able to do some aerobatics occasionally, as it wasn't in the commercial flying syllabus. Neither was formation flying, but we had a few opportunities for that when commercial cameramen came to take air-to-air pictures, as in the accompanying photo. This was taken on the 19th March 1952, when the Hawker-Siddeley Group sent down two photographers for publicity purposes. They were Cyril Luckham and Russell Adams, whom I had the pleasure of taking up. They were original and daring in their work, quite unperturbed by the close formation, noise and wind of the Tiger's open cockpit. This was a wonderful opportunity for Henry and me to do some close formation flying, which I liked very much (in fact I'd done it tied together at Cambridge a few years earlier). There was a happy sequel to this session, as many years later Cyril Luckham retired to the Isle of Wight; as I was still working at Hamble for the College of Air Training, as it was called by then, I flew over to meet him again for a very pleasant reunion.

The Oxfords were used for twin-engine conversion and instrument rating training. This became obligatory, and we all had to undergo annual renewal tests with examiners from the Ministry of Civil Aviation. This was good for us, as it reminded us what it was like to be on the receiving end of a test instead of giving one! Also, instructors had to undergo a renewal test every two years and medicals every six months. I used to go to RAF Thorney Island for mine, and I still remember the bottom line on the eyesight card – A E L O C H T! Later on we had our own resident Doctor at Hamble; not so long ago I passed him on our golf course as he was searching for a lost ball, and remarked to my golf partner that "apart from my wife, that man knows more about my body than anyone else!"

I mentioned earlier that we had some German pilots at Hamble. These were ex-Luftwaffe pilots doing a short refresher course ready for restarting the German state airline Lufthansa, which had not functioned since about 1940. We all got on very well; my pupil was Col. Eduard Neumann, who had flown against the RAF in the Western Desert. We had mutual respect for one another and became good friends.

For a short time we had two Hiller helicopters for training, although I was not in on that act. One had a disastrous prang, luckily without casualties. The two instructors on the Hillers were Len "Tubby" Fieldhouse and Dick Hazlehurst, who took me up on an air test in G-AOFK on September 1st 1955. He showed me a 'backwards autorotation' to overcome the unlikely situation of an engine failure just after passing the only suitable space for a forced landing. I was scared out of my wits: he dived to keep sufficient speed up for the rotors to keep going, and then went backwards, losing height rapidly, until the space came into view. He then changed quite abruptly to forward and downward flight to make a successful forced landing. Not for me, thank you very much, going backwards with a failed engine indeed!

AST also ran service Ansons on a navigator training contract, and there was a maintenance unit and the Southampton University Air Squadron on the airfield: a very busy place indeed.

A flight I did in Oxford G-AITF on the 17th April 1957 got into the "*Southampton Echo*," as I witnessed a fire breaking out in the New Forest. I radioed Eastleigh with a warning and they alerted the fire services. 1,500 acres were affected and it took eleven hours to extinguish.

Now an amusing incident very much tied up with a foreigner's reluctance to 'lose face.' On February 23rd 1950 our duty air traffic controller got a phone call from a solo Persian cadet on a cross-country flight in a Tiger Moth. Roughly, the conversation went something like this:

"Please, Sir, I was lost but I have landed and I know where I am. May I come back by myself?"

"Where are you, then?" the controller asked.

"Sir, I am at Uphill Landing."

"No! Stay where you are and we will fetch you."

I took the pupil's instructor to get him back. He had landed at Worthy Down, near Winchester, where there was a large notice cut into the chalk warning 'uphill landing' on a steep uphill part of that airfield. The cunning so-and-so had sneaked off to a public phone box to try and get out of 'loss of face'!

I would like to end with a tribute to the ground engineers. They were marvellous blokes (one had pulled me out of a crashed Oxford at Watchfield in 1942). Perhaps if I say that about half my total experience was on single-engined aircraft, and that I never once had an engine failure, that is the best way of showing my appreciation.

In 1960 Hamble was taken over by a joint BOAC/BEA consortium to train airline pilots from scratch. The work was subtly different and very interesting; I stayed on there for a further ten years or so. Then eventually Airwork took over most of the aircraft and unneeded equipment. Now Hamble is no longer an airfield, but as I said earlier, those were truly happy days.

CHAPTER 4

PAST THE POINT OF NO RETURN

by

Peter Amos

To set the scene we must first return to the 22nd June 1950, for on that day I got demobbed. At this point I was posted for a further four years service with the Supplementary Reserve to the 5th Battalion, the Queen's Regiment at Guildford in Surrey. To say that I was not impressed with being transferred against my better wishes to an Infantry mob when I had just served eighteen months with an 'elite' technical regiment was putting it mildly! I was not having any of that; if I was going to have to suffer four years on the SR and give up fourteen days a year to His Majesty, I wanted back in the REME forthwith or forget it! Whereas I might not have been too happy about having to join the army for my National Service in the first place, I had by this time become intensely proud of 'my' regiment. However, to cut a long story short, I duly reported to Guildford and signed in, made my point and thirty minutes later I was a relatively free man again. For the record, and following a considerable effort, I did get back into REME and actually went on three of the four fortnightly annual camps – I managed to lose the first one during the course of the stink I was making! We were working on the Supermarine Swift at the time (but we won't go into that just yet!) and this was considered to be a 'Super Priority' aircraft (I just cannot think why but perhaps I was biased in favour of 'real' aeroplanes), but I used this as an excuse to try to avoid having to waste valuable time 'playing soldiers' for four more years! I wrote letters to my MP, as did my boss, but in the end I had to admit defeat! Ah well! We tried. But I am getting ahead of myself.

Getting back to the rigours of civilian life in post-war Britain first entailed collecting my Identity Card and Ration Book, then on Friday the 23rd June I started eighteen days demob leave. I also began to think seriously about my future prospects as I did not wish to return to the Gas Company, although I had spent two happy years there as Personal Assistant to the Chief Engineer before being called up. Actually I had already made my mind up – it had to be the aviation industry or nothing!

I had left the Army with many happy memories, but while at Christchurch I had been smitten by the aviation bug! Before I left I had arranged with Derek, a friend and club member, to borrow the Auster IV G-ALYH from the club on Saturday 1st July for one last flight. Derek was to fly to my 'home' aerodrome at Redhill, pick me up and then take me to Pebsham near Hastings in order for me to spend some of my leave with my parents, who were holidaying in a bungalow on the beach at Pevensey Bay, midway between Eastbourne and Hastings.

Saturday duly arrived and I was pleased to see that the weather was perfect, with good prospects for an enjoyable flight. I rang British Air Transport Ltd, the owners of Redhill Aerodrome, to see if they had heard from Derek and, having received confirmation that the Auster was on its way, I cycled over to the aerodrome from my home at Merstham with a small holiday bag (no, I wasn't married then!) just in time to see G-ALYH join the circuit at about 9.30 am. Derek taxied in, shut the engine down and broke the news to me that the Auster was required back at Christchurch pronto for club flying; ah! well, at least I would be seeing the old place again.

We had already unintentionally made the first mistake of the day by shutting the engine down, but Derek had never been to Redhill so we decided that being a few minutes late would not make much difference and I showed him around the hangars. When the time came to leave however, the Auster's Lycoming engine just would not start – not a flicker of life could we coax out of it. Swinging the prop 'backwards' didn't help much either, nor did cursing it, and time was slipping by. Derek had also been asked to call in to Viv Bellamy at Eastleigh on the return journey to collect some spares for Tommy Marshall, so panic now began to set in! Then, luckily, a mechanic from F.G. Miles Ltd saw our plight and took pity upon us by kindly offering to clean the plugs.

Shortly after this the engine started and we were off! It was now 12.00 noon and we were worried about what might happen at Eastleigh! We therefore decided that Derek would rush to collect the parcel while I would stay in the aircraft and keep the engine running – it must not be allowed to stop at any cost. What happened to it after we returned to Christchurch we cared not but for now it was our biggest worry. We parked outside the spectators' enclosure at Eastleigh and I must admit to feeling a little embarrassed sitting in full view of the few spectators, gently blipping the throttle at regular intervals.

Arriving back at Christchurch we were met with the inevitable "Where the blankety-blank hell have you two been?" from our CFI Eddie Livermore. Livermore by name but 'Liverish' by nature! But it was a lovely sunny afternoon and having nothing better to do until the aircraft was released from training we lazed around on the airfield drinking tea and enjoying the flying. However, when teatime came with G-ALYH still grinding around the circuit, bumping in-between-times, I began to think that I was going to be marooned at Christchurch for the night. At last the time eventually came for it to be handed over to us but with it came the order from Eddie that "It's now too late to get to Pebsham, so you can only go to Shoreham: *he* [pointing to me] will have to go on by bus." Eddie had calculated that Derek could hope to return from Shoreham before dusk but not from Pebsham.

We eventually took off at 19.00 and headed south over Hengistbury Head before turning east on course with the sun behind us – just follow the coast, no need to set a course or even to map-read – it couldn't have been easier. It was such a wonderful evening, the view was magnificent, the sky was blue, as was the sea, and the beaches, now clearing of holiday-makers, looked inviting. I have often been asked why I like flying and this is not an easy question to answer until you try flying on such an evening; how can anyone describe the fantastic feeling, the freedom from earthly bonds, the fabulous view that stretched out before us to infinity, to which we were treated on that glorious, sunny evening? Perhaps if I were of poetic bent I could probably wax lyrical and express my feelings more eloquently but . . .

We flew over the Solent, the Isle of Wight, Thorney Island, Selsey Bill, Littlehampton, Worthing and – wait a minute – surely that was Shoreham passing below? Were we really going to Pebsham and to hell with Eddie? Derek was obviously so enjoying the flight that he too felt the need to complete its original objective.

I was naturally delighted. Shoreham was miles from Pevensey Bay anyway and the bus ride, even if there had been one at that time of the evening, would have taken hours. Peeved at having to wait for so long to get our hands on G-ALYH (we blamed Eddie of course for not letting us have it sooner – he could be a right so-and-so!), both Derek and I then agreed that perhaps we could just about get away with it provided we did not stop too long at Pebsham, and nobody would be any the wiser. We were soon passing over Beachy Head and Eastbourne and I saw our little bungalow on the beach at Pevensey Bay, where hopefully I would be within about an hour or so. However I had not allowed for the fact that we might not be able to find Pebsham – our second mistake of the day! When we arrived over the area where we had calculated it should be there was no sign of an airfield. More panic, then amidst a sea of greenhouses and the Hastings Corporation refuse dump I suddenly espied an Autocrat in the corner of a very small green patch. Shouting news of this important find to Derek and pointing to the 'postage stamp' airfield that was by now almost beneath us, he immediately wound the Auster down in true Army style – well, it was designed to land on a 'postage stamp,' and that it did in fine style! The time was now 20.15 – we had completed our objective.

A welcoming committee from the resident East Sussex Flying Club came out of their hut to meet us and they were thrilled to bits to find that we had come all the way from Christchurch especially to land at their field. From all accounts the club didn't get many (if any) visitors, which was not surprising really, seeing how difficult it was to find the airfield. They promptly enrolled both of us as Honorary Members of the Club (I still have the card as a souvenir of our visit), but it was getting late so, without stopping the engine (we did

EAST SUSSEX FLYING CLUB
HASTINGS AERODROME, SUSSEX
MEMBERSHIP CARD
Type of Membership *ASSOCIATE*
Expiring *1-7-51*
Name *SOUTH HANTS. ULTRA LIGHT AIR CLUB*
Address
Hon. Secretary.

not want *that* trouble again), I thanked Derek for a wonderful flight and we all waved him off into the by-now-setting sun.

This had been a truly memorable flight and one which will forever stand out as being the most enjoyable experience of my life. Thanking the members of the East Sussex Flying Club for their hospitality I wandered off to get my bus to Pevensey Bay and to enjoy my seven days leave with not a care in the world, even though facing an uncertain future.

We had made it, in spite of Eddie! What did he know anyway? Well, it transpired later, after I had read the letter from the Secretary of SHULAC (the club at Christchurch) upon returning from my holiday, that our Eddie knew a damn sight more than we did! He knew that G-ALYH hadn't been refuelled after the afternoon's flying and that the return journey to Shoreham was just about all that the Auster was capable of.

I learned later that Derek very nearly made it home but, while flying over the New Forest and luckily within sight of RAF Station Beaulieu, the engine died. Beaulieu was on 'Care and Maintenance' at the time with only a skeleton staff and, although his had been an emergency landing, I don't think they were too keen to see him! Having an aeroplane descend on them unannounced on a Saturday evening undoubtedly meant that they would have to raise some paperwork or some such when they should probably have been sleeping. They had no fuel, so there was nothing else for it: Derek abandoned the Auster to their tender mercies and, knowing the local form, walked to the main railway line at Brockenhurst and hitched a lift from a passing train. He arrived back at Christchurch later to be met by a very hostile welcoming committee!

Eddie, realising that Derek should have returned long since, had rung Shoreham, only to be told that we had not landed there but that they had seen an Auster heading eastwards earlier in the evening. Oh! dear, what *had* we done? To say that Eddie was not amused was the understatement of the century. He had then immediately instigated a search for a missing aeroplane. The best laid plans of mice and men . . . you learn from that as they say!

For a while after that episode we were not the most popular members of what had by then become the Christchurch Aero Club, but I was now 120 miles away and oblivious to the chaos we had caused. However, for the record, the day's flying had cost me the princely sum of £3-3s-9d (£1-4s-4d for the 1 hour 5 minutes from Redhill to Christchurch and £1-19s-5d for the 1 hr 15 minutes from Christchurch to Pebsham). Oh! dear, how times have changed – how far could you go for £3.20 these days?

Pebsham closed soon after this but I would like to think that it was not on account of our late evening visit!

Where were we? The problem with getting old is that you have so much to say and so little time to say it in! Ah! yes, the summer of 1950 and the prospect of getting a job in the aircraft industry. Well, I did find a suitable job *and* at my first attempt, as a junior design draughtsman with the de Havilland Aircraft Company in their London Design Office. This office was situated on two floors above Accurists, the watch shop, opposite Libertys in Regent Street in the West End. In those days it was fashionable for the major aircraft manufacturers to have a London design office, which in turn also made it easier for employees to work for a company without necessarily having to 'up sticks' and move to wherever they were based. It was quite easy for me to travel to London on the Brighton railway line from my home at Merstham, which was just a couple of miles north of Redhill aerodrome, as the crow flew. The idea of commuting (as we call it today) did not appeal to me overmuch as for one thing it meant getting up early, and for another, more importantly, it cost too much, even on the Workmen's train (which admittedly was cheaper than the normal fare but got you to London too early).

But it was a means to an end; I had achieved my aim – I had broken into the aircraft industry. I was reasonably happy at DH's and I certainly learnt a lot – apart from aircraft design that is! My office was on the first floor, and I recall that one of the more senior draughtsmen, whose desk was alongside the window overlooking Regent Street and Liberty's on the opposite side of the road, kept a pair of binoculars in his drawer for reasons which were not immediately apparent. After a while however, it dawned on me that the ladies' changing room was in his line of sight. It was not long before they caught on to this and put the blinds down before they stripped off. If the office had been a ship I feel sure that it would have capsized at regular intervals, such was the rush to our window!

It was during my time with DH that my love-hate relationship with aircraft tailplane design started. We were engaged on 'productionising' the prototype Heron, their new four-engined 'local' airliner and I remember drawing every rib in the elevators. Although I could not have realised it at the time I was to be stuck with the design of tailplanes in one way or another for a considerable part of my design office career! My drawing board was in front of George, an elderly draughtsman who had worked for Shorts at Rochester before they moved to Belfast, and it was from him that I learned about the 'joggle,' a very necessary device in the design of aircraft structures!

De Havilland were very proud of their new airliner and did not like it being called a 'four-engined Dove,' claiming that it was a brand new type. Nevertheless it really *was* just a four-engined Dove and in consequence the prototype was definitely a hand-built one-off – why else were we 'productionising' it? For the record they never did get the Heron quite right, and this fact was to be brought home to me many years later in no uncertain fashion whilst working for Hawker Siddeley Aviation at Dunsfold. I was returning from West Freugh one day in G-AVTU, a late production Heron Mk.2D, and this was the nearest that I ever came to being airsick – OK, so it was a bit bumpy, but the tail never ceased its 'fishtailing' manoeuvres for the whole flight, which was of 2 hours 25 minutes duration. I had never been so glad to step out onto mother earth back at Dunsfold, especially as the rest of the passengers had been airsick for the latter part of the journey!

It was whilst working for de Havillands that I had my 20th birthday and at that point I felt that I was due for a raise in salary. The mighty de Havilland however thought otherwise and I was politely but firmly told that it was not company policy to review salaries during the year, only at Christmas, and the fact that my birthday was in August was, in their considered opinion, tough! However I was young and impatient and if they would not give me a raise then I would be forced to take my services elsewhere. In those far-off halcyon days it was the weekly ritual to study the Situations Vacant pages at the back of "THE AEROPLANE" and "FLIGHT" magazines immediately they arrived in the office, in the hope that a job could be found with a more generous employer than de Havilland – DH were not renowned for their generosity! Draughtsmen were in great demand in those days and regularly moved to whichever firm was paying the best wages; allegiance was a word foreign to their ears. Ah! happy days, we will never see their like again!

I could not believe my eyes when shortly after this I saw an advertisement for draughtsmen wanted by a company on Redhill Aerodrome of all places – my home territory. The aforementioned company was Tiltman Langley Laboratories Ltd and they were looking for design draughtsmen "with experience"; they seemed to be offering good prospects, but more importantly they were on my doorstep and within easy cycling reach of home. I promptly applied and was pleasantly surprised by the immediate reply I received requesting that I contact them to arrange an interview. I got the job, which sounded not only more interesting than drawing elevator ribs but was also offering more pay – suddenly de Havillands were history! A job just two miles away on my home aerodrome which offered to pay real wages, and with no train fares to have to fork out – this had to be too good to be true. It was to change my life.

Founded in 1948 by Marcus Langley and Hessel Tiltman, late of Airspeed's, Tiltman Langley Laboratories Ltd was affectionately known by all its employees as Tiltmans; Marcus ran the company and I only recall seeing Hessel once. Marcus and the project engineers were all from Flight Refuelling, having worked with Sir Alan Cobham for many years. After the end of the war Marcus and Sir Alan had had a difference of opinion (row!) over which way they each thought the company should go. Marcus wanted to concentrate on research and development while Alan wanted to expand the company and continue to specialise in the development of flight refuelling.

In retrospect Marcus made the wrong move although perhaps with hindsight and better management he might have got away with it. Tiltmans somehow survived until the 1960s, albeit without my help as I had by then departed for pastures new, but Flight Refuelling went from strength to strength and is still a household name today.

Tiltmans however had by 1951 become well-established with a machine shop and drawing office in the original hangar at Redhill, the one with the control tower attached and the offices to one side. This control tower is sadly no more, having been replaced by a brick monstrosity in the middle of the airfield. They had also expanded into what had once been the pre-war purpose-built squash court of the Redhill Flying Club, situated on the left-hand-side of the entrance to the aerodrome, just inside the main gate behind the old Guard Room. This had recently been converted to have a mezzanine floor to take another drawing office on the first floor. This building is still there but is now surrounded by a ranch-style fence and used as a store by Bristow Helicopters Ltd.

The ground floor held the receptionist-cum-telephonist and the laboratories, as befitted the company title, and it was the clarion call "This used to be a squash court" which awoke us from our slumbers at regular intervals as Marcus came up the outside wooden stairs with a group of visitors or prospective customers on a tour of the works! The squash court was to be my second home for the next eight years, apart from some time in the late fifties which I spent in our 'quieter' design office on the first floor of the old control tower. I had moved there to assist Bill, one of the project engineers, with the design and construction of a ground test rig for the Skeeter helicopter's transmission. Bill was a brilliant engineer and had been one of the founder members of the old firm, but he had recently become infatuated by Mo, a rather voluptuous and clinging female tracer! Bill was however married and lived in a Nissen hut on the aerodrome; life was getting complicated, then one day it caught up with him and he left in somewhat of a hurry – I was lumbered! We were used to accepting challenges at the drop of a hat however, and as it was a very interesting project I welcomed the chance to see it through. I was ultimately to supervise the rig's construction and installation at Saro's flight test centre at Eastleigh. It was while I was there that I began to acquire a taste for the locality, which had such an historic aviation background.

But I am getting ahead of myself again. In the early fifties we were mainly engaged on sub-contract design work, first for Supermarine at Hursley Park, near Chandlers Ford (on the first variable-incidence tailplanes for the 517 and early Swift variants, the 525, 545 & 550), then Avro at Manchester (Shackleton for the SAAF and Vulcan) and then Saunders Roe at Eastleigh (Skeeter helicopter). This provided us with much experience and our 'bread and butter' for the next eight happy years.

This state of bliss was to be marred by just one incident (although I was not to know this at the time), as it was while I was working there that I met the girl who was later to become my first wife; she was working in an office below as the receptionist for the company. But that is unfortunately a story without a happy ending and one which ultimately I had to put down to experience.

As you will by now probably have gathered, I never aspired to obtaining my Private Pilot's Licence or even achieving my first solo flight at Christchurch, but I did try to keep my interest in flying alive with the odd half hour's flying, even after I had left the Army. It really was just too far to travel to Christchurch though, and much as I loved the place it was well over a hundred miles away from my home, and I only had a cycle in those days! This was a great shame but the experience gained there on my hard-earned (?) meagre Army pay put me in good stead for what was to come later at Redhill. Meanwhile, however, I did make one last flight with the club at Christchurch in the Taylorcraft Plus D G-AHUM on the 24th March 1951.

I soon settled in at Redhill and after a while discovered that there was another flying club on the airfield as well as the old established resident Redhill Flying Club, and this was the Experimental Flying Group of the Ultra Light Aircraft Association. This sounded very grand, but it was made up mainly of enthusiasts and did not actually own any aircraft of its own at the time (where had I heard that before?). They did however have access to two lovely little DH Moth Minors: G-AFPR, which was owned by the group's Chief Flying Instructor, Miss Jean Bird, and G-AFOZ (owned by a Mr Allan, I believe). Their 'club room,' for want of a better word, was in one of the tattiest Nissen huts that I had ever seen (and by then I had seen quite a few!), and this was situated next to what had once been the airfield fire section outside the Redhill Flying Club. They were the 'poor relations' and it was really surprising that the Redhill Flying Club tolerated them right next door to the hallowed turf outside their beautiful pre-war wooden club house.

Jean Bird, who had learned to fly at Hamble before the war, had gained her very impressive flying experience with the Air Transport Auxiliary during the war, and lived in an ancient minute caravan with her black Labrador dog in one of the dispersals around the Redhill perimeter track. She was to be tragically killed later in an Aerovan crash at Ringway but I will never forget her, not only because she had been one of those few intrepid ATA pilots of whom I have such lasting admiration and respect but because she was also such an excellent flying instructor.

The Experimental Flying Group had been formed by the ULAA after the war at Elstree and its original aims had been to examine new Ultra Light Aircraft as they were built and confirm that they were in fact fit to be flown by their enthusiastic owners/builders. The only trouble with the Group was that, apart from having too many members, not enough aircraft and the English weather to contend with, there was the problem of it not being an 'approved club.' This meant that to qualify for the minimum 30-hour course of instruction to obtain your Private Pilot's Licence, which had recently replaced the old 'A' Licence, your flying club needed to be equipped with toilets and be run on 'proper' lines! The Nissen hut did not have these essential facilities (bushes around the back did not count), which were an accepted prerequisite of such clubs as the Redhill Flying Club, and so you had perforce to do 40 hours to qualify for a PPL. This seemed to be most unfair but typical of what was to become the most anti-aeroplane Government ever to be in office (until the last lot which have fairly recently been disposed of!).

After a time at Redhill I took myself up to the black Nissen hut, introduced myself and was duly accepted as a member of the Experimental Flying Group. Shortly after this, on the 2nd June 1952, I made my first flight, of 20 minutes duration, with Jean in the lovely little Moth Minor G-AFPR. Of the two Moth Minors which tried their level best to keep everybody happy, G-AFPR was to become my favourite and it was in her on the 26th October 1952 that I was to successfully complete my first solo.

Meanwhile however, on the 20th July 1952, while on a cycling holiday in the West Country with David Freeman, we called in to St Just, Land's End Airport, as we wanted to fly in a BEA Dragon Rapide to the Isles of Scilly. Although we soon discovered that they were all fully booked, we noticed a chap seated at a table outside the airport restaurant reading a book, with the Proctor G-AKXK parked alongside. So putting two and two together, we decided that they might well be connected, and our polite enquiry confirmed our surmise that he was indeed the pilot of this machine, which was owned by Murray Chown Aviation Ltd of Cheltenham. Apparently he was there for joyriding, but that did not stop

37

us from asking him if he could take us to the Isles of Scilly. Much as he would have liked to have taken us across the twenty miles of sea, he had to decline as he did not have the correct crystals fitted to his wireless set. The best he could offer us was a trip around the Longships Lighthouse, so as business did not look very brisk (we were in fact the only visitors) we took pity on him, paid our 10/- each and went. It was a great flight, the sheer power from the Proctor's 200

horses was exhilarating in the extreme and after the 90 horse Gipsy Minor seemed quite awe-inspiring! I will never forget the return to the minuscule airport at St Just though; having negotiated the hill on the circuit he put the Proctor down just inside the boundary (he had obviously done this before) but it was quite horrendous just how fast the end of the runway in use came up and I seem to remember that even with full braking he still had to turn off with what was (in my opinion at least) too much speed, to save going through the hedge!

On October 5th 1952 I made my first flight with 'Fred Nurke,' alias Chris Dearden, with whose exploits you will by now be familiar. This was a pleasant ten-minute jaunt on 65 horses from Gatwick (all grass in those days) in the Piper Cub G-AJDS of A.J. Walters, and my most lasting memory of this, my sole Cub flight, was the noise it made on landing. No, it wasn't that it was a bad landing, on the contrary I thought it was a good one but the aeroplane sounded as if it was going to fall apart as it trundled across the grass: I was convinced that I had travelled on quieter trams!

The next year, 1953, I had arranged for a coach to take the best part of the office staff to the Coronation Review of the Royal Air Force, held at the RAF Station at Odiham in Hampshire on Wednesday the 15th July. Here we saw the might of the ancient, a little of what was to be the modern and a number of American and British aircraft of the 'modern' RAF, both on the ground and in the air. The ground display was impressive though and, much to my annoyance, although great play had been made about the fact that you would not be allowed to take photographs, after the flypast was over they dropped the ropes and let you wander at will amongst the static aircraft. Photographs were also allowed but, to my eternal regret, although I had still taken my camera on the off-chance, I only had one partly-used film in it.

At this point I should also just mention that during the fifties I attended as many local air displays as possible and these included the RNAS ones at Ford and Lee on Solent, alas both no longer now in service. It was at these stations that hundreds of Griffon, Merlin and Centaurus piston engines could be heard on the runway in readiness for the dress rehearsal of the Fleet Air Arm's Coronation Flypast at Spithead. Then there was the annual SBAC Show at Farnborough which I attended both on the Monday (our free "Technicians' Day") and on the Friday and sometimes the Saturday as well, when most of the interest centred around the rare and interesting visiting aircraft at Blackbushe. I would also visit the annual Battle of Britain displays at Biggin Hill.

In August 1953 I was again required to do my fourteen days annual training for Queen and Country (and this I hasten to add was still under some considerable protest, although a lot of good that was doing me!). The venue this time was Gainsborough in Lincolnshire but there was little to do in the town and nothing of aviation interest in the locality, so someone organised a coach to take us to Skegness on the middle Sunday, 30th August. While the rest of the lads took in the resort I went off on my own to find Ingoldmells airfield and to see what was happening there. To my surprise I found that Skegness Air Taxi Services Ltd were doing Pleasure Flights at 10/- with the Dragon Rapide G-ALBA. I had never flown in a twin-engined aircraft so I just had to have a go. The pilot took us for a very pleasant ten-minute flight along the coast from this very small airfield but it is with much regret that I have never again flown in a Rapide. Other aircraft there were Gemini 1A G-AKFU, Messenger 4A G-ALAW, Argus II G-AJPE (with flat tyres), Autocrat G-AHAL and the wrecked Auster IV G-AJYB.

When any opportunity to leave the ground came my way however, I would still grab it, and working at Redhill with 'A' Licence holder Chris Dearden enabled me to keep in touch. I made my first flight in the College of Aeronautical & Automobile Engineering's Tiger Moth G-AMNN with Chris on the 28th May 1954, and thereafter we made occasional flights in 'MNN during the lunch hour, mostly to photograph friends' houses and the like. Then there was the famous flight to Shoreham on the 4th May 1957 (described in the chapter "I Sure Am!" in the previous book), in which I was an interested passenger and also tame photographer of the new Gatwick Airport under construction as we flew past.

On 26th February 1959 we even had the audacity to ask (and much to our surprise were actually granted) permission to photograph the newly completed London Gatwick Airport from the air, before it had really got going. Unfortunately the chosen day turned out to be rather hazy but Air Traffic there could not have been more helpful.

We had no radio (surprise, surprise!) but they said: "That's no problem; just let us know when you expect to arrive, and then do a circuit at 1,000 ft so that our radar can identify you, but if you see a 'red' then go away! Otherwise you can have 15 minutes around the circuit."

We took off at 12.35 (there went our lunch again!) but we had to make the most of this once-in-a-lifetime opportunity. We duly presented ourselves in the correct place and proceeded to orbit and take air-to-ground photographs. These photographs confirm that the new Gatwick was indeed a very quiet place and not a bit like the madhouse it is today. Forty minutes later we landed back at Redhill and we then got told off for not letting Gatwick know that we had returned safely!

My last Tiger flight with Chris was on the 12th April 1959 when we decided to attend a Breakfast Patrol at Biggin Hill. We managed to beat the defenders but we had to go round again when a cheeky Hornet Moth slipped in underneath us on the approach. Anyway we somehow managed to indulge ourselves in a free breakfast at the Surrey & Kent Flying Club's expense!

By 1959 the writing was definitely on the wall at Tiltmans, but having enjoyed working at Eastleigh on the Skeeter helicopter I decided that perhaps a move to that part of the world would not be too bad. I received an acceptable offer from Sir A.W. Armstrong Whitworth Aircraft Ltd at Hamble, and said my goodbyes to Redhill Aerodrome (not without much regret) for the last time on Friday the 28th August 1959. I commenced work in the design office at Hamble on Monday the 31st, and surprise, surprise, I had been appointed section-leader working on the design of the *tailplane* of the Hawker Siddeley Group's first new 'failsafe' airliner, the Avro 748!

The drawing office at Hamble had previously been used by Air Service Training, another member of the Hawker Siddeley Group, and it was a happy office with a good atmosphere. Some of the draughtsmen had spent the war working on Spitfire repair schemes in the same office, and many tales were told about the state of some of the Spitfires which came to AST for repair. I was accepted into their midst as a friend and this was to mark the beginning of the next chapter in my life.

However, during the week prior to my leaving Redhill, without any warning in the form of rumours (remarkable!), notices began appearing on trees around the aerodrome announcing the fact that on Sunday, 30th August 1959, an Air Display was to be held at Redhill. The airfield was to re-open after five years of it being put down to agriculture, and I was going to miss all the fun – would you credit it? A poignant note in my diary records the fact that I did not attend the display but that I just drove past on my return from visiting my parents. I suppose that I was still harbouring some regrets at having to leave the old place which I had made almost my second home. I just could not bring myself to go in: it was a strange feeling, a large part of my life had gone forever.

These are just a few of my recollections of the fifties; I could probably go on (I never even commented on the Supermarine Swift!). Suffice to say that I enjoyed the fifties immensely, even though I never did aspire to my PPL!

We will never see their like again.

CHAPTER 5

A SPOTTING LIFETIME

(WELL, NEARLY!)

by

Mike Hooks

My first recollection of aviation was as a two-year-old being carried out to see the German airship *"Graf Zeppelin,"* LZ127, flying over the South Coast at Pagham Beach, near Bognor. Subsequent research indicates the time as 9.20 pm and the date August 18th 1930, when the ship was en route to various UK destinations as part of a European cruise. Few can probably pinpoint their first 'reggie' so accurately!

Subsequently, there were other hazy childhood memories, such as a biplane, probably a Moth or Avian, landing after engine failure and turning over in a field behind Pagham Church. I still have a fragment of its wooden propeller but would really like to know its identity; the period would probably have been around 1933 as we moved to Croydon in 1934. My first visit to an air display was the Gatwick Air Pageant of 1938, where the only thing I can remember was the famous Major Al Williams who flew the orange Grumman G.22 Gulfhawk biplane, NR1050, owned by the Gulf Oil Company. This aircraft is now exhibited in the National Air & Space Museum, Washington, and I have an unmade kit of it which I'll get round to sometime – after all, I have only had it for about 30 years!

Evacuation to grandparents at Chichester for the first eight months of the war enabled me to see masses of aircraft before being brought back to Croydon just in time for the Battle of Britain and to witness the famous first raid on Croydon Airport. My log books go back to 1945 and are still being kept. Since these recollections are supposed to cover the fifties, I will gloss over my RAF National Service in 1945-46 as an aircraft plotter in the ATC Area Control Centre at Gloucester, where I was a nuisance to my colleagues in insisting that the correct serial numbers/call signs were inserted on the large wall plaques!

On demobilisation, I was taken on as a clerk by a Scottish engineering company building a new power station at Croydon, barely two miles from the airport which was easily reached by bicycle in the lunch hour. By this time I was a member of the Royal Observer Corps (ROC) and by courtesy of an officer in our Group managed to get a pass for the airport, renewable yearly, which allowed access for photography and general looking around, although not in the hangars unless permission was obtained. This pass proved invaluable and was in constant use until the airport closed on September 30th 1959, although I still paid the occasional visit afterwards to see progress in the Rollason hangar where work continued. By then aircraft had to be moved by lorry, usually to Redhill, for flight test after repair or conversion.

However, back to the beginning of 1950. In February, various Magisters were to be seen, some wearing their newly-allocated civil registrations (G-ALNX-'LNZ, 'LOA, 'B, 'E and 'F) although only 'LOE was to survive on export to Belgium as OO-ACH (I was later to see it at Croydon in March 1955 as a coupé model). The other "Maggies" were cancelled as not converted, scrapped at Elstree. An oddity among them was the impressed BB666, registered as G-ALOG, but then restored to its pre-war marks G-AFXA, although even then it did not undergo conversion, being scrapped in 1956.

Magisters were not the only ex-military types to appear at Croydon: there were Ansons, Proctors and many Tiger Moths – rows of the latter were to be seen parked on the south-east corner of the airport. They flew in from various Maintenance Units such as Aston Down and Kirkbride, with roughly daubed civil registrations and their roundels crudely crossed out, and were received by local companies including Rollasons, A.J. Whittemore and R.A. Peacock Aviation for conversion. Constant checking of the parked lines was necessary, for as soon as one was taken for conversion another filled the gap. It was also interesting to note that some of the rough marks had been incorrectly applied and did not always tie up with official allocations. As an example of this, T5606 allocated G-ANMN was marked G-ANOY, while T5840, the real 'NOY, was marked 'NMN. It didn't really matter, as both eventually went to France where such minor matters would have been ignored!

Many of the Tigers were converted at Croydon; some had only a hastily-sprayed coat of silver dope before going to their new homes in France, while others, mainly from Rollasons, received a more complete overhaul – you got what you paid for! At Rollasons, they were given job numbers applied in chalk, and such was the new dope coverage that the previous identities were completely obliterated. To keep an eye on what became what, I occasionally pencilled, in very small letters, the allocated British marks on an undercarriage leg, since many of them never carried these marks after conversion before acquiring their foreign marks. I believe I am right in saying that the first post-war German civil aircraft to be registered was a Tiger Moth, possibly D-EDAR (ex-G-AOBR & T6904) which I saw at Croydon on July 31st 1955. In those early days of the post-war German register, vowels were used as the centre letter, and the first batch of Tigers were D-EDAR, 'DER, 'DIR and 'DOR.

Tigers were a great source of interest during the fifties, with other export customers including Australia, Belgium, Canada, Spain, Switzerland and Sweden; there was even a batch delivered to the Thai Navy. Several others were converted to Jackaroos, and to resemble Fokker D.VIIs for a film company; one, DE631/G-ANJX, was said to have been thrown into the sea after gale damage in January 1954.

Croydon was not the only place working on these early surplus Tigers; Thruxton and Eastleigh were also involved. Replacing the Tigers with the RAF were Chipmunks, and a visit to Fairoaks on April 23rd 1950 revealed WB604 to '611 (except '609) with the London University Air Squadron. All except '607 eventually followed their predecessors onto the civil market, in either the UK, Switzerland, Germany or Australia.

Croydon always had something of interest, be it the first batch of Beech Bonanzas in Europe, the first Cessna 120 (HB-CAA), or the famous Cessna Bobcat 331964 in USAF silver, reputedly belonging to Prince Peter of Yugoslavia, and which subsequently rotted away behind 'D' Shed.

The first substantial civil show in 1950 was at White Waltham on May 14th. Highlights were the Sokol G-AIXN with previous marks OK-BHA clearly visible beneath the paint, a French Air Force team of four Stampes (Nos 678, 680, 682 and 683), similarly with civil marks showing through, respectively F-BDNX, 'DNZ, 'DOB and 'DOC, first appearances in Britain of the tiny Fouga Cyclone F-WFOI with a Turboméca Pimène jet mounted on top of the fuselage behind the cockpit, the odd little Hurel Dubois HD.10 F-WFAN with its high-aspect-ratio wing, the Fokker F.12 PH-NDC tricycle undercarriage trainer based on the Instructor, and the silver and red Rapide VT-ARV. Returning home past Heathrow, it was a delight to see several Stratocruisers (N90944, N1028V, G-AKGI to 'L and 'LSA) and a pair of Languedocs (F-BATT and 'CUP).

Memory is not all that it might be these days, with senility creeping (rushing?) on, but it appears from my log that I had an Isle of Wight holiday in May 1950, and a visit to Aquila Airways on the slipway at Hamble on the 27th netted eleven of their Short flying boats: Sandringham G-AGKX and Hythes G-AGER, 'EU, 'HZ, 'IA, 'JJ, 'JK, 'JL, 'JM, 'KY and 'HER. It was a sorry sight, as some were partly scrapped already. I noted at the time that I went inside 'KY *"Hungerford,"* but I have no recollection of this at all. The airfield at Hamble had a mass of RAF Tigers and Ansons, a load of civil Tigers and five instructional airframes which wore dummy registrations: Ansons G-ERTY and G-RETA, Oxford G-ARBO, Auster G-ABBY and Proctor G-ARTA. Just up the road at Eastleigh were 21 Wellingtons and a pair of 'B-Conditions' registrations on Spitfire G-15-90 and Sea Otter G-15-84, while over at Cowes were Walruses L2306, W2688, G-AHFM and 'HFO, the last three, along with Cygnet G-AGAU, being on the scrap heap. It was at Cowes, maybe not on that occasion, that I saw Rapide G-ALAX being convincingly looped, a sight to behold and hear, as the rigging wires really sang!

The air racing and aerobatic contests at Wolverhampton and Coventry in the fifties were a must for enthusiasts. The 1950 King's Cup at Wolverhampton attracted a great many visitors and at the risk of readers salivating I would mention 47 Austers, 9 Rapides, 19 Tigers, 15 Geminis, 20 Magisters, 3 Falcon Sixes, 4 Whitney Straights, 2 M.28s, 24 Messengers, 18 Proctors, 2 Vega Gulls, 2 Q.6s and 3 Taylorcraft Plus Ds, among others which included Ercoupe VX147, Mamba Dakota KJ839, Lockheed 12A G-AGTL and GAL Hotspur HH196. On the coach journey we had a raffle and each drew an aircraft for the race. Mine was the Mosscraft MA.2 G-AEST (the MA.4 G-AFMS was also present), but unfortunately 'ST crashed at the Newport turn, killing the pilot. At the end of the race, Spitfire G-AISU (now better known as the BBMF's AB910) taxied into the Parnall Heck G-AEGI and cut off its tail; fortunately there were no injuries but it was the end of the road for the Heck.

I seldom went to the late-lamented West Malling, but a visit on July 2nd produced 24 Mosquitoes, a Hornet, Meteor and Anson. One could write a book about the RAF Display at Farnborough on July 7th & 8th, but I'll mention just a few figures (more salivating): 65 Lincolns, 3 Yorks, 3 Lancasters, 3 Balliols, 3 Hornets, 13 Mosquitoes, 36 Vampires, 7 Chipmunks, 32 Meteors, 7 Hastings, 2 Halifaxes, 25 Spitfires, 7 Dakotas, 6 Sunderlands, 7 Hoverflies, 5 Sedberghs, 11 Harvards, 4 Valettas etc. — and these were just the ones from which I got serials! Needless to say, many of these were in the flypast only, but some of the Mosquitoes replicated the attack on Amiens prison and were harried by Spitfires TE380 and TB750 painted to represent Bf.109s. A novel item was the snatch off the ground of Hadrian 274521, in RAF roundels, by Dakota KN641.

I was rather surprised at Tangmere on July 31st when nine P-47D Thunderbolts arrived, five with blue noses and tails and four with red. They were accompanied by C-47 348594 and I often wondered about the purpose of their visit to this RAF jet station, then equipped with Meteor 4s of Nos.1 and 43 Squadrons. Also there were four Martinets, EM955, EM697, JN672 and PX133, presumably used for towing targets to give the Meteor squadrons practice.

In the previous book, "Tails of the Fifties," Peter Campbell recalled the 1951 "DAILY EXPRESS" South Coast Air Race. It is worth mentioning that the year before, on September 16th 1950, that newspaper had held a similar race from Hurn to Herne Bay. This was particularly interesting, as among the 76 entries in addition to the usual Proctors, Geminis,

Messengers and Magisters were some real oddballs. They were the Mamba Marathon G-AHXU, Aerovan 6 G-AKHF, Balliol VR602, Hurricane G-AMAU (PZ865), Halifax 8 G-AKEC, Consuls G-AHEF and VX587 (the latter being the Alvis Leonides test-bed), Skyjeep G-AKVS, Argus G-AKIZ, Wicko G-AFJB, Hirtenberg HS.9A G-AGAK, Tomtit G-AFTA, Q.6 G-AEYE and a pair of welcome foreigners, BHT Beauty LN-JHC and Lignel 46 F-BCZJ. Nine aircraft scratched before the race, including Starck AS.71 F-PCIC, Mew Gull G-AEXF, Bonanza VT-CSF and the Youngman-Baynes High-Lift Monoplane G-AMBL, while six others retired, leaving a finishing field of 61. Winner was Proctor G-AHUZ at 164.5 mph, the Marathon was seventh at 280.5 mph, but the most remembered sight was the Halifax pounding its way through the smaller fry but failing to get a place in the first dozen.

Breaking away from the registration scene, I would like to say something about the Royal Observer Corps (ROC) in the fifties. I was on the Wallington Post, part of 19 Group, Horsham. Originally designated Y2 (Yoke Two), it later became Q2 (Quebec Two) and most of the younger post members were aircraft enthusiasts. Our older members included one who wore the Seaborne shoulder flash indicating that he had taken part in the invasion of Normandy, where a number of ROC volunteers had gone in with the Navy solely to identify friendly aircraft and lower the risk of loss by friendly fire. Our post was less than two miles from Croydon Airport, so we had a good view of their operations. Unfortunately, this also meant reporting everything, including the local circuits and bumps by resident Tigers which tended to become monotonous with "Tiger Moth airborne Croydon, Tiger Moth landed Croydon" every few minutes, or so it seemed.

There were one or two incidents which were memorable; on one occasion a USAF Thunderjet came across the airport so low that, so I was told, he lost a tip tank when it touched the ground. One night we had a Constellation with engine trouble which the various posts reported until it was safely down. On a very clear day we plotted a vapour trail away to the south-west until it turned back, later discovering that it was a Valiant on test from Wisley and it had turned over Portsmouth, almost 80 miles away. In those days, the RAF would put up aircraft specially for ROC exercises, in addition to their own exercises in which we would take part. You could of course be on duty for hours and see virtually nothing, but among the rewards were special ROC Open Days at RAF stations where one could go, with a camera, and see a special static show and flying display, and often go flying in a Valetta, Varsity, Hastings or Beverley. Being virtually on the border with No.2 Group, we often managed to get on their visits in addition to our own. I will come back to these displays later.

A visit to Wisley on June 3rd 1951 revealed Valetta VL275 fitted with a four-wheel bogie undercarriage that I noted as "presumably test rig for Vickers 660 bomber," which of course was the Valiant.

That June, the film *"Angels One Five"* was being made at Kenley, then mainly an Auster base. Involved were a pair of Hurricanes, both marked P2617, one coded B-US, the other P-US, while a third, L1592, was B-US also. Spitfires P9444 and K9942 and a Bf.110 tipped on its nose were present; I believe the Messerschmitt was subsequently scrapped.

Occasional 'Foreign Visitors' Days at southern England airfields were always worth investigating; one at Gatwick on July 18th brought a splendid assortment whose details I have on record although I will not mention them here. One of the large events of 1951 was the Jubilee Display at Hendon on July 21st which brought a wide variety of aircraft from the 1909 Blériot to a Meteor and Vampire.

It was always a pleasure to go to an event at Farnborough, but it was also rewarding on other occasions just to look over the fence. Most of the usual types were about together with various Lancasters and Lincolns with lumps and bumps in various places. Lancaster RT690 had a spike below the nose turret in place of the bomb-aimer's dome, Lincolns RF530 and RF560 had filled-in noses and Lancaster 2 DS708 was lying on its belly. Mosquito VT655 had a bulge just behind the glass nose, while Vampire VV215 had a rod in the nose.

A cycle tour around the Gloucester area in October 1951 was interesting. South Cerney was very active with several Harvards and many Prentices, while Kemble produced 19 Lancasters and 10 Lincolns, with 6 more of the latter at Hullavington. Lyneham was busy, with 19 Hastings, but the most interesting items there were four Hamilcar fuselages, including TK726, RR949 and 6770M (ex-RR948). I wonder what happened to them: probably they finished up as garden sheds! An odd find at Thruxton on November 11th was the wreckage of Puss Moth G-ABEH, both fuselage and wings showing signs of once being G-AAZP and, before that, RAF service. Since 'AZP is still with us, how much of it is genuine? That year finished nicely with a visit to Croydon of Catalina SE-XAD, seen on December 29th.

I wonder how many of us remember Rapide EL-AAA of Liberian National Airways, ex-G-AHGG, which was at Croydon on April 24th 1952, or the Avro Anson 19 EL-ABC, ex-G-AKUD and VM373, seen there in August 1955? A welcome visitor on May 24th 1952 was Dr J.N. Haldeman's Bellanca Cruisair ZS-DEN (ex CF-GLM) from Pretoria.

In those faraway days, the Royal Aeronautical Society held Garden Parties at White Waltham, still very much in use by Fairey for Firefly production, and it was possible to walk along the front of their hangars and see the line. On June 15th 1952 there were no less than 48 Mk.7s present ranging from WJ146 to WK356; these plus two Gannet prototypes were a good bonus to the 100-plus other aircraft there, which included Swedish Air Force Safir 91123.

I mentioned earlier the displays specially arranged for the ROC; one held at Biggin Hill on July 6th gives an idea of their scope. A height-and-speed-judging contest with a Meteor T.7 was followed by an aerobatic display by Vampire FB.5 WR872. Individual displays by Meteor NF.11 WD617 and Vampire NF.10 WP233 led to a Wing scramble by 16 locally-based Meteor F.8s, then a flypast and stream landing. Six Meteor F.8s from Waterbeach performed formation aerobatics, culminating in a break-away and high-speed low-level crossover from six directions. We then had a fly-over and beat-up by 12 Vampire FB.5s, Meteor F.8 WF686 aerobatted and this was followed by Washington WF492 in a flypast. Sabre FU-316 of the USAF performed some fast runs and the display ended with fast fly-bys by Canberra WE117. During the morning, pleasure flights were given to ROC members in Ansons VM367 and '393, Oxford LX162 and Valetta VL271. A number of aircraft were also on static display, so the RAF did us proud.

Breaking away for one day from the SBAC Display at Farnborough in September, I went to a Naval Air Display at Ford which produced a satisfying mix of types. A number were locally-based, but some of the Sea Furies bore CM, LM and JA tail codes. Sixteen Attackers were seen, most with J codes, and three were wrecks. A pair of Seafire 17s, SR478 and '631, were sacrificed as ground targets in an attack on the airfield. I was fortunate in being at Ford that day and not at Farnborough, for it was the day on which John Derry crashed in the prototype DH.110 WG236.

Battle of Britain Day, September 15th, was commemorated by a flypast over London consisting of 12 Lincolns, 12 Washingtons, 12 Canberras, 8 Attackers, the prototype Hunter WB188 and some Meteor F.8s and Sabres – I didn't note how many of these. The formation was led by Hurricane LF363, the only type connected with the Battle – where were all the Spitfires?

Some of you may remember the London-based Aircraft Recognition Society and its monthly meetings presided over by the urbane Eric Wilton. These were good for us recognition enthusiasts, and on October 11th the Society organised a trip to the USAF at Manston, where we saw no less than 43 F-84E Thunderjets, 4 SA-16 Albatross amphibians, a T-33 and a pair of Harvards. Visiting were three Dutch Thunderjets and two Dutch Meteor F.8s. The USAF F-84s had blue, red or yellow noses, while the Dutch ones had red and yellow rudders.

In May 1953, Little Rissington seemed to be a Dakota store with more than 46 there plus several Wellingtons. Brize Norton had 20 B-50s in that month but the mid-year high spot was the Open Day and Preview of the Fleet Royal Review Flypast at Spithead, with aircraft taking off from Lee on Solent. These comprised 112 Fireflies, 3 Gannets, 13 Skyraiders, 14 Sea

Hornets, 40 Sea Furies (including nine Canadian), and 19 Avengers (including 10 Canadian) — and I got all the serials!

My first overseas spotting trip was in July 1953 to the Paris Air Show. We flew from Northolt to Le Bourget in BEA Viking G-AMNJ and on the following day visited Toussus-le-Noble for the first time, logging 225 aircraft, the vast majority of course being French-registered. Several others included Norseman I-AIAK, Voyager I-VALB and KZ.7 HB-EPP. This was the first time I had been subjected to so many diverse French types – 35 Norécrins for instance – but it was an education! In any visit to Toussus one would always find something interesting. At that time there were plenty of vintage types around which had one way or another survived the war; they included MS.181 F-AJQK, MS.230 F-BEJO, MS.341 F-AMRO, Bagimer F-PFAR, Luciole F-BBAZ, very ancient but airworthy Dewoitine 482 F-AQMO with biscuit adverts, dismantled Farman 192 F-AKER, Monocoupe F-BBSN and Reliant F-BBCS. The splendid original Farman hangar, on the left as you enter the airfield, was noteworthy for its external roof-bracing struts. It always had a collection of unusual and forgotten types, gradually pushed to the back of the hangar to make way for modern equipment and usually access, easily granted everywhere else, was denied in the Farman hangar with the excuse "We are building a prototype for the government." Maybe, but the gestation period for the Farman Monitor F-WFOF couldn't have covered all the years this excuse was given! These days, permission can often be gained "for one only" so his logging needs to be accurate.

A half-hour's walk across the fields from Toussus was Guyancourt, a friendly field with the control office built in the top corner of a hangar. Here were another 19 Norécrins plus other treasures including Argus F-BFPO, Simoun F-BDXS, Bestmann F-BBPX, Courlis F-BEVI and the tandem-wing Louis Massotte F-APAG. Guyancourt is no more, becoming a housing estate in the early nineties.

Even closer to Toussus in the other direction, only about a field away, was the historic airfield of Buc, complete with a massive entry arch. Buc was an alternative to Le Bourget between the wars, but again has now been built on – I stayed at a Campanile there recently. At the time of my visit in July 1953 virtually all the 32 aircraft present were interesting, but to select a few: orange Anson F-BGOF (ex-MG199), Luciole F-ANTG, Phalene F-BBCH, the unmarked Caudron 690 (now in the Musée de l'Air), Ercoupe F-BCJI, Aubert PA.204s F-WWBQ and F-BFRU, unmarked Potez 32 F-AROY, the twin-boom Roussel 40 monoplane which was apparently never registered, 7 Navions including EC-AGR and a pair of Voyagers, F-BEDN and 'FXD.

Another airfield near Versailles was St Cyr, fortunately still with us. The military airfield at Villacoublay was fairly active, and at that time there was another small airfield on the other side of the road, opposite the eastern end. This was Villacoublay-Velizy, and was used by Morane-Saulnier; it has long since gone.

Back to England, and the static display at Odiham on July 15th 1953 for the RAF Royal Review, a splendid occasion. Statistics: lined up were 9 Oxfords, 6 Auster 6s, 7 Ansons, 4 Lancasters, 8 Lincolns, 84 Meteors of various marks, 6 Hastings, 4 Neptunes, 12 Harvards, 16 Sabres (including 12 Canadian), 4 Shackletons, 12 Prentices, 4 Provosts, 6 Balliols, 60 Chipmunks, 52 Vampires, 4 Venoms, 6 Canberras, 5 Valettas, 5 Varsities, 4 Washingtons, 2 Devons and single examples of the Sycamore, Bristol Freighter (RNZAF) and Slingsby T.31. This was a feast in itself, but here comes the flypast: a Sycamore, 12 each of Chipmunks, Prentices, Harvards, Oxfords, Ansons, Balliols and Varsities, 6 Valettas, 3 Sunderlands, 45 Lincolns, 12 Washingtons, 18 Shackletons, 5 Neptunes, 3 Hastings, 36 Vampires, 24 Venoms, 276 (yes!) Meteors, 48 Canberras, 60 Sabres, 6 Swift F.1s and single examples of the Victor (WB771), Valiant (WP215), Vulcan (VX770), Javelin (WT827), Hunter (WB555) and Swift F.4 (WK198). As if this cavalcade was not enough, we had an interval fly-over by Tiger Moth G-AHUT, Harvard FX283, Meteor T.7 WL368, Canberra PR.3 WE141, Canberra B.2 WE137, Hastings Met.1 TG567, Spitfire LF.16 TE401, Auster 6 VF543, Hastings C.2s WD475 and WD499, Anson VM383, Mosquito RG207 and a pair of Meteor FR.9s. Any other RAF event for as long as I can remember pales into insignificance after that!

An oddity at Aston Down's Battle of Britain display on September 19th was an air race. The starting order (with finishing order in brackets) was Chipmunk WZ846 (1), Provost XE506 (6), Anson TX225 (5), Varsity WL625 (3 tie), Spitfire RW352 (7), Canberra WJ608 (3 tie), and Meteor WX975 (2).

At this time, the racy B-47 Stratojets were based at Brize Norton; there were 19 visible on September 20th plus a C-124B Globemaster. I mentioned earlier some Hamilcar fuselages at Lyneham; on September 21st there were six rear fuselages, RR993, RR995, RZ411, RZ422 and RZ428 plus one cocooned. A number of airframes were being cocooned around that time and among those seen were a number of Spitfires at Lyneham plus Lincolns RE420, RF369, RF403 and RF512 at Hull-avington, the first three entirely cocooned and the last engines only.

Gales in January 1954 caused some damage to the picketed Proctors and Tigers at Croydon; Proctor RM188 had its port undercarriage smashed and tail damaged; NP387 also suffered tail damage, while the wings of Tiger DE631 (G-ANJX) were ripped off and the tail and prop smashed, and Tiger N5490 (G-ANHG) had its port upper wing broken in half; also the port tailplane and fin were smashed on BB726 (G-ACDC), precursors of the many replacements used on this aircraft still claimed to be the oldest Tiger flying, a case of grandfather's original axe with three new heads and two new shafts!

Passing through Croydon on February 27th, being ferried by the Airways Aero Club to Kuwait, were new Aiglet Trainers G-ANNV and 'NNW in silver with green trim and Autocars G-ANNX and 'NNY in silver and red. I'll finally leave the subject of Tiger conversions at Croydon with the readiness for departure on May 28th 1954 of F-BGZN, 'O, 'P, 'R, 'X, 'Y and 'HAP; 'GZY apparently had no British civil identity and was ex-T7400, so it had probably arrived at Croydon by road. A similar exercise with Austers was going on at Elstree, and 23 were there on May 30th, still in military marks.

My next overseas trip was in July that year, and included a visit to Zurich Airport. At that time, you could go to the operations office and request a pass, which allowed you to walk across the tarmac on a marked line between the Constellations, Convairs and others, stopping to take photos, to the light aircraft hangar, then situated in the centre between the runways. You could then click away as long as you liked. Things are now rather different, and that light aircraft hangar, which also housed the fire service, has long gone. I can remember seeing an old biplane at Thun airfield and writing to the Swiss military authorities to ask what it was. They sent me a nice picture of the type and said that it was a Fokker C.V "waiting his end in a fire-extinguisher exercise!" Switzerland at that time was still using Bf.108s, Mustangs, P-2s, EKW C.35s, Fokker C.Vs, Harvards, Storches, Jungmeisters and Jungmanns, plus of course the ubiquitous Ju.52/3Ms, and a number of these types were seen. At Berne, the antique Koolhoven FK.50A HB-AMA in cream and blue was a welcome sight.

Visitors to the SBAC Display in September flew into Blackbushe and it was always worth looking there. Oddballs in 1954 were Dove D-101 of the Arab Legion Air Force and Viking G-AJBX with Arabian Desert Air Lines titles. The old-timers among you may remember the USAF C-119 Packet 12611 used as the air-to-air photographic aircraft for the Press at the Farnborough shows, later replaced by a Hastings from the RAE.

This article has lasted somewhat longer than I intended and has still only reached the mid-fifties! I'll close therefore with a few final registrations which might stir memories: these were noted at the much-lamented Derby Burnaston airfield. On April 16th 1955 I was delighted to see 10 Mosquitoes for Spartan Air Services, Canada. CF-HML (ex VR796) was complete and awaiting flight-test, 'HMK (ex-VR794) was almost complete, 'HMQ (ex-VP189) was being sprayed, 'HMT (ex-RS711) was silver and blue and incorrectly marked CF-HMR, while unconverted in ferry marks were 'HMM (ex-TK623), 'HMN (ex-TA713), 'HMO (ex-TA696), 'HMP (ex-TK648), 'HMR (ex-TA661) and 'HMS (ex-RS700). I wonder if the error on 'HMT was ever corrected. Also there was Gemini CF-HVK (ex G-AJOH).

My apologies to those readers who are not interested in registrations, but I guess they will already have moved on before getting this far! To those who have come all the way, thanks, and I hope the foregoing will have stirred some ancient memories and perhaps even the odd "Oh! that's what it was!" And just in case anyone wonders, I am still spotting!

CHAPTER 6

EASTLEIGH AND WESTERLY

by

Vivian Bellamy

(as told to Peter Campbell)

When I think back on it, we operated a lot of different types of aircraft during the time I was at Eastleigh, including the Tiger Moth, Hornet Moth, Leopard Moth, Puss Moth, Chipmunk, Proctor, Dragon Rapide, Consul, Auster, Anson, Wot, Dragonfly and, of course, the last DH.86A Express.

I had left the Navy in July or August of 1945, shortly after the end of the war, and Jack Jones (who later started East Anglian Flying Services) and I had just the end of the summer season doing pleasure-flying together at Herne Bay. After that I bought a Puss Moth from him. Jack later went back to Southend to start the airline. He did very well during the fifties, operating Rapides, Doves, Bristol Freighters, Vikings and DC-3s that he bought from BEA. I remember that there was one dreadful time at Portsmouth, probably in the mid-sixties, when there were two accidents on the same day – I think they must have been Avro 748s. It had been raining heavily, and of course it was an all-grass airfield. One came in to land and slithered into the hedge. When the next one arrived, the controllers let it land and it, too, went into the hedge.

At the end of 1945 I was considering where would be the best place to start an aeroplane business, narrowed it down to Elmdon or Eastleigh, and finally settled on Eastleigh, where I started Flightways. We had a Puss Moth, the one that I mentioned earlier, G-AAZP – nothing better, a wonderful aeroplane, a beautiful thing, although we were a bit afraid sometimes of whether its structural reputation was true! I think that this particular one is still flying from Hungerford. We also specialized in converting Dragon Rapides to take Gipsy Queen 2 engines driving constant-speed propellers, making them into Mk.4s; this increased the permissible take-off weight and improved not only the climb but also the cruising speed and single-engine performance.

Amongst the more unusual aeroplanes that I was involved with in the early fifties was the Gladiator; more accurately, there were actually two of them! One, G-AMRK, is now with the Shuttleworth Trust. I was sitting in the bar one day (all good stories start like that!) and they were talking about aeroplanes generally. Then the discussion got round to Spitfires and Hurricanes, and then someone was saying that they were all good but that the Gladiator was *much* better than any of them. As you can imagine, there was then a deathly hush, a sort of "throw that man out" atmosphere, and then someone turned round and said that there was a Gladiator sitting down at Hamble with Air Service Training.

So I picked up the telephone and said to the chap on the other end: "That Gladiator of yours, what are you going to do with it?"

"We're going to scrap it," he said.

"Well, send it round here."

"You'll have to pay for it."

"How much?"

"A fiver."

So we got the Gladiator for a fiver! It was pretty well perfect. Then he said: "Do you want another one? We've got another one, but it's sitting out in the open at Ansty."

That one cost us another fiver, and of course we had to truck it down to Eastleigh.

The first one was in perfect order; it had only done 80 hours since new and had been operated by a Met. flight. The engine was rather rusted up, though help then came from an unexpected source.

Mr Dowty came to me and said: "It's our hundredth anniversary coming up; could we have the Gladiator to display?"

"Well, you could," I replied, "but we can't make the engine go."

"Don't worry about that!" he said. "Are there any other bits you want?"

"Not really; its just the undercarriage legs we've got a bit of a problem with."

"Well, I'll do those for you! You just send the engine along to Bristol's."

So we did, and they rebuilt the engine for us. Mr Dowty must have had a lot of influence at Bristol's!

We were intending to use the other Gladiator for spares, but in the event we didn't. As you'll remember hearing from Ted Gould [and reported in "Tails of the Fifties – Ed.], I did offer it to him in exchange for his Drone on one occasion, but then the Fleet Air Arm got hold of it. I believe that they eventually sold it on as scrap for something like £500,000. I should have been on a commission! It has been rebuilt at Duxford by a chap who already owns a Hurricane and several other aeroplanes.

Later, after I became the owner of the Hampshire Aeroplane Club, I was deeply involved with a Spitfire. I used to fly the MD of Vickers-Armstrong's Supermarine Works from Eastleigh up to South Marston

UPPER: Last-minute discussion before the Tiger Club display at Sandown,
May 26th 1958.
LOWER: A Tiger Club formation returning home, March 1959.
Photos: via Clive Elton.

UPPER: The Martlet G-AAYX flown by Tony Farrell in 1936. The "pilot" notice seems superfluous to say the least; on the starboard side was the even-more esoteric caption "hoofhearted." Photo: Tony Farrell.

LOWER: At the close of a photographic sortie on March 19th 1952 at Hamble. L. to R.: Cyril Peckham, CFI Wg. Cdr. Stratton AFC, Tony Farrell. Photo: Cyril Peckham via Tony Farrell.

UPPER: Bob Whitehead (instructor at AST from 1948 until the sixties), seen in Whitney Straight G-AEVG, March 1952. Photo: Tony Farrell.
CENTRE: Murray Chown's joyriding Proctor G-AKXK at Land's End, July 20th 1952. Photo: Peter Amos.
LOWER: Rex Nicholls with the Spartan Arrow G-ABWP at Croydon, May 9th 1954. Photo: Peter Amos.

TWO DETAILED VIEWS OF THE RAF REVIEW
AT ODIHAM ON JULY 15TH 1953.
UPPER: Hastings WJ327 & Meteor FR.9 WH542.
LOWER: Washington WF572 & Vampire FB.9 WR196.
Photos: Mike Hooks.

UPPER: Saunders Roe's Dragon Rapide G-ALAX at Cowes, August 4th 1949.
CENTRE: Youngman-Baynes High-Lift Monoplane G-AMBL at White Waltham, May 6th 1951.
LOWER: F.24R Argus F-BDAQ parked by the "Beehive" at Gatwick during the Foreign Visitors' day on July 18th 1951.
Photos: Mike Hooks.

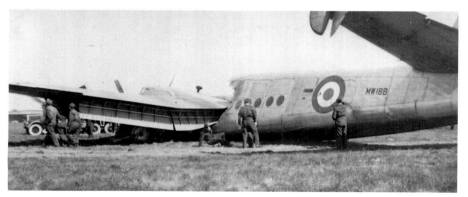

UPPER: 33 Sqn. Tempest PR689 after a forced landing in Germany, 1948.
CENTRE: Lancashire Aircraft Corp. Halifax G-AHWN at Gütersloh during
the Berlin Airlift in 1948.
LOWER: York MW188 after an emergency landing at Gütersloh in 1948.
Photos: Tim Webb.

near Swindon. Periodically he used to ring me up from just across the river, and I used to put him in a Hornet Moth and take him up there.

One day we got talking, me doing my bit about Hurricanes, Spitfires and Gladiators and all the rest, and he said: "We're going to scrap a two-seater Spitfire at Chilbolton."

"You can't do that!" I said.

"Do you want it, then?" he asked.

"Yes, please."

"All right, you can have it, but you mustn't come to me for spares."

So I went up to Chilbolton to have a look at it; it had only done 800 hours since new, and was on the civil register as G-AIDN. Then later I took John Isaacs up with me to collect it; John had always wanted to fly in a Spitfire. After completing all the necessary formalities, I said to him: "Well, jump in the back and we'll take it down to Eastleigh."

Mind you, I wasn't sure if I was as capable as I thought I was: I hadn't flown one of these things for a long time. So I sat in it to familiarise myself with everything, and it seemed all right. After we had finally got the engine going I taxied out for take-off, lined up and opened the throttle. As soon as the power came on, I felt that of course I could fly the bloody thing, all the old enthusiasm surged back.

So we roared into the air, I pulled the wheels up (after a reminder from the control tower that I hadn't yet done so) and then slammed it into a climbing turn. Halfway up the engine stopped. I just couldn't believe it! We were at about 500 feet then; out of sheer instinct I first checked whether the fuel was 'off' and, amazingly, it was. The undercarriage selector and the fuel cock controls were very close together and non-standard, and I must have switched off the fuel cock immediately after take-off instead of retracting the undercarriage. I turned it on again and the engine came back to life when I was about ten feet from the deck!

John, in the back, must have nearly died of fright, and a tremulous voice over the R/T said: "Did you know your undercarriage is still down?", which of course explained it all.

Anyway, we got back to Eastleigh all right, but I didn't make a very good landing, partly because I had never flown a Spitfire with a counterweight in it, which made it very hard to get the tail down – but perhaps the experience we had just gone through had got to me too.

We had a bit of trouble getting a C. of A. on it; everybody screamed their heads off saying that we couldn't have a dangerous thing like that flying around. Then the Israeli Air Attaché came to us and asked if he could borrow it for an air race, so I told him that I wasn't allowed to fly it.

"Don't worry," he said, "I'll put an Israeli C. of A. on it."

"Jolly good," I said. "But there is one problem we've got to get sorted out with the engine, there's white metal in the filters. What we really need is another engine."

The long and short of it was that Billy Butlin got us another engine, and for some years after that the Spitfire was a fairly common sight at air shows and air races; it's in America now. We also had the use of the Zaunkoenig G-ALUA for a while, which John Isaacs bought from the Ipswich PFA Group for £140. That was a fascinating aeroplane; it had a Zundapp engine, with single ignition. If one plug went out, it wouldn't fly. The problem was that, because it was so well known for its slow-flying capabilities, people thought they could act like 'silly b*****s' with it. Someone would do a climbing turn, it would go out on one 'pot,' and then they would get into some quite interesting and exciting positions. John wrote quite a bit about it and many of our other experiments and adventures in his wonderful book *"Aeroplane Affair." [Air Research Publications, 1988 – Ed.]*

Of course the other unusual plane I flew once at Christchurch was Ted Gould's Drone *[as described in "Tails of the Fifties" – Ed.]*. I'd always wanted to fly a Drone ever since the thirties. Finally Ted said: "There you are; off you go!"

I thought: "Ah! Splendid!" and took off. But by the time we got to a hundred feet it was boiling! I just crept round the bloody circuit. These simple aeroplanes, you think they'll be no trouble at all, but it bloody well was! I did get it down, and didn't break it, so that was the main thing.

We bought the DH.86A, G-ACZP, from the Lancashire Aircraft Corporation in 1956. They had advertised it for £500 (wonderful days, those, weren't they?), and we went up there to see it; it was perfect. We just pressed the starter buttons and flew it away! We used it for all sorts of trips and for giving joyrides at air shows, and I remember we once flew some strawberries up to Scotland. We came back via Pwllheli; we had the pleasure-flying concession at Billy Butlin's holiday camp there.

We finally pranged it at Madrid on the 21st September 1958. We were on our way to Tangier, which I was always very intrigued with; I had a house down there which we used for holidays. It was very sad; we had a lovely trip down to Madrid, and landed at dusk. Halfway down the landing run, I thought: "Hallo, something funny's happening." In fact a tyre had gone, and the aircraft slowly swung over to one side, until at about 15 knots it ground-looped. The axle cap had broken and let the wheel out, so we spun round on the stub axle.

Madrid, being Madrid, had no idea we were there. I was talking to them on the radio and said: "We've had an accident on the runway," but they kept on speaking in Spanish and obviously didn't understand us. Then a DC-4 came in, and the pilot saw us on the runway and spoke in more violent Spanish to the controllers. It was only then that they realised exactly where we were!

Eventually they organised a couple of stack trucks to have the aircraft moved out of the way. One of these trucks had long prongs and the other one short prongs, and they were carefully placed between each of the engines and the fuselage. However, on moving off, the aircraft unfortunately slipped off the short-pronged truck, which damaged the spar. That was the real reason we had to leave it there. The spar was certainly damaged, but with a lot more experience like we have now we wouldn't have been as concerned as we were at the time.

So we had to abandon the aircraft there; eventually the Spaniards burnt it. What a sad end, and especially so, looking back on it now, because it was so unnecessary.

The extraordinary thing was this; when we bought it, it had a lot of spares with it, including about a dozen tyres, all of which were brand new. We used two of them on a tyre change shortly after bringing the aircraft down south, and I remember that when we were landing at Lee on Solent one day, one of of the tyres went there, just the same thing as at Madrid, and we landed up right in front of the Captain's enclosure, which didn't make us very popular, as it was an RNAS Open Day and all the VIPs would soon be arriving!

On reflection, I think that all that batch of tyres were probably very old. They could have deteriorated quite a bit but still *looked* perfectly all right.

In more recent years there have been rumours circulating (which were quite correct, in fact) that we were intending to build a DH.86 from scratch at Land's End. However, the sponsorship money we were hoping for never materialized, and regrettably the project had to be abandoned. We had a complete set of DH plans available and it would have been a practical project.

The Currie Wot was an interesting aeroplane. After we had built the first one with a JAP engine, I thought that it just needed a few modifications and would really be jolly good. So we put a Mikron engine in it, and it *was* jolly good; we called that the 'Hot Wot.' Later we converted the second Wot to a seaplane (the 'Wet Wot'), having Saunders Roe design the floats. We had been a bit over-confident, and had told them that we wouldn't need them to be as long as they had drawn them, so they were made a bit shorter. Well, they turned out to be definitely too short; when we had the Wot on the water, the floats threw up so much spray that they drowned the engine. Anyhow, we never did get it off the water, although with a bit more forethought we could have done! After that, we put a Rover gas turbine in it (that was the 'Jet Wot'); John Isaac's book describes our trials and tribulations very well.

John then had a look at the Wot design and thought he would like to modify it to make a scaled-down Hawker Fury out of it, which he eventually did. But although it flew all right with a Mikron engine it proved to be rather underpowered, so we decided to put a bigger engine in it. John and I went out and got a 125 hp Lycoming out of an Auster, and that transformed it. It was a quite brilliant little aeroplane then. It was terribly good for aerobatics, I remember, especially when we had fitted proper flying wires instead of bits of string!

During the late fifties, Saunders Roe, who of course were by then building Skeeter helicopters at Eastleigh, also had a contract with the American Hiller Company to develop their small one-man helicopter. *[The prototype XROE-1 Rotocycle had its first flight at 16.30 on the 15th October 1959: I was there! – Ed.]* It was flown quite a bit, but some time later it pranged (or it might be more accurate to say that it tripped over) outside my office door, after a gust of wind came round the hangar. It fell on its back, and caught fire. If I remember rightly, it was a chap called Lamb who was flying it. He looked rather like a beetle trapped upside down, and there he was with this fire going on all around him – it was very unpleasant to watch. But he got out all right; the worst thing that happened to him in the end was that his legs got burned – his socks were nylon, and they melted and fused with the hairs on his legs!

I had also been an eyewitness some years earlier to the crash of the Cierva Airhorse just off the aerodrome. I was sitting in my office and saw it crash. I jumped in the Rapide and flew out to it, and the fire crew followed me. That was very very sad; the pilot, Marsh, was one of the early instructors with the Hampshire Aero Club.

The crash should never have happened. There was a little lever, used for changing the pitch of the rotors, on which the total loading was meant not to exceed 15 lb. In fact it was much much more than this. It let go, one of the blades got 'out of sync' and it chopped itself to death.

Then there was the Halcyon. That story fills me with a certain amount of sadness. After building two or three Curry Wots, we thought we ought to have a go at building something a bit modernish, and I thought it would be nice to have a little side-by-side two-seater Mosquito (all wood, of course) with a couple of Mikrons in it. That's where it started. So we got hold of Ray Hilborne, who was reputed to be a brilliant stress man, and started to make a go of it. When he saw the plans, he said: "Why don't you make it a four-seater? The stresses involved are much the same."

So we built it as a four-seater, but didn't put Mikrons in, because it had got a bit big for them; we fitted Walter Minors instead. In fact we went to Czechoslovakia to get those, which is a story in itself. We went out in a Rapide to collect them, and on the way out the weather clamped really right down. We got as far as Luxembourg, and had to almost climb up the hill, more or less; all I could see were the lights of the airfield. We left the aircraft there, and went on by car to collect the engines.

Unfortunately, it turned out that Hilborne can't have been quite as clever a stress man as I thought he was. We pushed the Halcyon out over the hangar rails and the nosewheel collapsed! Then, several months later, when we had got the engines going, I was taxying it over the grass and the rear spar collapsed!

After that I got a bit discouraged, as you can imagine, and abandoned the project. It was such a shame; it was a very pretty thing. In fact I was looking at the drawings of it only the other day, and was wondering if it could be made successfully out of more modern composite materials.

The United Nations suddenly offered me an enormous amount of money (!) to go down to North Africa and run a flying school for them, training would-be commercial pilots. This opportunity came up at a time when we had had a bit of trouble with the airfield at Eastleigh, and it didn't seem a very good place for flying clubs to operate from after that, so I decided to take up the offer, and went down to my favourite area, Tunisia.

After I came back I had an office and workshop at Blackbushe, and one day in 1966 the phone rang. It was Allen Wheeler: could I build him an Avro 504? So we did, in twelve weeks from scratch! It even had a proper Le Rhône rotary engine in it. This was intended to be used in a film called *"The Bells of Hell Go Ting-a-ling-a-ling,"* which was to be about the raid on the Zeppelin works in Freidrichshafen in 1915 or so, but the film never got made.

While I was at Blackbushe I also converted an Auster, G-AGVI, to take a Rover Gas Turbine; this engine had been developed from the one we had used previously in the 'Jet Wot,' and was more successful. I was also asked to build and test-fly a Pfalz for the fim *"The Blue Max,"* which we did back at Eastleigh; that was a beautiful aeroplane. When I applied aileron I saw the top and bottom wings come together and understood why the film pilots called it the "India Rubber Pfalz."

I then moved down to the aerodrome at Land's End, where I was based for many years subsequently. One day, the Honourable Patrick Lindsay came down and asked if he could have a ride in the scaled-down Fury which had been designed and built by John Isaacs (he was now involved with building a scaled-down Spitfire). So I said: "Yes, of course you can; off you go," and he flew it. Afterwards I said to him: "One day we're going to build a proper Fury!"

You see, I was always being told when I was in the Navy by lots of people who had flown Furies and Nimrods that "the Gladiator's a great 'ham' aeroplane in comparison; the one you really want is a Fury." So I'd always had the thought in the back of my mind that what I wanted was a Fury.

Patrick said as he was leaving: "If you ever find any drawings and decide to build it, do let me know."

Well, I was quite serious about this; I started a world search for some drawings and found *a* set, not for a Fury, but for a Nimrod, in the Danish Dockyard. They had been going to build them, but they didn't, although they did build Harts and things, and they had all the drawings there. Shortly after that we actually managed to get a proper set of drawings out of Hawkers themselves; we weren't supposed to have them, actually, but we got them. So Patrick commissioned us to build a full-scale Fury!

Getting the right engine was a big problem. But John Isaacs used to go out to New Zealand occasionally, as he was invited by other enthusiasts who had built Furies like his. After one trip, during which he had mentioned we were looking for a Kestrel engine, he had a phone call to say one had been located. He went out there again to a remote museum, and was introduced to four brothers who were all Rolls Royce fanatics; there underneath a table was nothing less than a Rolls Royce Kestrel engine complete! Needless to say, John was able to acquire it, so the Fury finally had the proper power plant.

We used to have a bit of trouble with the carburettor – at least I used to think we did! I didn't get very much chance of flying it, but when it came to stalling it, I was always a bit worried, not about the stall of the aircraft itself, but about the engine; it ran very rough at that slow speed, and being in Cornwall with very small fields, I didn't want to have to try and put this thing down with a dead engine. I was always a bit dubious about closing the throttle dead; someone else did at an air show in Belgium and it almost fell out of the sky!

Just one piece of the aeroplane was a genuine Fury part! One of the old boys at Hawkers, when he learned what we were doing, said: "Ah! I'll bring you a bit, the first bit I made as an apprentice at Hawkers." This turned out to be part of the rudder pedal assembly. The Fury eventually flew at the end of 1985, but very sadly, Patrick Lindsay, who had commissioned the aeroplane, never got to see it or fly it; at the time of the first flight he was very ill with cancer, and he died shortly afterwards.

During the seventies and eighties we built quite a range of vintage replicas at Land's End, including a DH.2, Sopwith 1½ Strutter, Albatross, Spad, Fokker Triplane and a Camel for a Biggles film. But unfortunately we couldn't get a rotary engine at the time and had to put a Super Scarab in it.

I had had a real urge to see what these older aeroplanes were *really* like, especially the Camel, and was determined to build a *real* one. Eventually we did, complete with the proper Clerget rotary engine, and that's now in the Brooklands Museum, by the way. We made it for Leisure Sport, who used to fly it against a Fokker Triplane we had also built. This one I really tried to get dead right; we had all the drawings, and finished it with the optimistic view that no one would be able to fault it. I remember that after about half an hour on its first public viewing, the inevitable small pimply boy came up to me and he said: "You've got the drain holes wrong."

"Drain holes? Drain holes? They're there, I can see 'em," I retorted.

"Yes," he said, "but you haven't made them of the right stuff. You've made celluloid ones, like Tiger Moths. They were all done in 'pen' steel in those days."

There's always someone!

The rotary Camel was very heard to beat, so we thought we should make a rotary Triplane; we eventually built this for ourselves, although when it came to it we weren't able to get a rotary engine after all. Then later on the Army came along and wanted to buy it, and that's now flying successfully.

[Editor's note: It is very sad to have to report that Vivian Bellamy passed away on the 26th February 1998.]

CHAPTER 7

RAF SWINGS AND CIVIL ROUNDABOUTS

by

Tim Webb

When it was suggested that I might contribute to this latest collection of aviation memories of the fifties, I found my 'memory bank' went back to my very first flight. Strictly speaking it occurred before the fifties, but just after the war there were many unusual events worth recording.

It was towards the end of June 1946 when, as a new Air Training Corps cadet, I took off for the first time at Ford in a Fleet Air Arm Airspeed Oxford. I can remember sitting in the right-hand seat alongside the pilot, much to the envy of my other companions, and stooging about over the Sussex countryside for about an hour. There was nothing very remarkable about the event itself, but Ford at the time held many interesting ex-Luftwaffe aircraft and these were, of course, quite unique. Unfortunately I had not at the time developed the habit of recording aircraft numbers, but there was a Ju.88G and what I now believe to be an He.219 full of interesting radar aerials in the nose. We were allowed unrestricted access to them as they were parked quite close to our Oxford. Later we discovered the real prize in a blister hangar, an Me.262B jet, which was the two-seater night fighter version also equipped with radar antennae. We learned that it had burst a tyre after a high-speed landing, but otherwise it was in good shape.

From *"Air-Britain Digest"* (Winter 1997) I have just discovered reference to these aircraft complete with the serial numbers! The Ju.88G was 622311/3C+DA, the He.219 was 310215, and the Me.262B was 111305. It is indeed strange how little snippets of information fit into place years after the actual event!

I eventually joined the RAF at the end of 1947 as a National Serviceman and served in the somewhat lowly capacity of an airframe mechanic's assistant, but at least I was involved with aircraft.

I was trained at Cosford (long before it became a museum) and eventually found myself posted to the Central Fighter Establishment at West Raynham in the wilds of Norfolk (recently closed). It was a bleak place exposed to the chilly winds which they said came direct from Siberia, but there was an event which certainly warmed us up one night.

Around 2.00 am I became aware of some muffled bangs coming from the nearby hangar, and looking out of the window I could see what appeared to be smoke and a dull red glow behind the doors. I hastily alerted our Corporal, and the entire billet was soon rushing over to the hangar. Inside we found a brand new Mosquito 38 well alight, and surrounded by other parked aircraft which included Mosquitos, a Wellington, an Oxford and a Harvard.

Chaos reigned supreme as we tried to push the other aircraft clear, all the time being showered by red-hot fragments from the now furiously burning Mosquito. Our Wellington had been parked with the brakes on, and as a brave young AC2, I offered to climb into the cockpit to release the brakes, which I did. It was only later I realised why the Corporal let me do it – the cockpit in a Wellington bomber surrounded by exploding petrol tanks was hardly a safe place – but I survived. While nothing could be done to save the Mosquito, all the other aircraft were successfully dragged clear. The investigations led to a disgruntled airman who was later charged with the destruction of one of His Majesty's aircraft.

It was at West Raynham that I got my one and only flight in a Mosquito 36 flown by our CO of the Night Fighter Leader School. Formating on a second Mosquito was the highlight of the twenty-minute flight, and I can recall being almost blacked out as the CO peeled off in a steep turn!

West Raynham was full of parades and AOC's visits, so when they asked for volunteers to serve with the occupation forces in Germany, I grabbed the chance.

Working with 33 Squadron on its Tempest IIs at Gütersloh was much more fun and the squadron life suited me. One day the engine failed in one of the Tempests, and the pilot made a successful wheels-up forced landing in open country near a farmhouse.

Quite suddenly I found myself sharing the farmhouse with the farmer and his family, where we set up a temporary guard. In 1948 the German population did not love the RAF, but this was not the Germany of complete destruction we had seen in cities like Hamm. We managed quite well with sign language.

This was the period of the Berlin airlift and from time to time we got diversions to Gütersloh. Visiting aircraft included an RAF Hastings full of coal dust, a USAF Skymaster full of Coca-Cola (as would be expected) and some of the freighters on the British civil register like the Halifax C.8 G-AHWN and Flight Refuelling's Lancastrian tanker G-AKFF.

One day an RAF York MW188 with a load of flour sacks on board suffered a tyre blow-out on take-off from Wunsdorf bound for Berlin and was diverted to Gütersloh. During the subsequent landing it developed a violent swing to port. Then there was an almighty crack as the port undercarriage failed and the entire centre-section collapsed with the props slicing into the fuselage, fortunately without injury to the crew.

When 33 Squadron was sent to Malaya to help deal with the communist uprising, I went to 26 Squadron which was flying Vampire 5s. I was offered the chance to go with 33, but my demob was coming up, and so I declined.

Shortly afterwards I was due for leave and flew home to the UK in an RAF Dakota from Buckeburg to Oakington, a trip of about two hours. It was a pretty noisy flight, and hardly airline quality; the seats were arranged along the side of the fuselage, and all ranks sat together. Next to me I had an Army Major, and I recall being roundly ticked off by an RAF officer for taking the Major's seat belt as we buckled up!

My leave in the UK had a surprise in store for me. Shortly after arrival I was stricken with acute appendicitis and was operated on at a hospital in Poole, Dorset. The operation went off quite well, but then they discovered I was an airman on leave from the RAF. All too quickly an RAF ambulance arrived and I was whisked away to the RAF Hospital at Wroughton, near Swindon. My driver was most concerned for my welfare and stopped at intervals to see how I was. This concern continued at Wroughton, and I was most impressed at the attention the nurses gave me. But I was somewhat puzzled when they put thick woolly socks on me, and a nurse appeared with a razor to shave my nether regions! Surely this was a repeat of pre-operative procedures? Seconds later, when it dawned on them that I had already had the operation, all concern for me evaporated!

I had one more incident in the RAF before demob in late 1949. After my operation I duly returned to Germany, but found that 26 Squadron had left Gütersloh and gone on detachment to the island of Sylt, just off the German coast, close to the Danish border. This meant a train journey across Germany, and I set off in company with one other airman who also had to rejoin the squadron. All went well until we reached Hamburg, which of course had been heavily bombed during the war, and the evidence was everywhere. Members of the RAF went in peril of their lives. I can't remember just how it happened, but we had to change trains and this involved a short walk. Somehow we took the wrong turning into a devastated area, and in moments a military jeep pulled up alongside us and we were told in no uncertain fashion to get aboard. It appeared that, only a few days before, RAF personnel had been attacked in the area, and we were very definitely in a no-go zone . . .

Sylt by contrast was still very much a holiday resort complete with casino and pretty Fräuleins, and not a bad place to finish a spell with the RAF!

I travelled back to the UK for demob via the overnight ferry from the Hook of Holland to Harwich. Like most returning servicemen I had with me one of those delightful German cuckoo clocks. The only trouble was, it had been purchased with some German marks which had come my way outside official channels. This meant that the clock could be confiscated by customs, so with it hidden just inside my small pack I sailed through customs without declaring it. "If you get through never give a sigh of relief," I had been warned. Ten yards after leaving the customs man I heaved up the pack and there was a distinct "cuckoo" from within! I will never know if the customs man heard it . . . I did not dare look back.

Early 1950 found me at the College of Aeronautical Engineering in Chelsea as related in *"Tails of the Fifties"* in my chapter about the notorious "Maggie" 'JDR.

My first flight as a civilian again came in March 1950 when Chris de Vere flew me from Denham to the home of Miles Aircraft at Woodley in his blood-red Maggie G-AKMU. Chris was going on elsewhere and he took off again without even stopping the engine. I then made my way to pay a surprise visit on my aunt Molly who lived to the north of Reading. Far from being pleased to see me, I recall that she gave me a scolding for flying in these dangerous aeroplanes and that I should spare a thought for my mother . . . Oh dear! My mother, bless her, had long since given her blessing on my chosen career, even if privately she may have held her fears. On a few occasions her fears were in fact well-founded.

One such occasion was at Redhill in 1952 while working on the sole surviving Robinson Redwing G-ABNX. It had been restored by the students with many parts having to be scratch-built. The engine was a five-cylinder Genet radial which was particularly hard to start. We were working just inside the hangar door checking the timing, and this involved removing the magneto covers to spot the moment the points opened. My companion, a student from Pakistan, was sitting in the cockpit keeping the throttle fully closed and was well aware that the engine was 'live' with the magneto cover off. Very slowly I turned over the prop several times to check the points, when to my horror the engine suddenly fired! My companion could do nothing to stop it, of course, with the switches isolated. Without chocks the Redwing threatened to move forward into the hangar door behind me. In a second I had leapt away to the leading edge of the

65

wing, pushing like hell against the Genet! It seemed like an eternity before the sound of the engine running in the hangar brought help and the magneto cover was replaced. The following heavy silence can be well imagined and a couple of students had learned by experience . . . I don't think I ever told my mother.

Only a short while later I was to have another close call when John Derry's DH.110 broke up over the 1952 SBAC Farnborough Air Show. I had already been to the show once that week, but an old school friend, Peter Gass, had persuaded me to go again. We were standing in the crowd where one of the engines landed, and I can vividly recall the dawning realisation that the engines, which appeared to be going upwards, were in fact traversing an arc and coming directly towards us. Everything seemed to be happening in slow motion, and I can still see one engine passing overhead, and the other turning end-to-end before hitting the ground some thirty feet to our left . . . Instinctively we threw ourselves to the ground as debris flew everywhere. As I got to my feet I dusted myself down and got roundly told off by the woman next to me for spoiling her clothes! That of all things, despite the surrounding carnage (26 dead and 65 injured) – a very tragic day.

Between 1952 and 1954 I worked as a ground engineer at the Wiltshire School of Flying at Thruxton near Andover. We had a fleet of Tiger Moths and Proctors, and a collection of privately-owned types such as Geoffrey Marler's beautiful Miles Falcon Six G-ADTD. John Currie was the chief engineer, and he will be recalled as the designer of the Currie Wot. He was a hard taskmaster at times, but one of the old school who really knew his craft.

One day one of our Tiger Moths turned over on landing at Filton, so the next day we flew over to Filton on a rescue mission in an Auster Autocar piloted by one of the instructors called, I think, John Heaton. John Currie sat up front and I sat in the back with another pilot. We found our Tiger back on its feet, but with a dented rudder and other superficial damage. We had no idea whether there was damage to the wings, but here John Currie revealed a technique born of his experience. I am not sure now of the precise sequence, but John Currie got hold of one of the wingtips and shook it up and down while he got John Heaton to count the number of times the structure vibrated (rather like the action of a tuning fork). I believe his theory was that a fractured spar would not transmit vibrations. Anyway he managed to persuade our pilots that the Tiger was safe to fly, and it was duly flown back to Thruxton without incident.

Our Proctors at Thruxton were contracted to fly at night for the Army anti-aircraft units, and this was not without its hazards in poor weather. One night one of our pilots, Jack Simlar, flying the

Proctor III G-AKZN, became lost in poor visibility and with fuel running low he had a real problem. Then through the murk he saw a large runway, brilliantly lit; he had no radio, so without further ado he put down safely and thankfully. Much relieved, he taxied off the runway along a taxi-track. However his relief was short-lived for he had landed at the top security USAF airfield at Greenham Common!

He found himself under spotlights with armed American Military Police in jeeps either side. He was escorted into a nearby dispersal and curtly ordered out of his aircraft. He was then subjected to intense questioning for his unauthorised landing and his aircraft impounded. We eventually got a phone call from Jack to say he was at Greenham Common, which relieved us somewhat as by our calculations he was long out of fuel . . .

Early next day we drove over to rescue Jack, and put in some 39 gallons (his total tankage in the Proctor was 40 gallons): I think the Americans were finally convinced Jack needed to land. I flew back to Thruxton with Jack and got a magnificent view over rows of B-36s and the like.

(Jack's Proctor was not the only British civil aircraft to make an unauthorised landing at Greenham Common. In 1956 Ted Gould force-landed his Messenger G-ALAJ in poor weather and got similar treatment, as recalled in *"Tails of the Fifties."*)

Jack Simlar later flew another Proctor III, G-AKZS, out to Australia. He invited me to come with him, but with marriage on the horizon I declined. I often used to wonder whether he got there, and only recently found out from Australian aviation historian John Hopton that G-AKZS did indeed reach Australia in January 1954 and became VH-BEG.

We saw many different types at Thruxton in for C. of A., mainly Austers, Tiger Moths and Proctors with an occasional Gemini or DH.89A Rapide. But among the more unusual was the Fox Moth G-ACEJ which arrived in a rather sorry state after being exposed to salt water and sand on the beach at Blackpool where the owner used it for joyflights. We struggled with it for some time, particularly with corroded metal fittings, but eventually got it back into the air. It was nice to see that the same aircraft was still flying in 1997.

I mentioned that John Currie was a hard taskmaster, and he was always quick to size up a situation and its possible ramifications. One day, one of the Tiger Moths had just taken off when we heard a distinctly unhealthy sound coming from the engine. We ran outside just in time to see the Tiger execute a neat turn and arrive back on the airfield it had just left, fortunately with just enough height to do this successfully. John Currie and I arrived on the scene and I opened the cowling to find one of the two plugs to the front cylinder dangling in the breeze . . . I announced that I had found the problem, only to have John Currie slam the cowling down and call out to the instructor still sitting in the cockpit: "Blown head-gasket, skipper." John Currie was not about to have his team accused of sloppy maintenance, and the Tiger was ceremoniously wheeled back to the hangar for a "top overhaul" – a case of what the eye didn't see etc.

One day our oldest Tiger Moth G-ADGX was being used by a student pilot on circuits and bumps. He had made several landings and take-offs without incident and appeared to be managing very well. Nobody noticed after his third take-off that he had not landed again, so it was with some amazement to all of us that a little later he walked into the hangar and announced he had crashed! He was quite uninjured, but somehow he had managed to stall the Tiger over trees on the far boundary during his approach, and mushed it into the top branches; these were sufficient to break his fall and the Tiger ended up nose-down between trees in a relatively soft impact. But the poor old Tiger Moth G-ADGX had ended its flying days. Of course the question was raised why nobody had seen him go in and the need for a continuous watch was highlighted.

John Currie started work on the Thruxton Jackaroo project about this time using an old Tiger Moth fuselage to make the wide-body version. Little did I think some 43 years would pass before I would eventually get to fly in one at Shoreham, when Ian Oliver so kindly gave me a quick trip round the circuit in his beautiful example G-AOIR, on the occasion of the launch of my book *"Shoreham Airport, Sussex"* on June 15th 1996.

Thruxton days could not last for ever and from there I went to Flight Refuelling Ltd at Tarrant Rushton in Dorset to work for Sir Alan Cobham in his drawing office. The world of Tiger Moths and Gipsy Major engines began to recede, but they live on in my memory as the golden age . . .

CHAPTER 8

JACKSON'S JOTTINGS

by

A.J.Jackson

(edited by Peter Campbell)

[Jack Jackson (normally referred to as A.J.J. or "Jacko" to his friends) was an early member of Air-Britain and edited their "British Civil Register Bulletin" from its first issue dated July 30th 1948. The publication changed its name on two subsequent occasions, first to "British Civil Register News," and then to "British Civil Aviation News," but the intention always remained the same: to keep enthusiasts up to date with goings-on in the world of civil aviation, whether it be airliners or smaller business and private aircraft.

After nearly nine years at the helm, he handed over the editorship to Denis Fox (extracts of whose articles were included in "Tails of the Fifties"), to concentrate on completing his major and well-known work "British Civil Aircraft 1919-1959."

During the period of his Editorship he was an active pilot based at Southend, and frequently visited events such as breakfast patrols in either the Dart Kitten G-AEXT or, in later years, a Tiger Moth or Auster. His contributions to the journal had a special personal touch, therefore, because of his intimate knowledge of both the aeroplanes and the people who flew them.

I have made a selection of various contributions which seem to me to reflect the spirit of private and recreational flying at the time; reading through them, it seems as if flying events were plagued just as much by bad weather as they are now, belying the belief that we used to enjoy better weather fifty years ago!

These sections are reproduced here by kind permission of Air-Britain (Historians) Ltd; the dates shown in the headings are issue dates – Ed.]

MAY 19TH 1951: PANSHANGER PATROL

Yet another flying club breakfast patrol was staged on Sunday April 29th 1951, when over thirty visiting aircraft converged on the London Aeroplane Club.

Air-Britain, represented by "Maggie" G-AIUA flown by C.A. Nepean Bishop and the editorial Kitten G-AEXT, succeeded in eluding the defence to the tune of a brace of plates of 'the usual.'

In addition to the usual line-up, a grey and red Tiger G-AMHP and Swallow 2 G-AFCL came all the way from Thruxton, Geoffrey Alington's Q.6 G-AEYE arrived from Wolverhampton, and the red Proctor G-AGTE turned up from Luton. Broxbourne, being only five minutes away, sent nine aircraft including Rapide G-ALXT, Autocrat G-AGYD, Cub G-ALMA and Swallow 'EMW.

Quite the most interesting find of the day was the fuselage and other major components of the Chipmunk G-AKEV. These were in a blister hangar.

* * *

MAY 19TH 1951: THE 1951 ROYAL AERONAUTICAL SOCIETY GARDEN PARTY

On the afternoon of May 6th White Waltham presented its annual collection of old-time aircraft, the kind with two wings that fly properly.

The weather was unkind. As we came down the railway in the strong wind in the Dart Kitten with 45 degrees of drift, the airfield remained obstinately invisible in the gloom ahead until the leering countenance of the kite balloon emerged weaving at the end of its cable. As in the ill-fated 1938 show, visiting aircraft were few and confined to the mounts of the hardy band of enthusiasts that the weather seldom defeats.

The proceedings commenced with the arrival of the President of the Society in the red and gold S.51 "Smart ALIK," emitting a noise rivalling the band it manoeuvred so adroitly to avoid.

The first serious event was a demonstration of the one and only Aerovan Mk.6 by the Miles test pilot Ian Forbes. With Lycomings chattering merrily, its corpulent silhouette came and went in a variety of unseemly postures. After the Youngman-Baynes and the Macchi had gone, and after the kite balloon (type R!) had been gingerly winched up to about 100 ft with two intrepid birdmen in the basket, and had been hastily hauled down, deflated and sat upon, Mrs Ann Douglas towed off the Olympia Eon sailplane BGA537 which was very obviously ex-G-ALKA.

The populace then settled down to enjoy the main purpose of this meeting, the annual circuits and bumps by a selection of the surviving ancients of the aeronautical world. The Brisfit D8096, flown by "Brabazon" Pegg, came as quite a shock to some of the younger generation. With the Falcon roaring lustily it positively leaped out of the aerodrome. His landing will be remembered for many a long day – a thistledown three-pointer which didn't even stretch the bungee on the tail skid.

And so it went on. The little Hawker Cygnet was followed by the recently rebuilt Carden-Ford-engined Drone flown by John Fricker, and by the Sopwith Pup N5180. This is without doubt ex-G-EBKY.

Next came the Blackburn B.2 in which Harold Wood executed a rate 4 turn at an altitude equal to half his span! He didn't do this on Hillman's old Fox Moths!

The show than became comparatively orthodox and consisted of the flypasts and beat-ups of Hirtenberg G-AGAK, the Dragon, the Tomtit, the Hurricane, the Bristol 171 Mk.3, the 1912 Blackburn and the inevitable Chipmunk.

With the wind gusting up to 28 mph from the north east, the Kitten was very regrettably hangared with the West London Aero Club, and the homeward journey made by a less agreeable form of transport.

*   *   *

JUNE 30TH 1951: THE 1951 KING'S CUP MEETING

The weather on June 23rd was exasperating in the extreme, a first class 'clamp' covering the King's Cup course, while the rest of the country enjoyed a day of blue skies. Even so, the members whom we had the pleasure of meeting at Hatfield were obviously enjoying themselves, and we too departed with few regrets at the end of the day.

Despite the lowering skies, an outstanding flying programme and the large number of thoroughbred aeroplanes on an historic aerodrome made it a connoisseur's day indeed. A browse among the visiting aircraft is almost a ritual at an event of this kind, but of about a hundred expected only seventeen managed to get through. The little Kitten brought us safely in from Southend, but it was never possible to fly higher than 500 ft or to see more than a mile or so. It was all very unpleasant, but one simply can not miss the King's Cup! Rapide G-AKNX, bringing some members of our Birmingham branch, was unable to find Hatfield and had to return to Elmdon. Fred Dunkerley, practising round the course on the eve of the race, 'blew' an engine of Gemini G-AKKB and force-landed at the Hunsdon turn. After a feverish engine change he took off on the morning of the race but such was the 'vis' that he was not able to locate Hatfield only 13 miles away. He eventually landed at Southend, returning to make that tricky cross-wind landing we witnessed around 2 o'clock.

Six racing aircraft were scratched and with one exception failed to appear. This was the Taylorcraft Plus D G-AHUG, which was parked behind the line alongside the Lancashire Club's G-AHHB which had lost its tailwheel on landing. The other non-starters were the long awaited

Bombardier Messenger G-ALAC, the Heck G-AEGI, Mercury G-AHAA, Gemini 3 G-AKDC and the crashed Hawk Tr. 3 G-AJDR.

The biggest surprise of course was the presence of the dear old Avian G-ABEE which in view of the remarks on page 49 of this issue must have been subjected to some pretty intensive effort by keen types at Denham and ARB alike. *[Page 49 of BCRN had reported: "It seems that the most interesting of all the King's Cup entries, Avian 4M G-ABEE, is unlikely to be ready in time because as recently as June 3rd none of the major components had been assembled to the fuselage. The latter was in the open at Denham, without letters, being done up in silver and blue." – Ed.]*

Numerous old friends appeared this year in new colour schemes and included Doc James' little Chilton G-AESZ (pale blue with Picasso 'Z's), Moth G-ABJJ in a dirty green but sporting stub exhausts, with G-ABAG proclaiming a Scottish ownership with a red Bruce's lion upon the rudder; J/1 G-AGXT had forsaken its usual foul hue for honest silver and black as also had the Falcon Six G-ADTD. We were very pleased to meet the immaculate M.38 EI-AFH and also the Aiglet G-AMIH *"Lady-Lady."* The Moth Minor G-AFNJ was quite unusual in all-red with rear seat faired in for the race.

The inevitable Hawk Trainer G-AIUE was resplendent in black and yellow and had the front seat faired in as usual, but by and large, 'mods' were noticeably few this year. The one and only Gemini Mk.1B (G-AJTG) had become the one and only Mk.3B overnight by the installation of Gipsy Major 10-1 motors, and Jimmy Rush's old Falcon Six G-AECC had been resprayed in all-black, but there was little else of note. Our own personal triumph lay in tracking down and photographing Eagle Aviation's Proctor 1 G-AHES which, having flown but a single hour in all its civil life and been four years in storage, had long remained a blank in editorial files.

The first event was to have been a demonstration in two of the Surrey Gliding Club's Olympias, but they were not able to tow them over the North Downs and they remained on *terra firma* at Redhill. The Bristol 171 Mk.3 G-ALSX therefore performed its usual antics and was followed by equally familiar precision aerobatics by four SV.4As of the *Patrouille d'Étampes*. The tops of loops inevitably came well up in the cloud base and made the tight formations in which these creatures fly even more dicey than usual.

Not since the early 1930s however have we had the pleasure of witnessing that extinct manoeuvre, the flick roll. Prince Cantacuzene gave even the hardy veterans something to enthuse over with his performance on Jungmeister EC-AEX. The rate of roll of this diminutive biplane has to be seen to be believed and two of his pranks were outstanding, not only for originality but also for quite the most impressive split-second timing we have ever seen.

The first consisted of beating up the enclosures and, when climbing away, doing one and a half flick rolls in the twinkling of an eye to enable the climb to be continued inverted. The second is dependent on perfect judgment and timing, for when gliding in, apparently at about seventy, a flick roll in the last hundred feet or so puts the machine on the ground straight out of the roll and it's all over!

With the final cancellation of all the racing because of the weather, hopes of getting home faded also. Not wishing to cause a vacancy for a BCRN editor in the height of the season, 'EXT was left to its own devices for the night.

AIRCRAFT DEMONSTRATED

G-ALSX Bristol 171 Mk.3 Helicopter
G-ALYP DH.106 Comet (BOAC livery)
WA780 & WA988 Gloster Meteor F.Mk.8s
(from No.66 Fighter Squadron at Linton on Ouse)
EC-AEX Bucker Jungmeister

The *Patrouille d'Étampes* quartet's SV.4s were numbered 7, 10, 677 & 678.

Yellow Tigers G-AHUB, 'HXC and 'LIX from the London Aeroplane Club at Panshanger stood by to uplift the parachute experts, but even that was 'scrubbed.'

VISITING AIRCRAFT

With few exceptions these were put right at the eastern end of the runway:

G-ACRW Leopard Moth	G-AIEH Proctor 1
G-AEXT Kitten	G-AIGG Autocrat
G-AFRE Hornet Moth	G-AIJM Auster J/4
G-AGBN Cygnet 2	G-AJIH Autocrat
G-AHAO Autocrat	G-AKKY Hawk Tr. 3
G-AHBJ Proctor 5	G-AKPA Rapide
G-AHFP Messenger 4	G-ALZG Gemini IA
G-AHGJ Proctor 5	VM341 Anson 19
G-AHHB Taylorcraft Plus D	VR303 Prentice

KING'S CUP AIRCRAFT

The following were lined up on each side of the runway:

G-ABAG Gipsy Moth	G-AHVG Proctor 1
G-ABEE Avian 4M	G-AIAG Proctor 5
G-ABJJ Gipsy Moth	G-AIET Proctor 5
G-ABMR Hart	G-AITO Hawk Tr. 3
G-ABUS Swift	G-AIUA Hawk Tr. 3
G-ACMA Leopard Moth	G-AIUE Hawk Tr. 3
G-ACMN Leopard Moth	G-AJTG Gemini 3B
G-ADGP Hawk Speed Six	G-AJUR Autocrat
G-ADMW Hawk Major	G-AJYD Chipmunk
G-ADND Hornet Moth	G-AJYZ Messenger 2A
G-ADTD Falcon Six	G-AJZH Hawk Tr. 3
G-AECC Falcon Six	G-AKDN Chipmunk
G-AELO Hornet Moth	G-AKHV Gemini 1A
G-AESZ Chilton	G-AKKB Gemini 1A
G-AEUJ Whitney Straight	G-AKMN Hawk Tr. 3
G-AEXF Mew Gull	G-AKPE Hawk Tr. 3
G-AFEA Vega Gull	G-AKRT Hawk Tr. 3
G-AFJB Wicko GM.1	G-AKRV Hawk Tr. 3
G-AFLT Gemini 1A	G-AKRW Hawk Tr. 3
G-AFNJ Moth Minor	G-ALBE Messenger 4A
G-AFOJ Moth Minor	G-ALCK Proctor 3
G-AFTA Tomtit	G-ALGJ Hawk Tr. 3
G-AGTC Proctor 1	G-ALMS Proctor 3
G-AGXT Autocrat	G-ALWB Chipmunk
G-AHES Proctor 1	G-AMCO Proctor 1
G-AHGR Proctor 1	G-AMIH Aiglet
G-AHKO Taylorcraft Plus D	EI-AFH Messenger 2A
G-AHUG Taylorcraft Plus D	(ex-G-AKBL)

JUBILEE TROPHY AIRCRAFT

These were parked near the western end of the runway:

No.1	VX283 Hawker Sea Fury T.Mk.2
No.2	PK542 Supermarine Spitfire F.22
No.3	WP240 DH.100 Vampire NF.Mk.10
No.4	WE256 DH.112 Venom F.Mk.1
No.5	TS409 Supermarine Attacker F.1 (fitted dorsal fin)
No.99	G-AMAU Hawker Hurricane Mk.2C

*　　*　　*

74

AUGUST 11TH 1951: FIFTY YEARS OF FLYING –
THE "DAILY EXPRESS" EXHIBITION AND DISPLAY

This truly remarkable occasion has been dealt with very fully in both technical and lay press alike, and all the usual superlatives have had their periodic airing in praise of men, machines and organisers. Although we thoroughly endorse all these paeons of praise it is felt that our function is to subject, to an 'enthusiasts' dissection,' certain of the more important exhibits rather than to repeat general descriptions appearing elsewhere.

Among the 'ancients,' Ken Waller's Caudron G.3 OO-ELA was making its first post-war appearance. It has been stored at Brooklands ever since being rescued from a hangar fire there in 1937. It was to be G-AETA but somehow it never was. Nearby our old friend the Pup N5180 needed no introductions and was, of course, Dove G-EBKY in disguise, and must not be confused with the real N5180 which occasionally appeared pre-war.

Equally familiar was the 'Brisfit' D8096, at one time destined to become G-AEPH. It is literally a new machine, and its performance is a testimonial to the Filton fitters.

Mere words are inadequate to describe one's reactions on coming face to face with the dear old Avro 504K, but a glance at the serial on the poor thing is enough to destroy even the most concentrated nostalgia. H2311 was the aircraft in which the present King learned to fly, and this particular machine certainly isn't it! The sole Avro 504K in R.G.J. Nash's sheds at Brooklands in the summer of 1939 was G-ABAA, so a very obvious conclusion can be drawn.

Next in the World War 1 line (how very like the dump at St. Omer in 1917!) was the SE.5A B4563. This equally bogus serial proclaimed the presence of another old friend, G-EBIC, reduced to a shadow of its former self in 1950 at 39 MU Colerne, so that it is doubtful if even M.L. Bramson would recognise it.

And so to the 1919-31 era! For the benefactors who gave us G-EBLV, we have nothing but praise, but would it not be more fitting to redope it in its original Lancashire Aero Club colours? G-AACN was looking just as decrepit as usual, a sharp contrast with immaculate Shuttleworth aircraft. We noticed L.A. Jackson the chief engineer at Old Warden moving lovingly among his charges. Gipsy Moth G-ABYA won many a Concours d'Elegance a decade or so ago, and is still in first class condition, while the Elf, the old Hermes Moth and the Spartan Arrow look in even better condition than they did at Heston twenty years ago.

Queerest of the bunch however was undoubtedly the erstwhile Desoutter 1 G-AAPZ. With a longer nose to house the newly-fitted Menasco Buccaneer motor, a revised windscreen and modified rudder, it was a hybrid likely to satisfy even the most fanatical variant fiends. Redwing G-ABNX, newly graduated from BCRN Wrecks and Relics columns, was spruce in silver and red, and vied with the bright yellow Tiger G-ALIX and part-blue Avian G-ABEE. The knowing ones were wagging accusing fingers at them because during conversion a pair became mixed, and the airframe of G-ALIX is actually the one that should have become G-ALIZ. As for the Avian, it is becoming clearer every day that a restoration of G-ACKE would have been a more accurate procedure.

The fragile undercart of the Drone G-AEKV had evidently given up the ghost at a most embarrassing moment and a part of it lay crumpled beneath the fuselage, but the Pou du Ciel G-AEHM was a shock! Named *"Blue Finch,"* it still had a constructor's number HJD.1 painted on the side, the machine having been built by H.J. Dolman at Bristol in 1936.

Among the comparatively modern aircraft we found the Swordfish LS326 that was once destined to become G-AJVH, and obviously never will. Camouflage on the Hurricane with fictitious serial P2619 and coded US-B fooled no one. The registration G-AMAU was fairly obvious and it is now well known that it starred in the film *"Hawks in the Sun"* at Kenley. Spitfire 5 G-AISU still bore its 1950 racing number 40, in spite of the fact that it was alleged to be in the USA.

Among the gliders, Krajanek G-ALMP was flown aerobatically by Marmol, and Olympia G-ALJN was sporting the legend BGA434, but the others were not on the civil register.

So with a couple of minutes quiet homage before the poor Gipsyless G-ABLM back from the tomb, we said goodbye to dusty old sun-baked Hendon, and wondered if there were enough old-timers left after this to keep a Wrecks and Relics Section going!

A full list of those present is on record for reference purposes:

Blackburn Type C	G-AAPZ Desoutter 1
Bleriot XI No.14	G-AAZP DH.80A Puss Moth
Bleriot XXVII	G-ABEE Avro Avian 4M
Deperdussin Type 143	G-ABLM Cierva C.24
Maurice Farman	G-ABMR Hawker Hart
B4563 SE.5A	G-ABNX Robinson Redwing 2
D8096 Bristol Fighter	G-ABUS Comper Swift
H508 Sopwith Camel	G-ABWP Spartan Arrow
H2311 Avro 504K	G-ABYA DH.60G Gipsy Moth
J8067 W/H Pterodactyl 1	G-ACMA Leopard Moth
N5180 Sopwith Pup	G-ACUU Cierva C.30A
N5912 Sopwith Triplane	G-ADGP Hawk Speed Six
G-EBLV DH.60 Moth	G-ADKC Hornet Moth
G-EBMB Hawker Cygnet	G-ADMW Hawk Major M.2H
G-EBWD DH.60X Moth	G-ADPR Gull Six
G-AACN HP.39 Gugnunc	G-AEBJ Blackburn B.2
G-AAIN Parnall Elf	G-AEHM Pou du Ciel

G-AEKV BAC Drone
G-AEUJ Whitney Straight
G-AEVS Aeronca 100
G-AEWZ Dragonfly
G-AEXF Mew Gull
G-AEXT Dart Kitten
G-AFFD Percival Q.6
G-AFHS BA Swallow 2
G-AFJB Wicko GM.1
G-AFJU Monarch
G-AFLT Gemini 1A
G-AFTA Tomtit
G-AFVR Cygnet 2
G-AFZE Heath Parasol 1
G-AGPG Avro 19 Ser. 1
G-AGVX Mercury 4
G-AHET Vega Gull
G-AHGL Proctor 5
G-AHRH Dragon Rapide
G-AHXE Taylorcraft Plus D
G-AIBE Fulmar
G-AISC Tipsy Trainer 1
G-AISU Spitfire 5
G-AJIZ Autocrat
G-AJVD Chipmunk
G-AJYO Autocar
G-AKHF Aerovan 6
G-AKLN Sealand 1
G-ALBE Messenger 4A
G-ALBM Dove 1
G-ALIK S.51
G-ALIX Tiger Moth
G-ALJN Olympia
G-ALMP Krajanek

G-ALSX Bristol 171 Mk.3
P2619 Hurricane 2C
DE164 Tiger Moth
EB806 Oxford 2
EK770 Firebrand TF.5
JN180 Sea Otter ASR.1
KK990 Sikorsky R.4
LS326 Swordfish
NG892 Wellington T.10
NP307 Proctor 4
NV699 Tempest TT.5
PP549 Firefly 1
RA476 Meteor 4
RJ796 Barracuda TB.3
RZ155 Horsa 2
SP349 Seafire F.17
TW449 Auster 5
TW584 Auster AOP.6
TW655 Lancaster 1
VP538 Anson 19 Ser. 2
VT592 Mosquito T.3
VV695 Vampire F.5
VZ353 Sea Fury T.20
WD881 Firefly 6
WE241 Sea Hornet F.20
WE600 Auster T.7
G-35-1 Aries
BGA162 Willow Wren
BGA625 Prefect
W-2 Weir Autogiro
Dagling Primary Glider
Hafner R 2 Giroplane
Focke Achgelis Fa.330
CARD 1 Spherical balloon

*   *   *

FEBRUARY 9TH 1952: VINTAGE AEROPLANE CLUB WINTER RALLY

Saturday January 19th, although a very cold and windy day, was sunny
and dry enough to enable quite a few of the oldest registered aircraft to fly
into Denham for the Rally. The greatest surprise of the day was of course
the arrival by air of the Cirrus Moth G-EBLV. This had been flown over
from Panshanger by W/C C.A. Pike on a permit. It made quite a few feel
young again to see the old 'straight axle' undercarriage airborne once

again. Long distances against that strong headwind were flown by the Tipsy G-AFSC from Cardiff and the Pobjoy Swallow G-AFCL from Thruxton.

Near-neighbours to turn up were a trio from Langley – Hart G-ABMR, Tomtit G-AFTA and Whitney Straight G-AEUJ, and the Bianchi Puss Moth G-AAZP from White Waltham. The Hart and Tomtit, flown by Messrs. Bedford and Duke, arrived in formation with Frank Murphy in 'EUJ behind. The remaining old-timers consisted of a pair of Aeronca 100s G-AEWU and G-AEVS, another Tipsy G-AFRU brought over from Redhill by Ian Forbes, and the last of all the Tipsies – G-AISC. Among the 'unmentionables' present were the Auster V G-AJVV, Autocrats G-AHAY and G-AJAB, a Gemini 1A G-AJWF and Hawk Tr.IIIs G-AIUE and G-AJZH.

The results of the various events are by now well-known, but we were particularly impressed by the slow-flying characteristics of the Moth G-EBLV which we took for granted a generation ago, but which look quite amazing today. It won the landing competition with a mean distance of five yards from the circle!

In contrast with feverish efforts by the Taylorcraft Plus D G-AIIU at getting in, Bill Bedford's slow approach in the Hart with that huge prop idling, followed by hardly any landing run, was just ludicrous. Some time later, on take-off, he raised a laugh by getting the front wheels off immediately the throttle was opened, leaving the tailwheel firmly on the ground doing astronomical revs!

After the slow race, which was won by the Swallow 'FCL, the first of this season's series of aerobatic 'Farewell Performances' by C.A. Nepean Bishop with Hawk Trainer G-AJZH, a superb show on the Tomtit by Neville Duke, and the assessment of P.J. Colbourne's red Aeronca G-AEWU as the winner of the Concours d'Elegance, members adjourned to hear the talk by J.C.C. "Joe" Taylor of Shell.

* * *

MAY 9TH 1953: REDHILL BREAKFAST PATROL

Sunday morning, April 26th, brought fine weather for this popular annual event and a larger number of 'attackers' than ever before converged on the airfield from all directions in the half hour after nine. Finding a gap in between several familiar yellow London Club Tigers and a gaggle of Taylorcraft Plus Ds, we somehow managed to put Tiger Moth G-AMSY onto the last remaining empty acre of the airfield without touching anybody else.

It was good to see real enthusiasm present in the shape of the cabin Tiger G-AIZF and the Gemini 1A G-ALZG, which had come all the way from Baginton. The rest were the 'usuals' except that this was the first time we remember seeing a representation from Portsmouth and

Eastleigh. Southern Flying Schools sent the ex-Air Service Training Tiger Moth G-AHWB and several others, while the horrible mustard and pale blue of the Hampshire Club Tiger G-AHUO and Taylorcraft Plus G-AHCR are not easily forgotten.

The Zaunkoenig G-ALUA was on a visit to the Redhill UItra Light Group and had been seen passing over Southend on the previous evening en route from Ipswich.

*　　*　　*

JULY 11TH 1953: THE OPENING OF RAMSGATE AIRPORT

Ramsgate Airport was built in 1936 and is situated about three miles east of Manston at the junction of the Margate to Ramsgate road and that from Sandwich. We well remember being present at the original opening ceremony on July 3rd 1937 and although we have no record of *all* the machines present that day, the following were seen then for the first time: Aeronca 300 G-AEVE, Drone G-AEEN, Hawk Major G-AENS, Hornet Moth G-ADKV, Swallow 2 G-AERK & G-AEYV, Tipsy S.2 G-AEYG.

The main buildings and hangar were damaged by enemy bombing during the war and until last year the airfield was in agricultural use. All has now been put in order and on June 27th we crept under a lowering cloudbase in the Southend Autocrat G-AGYF to attend the reopening ceremony. This was performed by the Minister of Civil Aviation who arrived per S.51 G-AJOV from Shoreham.

Although hampered by the low cloud the flying display was of above average quality, starting with simultaneous gyrations by Dart Kittens G-AEXT and 'MJP and the Fairey Junior G-AMVP. Next came a demonstration by the prototype Heron G-ALZL, its 'small-field' performance being shown off in natural surroundings.

Marmol then shattered the populace with a gliding display in the Aerovan 4 G-AJTC with dead 'sticks.' If the ceiling had been higher he intended to take up the dance band and let it play sweet music through the open rear door on the way down. Then came the age-old instructor and pupil act on the Ramsgate Club Tiger Moth G-AHND followed by a demonstration by Sikorsky H.19 51-3889 of the USAF.

The SV.4s used by the *Patrouille d'Étampes* were Nos. 7, 9, 54 and 62. Their performance is too well-known to need a description here, but it was especially good on this occasion below the clouds. John Ralling then ejected himself from Autocrat G-AIZZ of the Ramsgate Club to land by parachute in an adjacent field. 'Bish,' otherwise our old friend C. Nepean Bishop, then gave the 1953 edition of his well known 'Maggiebatics' in the Redhill Hawk Trainer 3 G-AJRT. The programme then ended with flypasts by the Meteors of No.500 Squadron and a lonely F.86E Sabre 19154 of the RCAF.

APRIL 24TH 1954: THE BITTER END

A few stalwarts foregathered at Redhill on April 11th to say goodbye to a famous club. We probably qualified as the last visiting pilot with a final editorial sortie in Tiger Moth G-ANGD using the Hon. Gen. Sec. of Air-Britain as ballast.

Rigor mortis was everywhere apparent, even among the rats that eat the corn that fills the hangars that used to house the aeroplanes that Bish flew. Even the faithful Flamingo G-AFYH has been cast outside and by the time these words appear will be in an advanced state of dis-memberment.

The club Austers and Hawk Trainers were making a brave show of flying, as if not doomed after all, but apart from the Moth Minor G-AFPN, Messenger G-ALBE, Heath Parasol G-AFZE, the remains of the famous Tipsy G-AFRU and a few Ansons, the place was deserted.

So for the last time we set 065 on the compass and with a final beat up shook the dust of Redhill from our wheels for ever.

[In fact Redhill never did really close completely! Peter Amos, who was working there during the fifties, has said that until 1959, when the Tiger Club made it their home after the closure of Croydon, landings were still possible on a PPO basis and at the discretion of the airfield manager. Various business aircraft, such as those belonging to Saunders Roe and Marshall's of Cambridge, were fairly regular visitors, occasional emergency landings were made, and Chelsea College's Tiger Moth was flown. – Ed.]

*   *   *

SEPTEMBER 11TH 1954: THE GOODYEAR TROPHY RACE

This, the last event of the air racing season, was staged in fine weather by the Southern Aero Club at Shoreham on August 28th. The line-up of competitors would have fitted almost any air race programme printed in the last few years and consisted of L. Atherton's Cub J-4A G-AFSZ, A. J. Spiller's Messenger 2A G-AKIN, Geoffrey Marler's Falcon Six G-ADTD, Miss Freydis Leaf's Hawk Major G-ACYO, Jan Christie's Globe Swift LN-BDE (ex-G-AHUU), "Buster" Paine's Proctor 1 G-AHNA, Percy Blamire's Gemini 1A G-ALZG, "Nat" Somers' Gemini 3 G-AKDC, the Mew Gull G-AEXF flown by P.S. Clifford, J.M. Donald's Tiger Moth G-AIVW, E.W. Westbrook's Messenger 2A G-AJDM, Harold Wood's famous borr-owed Messenger 2A G-AKBO, Proctor 3 G-AIFE flown by D.W. Phillips, Walter Bowles's Gemini 1A G-AKDK, Ron Paine's Hawk Speed Six G-ADGP and Fred Dunkerley's all-white Sparrowjet G-ADNL.

One of the first visiting aircraft was the Puss Moth G-ABDF, now resplendent in red and white, flown by our member John Jakeman, hotly followed by John Bagley in the now well-known Tiger G-AMCM and another of our members, Peter Keating, in the Aiglet Trainer G-AMTD. Other visiting machines were Aiglet Trainer G-AMTE, Auster J/4 G-AIJM, Autocrats G-AGYM, 'HAT, 'HHW & 'JEE, Chipmunk T.10 WD377, Consul G-AIDX, Gemini 3A G-AKHC, Hawk Trainer III G-AIDF & 'LIO, Messenger 4 G-AKKG, Mosscraft MA.2 G-AFMS, Puss Moth G-AAZP, Proctors G-AHMP, 'IED & 'IHG, Swallow G-AEMW, Tiger Moth G-ANON.

The proceedings were opened by the Autair S.51 G-AJOV, . . . after which Miss Leaf flew G-ACYO to victory in the first heat of the Goodyear Race with Spiller second in G-AKIN. Then followed a demonstration by Silver City's S.51 G-ANLV, a parachute drop by "Dumbo" Willens from Tiger Moth G-ANCN, and some masterly aerobatics by a Biggin Hill Meteor 8 WL179. A third S.51 then appeared, Royal Navy WN496 with c/n 73, which rescued the inevitable dinghy dweller from the imaginary "drink." Shorn of his nether garments and wearing a stove-pipe hat the same brave gent was then conveyed twice round the arena on a bicycle fitted with a prop and some fin area. Only Doug Bianchi thought of what his fate might have been if the engine had failed. Rapide G-AKNY and Gemini 1A G-AKEL joyrode incessantly with masterly disregard for either the racing and demonstration machines or for the direction of the wind. They were only rivalled by the seemingly endless comings and goings of the East Anglian Rapides G-AEMH, 'KJZ, 'KRN & 'KSC between Southend, Shoreham, Paris and Jersey.

The second heat gave us a chance at long last to see the almost mythical Sparrowjet in the air – a graceful shape indeed, but only a shade faster than the veteran Mew Gull after all. The heat was won by J.M. Donald in the good old Newcastle Tiger G-AIVW, with Harold Wood second in G-AKBO.

The final started rather late, to give the Sparrowjet a sporting chance to replace a burst tyre, and to everyone's intense delight the Trophy was won by Miss Leaf and G-ACYO, with J.M. Donald and G-AIVW second. Miss Leaf was thus the 1954 Air Racing Champion also, but J.M. Donald's performance in pushing that old Tiger all the way down from Woolsington, winning his heat and beating all the "hot rods" for second place in the final, will live for ever. He flew it from the front seat and, sportsman that he is, waved congratulations to the Hawk Major even as they both dived past the finish. While the prizes were being presented the bowser was already refuelling 'IVW and he left in it straight away on the long haul northwards. What a man!

The well-known "radio-controlled" aerofoil then performed, Cadet G-ACHP being the aerofoil with Ron Gillman as the electronics.

The day finished with the invitation race which was won by Nat Somers in Gemini 3 G-AKDC, with the oft-disappointed Geoffrey Marler second in the Falcon Six G-ADTD.

A final round of the hangars laid bare Aerovan G-AJKP which flew during the afternoon, the remains of Tipsy G-AFRU, Martlet G-AAYX, Hawk Trainer III G-AITS, Geminis G-AJOJ and 'MRG, Swallow G-AFHS, and the remains of Proctor G-ALMS.

*   *   *

APRIL 9TH 1955: A CROYDON OCCASION

Saturday March 19th 1955 brought sunshine and extreme visibility in the Thames Estuary, but the Editorial Tiger Moth was confined to its blister by the very gale which brought the good "vis." Croydon was approached therefore in state in the Gemini G-AIRS belonging to the Mayor and all the Whatsits of the County Borough of S-on-S. It was QBI *[foggy – Ed.]* at Croydon of course – it always is – but such trifles were not likely to stop John Bagley, Air-Britain's uncrowned king of aerial rallyists, and sure enough before many minutes had elapsed, George Able Mike Charley Mike hove in sight and brought off a veritable Argosy-like landing.

Air-Britain then proceeded to get the new Club house of the Surrey Flying Club opened. Our well-known member C.A. Nepean Bishop, otherwise "Bish," steered the Mayor of Croydon behind the microphone, and he was soon reminiscing about welding up the leaks in the water jackets of the Napier Lions of the Instone Air Line DH.34s thirty years ago. The door was then unlocked and the shivering concourse flocked within. Pinned to the wall was a list of guests of the SFC which might well have been part of Mr MacGeorge's list of A-B members!

Thereafter the club Tigers G-ANRA, 'NRY, 'NSG and the newly C. of A'd G-ANYN took the air in formation, much, no doubt, to the alarm of the control wizard. After all it was QBI – it always is!* The Mayor was then coaxed into the newly-repaired Messenger 2A G-AILL and flown round his domain by "Bish."

Yes, it was a grand little show and soon the famous Varcoe Messenger G-AKKG, the Hofer Gemini G-AJZS, the MTCA Chipmunk G-AMMA, John Bagley and ourselves were fast leaving dear old Croydon in the failing light, until only the flashing beacon remained in the murk. Ten miles away visibility suddenly increased to infinity!

[I am grateful to Chris Dearden for confirming the full significance of 'QBI' – part of the old 'Q' code wireless system; I had correctly assumed that it must refer to foggy conditions, but Chris has sent me an explanatory extract from Newnes' "Aeronautics" Vol. III, which reads as follows:*

"The procedure in force under bad-weather conditions will be dealt with in this article. However irksome pilots may at times feel Control to be, they will agree that under bad conditions Control is their best friend.

Under QBI conditions implicit trust in the Control Officer and rigid adherence to his instructions are imperative.

'QBI in force' spells a great deal to a pilot and warns him that he will be required to obey to the letter every instruction given him from the Control tower. 'QBI' is the 'Q' code signal for promulgating the information that the fog regulations are in force and it means that as the horizontal visibility has fallen below 1,000 ft, the Control Officer has decided to bring into force a controlled zone into which no aeroplane is allowed without permission from him."

In practice this meant that only one aircraft at any one time was permitted to be within the controlled zone, which normally included an area within a radius of five miles of the airfield. If one aircraft had permission to land, others had to wait their turn at specified heights. There is an apocryphal story that, unofficially, 'QBI' was considered by some pilots to mean "Quite Bloody Impossible!" – Ed.]

*   *   *

MAY 14TH 1955: RAMSGATE BREAKFAST PATROL

The Ramsgate Aero Club staged a highly successful Breakfast Patrol on Sunday April 17th. Manston frowned on it because the "vis" was below minimum. Ramsgate, with both eyes on the bacon frying, said: "Get cracking."

Off the tip of Sheppey CFI Quinn in Autocrat G-AIZY was making our modest 500 ft in Tiger Moth G-AMSY look like the height record! Somewhere in the low stuff ahead sat John Bagley in the back seat of the Mayoral Gemini G-AIRS – yes, the tables were turned after the Croydon trip a month back! The residents of Herne Bay muttered imprecations on fools that disturbed the peace of that "put the clock forward" Sunday morn, but we were preoccupied with keeping station with Zebra Yoke and with thumbing David Ogilvy, just shooting past in the Elstree Gemini G-AJTL.

Keeping well clear of Manston – they say there were some who had never heard of it, who flew straight up the main runway! – we were attacked with considerable vigour by Edward Day in the one and only Gemini 3B G-AJTG before we sat down abruptly on Ramsgate Airport. The one and only Gemini 3B with its retractable flaps and Gipsy Major 10s proved too much for the attackers of Ramsgate.

Parked outside in the now brilliant sunshine were the Southend fleet consisting of Autocrats G-AJEO, G-AJID and G-AJUE in addition to those already mentioned, Percy Blamire's Gemini G-ALZG all the way from Baginton, Hawk Trainers G-AKUA and G-AHNW and Autocrats G-AGTP, G-AGXT, G-AHAP and Auster 5 G-ANHU from Elstree, Wicko G-AFJB and Hawk Trainer G-AJJI from Denham, Surrey Club Tigers G-ANRY and G-ANSG, Tiger Moth G-AIDS and Hornet Moth G-ADOT from

Stapleford, and the Messenger 2A G-AILI, Moth Minor Coupé G-AFNI and Hawk Trainer G-ALIO.

The defenders were the local Autocrats G-AIRC and G-AIZZ, Day's Gemini G-AJTG specially up from Lympne and the Air Kruise Rapide G-ALWK.

All good things must come to an end and soon Sugar Yoke, with tail well up, was showering the public enclosure with the good earth. An obvious Air-Britain member was faithfully recording those present, even at that hour of the day. Could it have been our correspondent D.H. Bird we wonder? If so, apologies for all that slipstream!

*   *   *

MARCH 10TH 1956: RECORDS

The Royal Aero Club recently published a list of the officially recognised records held by Great Britain, and it is of some interest to see which records are held by the pilots of British civil aircraft. There are four Class records. In Class C.2 – seaplanes – the distance record is held by Air Marshal D.C.T. Bennett, for a flight of 5,997·47 miles from Dundee to Port Nolloth (South Africa), in the Short S.20 *"Mercury"* G-ADHJ, on October 6th-8th 1938. This record led to a certain amount of dispute at the time, since *"Mercury"* was assisted into the air at take-off by being carried on top of the Short S.21 *"Maia."* However, it was duly homologated by the FAI, and has stood unchallenged for seventeen years.

The other three Class records are for speed round a 100 kilometre closed circuit, and were all set up at the National Air Races meeting at Wolverhampton on May 17th 1950. Ron Paine, with the Hawk Speed Six G-ADGP, holds the record for Class C.1b – aeroplanes between 500 and 1,000 kilograms all-up weight – at 192.83 mph. Miss R.M. Sharpe set up the Class C.1d record (1,750 to 3,000 kg) with the Spitfire 5B G-AISU, at 322.79 mph, and P.G. Roberts gained the record in Class C.1e (3,000-4,500 kg) at 328.48 mph in the Spitfire T.8 G-AIDN.

Point-to-point records are, naturally, almost all held by jet aircraft but memories of a past era are recalled by the discovery that A.E. Clouston still holds the London-Sydney, Sydney-London and Wellington-London records. These were set up in the Comet *(the* Comet – the DH.88 with two Gipsy Sixes) G-ACSS in March 1938. He and his co-pilot Victor Ricketts left Gravesend on March 15th, and arrived at Sydney on the 19th, taking 3 days 9 hours. The official record time is adjusted to the distance from London to Sydney, and stands at 80 hours 56 minutes, giving an average of 130.2 mph. Eleven hours after arriving at Sydney, Clouston and Ricketts took off for New Zealand, and landed at Blenheim 7.5 hours later. After an overnight stop, they left again for Sydney, arriving on March 21st. Eventually they arrived back in Croydon on March 26th, having covered 26,450 miles in just under 11 days. The outward record to

New Zealand was beaten by the Canberra 3 WE139 in the London-Christchurch Race in October 1953, but Clouston and G-ACSS still hold the Wellington-London and Sydney-London records, at 140 hours 12 minutes and 130 hours 3 minutes respectively.

De Havilland's other Comets figure prominently in the record lists: John Cunningham in the Comet 1 G-ALVG holds the London-Cairo, Cairo-London, London-Rome and Rome-London records, with average speeds between 385 mph and 453 mph. The same pilot, in the Comet 2 G-AMXA, set up the London-Khartoum record on January 22nd 1954, at 481.1 mph. The last civilian record is London-Melbourne, set up by Capt. W. Baillie in the Viscount G-AMAV in the London-Christchurch Race, on October 8th-10th 1953.

Point-to-point records for light aircraft are also officially recognised by the FAI, and in Class C.1b Tom Hayhow set up 27 records between London and various European capitals in his Aiglet Trainer G-AMOS during 1952, before losing his life while trying to set a record for the London-Belgrade trip on April 10th 1953. In the same class stands Alex Henshaw's flight from Cape Town to London in February 1939, in the Mew Gull G-AEXF at 151.45 mph. In Class C.1c, Fred Dunkerley holds ten records between London and various European capitals, established in June and July 1953 with his Gemini G-AKKB.

CHAPTER 9

THE GRAND TOUR

(WHO NEEDS RADIO?)

by

Peter Amos

I noticed while reading *"Tails of the Fifties"* that one of the authors was Rex Nicholls and that he had written a chapter on the Experimental Flying Group. I met Rex at Redhill for the first time in early 1953 and from the start it became obvious that we shared a common interest in flying and a love of light aeroplanes. In that chapter he mentioned that after his tour of France in a Moth Minor in 1952 he was yearning for a more ambitious foreign tour and how this had materialised in the summer of 1953 but this time in a Magister. (I still have trouble getting around their official title of Hawk Trainer III: "Maggies" they were and "Maggies" they will always be!) Suddenly the memories of this foreign tour came flooding back for I was also a part of it! At long last I have now finally achieved a lifelong ambition (and it's only taken me forty-four years!), that of committing the story of this tour and a few more flying memories to paper for posterity!

Rex was a man after my own heart; he was very interested in civil aircraft, their registrations and taking photographs of them. Rex also knew R.S. Spackman, who owned the beautiful red and yellow Moth Minor G-AFNI at Croydon, and which he borrowed to visit other airfields and attend various Dawn, Lunch or Tea Patrols. Sometimes I went with him, and on one occasion, on the 17th of August 1952, we went to Bembridge on the Isle of Wight to attend a 'do' which was supposed to be taking place there. We had planned to arrive in plenty of time but noticed as we neared the island that there were no other aircraft to be seen. We soon discovered the reason for this after we landed, when we were told that it had been cancelled sometime earlier, unbeknown to us; perhaps we should have telephoned to confirm, but what the hell? It was a nice day so we went anyway!

We strolled down to the beach, threw pebbles in the sea (we should have taken our swimming trunks) and watched the world go by until we had enough – and never mind, it had made a good day out! We landed at

Eastleigh on the way back to Croydon and our course from there took us right past Leith Hill Tower in Surrey. The Tower was a local tourist attraction, and so as we passed by we gave a wave to the sightseers! As we were at normal cruising height I recall being surprised at just how high above sea level the tower must have been.

On the 30th of August we attended a Lunch Patrol at White Waltham, and then on the 13th of September we went to a Breakfast Patrol at Shoreham, where we really 'stole' a free breakfast by arriving somewhat unofficially from the direction of the sea and at a great height about five minutes after the official opening time: the defenders never stood a chance! Then Rex decided that he would like to add the Proctor to his vocabulary and I flew with him from Croydon to Redhill in G-ALJH on the 11th of October. This was a prelude to a cross-country from Croydon to Southend on the 18th of October in the same machine, a modified Mk.III, with four on board. This was a super flight and I still remember the argument we had with the airport authorities over their interpretation of the fact that the original Mk.III was a supposed to be a three-seater. We stuck to our guns because, although we couldn't argue with the fact that there were four of us on board, a Mk.III was normally charged a lower landing fee, and as G-ALJH was still officially a Mk.III we eventually got away with the lower charge! The relatively enormous power of the Proctor still took some getting used to, as did the diminishing forward visibility as the propeller started spreading oil all over the windscreen, but it was quite an aeroplane, and we had a very enjoyable flight.

On the 26th April 1953 Rex borrowed the Tiger Moth G-ALOX from Croydon in which to help to defend Redhill at their Dawn Patrol and I went along as spotter: 50 minutes of great fun for a £1 share of the costs, couldn't be bad! I can't remember if we bagged any attacker's registration but it was all good fun.

Then one day Rex mentioned that he would like to do another foreign tour in the summer but this time in a "Maggie." He wanted to include Switzerland and the Paris Air Show in the itinerary and would I be interested in joining him? Wouldn't I just! We obtained some maps of the Continent and started to plan our route to take in as many airfields as possible in order to see all the weird and wonderful French aircraft that we had heard so much about and also, hopefully, to see some of the many British-built aeroplanes based in Switzerland.

Jean Bird had realised by this time that, as the spares situation for both the airframe and engine of the Moth Minor was becoming rather acute, another suitable type would have to be obtained soon in order for the Group to continue to function. Apart from a few Short Scion 2s the Moth Minor was the only aircraft to be powered by the Gipsy Minor engine, and as only relatively few had been built before the war this was certainly not helping the situation. Something more rugged with a ready supply of spares was urgently required and the ex-RAF Magister finally became the obvious choice; there was a ready supply of these at not too desperate a price, so by February 1953 we became the proud owners of G-AMBM. The Moth Minors were disposed of, not without a little regret from yours truly as I had come to love the dainty little aircraft and the lightness of its controls. Then with the assistance of Col. Busk, a Director of the Group, another "Maggie"was added to the fleet in March. This was G-ALIO, soon to be named *"Pongo"* by Rex in memory of his time in the Army; he had done his time in the Signals, so we were the only two 'brown jobs' in the Group!

On the 15th February Rex took me for my first "Maggie" flight in G-AMBM and the first thing that struck me, apart from the sheer size of the beast, was the large diameter of the 'pole.' After the dainty joystick in the Moth Minor the one in the "Maggie" felt like a telegraph pole, but after a while I got used to it and I also liked the extra power that the reliable Gipsy Major produced. I enjoyed flying the "Maggie" very much and was not even worried when the dreaded word 'spinning' was mentioned! In the very early days of the "Maggie" before the war it had gained somewhat of an evil reputation for not recovering from spins, but this problem had been rectified in due course and I found recovery to be quite straightforward and positive. The initial reaction to entering the spin was one of considerable surprise, however, as the entry was quite vicious, with the nose disappearing from its usual place on the horizon to somewhere underneath your seat, leaving you hanging on the straps looking at the countryside below. But you soon got used to it.

My "Maggie" solo was made in G-ALIO on the 22nd April, after a very intensive session of simulated engine failures on take-off with Jean Bird. Woe betide you if you didn't react quicker than instantaneously after she chopped the throttle! When taking off to the east Jean expected you to point the nose between the two bungalows on the opposite side of the road at the end of the overshoot pretty quickly, without turning too much or reducing flying speed: never mind about taking the wings off as you went between the bungalows if you wanted to live to fly another day!

I often wondered what the occupants of these bungalows would have thought if they had realised that they were on the receiving end of all these simulated engine failures! Jean knew the dangers of engine failure on take-off only too well though, as while ferrying with the ATA she had been fortunate to survive a horrific crash at Gosport in a Hudson when both engines failed.

I made a couple of dual cross-country flights in "Maggies" with Rex, the first to Hamble on the 27th March in G-AMBM and then to Broxbourne (via Hornchurch which we overflew) in G-ALIO on the 6th

April. On reflection I am now very glad that I did, as both of these interesting airfields are sadly no longer with us.

On the 28th June Rex took G-AMBM and I to the Tea Patrol at Fair Oaks for the reasons he explained in his previous story, but he omitted to mention the toilet-roll-streaming episode on departure – perhaps, on reflection, for very good reason! The next day, Monday the 29th June 1953, we were due to leave Redhill in G-AMBM on the first leg of our foreign tour: we could not have gone over the weekend, much as we wanted to, as both "Maggies" were busy on training and procuring free teas for two at Fairoaks.

The great day had finally arrived and we were pleased to see that it had dawned bright and sunny for our big adventure. We gave 'BM a last-minute test flight to check that everything was in order and left at 12.20: first stop Lympne to clear customs. We 'Bradshawed' it along the railway line to Lympne, arriving 50 minutes later, and after the usual customs formalities we stopped for a quick coffee before taking on the English Channel. It was at this point that I realised just how efficient the Silver City car ferry service was.

As we sat in the coffee lounge I noticed G-AHJP, a Bristol Freighter, leaving for Le Touquet, and before we had finished our coffee (or so it seemed) it had returned and was taxying in again: total elapsed time could not have been more than about an hour! We took off from Lympne and headed out across the Channel at the narrowest point – first stop Lille. We had life jackets but I recall that they were stowed under the seats – I can't think why! The trusty Gipsy Major never missed a beat and although they do say that immediately you fly over water the engine always sounds different I don't remember that it did in our case. Shortly after we crossed the French coast I saw my first live 'Frog' riding a bicycle (I don't remember seeing the onions though!). We soon saw the large aerodrome at Lille and landed there after a flight of 1 hour 20 minutes. Lille was a combined civil and military aerodrome and as we cleared French customs we were surprised by the official who questioned the number of rolls of film we were carrying. We could not convince him that we were aviation enthusiasts and not spies so we gave up and so did he. I can imagine him thinking: "Ze mad English!"

At Lille we saw a number of French Air Force machines which included two MS Criquet; two Nord 1000 Pingouin; six MS 474 and a Caudron Goeland, while amongst the civilian populace were F-BBCY Leopoldoff L.6; F-BCNY & F-BEJP MS 502 Criquet; F-BBMR, a dismantled Bu.181 and F-BBKV Nord Norécrin. Our next stop, where we intended to stay the night, was Mezières on the French/Belgian border and after a flight of 1 hour 20 minutes we landed on the one narrow 'runway,' which had just been cut out of the crop of wheat still growing over the whole of the remainder of the field! We taxied up to the clubhouse, where we were met and made very welcome by the members of the local flying club, black berets and all. Joking aside, though, they were really very friendly and fortunately most of them spoke good English, which was just as well because although Rex had a smattering of the language I, being typically English, knew none!

We had touched down at 18.40 and before we knew it another little Frenchman with the inevitable black beret arrived on a bicycle (still no onions!) and proclaimed he was the local customs official and that we would have to clear customs. The fact that we had already cleared customs at Lille went unheeded and this brought forth an incredible exhibition of the French 'discussion' with much shouting and waving of arms by all concerned, most of it being directed by club members in our defence against this unfortunate individual! I thought at one point that they would all come to blows as the club members surrounded him, taking our side in trying to convince the "stupid little 'Frog' bureaucrat" (at least that is how they translated it for us afterwards!) that we had already cleared customs at Lille. We discovered later that most of the fuss had been about the fact that he wanted to charge us the equivalent of 5/- for his services in having to come out from the local town, all that way on his bicycle. That we had not asked for his services and did not want to see him anyway was beside the point and the club members were having none of it! They told him in no uncertain manner that they felt it was an insult to their English visitors, who had been kind enough to come all that way to visit them, to be asked to pay for something which they certainly did not want. Eventually we paid him just to keep the peace, as he wouldn't go away and was beginning to get on everyone's nerves.

The club members were genuinely pleased that we had landed at their small airfield, as few if any British civil aircraft had landed there since the war, and before we knew it we had been taken under the wing of a charming French couple. They spoke excellent English and had apparently already decided to wine and dine us at the Station Hotel in the nearby railway town of Charleville.

In conversation we learned that the couple who had befriended us had an interesting and sensible philosophy: they were both qualified pilots, but they had a young family so never flew together or even at the same time. They felt that one or the other of them should keep their feet firmly on *terra firma* if the other was flying. Incidentally, I cherish a lovely memory to this day of seeing my first bare female midriff (I had led a very sheltered life!) as the wife wore a very fetching white cross-over blouse which tied at the back and exposed the relevant feature beautifully!

We had a wonderful evening but I was not used to all this generous Gallic hospitality, having been brought up on tea and 'meat and two veg'! Drinking rot-gut French red wine by the bucketful and eating what must have been at least a ten-course meal was a new experience for me.

However, after a most enjoyable evening we bade our farewells and eventually retired to our rooms exhausted: it had been a very full day. What I did not realise at the time however, was that my room, from memory on about the fifth floor, overlooked the railway marshalling yards and the French railways shunted all night! The quite incredible noise this produced, coupled with the heat of the room (the central heating appeared to be going flat-out even though it was mid-summer) and the results of the large meal (and all the wine) combined to give me the worst nightmare that I have ever experienced; I lost count of the number of times I awoke bathed in sweat as imaginary foreign people kept entering my room, turning all the lights on and frightening me half to death. I will never forget the first night I spent abroad!

Enough of this revelry: we should not forget the purpose for which we had come thus far – to look at foreign aeroplanes! I still have a complete list of the weird and wonderful aircraft which we saw in France and the immaculate ones in Switzerland, but unfortunately, while this makes fascinating reading for the *aficionado* it is perhaps inappropriate to include all the details here (shame!).

Some of the more interesting types at Mezières (they were *all* interesting to us) included: F-BBCA Caudron Luciole; F-BBXL & F-BBSE Bu.181; F-BGMG GY.20 Minicab, F-AMGJ Caudron Phalene 282-9 *"Jean Bivoit"*; F-WFDD Roger Druine *"Le Turbulent"* c/n 106; F-BDJT Caudron C.600 Aiglon c/n 2 (rebuilt since the war by Peitz); F-BEQH Nord 1203 Norécrin and F-BCJC Proctor.

Although I presumably had a hangover we somehow managed to take off quite early next morning, at 09.45 in fact, en route to Nancy, which we reached in 1 hour 25 minutes. It was while landing there that we had our one and only slightly hairy moment of the tour. The airfield did admittedly look rather small from the air and somewhat deserted, but there was the inevitable little hangar in one corner and apparently nowhere else to go, so in we went. As we approached we thought that it would not have hurt them to have cut the grass once in a while; it turned out to be about three feet long as we descended through it! The natives encamped around the perimeter (possibly Gypsies) looked none too friendly either so without stopping to enquire further Rex opened the throttle and we left forthwith. Fortunately, as the wheels cleared the top of the grass an enormous ditch appeared at right angles across our path – it had been a close thing. Who had left that across the middle of what was by now fast becoming apparent to us to be an abandoned airfield we knew not. As we gained height a larger aerodrome which we had not seen on our approach appeared beneath us and we had found Nancy proper! We never did discover what the other field was called and, discretion being the better part of valour, we chose not to try to find out.

Now, for those of you who are unfamiliar with the ways of the French at that time, Tuesday was their day of rest (thinks: "only Tuesday?") but by this time we felt the need to refuel. What followed was the nearest thing to a pantomime that I have ever nearly been a part of. If I had not witnessed it with my own eyes I would not have believed it: it could only have happened in France. The first act opened with a kindly English-speaking air traffic controller taking pity on us; after he had explained that the place was shut until the morrow due to their quaint habit of Tuesday closing, he said that if we were to follow him we would be refuelled but we weren't to ask any questions.

At that moment the second act opened with the two occupants of F-BEXN, a Fairchild Argus 3 which had just landed, coming in. Dressed in black leather jackets and black berets, the two garlic-smelling Frenchmen vociferously demanded fuel but equally chose to forget the fact that it was a Tuesday, their national day of rest. Unperturbed by this fact which was patiently explained to them by the air traffic controller, they then demanded and were given a telephone. Into this incredibly ancient upright device the pilot then proceeded to vent his feelings on the the subject to an unknown personage at the other end. Whoever this person was, it was obviously all his fault that the place was closed and it was at that point that the fun really began when his mate grabbed the secondary earpiece, which was only really meant for listening into, and then proceeded at strength five and speaking very fast to add his 'fourpennyworth'! Of course all this was accompanied by the inevitable Gallic habit of arm waving, and although no one but us could see them, this mattered little. It was as much as I could do to refrain from 'rolling in the aisles'!

Unfortunately, we had to leave them to their reveries as by then our English-speaking controller was saying "Follow me" as he rushed out of the door (he had obviously had more than enough of the other two), clambered aboard his open-top Cadillac and departed in a cloud of dust along the perimeter track.

We swung 'BM's prop and clambered aboard, not bothering with our straps as we had only intended taxying slowly to wherever we were going, but on reflection it might not have been a bad idea to have done them up as although seven years had elapsed since the end of the war you would never had known it by the state of the airfield. The perimeter track was still covered in bomb holes and heaps of rubble which we had to negotiate as we endeavoured to follow the cloud of dust in which the Cadillac was hidden. It soon became apparent that our destination was the French Air Force base, and by the time we arrived the controller had already rousted the drunken duty officer from the mess and demanded that he arrange for our tanks to be filled forthwith.

Warming to this happy turn of events we watched helplessly as a few of the less inebriated mechanics attempted to refuel us. Upon completion of the task we feigned total ignorance of the language when one of them held his hand out for a tip – well! We travelled around Europe on a fuel carnet but we were told to keep quiet at this point and so we did: we never did pay for this fuel!

The more interesting aircraft at Nancy were: F-BFSQ NC.853S; F-BBCG Caudron Phalene; F-BENS Proctor; F-BDOK Tiger Moth; F-BCRL Bu.181 "Charles Chaon"; F-BGOA Dove and the dismantled Auster LX-ACD. The French Air Force had Dassault Flamant (c/n 10), two Nord 1000 Pingouin and about a dozen Piper Cubs scattered about.

With 'BM suitably refreshed we took off and climbed to some 2,000 ft over the Vosges Mountains en route for Basel Mulhouse where we cleared French customs, taxied around the corner and then cleared Swiss customs! Dakota G-AMNL came into the circuit while we were in the tower reporting in, and I distinctly remember the controller complaining about the poor quality of the British radios compared with those of the American ones. I must admit that I could not understand a word of what the pilot said but I supposed that the ATCs eventually develop 'RT ear'! Without the benefit of such modern luxuries in 'BM I was quite happy to scream down the Gosport tube when I wanted to communicate with Rex, and to keep my eyes peeled at aerodromes! The Swissair DC-4 HB-ILU was on the tarmac (this was 44 years before the recent event to mark the 50th anniversary of Swissair's first trans-Atlantic crossing: it is this sort of thing which makes you feel really old!), and also in evidence were HB-UOL & HB-UOM Avia FL.3, HB-DUC Luscombe Silvaire and HB-EIM Argus 3.

We had planned to make Zurich in good time so at 16.55 we were on our way again. A 45-minute flight took us to Zurich International Airport where we had been assured it would be all right to land! I must say that it was somewhat disconcerting to join a circuit full of airliners including DC-6Bs of Swissair, DC-3s of Swissair & Air France, Convair 240s of Sabena and KLM, BEA Ambassadors and the like, but just as I was beginning to get worried we espied a large grass strip to one side with its own control tower, from which an Aldis lamp was flashing a green. We joined its circuit, landed on the grass and parked in front of an enormous hangar with an equally enormous up-and-over door. The air traffic controllers were shortly going off duty and kindly offered to take us to a hotel at Kloten, near Zurich, on their way home, where they assured us we could get good accommodation at reasonable rates. While we waited for them we took the opportunity to wander round the hangar. This contained many exotic types, all in absolutely immaculate condition, as indeed were all the Swiss aircraft which we ultimately saw in our travels through that exceptionally clean country.

These included: HB-EKE, HB-EVA & HB-EVE Bücker Jungmann; HB-EAM & HB-EAX Argus 2; HB-ERE & HB-ERO Argus 3; HB-EEA Gemini 1A; HB-EPI Whitney Straight; HB-OKO Leopard Moth; N9978F Fairchild Cornell; HB-UXC Klemm KL.35D; HB-EUS Globe Swift; HB-EPB & HB-EPT KZ.VIII and eight Swiss-registered Bonanzas.

How we all managed to cram ourselves into the Fiat 500 which ultimately arrived to collect us I will never know; perhaps the fact that it had a folding canvas roof helped as I seem to remember that some of the passengers were sticking out through it! Following a much quieter evening and a much better night in what turned out to be a very nice hotel, we returned to the airport next morning to find five Swissair DC-3s, a DC-6B, the Dragon Rapide HB-APA and a wing from DC-2 HB-ITO.

We left Zurich at 10.50 for Berne, arriving there at 11.40 to be met with what was to become the usual Swiss efficiency, where unlike France all our details were presented to us for confirmation after we had landed, without having to be asked for them. Due to the inhospitable terrain of most of the country it was their standard practice to notify the destination airfield of the time of departure, full details of the aircraft and occupants together with the ETA. If we had been late in arriving we gathered that all hell would have broken loose with search and rescue parties being sent out – most impressive.

At Berne we found amongst others HB-ALI Leopard Moth; HB-AMA Koolhoven FK.50; HB-IKI Nord 1000; HB-EOC Auster 5; HB-RAA Dewoitine D.26; HB-TRY Vultee Sentinel; HB-AXA Comte AC.12 Moskito and HB-EMI Argus 2.

After we had looked round the hangars, we took off at 12.30 for Lausanne, arriving there 40 minutes later. At this lovely grass airfield we found, amongst other rarities, three British-built aeroplanes (Leopard Moth HB-OTA, Moth HB-OBA, Moth Major HB-UPE), and an indigenous population which included HB-KIL Comte AC.4 Gentleman; HB-KIN Comte AC.12 (with an A/S Genet Major engine); HB-OLU Comte AC.12 (with a Gipsy Major engine) and HB-RAC Dewoitine D.26.

Next stop was Geneva, and at 14.30 we were off again, to arrive at 15.05. The airfield at Geneva consisted of acres of concrete with a very long runway and I recall that we had to taxi to the end of this and backtrack along the equally long perimeter track to return to the terminal building. However it was all worth it as the reception we received when we finally arrived was quite something. A marshal with bats appeared, guided us onto a yellow line painted on the vast expanse of concrete and parked us with all due reverence alongside the Alitalia DC-4 I-DALZ "Citta di Roma"! We both shared the ramp (why 'ramp'? It was quite flat.) with four USAF Skytrains, a Constellation N6008C "City of Indiana," a Swissair Convair 240 and DC-3, a Ryan Navion and a Piper Cub. Around and about were nine Swiss Piper J/3C-65 Cubs, two Bonanzas, HB-ETB

Aeronca Sedan, HB-OXO Leopard Moth, HB-OMU Moth Minor (wonderful!), HB-OFU Percival Gull Six, HB-EEF M.28 (more joy!), HB-EMO Argus 2, HB-URO Whitney Straight (we must have seen nearly all the Swiss-registered British civil aircraft in our travels). Up to now the weather had been extremely kind to us and this is borne out in the photographs we took but it was now time to commence our return through France and it began to look as though we were in for a change.

As usual time was of the essence and at 16.40 we took off for Lyon, where we intended to stay the night. The hour's flight took us over the Jura Mountains and while cruising over these at about 4,500 ft we encountered some rather black-looking weather to one side. We were not precipitated upon but thinking it would be 'one for the book' I took some photographs of this stuff over the mountains. Upon our return I made the mistake of showing our photographs to Jean Bird and when she got to these we were suitably dressed down for flying in such weather. In all honesty it was not as bad as it looked in the photographs: the camera *does* lie, at least that was my story and I was sticking to it!

At Lyon-Bron were a number of very interesting aeroplanes including F-BFLM a Boisavia B.601 Mercurey, which Rex especially wanted to see and was the *raison d'être* for planning our trip around Lyon.

Also there were F-OABY Dakota of Air Atlas; F-BFPP Gemini 1A; F-APPZ Whitney Straight; F-BEDV Expeditor; F-BDAR Argus 3; F-BCUT Aero 45; F-BFPQ Auster Autocrat; F-BFPH & F-BBSV Stinson Station Wagon; F-PBOB Jodel D.93 Bébé; F-BAOT MS.502 Criquet (dismantled and still camouflaged, with the Cross of Lorraine on the fin); F-PEAT AAL.28X; F-BFXA KZ.VII; F-BCIH Stark AS.57; F-BCZG Brochet MB.71 and F-BDJK MS.230. The French Air Force had a small presence there also.

We stayed that night in Lyon, departing for Nevers the next morning at 10.00 and landing there 1 hour 30 minutes later. The one small hangar there produced F-AOET Potez 60; F-BDMQ Tiger Moth; F-BBUA MS.502 Criquet; three Jodel Bébés and a couple of gliders.

Next stop was to be Toussus-le-Noble, the centre of light aeroplane activity for Paris, which we reached in a further 1 hour 30 minutes. I well remember my first glimpse of the Eiffel Tower as Paris hove into view, but nothing could have prepared me (Rex had been there before and knew what to expect) for the sight which awaited us on landing. Toussus was without a doubt *the* aerodrome for light aircraft, although in typically French style it was still sporting the wartime steel mesh runway which clattered something rotten when larger aircraft landed on it! The hangars contained somewhere in the region of 200 aircraft and it took us quite a time to record these and try to identify many of them. It fair took my breath away: I wonder what happened to them all?

A few of the more exotic ones were: F-BEKQ & F-BEVZ SUC.10 Courlis; F-AKER Farman 192 (dismantled); F-WFOF Farman F.500 Monitor; F-BBAZ Caudron Luciole; F-BCZJ Lignel 46; F-AJQK MS.181 (flying!); F-AQMO Dewoitine 484; F-AJTE Dewoitine Hispano D.27; F-AMRO Caudron Phalene; F-BEJO MS.230 E.T.2; F-BGOP Consul; nine French civil Tiger Moths; F-BFVH Gemini 1A (F-BFXH wrongly registered!); F-OAKG Dove, F-BDPA & F-BDPH Magisters; F-BCJY & F-BATL Beech Travellers and I-AIAK Norduyn Norseman.

The object of planning our trip to end at Toussus on Thursday 2nd July was, apart from the opportunity to examine the inmates of that famous aerodrome, to take in the Paris Air Show on the Friday before returning home on the Saturday. Somehow, after thoroughly checking out all the hangars and parked aircraft at Toussus we then managed to get to Buc by road but quite how we achieved this is now beyond my recall. It was well worth the visit though because that was where it had all started, being once the home of no less a personage than Louis Blériot himself, or so we were told.

A truly wondrous collection of ancient and modern aircraft were there including the following: F-WBBQ PA.204 Cigale Major c/n 01 *"Old Chap,"* built by Avions Paul Aubert (we were introduced to him); F-BFRU PA.204 Cigale Major c/n 02; F-AROY Potex 32; F-BBCH Caudron Phalene; F-ANTG Caudron Luciole (less engine); F-BGOF Anson (ex-l'Armée de l'Air); F-BFPS Proctor and, wonder of wonders, the beautiful but dismantled anonymous Caudron C.713 pre-war lightweight fighter, while a Se.3120 helicopter, F-WGGD, which had just completed a closed-circuit record for a 1,252 km course a few minutes before we arrived, was the centre of attraction on the tarmac.

We stayed somewhere in Paris that night, and next morning we were up bright and early to board the most ancient Air France bus to take us right across Paris to Le Bourget airport to the famous Paris Salon. Visiting aircraft were not encouraged, to the point of being banned altogether at Le Bourget while the show was on, so we left our trusty steed at Toussus for the day. Having to resort to using this fascinating if highly dangerous mode of transport to take us to the Show was an act of desperation as we were not in any way in control of our destiny, and having to travel at breakneck speed in such a decrepit vehicle driven by a typically mad Frenchman through the centre of Paris was an experience we could have done without!

96

Details of all the extremely exotic stuff at the Paris Salon were covered in "THE AEROPLANE" and "FLIGHT" magazines at the time, but a few of the static aircraft noted and airline movements during the course of the day included fourteen Dakota variants from four different countries, F-BFPF Aerovan 4, F-BGOP Consul, seven DC-4s including EC-AEO and SE-BBA, SP-LHB IL-12, EC-WHT Languedoc, F-BAKN AAC.1 Tougan, four Liberators including F-BESL with a single fin and rudder, F-BGSA Comet, F-BBFS NC701-2 Martinet, four So.95 Corse, four civil Expeditors and last but by no means least, F-BELV, one of the very few surviving Boeing Stratoliners. On reflection it was all somewhat mind-blowing!

We spent another night in Paris and Saturday came all too soon. At Toussus the weather looked none too promising with low cloud and poor visibility but while we were waiting for clearance we noted that some new aircraft were in evidence in the form of F-BFVM Dragon Rapide, F-BFPC & HB-ECT Bonanzas and the Comte AC.12 HB-KIN which we had last seen at Lausanne.

But the time had come to leave: not only would 'BM be wanted for instruction over the coming weekend but by this time we were also practically out of funds. However the French Air Traffic types had expressly forbidden us to depart because of the weather, so we waited despondently in the tower for it to improve, purposely getting under their feet in the hope that they would get fed up with us. The visibility was a bit poor really, I suppose, but we felt that it was flyable. Then, just as were beginning to despair of ever getting away, we were very pleasantly surprised to see the Miles M.18 G-AHKY of S/L Brian Iles suddenly appear out of the gloom and join the circuit. We were outside in a flash waiting for him to taxi in so that we could ask him his starting point. When he said "England" that was enough! We almost frog-marched him up to the tower and after he had convinced them that the weather was flyable they had to let us go! Once airborne we discovered that the visibility wasn't so bad after all, and we reached Le Touquet without any difficulty.

Upon our arrival there 1 hour 30 minutes later we could have been excused for thinking that we had landed in England already as parked on the grass were twenty-two British-registered aircraft!

These included seven Silver City Bristol Freighters, G-AMZM the Provost demonstrator, G-AERV Whitney Straight (now languishing in a hut in Northern Ireland), G-AEWZ Dragonfly of Silver City Airways, G-AKPE Hawk Trainer, various Geminis, Rapides, Proctors and Austers (including G-ALYH with which I was very pleased to make my re-acquaintance) and G-AJVI, an Argus 2 with a damaged undercarriage. French-registered aircraft included F-BBSL Gemini 1A, F-BFVM Dragon Rapide and F-BGTF, F-BDRP & F-BBRU Austers.

We cleared customs and finally left Le Touquet at 15.40 en route for Lympne, which we reached after 40 minutes of flying in slightly hazy conditions over an inhospitable-looking English Channel. Imagine our surprise, however, when upon arrival at Lympne the first aircraft we saw was F-BFLM, the Boisavia B.601 Mercurey which Rex had been so pleased to see at Lyon! To think that we had detoured there especially to see it! Two of the Freighters we had seen at Le Touquet joined us soon after and in all six were soon in evidence, including the ancient G-AGVB. The 'usual' Oxford, Consul, Autocrats, Proctor, Gemini and three Dragon Rapides were also to be seen (if only they were around today they would be anything but 'usual') but time was pressing, and after clearing customs, we were soon airborne and following the railway to Redhill and home.

We had been away for six very full and satisfying days and now, suddenly, it was all over. I had managed to add another 15 hours 40 minutes dual to my flying time, and we both had to admit that it had been a wonderful experience and one which will live forever in my memory. Thanks again, Rex!

I still managed to get the odd hour's flying in from Redhill after this, but the writing was on the wall and unless you were prepared to camp out on the aerodrome over the Friday night in order to have half a chance of getting airborne first thing Saturday morning (always assuming that the weather would be OK and the aeroplane serviceable), your chances of actually flying at all over the weekend were becoming slim to say the least. Therefore, to gain any form of continuous flying instruction was really very difficult and this was a problem which was to remain with us for all time as far as I could see. I was also embroiled in my part-time engineering studies by then and it soon became apparent, even to me, the born optimist, that something would have to go. When Redhill aerodrome closed to flying in April 1954 following a Government economy drive which closed the Reserve Flying Schools, and not least of all No.15 RFS at Redhill, it soon became apparent that all resident club and private owners would have to find somewhere else to go.

Croydon was the nearest suitable alternative, so on 15th April 1954 I made my last flight with the Experimental Flying Group from Redhill Aerodrome, a very pleasant evening dual cross-country to Southend in G-ALIO with Vernon Burgess, marred only in the initial stages by me flying up the wrong line on my map! This fact became apparent as I realised that the airfield over which I was flying was Kenley and not Biggin Hill. Hoping that Vernon had not spotted this error (he was having his tea at the time, as the sundry debris and orange peel which drifted past the rear cockpit bore witness), I smartly corrected course and proceeded as if nothing had been amiss! The landing at Southend will forever remain in my memory, however, as it was there that I learnt that it was not always necessary to use full flap when you were landing into a 'straight windsock' wind! Our descent resembled that of a helicopter and we touched down neatly just inside the boundary fence, stopping almost immediately; Vernon let me learn that one the hard way!

My next flight, also in G-ALIO, was made on the 20th June from Croydon, where the Group had by then taken up residence. For reasons that I can no longer recall, I did not fly again until the 5th September and this was with Rex. I was very pleased to find that even after all that time I must have still 'had my hand in' for after 50 minutes dual he let me have my one moment of glory – my one and only solo flight from that most hallowed of aerodromes. Ten minutes of bliss, but halfway around the circuit and terrified of what the natives might do to me if I had to force-land for any reason, I suddenly found myself with another 500 ft on the clock: I had just passed over the electricity station's cooling towers – never a dull moment!

I made my final flight with the Group in G-ALIO, a local dual with Ken Sirett on the 26th September 1954, and with that my flying career ended. I could no longer (i) really spare the time as I was deeply involved in my part-time engineering studies (ii) justify the cost and (iii) stand the frustration of cycling all the way to Croydon to have to wait around for ever in the hope of getting a flight. It had been good fun while it lasted and it was all very sad but something just had to go.

And we had done it all without radio!

CHAPTER 10

ADDICTED TO AVIATION

by

Alan Hartfield

[NOTES ON THE AUTHOR: Alan Hartfield was born in London on the 20th November 1935 and his early years were influenced by World War 2. After an interrupted education he was accepted for a Royal Air Force Apprenticeship in the trade of Airframes at No.1 School of Technical Training, RAF Halton, in January 1951. This was the start of his life-long career in aeronautical engineering. On completion of his Apprenticeship he served for twenty-two years in many parts of the world and on many different types of aircraft, the work varying from repairing Meteors to five years as a Nimrod Crew Chief. On leaving the Royal Air Force he worked at Redifon Flight Simulation for three years and then returned to RAF Halton as a civilian instructor, teaching the Airframe trade to young Apprentices, Technicians and Mechanics until early retirement in 1995. He was the Safety Officer of the Vintage Aircraft Club for eight years and is a Popular Flying Association Inspector.

However, he always wanted to fly, but having a slight loss of hearing due to an early operation, he was unable to be accepted for aircrew. After many years of gliding during the 1950s and 1960s he gained a Private Pilot's Licence in 1974 and has flown continuously to date. For the past fifteen years he has flown vintage aeroplanes and is the proud owner of the 1937 Dart Kitten G-AEXT.]

It is often said that those of us with an interest in aviation have been "bitten by the bug"; this seems to imply that there is something wrong with us or that we are not normal! Be that as it may, I have found aviation enthusiasts to be agreeable, humorous and genuine men and women, many of whom have become my true friends. I have often paused at aviation gatherings and wondered what motivated each of us to become so enthusiastic about aviation. This thought led me to look back over my life and write the story of how I became addicted to aviation.

When World War 2 began I was four years old and living with my parents in Willesden, London NW10. One of my earliest memories is of my mother talking over the wall with the next-door neighbours and of all of them looking up at a formation of German bombers flying over us. The adults were expressing their horror at the sight of the aeroplanes, but being so young I did not realise they were hostile, and I clearly remember wishing that I was in one of the aeroplanes and wondering what it would be like to be flying. The progress of the War, especially in the air, became more and more exciting to growing lads and in spite of our home being bomb-damaged twice, causing me to be evacuated to the countryside, my interest in aeroplanes grew.

Living in London was becoming dangerous, so my father moved us to Wingfield Way, South Ruislip. As its name suggests, this road adjoined the aerodrome at Northolt, and you can imagine my delight at finding that I now lived only yards from the aerodrome boundary. I soon met other boys (and a few girls) at the aerodrome fence and we spent hours watching the activities on the ground and the aeroplanes flying. Most of the aeroplanes were Hawker Hurricanes flown by the Polish Squadrons and I well remember the late-night parties and revelry at the nearby Club; it is fitting that the memorial to those brave airmen now stands at the south-east corner of the aerodrome only a short distance from the site of that Club. When I stand at the memorial now I not only remember the sound of the Hurricanes quickly taking off in formation but can almost hear the singing and laughter of those crazy Polish airmen and see the sweets which they often pressed into my hand.

Later, like any boy of about eight or nine years old and keen on aeroplanes, I wanted to fly. This was not possible, but I can remember lying in bed and closing my eyes to see the instruments and controls of a Spitfire and feeling that I was sitting in the pilot's seat. Keeping my eyes closed and taking hold of the controls, I would hear the sound and feel the vibration of the engine as we climbed into the sky. I can clearly remember the motion of the aeroplane as we turned, climbed and dived; years later when I *did* fly, I was amazed at how accurate my early dreams of flying had been.

Shortly after the end of the war, Northolt aerodrome became London Airport and I was ideally placed to start aeroplane-spotting. There were no books published at that time and I listed every aeroplane by writing the registration and type, date and place, in a notebook. Many of the aeroplanes were converted military types such as Dakotas, DC-4s and DC-6s, Lancastrians, Yorks and Halifaxes. Soon other types appeared, such as Vikings and Convairs. It was thrilling to see the aeroplanes so close and my geography lessons began to have meaning when I saw that they were operated by Swissair, Scandinavian Airline System, Portuguese Airlines, Aer Lingus, Sabena, KLM, to name but a few. My face must still bear the marks made by the fencing as I peered through to enjoy and record the details of every aeroplane.

Someone mentioned that if you wrote to the airlines they would send their brochures to you; school homework now had to wait as I wrote numerous letters to airlines explaining my interest in their aircraft, and every one of them replied, enclosing generous amounts of information. I can still remember the feeling of excitement when the post arrived and I feverishly opened the large envelopes containing the airline brochures and posters, and photographs and cutaway drawings of their aircraft. I read every word and studied every detail and soon my bedroom wall became an aeronautical exhibition, much to the consternation of my parents.

I now realised that there were other aerodromes not far away and, to save having to give me bus fares or finding that his bicycle had disappeared for the day, my father bought me my own bicycle. Being independently mobile, I could now spend happy hours at Denham, Elstree, Heston, Langley and Heathrow, observing and recording aeroplanes large and small. I often found open gates and could not resist walking across to look into the hangars, which were full of delightful aeroplanes. At Heston, I remember seeing a strange-looking craft; it was a large single-engined aeroplane with a high wing and had the main undercarriage mounted on short lower stub wings (a sesquiplane) and was a shocking lime/pea-green colour. It did not appear in any of the aeroplane recognition books which were now being published but I later learnt that I had seen the rare Heston Phoenix. Usually when looking in hangars I would be told to "leave immediately and not come back" by a grumpy old so-and-so, so now whenever I see youngsters interested in aeroplanes I like to encourage them by showing and explaining everything to them. On a visit to Langley I saw lines of Typhoons and Tempests waiting to be scrapped; to economise on space when a row had been formed, the following aircraft had been dumped on top of those already there! There are no Typhoon or Tempest aircraft now flying and it is like a nightmare come true; hands up those responsible! *[The good news is that at least two Tempests are said to be currently undergoing restoration – Ed.]*

At twelve years old I really did want to fly, but whenever I mentioned it my parents discouraged me; they thought that flying was dangerous, and of course they could not afford to fund me. I decided that I must earn my own money and duly took up a newspaper delivery round. My savings seemed to increase rather slowly at a few pence a week (old money remember), so I helped the milkman on Saturdays and during holidays.

Northolt aerodrome now had a public enclosure and although I could not afford to pay the entrance fee I had found a gap in the fencing which I seemed to easily fall through! At the far end of the public enclosure stood a beautiful DH Rapide and nearby a caravan with a notice proclaiming that 7/6d was the cost of a flight over London. One Saturday afternoon I found that my savings amounted to 7/6d and, without saying anything to my mother or father, I slipped the money into my pocket. I almost ran up the road to the public enclosure and fell through the gap in the fence. I tried not to let my excitement show and to look grown-up as I reached up and tapped on the window of the caravan; the window slid back, and in exchange for my hard-earned cash, a lady in a dark blue uniform kindly gave me a ticket and asked me to sit and wait next to the gate leading to the DH Rapide. In a few minutes a small family group had also paid and came over to wait. The lady in the dark blue uniform let us through the gate and directed us to the aeroplane. After the family group had entered I quickly stepped up and took the first seat on the left, just in front of the door. The uniformed lady was so attentive as she made sure our seat belts were correctly fastened and I expected her to leave the cabin for the pilot to board. She then entered the cockpit, and I realised that she had already taken the steps away and had closed the door. I was being flown on my first flight by a woman pilot!

I clearly remember the thrill I felt as the Rapide accelerated along the runway, and of seeing the rubber skid marks which landing aircraft had made flash past under the window. Next I noticed that the ground was falling away and I was at last flying – yippee! Of course I was interested in looking down and seeing the sights of London, but it was the sensation of flying and the sound and smell of the aeroplane which thrilled me the most. Too soon we were approaching to land and I heard the quiet 'eeck!' as the lady pilot made a gentle landing and the tail lowered as we slowed before taxying in. Unfortunately I did not record the registration or operator of the Rapide, nor did I ask the lady pilot her name; almost certainly she was an ex-wartime Air Transport Auxiliary pilot, maybe Monique Agazarian? I rushed home so happy and found my mother; she listened carefully as I enthusiastically told her every detail of my first flight. Seeing how thrilled I was she did not scold me and said she would explain it to my father. Fortunately he realised that his son was committed to aviation and he forgave me for not telling them that I was going to fly.

A few of us aviation-bitten boys learnt of The Air League of the British Empire. This was an organisation for aviation enthusiasts and especially encouraged boys such as us. Again I raided my money box and paid to become a member; how proud I was to wear the 'speedbird'-image lapel badge of membership. In 1949 The Air League of the British Empire held a summer camp at Hamble aerodrome near Southampton and I was overjoyed when my father agreed to pay for me to go. Two of my friends also went to the summer camp and we looked forward in great anticipation to the programme which The Air League had planned for us, so much so that we did not feel homesick nor mind being accommodated in tents.

Hamble was the home of Air Service Training and we were not only shown round the technical and flying training classrooms, workshops and hangars, but also given some informal instruction; it was all very interesting to this aviation-struck boy. We had two external visits during our camp, one to the Folland Aircraft factory just down the road from Hamble and the other to the seaplane base at Cowes on the Isle of Wight. At Follands they were building a beautiful looking "hush-hush" jet fitted with their own-designed ejection seat because the cockpit was rather small; this lovely aeroplane became known as the Gnat. We were not treated as "just another nuisance visit" but had the production of modern aircraft explained to us by many enthusiastic workers. We boys soaked it all up.

To visit Cowes we walked through the Shell petroleum storage area to their jetty where a launch awaited us. As we crossed the Solent, one of the beautiful prototype Saro SR.A/1 jet fighter flying-boats came in to land. It appeared to be travelling quite fast as it touched down on the water and we were horrified to see it bounce up and then crash into the Solent. [Also see Chapter 27 – Ed.] All boats in the vicinity, including ours, sped towards the Saro and we were pleased to see the pilot bobbing up and down in the water and a boat rescuing him. Our launch then changed course towards Cowes but I believe the Saro rapidly sank. When we reached the slipway, another Saro SR.A/1 aeroplane stood there, and looked beautiful even on its beaching gear. We were shown round the large hangar where the Saunders Roe Princess flying boat was being built; it seemed enormous and all of the personnel were enthusiastic about it. What a shame that it was uncompetitive and was scrapped.

For me, the highlight of the Air League summer camp was going flying in Tiger Moths. I can still remember the feeling of anticipation as I struggled to fit the seat-type parachute; anyone who has worn this type of parachute will know how difficult it is to walk, because the dangling pack knocks the legs forward with every step, but oh! how excited I was as I walked out to the Tiger Moth, kitted out with parachute and flying helmet. On one flight the pilot asked if I had ever experienced "a falling leaf" manoeuvre or a practice forced landing; I replied, via the wobbly mask known as a Gosport tube, that I had not. My pilot pointed out a stubble field in which a tractor was working at the edge and said that "we will do a falling leaf down to a landing in the field"; this sounded very exciting, and it was! We stalled and side-slipped, first one way and then the other, many times, as the pilot descended and positioned the Tiger Moth on approach to the field. With a last side-slip, we straightened and landed on the stubble, which I remember seemed much more smooth than I had expected. Taxying back down the field we had to pass the farmer, who had stopped his tractor and was looking most puzzled! My pilot suggested that I give him a wave and this I duly did; this seemed to reassure the farmer and he happily waved back to us. Without stopping, the Tiger Moth was turned into wind and we started the take-off. As the aeroplane was about to leave the ground I saw a large rabbit running fast from our left and it disappeared underneath us; the pilot was worried that the Tiger Moth had hit the rabbit, but having turned my head quickly to the right I saw the rabbit still running in the same direction, perhaps a bit faster, and was able to confirm all was well.

After landing at Hamble I am sure that my pilot could see how happy he had made this aviation-struck boy! Some forty years later I met the aviation artist Gerald Coulson and was amazed to find that one of his paintings, *"Happy Days,"* shows a Tiger Moth flying low over a field and a rabbit running across in front; a limited edition print of *"Happy Days"* now adorns one wall of our dining room.

An enduring memory of my Tiger Moth flights at Hamble is of looking ahead through the slowly-rotating propeller, and of the sound of the throttled-back Gipsy Major engine during the glide approach on finals to land. Everyone who has experienced this sensation and sound will know what I mean when I say that it was at this moment that I knew that I must fly.

Like all boys 'bitten by the bug' I made model aeroplanes. Some flew successfully and others did not! One of the latter, which at least proved spectacular, was a Vampire fitted with a Jetex solid fuel 'rocket'-type motor. Whether the instructions were not clear, or whether in my haste to see it fly I failed to fit heat protection above the Jetex exhaust, we shall never know. The weather was fine and my friends were at the field to witness the first flight of the Vampire jet. Having already trimmed it to fly unpowered, I primed the Jetex engine with the solid fuel and fuse wire, and lit the end of the fuse. I duly waited until the smoke, sparks and noise pronounced the engine ready to propel the Vampire and hand-launched it. How excited I was as the model flew up fast to some 100 feet but then I noticed the increasing amounts of smoke, and even flames, coming from the fuselage. The Vampire was now gliding nicely but was on fire. Soon the fire caused it to crash in flames and burn out, much to the amusement of my friends! One could say that "I learnt about (model) flying from that."

Due to the activities of Adolf Hitler's men, and much time in hospital concluding with an ear operation, my early schooling had been badly interrupted and I never seemed to catch up. Being in the last year at the Bourne Secondary Modern School meant that approaching the age of fifteen I faced leaving to find a job with no academic qualifications. One morning, to the surprise of our class expecting a maths lesson, the teacher came into the classroom and asked us to close our notebooks. He said that he considered it far more important for us to decide what work or career we were going to do or follow than to do the maths lesson. He told us that it was important to choose something which interested us and asked each of us to write down our three choices. I remember that I wrote "journalism, meteorology, and aeroplanes." The teacher came round to each of us in turn and, on seeing my choices, he explained in a tactful way that the first two were not possible without high academic qualifications. However, he questioned me about aeroplanes and suggested that I might like to apply for a Royal Air Force Apprenticeship in an aircraft trade, with the possibility of applying for flying training later. Thank you, Mr Anderson, for your foresight and advice, which led me into a satisfying career in aeronautical engineering.

I applied for a Royal Air Force Apprenticeship and to my delight I passed the initial entrance examination, the first exam of importance which I had ever passed! I attended the selection board at RAF Halton, the last part of which was an interview with Group Captain Donald Finlay. We sat in the corridor as we waited for our interview and I noted that the other applicants were older than me and had qualifications. Occasionally a lad would come out with a smile and say that he had been accepted but most came out from their interview gloomily, and many were crying. When my name was called I did not think I had much chance of becoming an RAF Apprentice but I respectfully tapped on the door to hear a stern "Come in."

Closing the door behind me I was instructed to "sit down," and walked forward to the one chair in front of the large desk, behind which sat Group Captain Finlay.

Without looking up he said: "Not very good at mathematics, are you?" and I truthfully had to reply: "No, Sir."

He then said: "If I accept you for training, will you improve your mathematics?" and I replied: "I will try, Sir."

He then looked up and asked me why I had only applied for the Airframe trade and had left the other options blank. I made my answer brief but had to explain it from my heart, and my enthusiasm must have convinced him because he then said: "I accept you for training as a Royal Air Force Apprentice in the trade of Airframes."

I did not gloat, but how proud I felt that day as I was about to start my lifelong aeronautical engineering career. It is a coincidence that Don Finlay won the Gold Medal for the 100 metres hurdles at the 1936 Olympic Games at Munich, much to the displeasure of Adolf Hitler, the very man responsible for interrupting my early education. Don Finlay, now a Group Captain, was accepting me for an Apprenticeship in spite of my weak educational standard. Who says there is no justice in life!

And so I entered No.1 School of Technical Training, RAF Halton, in January 1951 to start my Apprentice training as a member of the 67th Entry. For three years the life and the training was hard; I started as a young red-faced school-leaver and became quite mature by the time we

106

'Passed Out' in December 1953. Our training was the best in the world and I am proud to have been one of Lord Trenchard's 'Brats.' In addition to the training we were encouraged to partake in sports and hobbies. Still wanting to fly, I joined the Gliding Club, and started by being seated on a Dagling Primary Trainer faced into wind and being instructed to "keep the wings level" using the aileron control. Next, I was told to do the same as the winch cable was attached and the Dagling did a ground-slide across Halton airfield. When the instructor was satisfied, the winch driver was told to increase the speed and, with the elevator control stop adjusted to prevent too much elevator movement, I was instructed to "do a low hop" and glide to land just before and to one side of the winch. After completing twelve ground-slides I flew fifteen instructional flights in a Sedbergh T.21B. My old log book records that my instructors were Flight Lieutenants Crampton and Pocock, who were then satisfied enough to brief me on the single-seat glider, which was either a T.31 Mark 1 or Tutor. I was told to do "a high hop of 30 seconds" and to land ahead. The first 'hop' was timed at 28 seconds, and so I had to do a second which was 32 seconds. This qualified me for the British Gliding Association 'A' Certificate. At this point in May 1953, with only a few months to my final examinations, I reluctantly had to cease gliding at Halton.

Having 'Passed Out' from Halton as a Junior Technician, January 1954 found me posted to No.32 Maintenance Unit at RAF St Athan in South Wales. My work was the rebuilding of Meteor aircraft which had suffered considerable damage, often from wheels-up landings, and I enjoyed the work. When the repairs were completed and we had prepared an aircraft for air test, the whole team, or 'gang' as we were called, would stand outside the hangar and watch as the test pilot started up, taxied and took off in 'our' Meteor. We were relieved when it landed and quite delighted when the test pilot said it flew well and only needed a small adjustment, such as to the aileron trim.

Having been promoted to Corporal, I was selected to work on the RAF team for the 1954 Royal Tournament. We modified two Meteor aircraft, one of which was a spare, so that the ejection seat could be fired out of the cockpit into a net and so that the aircraft could be 'taxied' out of the Earls Court arena. We had to design the modifications and had great fun devising ingenious methods to make it all work as required.

Two weeks before the Royal Tournament found us at the R101 airship hangar at Cardington for practice. Having assembled the modified Meteors, and proved that they could be taxied, the 'boffins' arrived to advise on the ejection seat trajectory. They chalked a cross on the hangar floor for the position of the Meteor nosewheel and, with slide-rules working furiously (no computers in those days), instructed that the net to catch the ejection seat should be hung from the roof in an exact place. Having positioned the Meteor we stood well back, for we had a feeling about the next event. Yes, when fired, the ejection seat flew majestically through the air, missed the net, and crashed onto the hangar floor. The faces of the 'boffins' went very red and the slide-rules flashed even more furiously as they recalculated and asked for the positions to be changed. I am pleased to be able to say, especially for the success of the RAF display in front of the public at Earls Court, that although the ejection seat sometimes came perilously close to the edge of the net, it did not ever miss it.

Another part of the display was the pilot ejection-seat training rig. This was a tower mounted on a 'Queen Mary' articulated lorry, and with a small primary cartridge fitted in the ejection seat the pilot could be trained to correctly fire the seat, which would travel up the tower rails and stop near the top on a pawl and ratchet. From there, the seat could be lowered by a hand winch. A few days before leaving the airship hangar at Cardington for Earls Court, the NCO in charge of this ejection-seat rig found that he had not used all of the seat cartridges allocated for practice and that their expiry date was the next day. He explained that to return them to the depot involved much administration and a vehicle travelling with an escort, so "please could you Airframe chaps help by 'volunteering' to be trained on the use of an ejection-seat" and he could put it down as practice use. Being an ex-Brat, I waited to see what happened to those who readily volunteered, but after several had been shot up the tower without any apparent effects I could not prevent myself from asking to experience this 'ride from hell,' or should that be 'to'? The NCO in charge firstly strapped me onto the seat without any cartridge fitted and instructed me in the exact way to sit and to pull the face-blind handle (no seat pan-handles on the early seats) without moving my spine from the back of the seat. Being satisfied, he asked me to vacate the seat, fitted the explosive charge, and invited me to retake my seat. I can assure you that I sat down and strapped into the seat more gently than I had ever done before and felt very vulnerable as the safety pin was removed! Then "Ready!" was shouted, and I found myself carrying out the actions exactly as I had been instructed. "Fire" was commanded, and I duly pulled the face-blind handle out and down. I heard a loud bang and felt a slight jolt; it was all over in the time it takes to snap your fingers. I had thought it would be great to peer out to the side of the face-blind as I went up the tower but I just found myself sitting up there, the slight jolt having been the pawl and ratchet engaging. What effect all this has had on my body or brain I do not know, but at least I do have an excuse!

On arrival at St Athan, along with my friend Gerry Wells from the 67th Entry at Halton, I had joined the Gliding Club and we flew every weekend possible. The members, although few in number, were high in spirit, and many happy days were spent out on the airfield. The atmosphere was light-hearted but the flying instruction was of high

UPPER: Proctor G-AKZS at Thruxton in 1953, shortly before its departure to Australia piloted by Jack Simlar. Photo: Tim Webb.

CENTRE: The same Proctor, now registered VH-BEG, seen in Australia in 1964. Photo: John Hopton via Neil Follett.

LOWER: The Handley Page Gugnunc, G-AACN, at the 1951 "DAILY EXPRESS" Exhibition & Display at Hendon. Photo: Mike Hooks.

UPPER: Moth Minor G-AFPR, operated by the Experimental Flying Group at Redhill, shown just after Peter Amos' first solo on the 26th October 1952. LOWER: The Experimental Flying Group's "Maggie" G-AMBM parked at Geneva next to Alitalia DC-4 I-DALZ during the 1953 "Grand Tour." Photos: Peter Amos.

UPPER: Saunders Roe SR.A/1 TG271 at Cowes in August 1949, shortly before its landing accident in the Solent. Photo: Alan Hartfield.

LOWER: Tiger Moth G-ALOX, borrowed from Croydon on April 26th 1953 by Rex Nicholls to 'defend' at Redhill's dawn patrol.

Photo: Rex Nicholls via Peter Amos.

UPPER: Members of the St. Athan Gliding Club in 1954 seen with their Slingsby T.31; Alan Hartfield is at far left.
LOWER: A night view of 52 Sqn. aircraft at Changi, Singapore in 1958, including Valetta C.1 VX529, Hastings C.2s WD495 & WD498 and two Beverleys.
Photos: via Alan Hartfield.

UPPER: Two of BSAA's Avro Tudors engaged on the Berlin Airlift, 1948-9.
LOWER: BOAC Argonaut outside the International Terminal at Teheran, Iran, c.1958.
Photos: via Archie Jackson.

UPPER: A panoramic shot of the RAF Review at Odiham in July 1953. The RAF had a few more aeroplanes in those days!
Photo: via Mike Stroud.
LOWER: Some of the unconverted "Panshanger Proctors," including G-AOAV & G-AOBE. Photo: Mike Stroud.

standard. I flew in T.31 two-seat training gliders until I qualified for the British Gliding Association 'B' Certificate, then I was allowed to fly the single-seat Tutor glider. Our Chief Flying Instructor was Les Reed and his deputy was Brian Coles. They were both experienced glider pilots and told us of gliding in Germany; they were also very humorous. I often wish I could meet them again.

Whilst at RAF St Athan I applied for aircrew and attended the Aircrew Selection Centre at RAF Hornchurch. I seemed to be progressing OK through the tests but on the morning of day two I was taken out and asked to go to an interview. The Squadron Leader told me that although I had passed all of the tests so far I could not be considered for any grade of aircrew. The medical board had discovered that the hearing in my left ear was poor due to the mastoid operation I had had at the age of seven. He asked if I would be willing to be trained as a pilot in the event of hostilities and I said that I would, but I believe this was said to soften the blow. On the train journey back to South Wales, as I watched the fields passing by, I clearly recall the disappointment that I felt, and how I swore that one day I would fly powered aeroplanes as a pilot.

After a year at St Athan I was posted to No.231 OCU at RAF Bassingbourn in Cambridgeshire to work on Canberra aircraft. As a Corporal, I found that when on night-shift I was the only Airframe Trade NCO, with one Technician and five Mechanics; we were servicing more than ten Canberras and with full flying programmes were kept very busy, sometimes until the day-shift arrived! Often I, or the Electrical Trade, required the engines to be run whilst we made adjustments or proved the aircraft serviceable to fly after rectifying a fault, but there would be no qualified engine tradesman available. So I soon became qualified to run the engines. How exciting it was to be sitting in the cockpit at night, with the Canberra feeling so alive and powerful. On reflection, the responsibility alone made it all very exciting . . .

May 1957 found me at Southampton docks boarding the Troopship "Dilwara" whose destination was Singapore. Because the Suez Canal was still blocked we 'sailed' round Africa. Perhaps it would have been better if the "Dilwara" had been fitted with sails because it took six weeks to reach Singapore; I began to wonder if I would ever live on land again or see another aeroplane, and anyway, where is this place called Singapore?

On eventual arrival at this exotic island in the Far East I was posted to RAF Changi to service Valetta and Hastings aircraft, which were mainly carrying out supply drops to Army patrols on operations against the CTs (Communist Terrorists) in the Malayan jungle. It was very hot and humid and the work quite hard; weightwatchers may like to note that my eleven stone became just over nine and a half stone, but I cannot recommend this method of slimming! I was conscious that it was only just over ten years since allied prisoners of war, and some of the local population, had suffered so much here at the hands of the Japanese.

Soon after arrival, I was introduced to an elderly Chinese lady who was officially authorised to enter any barrack block to sell fresh fruit, or to mend or sew for us. She was called Mary, and she loved to laugh and joke with all the young men, especially if one of the lads happened to be walking about in the nude. She was very sweet and everyone loved her; I was later told that she and her husband had helped the allied prisoners during the Japanese occupation of Singapore by secretly passing them food, but that her husband had been caught and later hanged on the tree alongside the main road outside the post office and left there as an example. How poor Mary had suffered.

To this day, a couple of my experiences are mystifying. The apron where I worked servicing the aircraft had been built by the prisoners as a runway and I soon noticed that an area of land between the apron and the barrack blocks had no paths and was never walked upon, even though it would be the easiest route. When the wind blew during the monsoon storms I noticed that the trees on this area of land did not move, and so I made some enquiries. I was told that many allied prisoners had been cremated there, and one day some of us decided that we ought to have a look at this piece of ground. We walked slowly and carefully, partly because of the large number of snakes but also out of respect, or fear! Near the centre of this area we found some overgrown foundations and remains of concrete pillars, and they showed signs of fire. We walked carefully away, and I never did see the trees move in that area.

One night, I was repairing the flap on a Hastings aircraft and heard footsteps on the gravel behind me. This was not unusual because the locally-recruited RAF Policemen patrolled at night and often walked along the strip of gravel between our servicing apron and a very deep and wide concrete-built monsoon drain. Our apron was well lit, and as the footsteps came closer I turned to pass the time of night. As I did so the footsteps stopped and I was surprised to find that there was nobody in sight. Thinking that the heat was getting at me I carried on working. In a few moments I heard the footsteps again and, believing that my workmates were having some fun, I very quickly turned to catch them. Again, the footsteps ceased and there was no sign of anybody.

It would be quite easy for my workmates to tie a large stone with thin string, place it on the gravel and from a hiding place pull the string so that the stone made the sound of footsteps on the gravel. Being quite convinced that this was the explanation I searched everywhere, including the deep monsoon drain and around the other aeroplanes. My careful search revealed nothing at all, so I went back to my work on the flap. The footsteps started again and were getting nearer all the time; I put down my tools and with a last quick look behind me and seeing nothing, I dashed across the apron to our crewroom. A few of my workmates said I looked pale, but I convinced them that, like them, I just needed a break. I later learnt that some of the prisoners had lost their lives when working on the construction of the runway, which was now our servicing apron, and that other unexplained happenings had occurred; some said it was their ghosts – I wonder?

During the war the Japanese had allowed the prisoners to convert the downstairs room of one of the barrack blocks to a Christian Chapel. On visiting this room one day I saw the mural painted on the end wall by the prisoners; it showed Jesus preaching and in a scroll across the width of the beautiful painting were the words: "Forgive them Lord, they know not what they do." . . .

At the end of 1959 I returned to Britain and the wheel turned a full circle, for I was posted to RAF Northolt. I worked on Ansons, Devons, Pembrokes, a Dakota and Sycamore helicopters. The Sycamores were used to fly VIPs, but we had one which was 'borrowed' and was used for training; it was camouflaged and had "ARMY" painted on the side. When there was a seat available on a training flight we were allowed to fly with them.

On one occasion we flew around the west and south of London and the route was then going to take us to the river Thames, from where we could turn left to fly up the Thames to about Chiswick, then turn right back to Northolt. All went fine for the first half of the flight but as we headed for the Thames from south of London the visibility, which had been poor all the morning, suddenly decreased. The pilot and navigator were getting 'unsure of position' and descended; I could clearly read "Chislehurst" on the station platform sign. After flying on for a short while at low level the crew indicated to me that we were going to land, and as a sports field appeared out of the fog, we passed between the rugby posts and without claiming any points we landed and shut down. In moments we were surrounded by many schoolchildren and a couple of teachers, for we had landed on Eltham College sports field. While the crew went to make some telephone calls I remained to guard the helicopter from many small hands, and to answer numerous questions, except any such as: "Where have you come from?" In less than an hour the fog had thinned and we took off to continue our flight. Imagine my surprise that evening to hear on the Home Service news that "an Army helicopter had made a forced landing in Eltham College grounds." The Army must have been quite 'miffed.'

By the end of the 1950s I was suffering badly from having been 'bitten by the bug' and my urge to fly was as strong as ever. And so during the 1960s I took up gliding again under the excellent tuition of Norman Smith, and gained a Silver 'C' Certificate, plus a Gold height with a flight to 17,500 feet. I became a gliding instructor and found it quite satisfying to see student pilots progressing successfully. In the early 1970s I just had to gain a Private Pilot's Licence, and was most fortunate to go to the Peterborough Aero Club at Sibson aerodrome to be taught to fly by the late Godfrey Bell, truly one of life's gentlemen, and to have been tested by none other than Barry Tempest. I have continued to fly continuously since then, and for the past fifteen years I have flown vintage aeroplanes, such as Chipmunks, Tiger Moths, and my beloved 1937 Dart Kitten. These were amongst the very aeroplanes which obsessed me all those years ago. Friends and family tell me that I am fully absorbed with aeroplanes and flying them, but I have not noticed this! I guess that there is no known antidote to aviation addiction.

CHAPTER 11

THE WAY WE WERE

by

Rex Nicholls

I began flying training for a PPL in August 1950. I joined the Experimental Flying Group of the Ultra Light Aircraft Association, to give it its full title. This was later abbreviated to EFG Flying Services Ltd after the Group left the ULAA (later the Popular Flying Association) and was affiliated to the Association of British Aero Clubs.

Flying training was carried out at Redhill Aerodrome, where the Group had moved from Elstree a few months earlier. A small Nissen hut did duty as an office, clubroom, bunkhouse and workshop. The latter contained various small bits and pieces of aircraft and engines, mostly of little use, I suspect. The Group's fleet comprised de Havilland Moth Minor G-AFOZ, which belonged to the then Secretary, while another, G-AFPR, was owned by the CFI, Miss Jean Bird. 'PR was unairworthy and had been towed, wings folded, on its own wheels behind Jean's Morris Coupé all the way from Elstree. Likewise, the Heath Parasol G-AFZE had been towed behind another car with its wings dismantled and strapped alongside the fuselage. A fourth aeroplane, the Taylor Watkinson Dingbat G-AFJA, had somehow made the same journey, to be dumped in a dismantled state in another Nissen hut and more or less abandoned. Eventually it was sold and made airworthy for a brief period.

Only 'OZ was available for flying when I joined the Group, but it was adequate for the demand as there were very few members. Another person joined on the same day as myself and I suspect that the two of us enlarged the membership by a sizeable percentage!

Another aeroplane, on loan to the EFG from the ULAA, was the Braunschweig Universität Zaunkoenig G-ALUA; it had done some flying when I joined the Group but by the August was being overhauled prior to being passed on to another ULAA Group. The "Koenig," as it was referred to, was a German single-seat ultralight parasol monoplane with a 50 hp Zundapp in-line engine. It had been brought over from Germany after the war to study its STOL abilities, for which it had a fixed full-span leading-edge slat, fairly potent flaps and ailerons which drooped with the flaps but had only 50% of the travel. It was said to be unstallable but I saw it

113

stalled, near the ground, when being demonstrated at an air show, fortunately recovering in time. Later I was able to fly it on two occasions.

The DH.94 Moth Minor was the last British light aeroplane produced for the civil market in significant numbers before the war. It marked the end of the biplane era and was a shapely low-wing tandem-cockpit aeroplane. Some were built or modified to have an enclosure over the cockpits. Production and development were abruptly terminated at the outbreak of war; it would have been interesting to see, had this not happened, if the enclosed model would have found greater favour than the open version.

The latest DH airframe also boasted a new DH engine, the Gipsy Minor 1; rated at 90 hp, it gave the impression of a scaled-down 130 hp Gipsy Major 1, as presumably was intended. One difference was the combination of the two magnetos into one unit as distinct from the more common arrangement of separate ones. It also seemed more prone to carburettor icing and on certain days would gradually lose power until, for no apparent reason, there would be an abrupt *increase* in power, meaning that the problem had cured itself; then it would begin all over again. However, we never had a complete stoppage. There was no carburettor heater control to rectify the situation.

Another interesting feature, fitted because the Moth Minor was a very clean aeroplane with a high-aspect-ratio wing, was the airbrake. This had two rows of holes about four inches in diameter, totalling twenty in all. No less than four 'down' positions were available, selected by a large lever in the front cockpit. The airbrake was treated as a non-lifting device and could be raised rapidly and fully in one deft arm movement. However Jean insisted that we treated it as a flap and raise it in stages, against the time when we might fly flapped aircraft. The Moth Minor's narrow-track undercarriage meant that it would ground-loop readily and we learned to take great care about this, especially when taxying cross-wind. Its cable brakes, like many aircraft of its era, were prone to fade if used excessively and various tricks were learned to try to remedy the situation.

This then was the equipment on which EFG members learned to fly and I completed the whole PPL course on G-AFOZ. Both the Minors were sprayed silver overall with registration letters in black on 'OZ and green on 'PR. Jean deplored the letters being writ large across both wings and as large as possible on fuselage sides; she considered the silver streamlined Moth Minor as a thing of beauty, not deserving to have official graffiti daubed all over it! Whether we shared her views or not, we all had great fun learning under Jean's tuition, there was much laughing and joking when we'd finished flying for the day, and, if anyone did, we certainly "danced the skies on laughter-silvered wings."

Redhill's flying operations were fairly typical of most small aerodromes in the early fifties, flying left-hand circuits. This led to pilots being good at left-hand turns and somewhat shaky when turning right whilst away from the circuit. Circuit height was 1,000 ft above aerodrome level, which at Redhill meant that we flew with 1,250 ft showing on the altimeter. I doubt if in those days we knew anything about QFE, or QNH for that matter. These were just two of scores of complications to be introduced into light aircraft flying down the years. In any case, nearly all club aeroplanes operated extraordinarily well without radio so there was no way we could learn what the QFE value was whilst flying.

The circuit at Redhill was frequently busy, as it was home to No.15 Reserve Flying School of the RAFVR. It operated about two dozen Tiger Moths and a few Oxfords and Ansons. The aircraft mostly flew details away from the aerodrome and thus tended to return all at once for morning coffee break, lunchtime, afternoon tea break and at the end of flying for the day. Together with the club aircraft, private owners and any visitors, the circuit could thus be very crowded for a time, which meant learning about keeping a good look-out. Apart from the Ansons and Oxfords, all this was non-radio traffic. Although the controller in the tower had a radio he could not talk to most aircraft operating in or out of Redhill and I don't recall him making much use of his signal lamp or Very cartridges either. In other words, pilots retained the full initiative – no bad thing.

While the VR did its training with Tiger Moths, all circuits flown at Redhill called for glide approaches. Once on base leg, the point would be judged where the throttle could be fully closed and not opened again till after landing. If this was misjudged, the throttle was opened to cruise power, the aeroplane flown level and the throttle fully closed again to complete the glide approach. If one's misjudgement meant that the approach was too high, an overshoot was flown. At no time were 'touch and goes' contemplated or flown unless the landing was severely botched. Each landing in a session of circuits meant a return to a point near the downwind boundary, take-off checks performed and, if the approach was clear, another take-off flown. When Chipmunks replaced the Tiger Moths, the VR elected to fly long draggy approaches, which could at times interfere with our glide approaches. In fact, this was when the enormous circuits frequently flown these days originated. So today, often a small aeroplane, needing little more than 200 metres in which to land and stop, is set up for a two-mile final to achieve this. Long, slow, powered approaches were looked upon as an advanced exercise in EFG.

Part of the Redhill scenery included two Supermarine Walrus and two Sea Otter amphibians. These were abandoned on the aerodrome's northern perimeter still in their rapidly-fading camouflage and marks. They had been allotted civil registration marks but never wore them. Their intended use was mind-boggling; it seemed their owner had a bizarre idea to get round the UK's gambling laws. A ship was to be moored somewhere outside the offshore three-mile limit, its sole purpose to be a gambling den. The punters were then to be flown out in the amphibians from some airport or other and later returned. Probably it was just as well that the scheme fell through, the four aircraft eventually going to a scrap dealer.

One Sunday two dignitaries of the ULAA paid a visit to EFG. Thus Group Captain Edward Mole and Edward Davis (usually called "Teddy") flew into Redhill from Croydon in Teddy's new Proctor 5, G-AHGL. Having chatted to Jean and sundry members, flights were offered in the Proctor; I flew with Teddy on a wide circuit of the aerodrome. Teddy came across as a cautious pilot and it later transpired that he liked to have another pilot with him on most of his flights. One such recounted a trip he did with Teddy in 'GL to Le Touquet. When preparations were made for the return to Croydon, they dutifully visited the French Met-man to check on the weather. In those days Met-men prepared a chart which they covered with information received from a great many aerodromes, details such as wind strength and direction, visibility, barometric pressure and cloud amounts. Peering at his chart the Met-man informed Teddy of the en route weather. Now Teddy and his brother owned and managed the Davis Theatre in Croydon, alleged to be the largest in the land. The Met-man completed his weather synopsis with the weather reported at Croydon and, using the abbreviation for cumulus cloud, said he could see "cus" building up over Croydon.

"Can you see any queues building up outside the Davis Theatre?" asked Teddy, guffawing loudly and leaving the Met-man totally confused!

One of the drawbacks in operating the Moth Minors was the lack of spares. Usually only one was serviceable at a time, the other grounded and acting as a source of spares. Something had to be done, so 'OZ was sold and replaced by the Hawk Trainer 'MBM. In due course 'PR also went, to be replaced by Hawk Trainer 'LIO. The "Maggies" formed the Group's equipment over a period of about eight years. During that time both 'BM & 'IO became casualties in minor accidents which nevertheless were uneconomic to repair, and 'ITN & 'KAS took their place.

The arrival of 'BM was the signal for me to commence an Assistant Flying Instructor's course, and Jean and I did some comprehensive flying. I had always wanted to fly a "Maggie" and found the aeroplane to my liking. It was more robust than the Moth Minor, and had a greater speed and rate of climb. Half as powerful again, it could aerobat well and could be flown comfortably in winds gusting up to 30 knots. In such conditions one had to forget about taking a Tiger Moth out of its hangar, let alone fly it, and Jean spurned the biplane when the question about replacing the Moth Minor arose.

The AFI course lasted quite a long time as there seemed to be no laid-down curriculum but I enjoyed every minute of it. The "patter" had to be projected to the other cockpit by shouting down the Gosport tubes fitted for the purpose. These had been invented during the First World War and nothing better had been devised for aeroplanes which lacked any form of electrical equipment. The trouble with instructing using Gosports was the need to hold the throttle with one hand and the stick with the other whilst using a third hand to hold the Gosport's rubber mouthpiece tight up against the lips so that little if any of what was shouted should escape away into the slipstream. In time one became quite adept at using just the two hands for this three-handed activity. Later, the transistor became available and one of our members designed intercom units powered by dry batteries which did a magnificent job.

Transistorised intercom units called for the use of ex-RAF flying helmets together with oxygen masks. We weren't expecting actually to use oxygen but the mask had a convenient microphone incorporated, along with an 'on/off' switch. So our aviation lifestyle involved learning about which Goverment surplus shops sold those items including, most important of all, earpieces of the correct impedance. I recall several visits to a shop in the Tottenham Court Road, for example, and all members were asked to keep their eyes open for other sources of supply. Enough stock needed to be bought in so that new members could be kitted out as soon as possible. Loaning one's helmet and mask to a new member was often done but it wasn't much fun if he or she decided to be airsick! When we eventually said goodbye to our faithful "Maggies" we were not sorry to dispense with our flying suits, helmets etc., especially as supplies of these items had virtually dried up. Our replacements, Auster Vs, had side-by-side seating, were reasonably silenced and had heaters.

The RAFVR recruited its pilots from those already possessed of 110 hours flying experience. When new material such as ourselves could not join because we had nothing like as many hours, and the availability of those wartime pilots who *did* have were drying up, the VR lowered its requirement to the 40 hours of the bare PPL. This signalled the start of something like an indecent rush by some members of the two gliding clubs based at Redhill at the time to get a PPL; those were the gliding pundits possessed of Bronze or Silver 'C' qualifications, the 40 hour period for PPL qualification being considerably reduced in their case. Up until then they were prone to tell us of the "purist" activity they indulged in – none of your nasty noisy smelly engines with their *infra dig* propellers. It was interesting to see the effect of the £30 per annum bounty given to its pilots by the RAFVR, plus all the free flying, of course!

For myself I volunteered for the VR and was given a trial flight by the Deputy CFI of No.15 RFS in Tiger Moth T5717. Being obliged to sit on a parachute has led me to regard this half-hour flight as the most uncomfortable I ever made. I passed the flight test but as the VR was by now inundated with its new influx of pilots I was offered any of the other trades; these I declined and so did not fly with the VR, but in any case my instructor's course was keeping me busy. I missed about three years of VR flying before the flying side of the Reserve was completely closed down in March 1954.

I did other types of flying as well as pursuing the AFI course, including the Proctor III G-ALJH; Jean checked me out on this, including a practice forced landing from 2,000 ft over Redhill. It was not unknown to hear those who considered themselves wise in the matter of Proctor-flying stating that one should never ever glide a Proctor: "Falls out of the sky, old boy!" for instance. I was pleased to find, therefore, that although nearly double the weight of the "Maggie" and 50% more powerful, it could be flown like any other aeroplane. The point about Proctors was that they were just about the only sensible four-seat equipment available with reasonable speed, endurance and price. The only drawback I ever found with them was their noisy interiors, bearing in mind that we had no radios and therefore did not wear headphones which to some extent would have acted as ear defenders.

During the AFI course I learned not only a lot more about spinning and recovery but also how to talk about it. Here again there were the pundits who knew it all. "Those 'Maggies' won't come out of a spin, you know." Some of this stemmed from an interesting idiosyncrasy of the aeroplane – its rudder could blanket the elevators when deflected. In recovery from a spin it was important to centralise the rudder when pulling out of the ensuing dive; otherwise the recovery was slow but could result in a sharp pitch-up if the pilot suddenly realised what the problem was and put the rudder straight! When Miles designed a replacement of the "Maggie," the M.18, the fin and rudder were set well forward of the tailplane to eliminate this problem. Since then quite a few aircraft have been designed with a similar arrangement. On the course I practised aerobatics for the first time and I thoroughly enjoyed it.

Jean arranged for me to fly with some of the VR instructors to see how I was getting on. Soon after that I took the flying test with the CFI of No.15 RFS, Sqn. Ldr. Lash. He didn't pass me first time although the only criticism I heard from him was that I had frightened him when I suddenly shut the throttle soon after take-off and "pattered" the 'engine failure after take off' exercise. This had become almost second nature to me during the course and I hadn't expected that I could alarm a seasoned pilot. The next test with him occupied a mere 20 minutes and he passed me.

I began using my instructor's rating at Croydon rather than with EFG at Redhill. There was little instructing to do with EFG and Ken Sirett, who had gained his rating before me, could cope with the demand, operating under Jean's supervision. However, I did make just one instructional flight at Redhill, and that was with Peter Amos, a member of EFG, in

G-ALIO on the 10th January 1954. The next day (or rather night) I began a night-flying course at Croydon, flying with Brian Stead in the Vendair Flying Club Auster Vs G-ANEP & 'NLU. The next month saw me flying the Airways Aero Association's Auster Aiglet Trainer G-AMTA, one of five purchased by AAA in 1952. I was to be flying it frequently some 43 years later!

I also met up with two middle-aged fellows who had purchased the Spartan Arrow G-ABWP and then proposed learning to fly on it. I did a certain amount of training with them in it but they soon ran out of funds and sold it on; it still flies today. The Arrow was one of those pre-war aeroplanes that fell under the title of "gentlemen's aerial carriages." Although it was about the same size as a Tiger Moth it stood on a taller undercarriage and had unstaggered wings, which to me gave it something of a haughty look. Its stalling characteristics were of the text-book variety: the nose would sweep gracefully down once the stick was right back, the wings remaining perfectly level. In contrast, quite a few specimens of ex-RAF equipment could produce a violent roll at the stall. The Arrow's stick protruded through the floor of the rear cockpit so that the aileron cables passed into the rear of each lower wing, which was below the line of the bottom longeron. The resulting hole in the cockpit floor produced a considerable updraught of air at the stall and this would whistle up one's trouser legs. It occurred to me that this very efficient warning of potentially dangerous flying could be patented as the "Gooly Stall Warner"!

Soon after this the EFG moved from Redhill to Croydon, following the closure of the former. Many members of EFG decided against flying at Croydon and membership figures dropped as a result. Apparently, the problem for those who gave up flying was the thought of more air traffic control at an airport with a certain amount of commercial flying which was situated in, and influenced by, the procedures required by the London Control Zone. This was a much larger affair than it is today, brought about by the piston-engined airliner types using Heathrow; these had a limited rate of climb and were afforded the protection of a zone large enough to get to an altitude well away from other traffic such as our activities. The zone's eastern boundary followed the Greenwich Meridian with its southern end positioned at Godstone in Surrey.

The terms IMC & VMC had yet to be introduced and we merely spoke of IFR & VFR. IFR came into force when there were less than three nautical miles visibility, and here the notorious London smog played a big part. The duty controller would declare Croydon's corner of the zone "QBI," the code for Fog Regulations being in force, and would switch on two amber lights on the control tower, complemented by a red light in the briefing office. QBI was being phased out, replaced by IFR. Flights by club aircraft and those of private owners where no radio was available then followed one of two 'Free Lanes' out of or into the zone. One Free Lane went in a straight line to the north-east, exiting the zone near Bromley, Kent. This one lacked good landmarks and was the less popular. However, when using it we flew past the BBC TV transmitter sited at Crystal Palace. The other Free Lane followed a slightly curved track, aligned as it was on the A22 road from Purley to Godstone. On each side of the road were railway tracks, the right-hand one terminating at Caterham, where one then followed the bypass which was dual-carriageway as far as Godstone; it was thus much easier to follow. Flights in the lanes were limited to 1,250 ft amsl (above mean sea level) and this set up a problem. Keeping the Caterham railway on the left as required by one of the rules of the air put one neatly into Kenley's circuit, flown at around 1,250 ft. There one could come face to face with one of Kenley's Ansons, Provosts or Chipmunks on their downwind leg in the circuit! The problem was eventually solved when powered flying ceased at Kenley.

Sometimes we would fly down the south-east Free Lane, only to observe landmarks such as Chanctonbury Ring on the South Downs near Worthing (largely destroyed in the 1987 gales) some thirty or more miles away. On landing we would remonstrate with the controller who would say that *he* hadn't made it IFR, the Met-man had. So we would beard the Met-man in his den and he would point out of the window to the north and the belt of London smog lurking less than three miles away. He had to take the worst case, so on went the amber lights and we had to play the 'Free Lanes' game. Sometimes of course the prevailing light winds would vary their direction slightly, enough to bring the whole sorry mess across the airport and give us real problems. Bear in mind that in those days a London smog could reduce visibility to no more than five yards in extreme cases.

Once having flown down a Free Lane on a local flight it was necessary to arrange the return trip. This was achieved beforehand by calculating the time it might take to taxy out and get a green light from the control tower authorising one's flight to, say, Godstone; the flight time to that exit point; the time for the detail, perhaps half an hour for some stalls, followed by forced-landing practices using Redhill for this (but not touching down). One then booked out giving ATC the time we wished to re-enter the zone for a landing at Croydon. We became quite adept at this sort of thing and, in order not to lengthen a training detail too much to the detriment of the pupil's bank balance, I often flew out via the north-east Free Lane and returned via the south-east, or vice versa. Care had to be taken when routeing via both lanes not to infringe Biggin Hill's airspace. Mind you, Biggin's aircraft were not averse to infringing *Croydon's* airspace; on one occasion, I was on finals for runway 24 at Croydon about half a mile from touchdown when a Meteor passed between me and the threshold at 90° to my heading and at about 200 ft, going quite fast, of course. Croydon ATC seemed disinclined to do anything about it but I thought a call could have been made on the phone to Biggin asking their pilots not to be so silly.

Circuits at Croydon were normally flown at 1,000 ft aal (above aerodrome level) in a left-hand pattern. The runway in use would be displayed on the control tower for the information of those taxying out for take-off. Those approaching Croydon could overfly above circuit height and view the landing tee which was electrically controlled from the tower and was situated, together with a windsock, close to 'D' Hangar. Small wooden tees were placed beside the touchdown point of the duty runway, having been positioned by the fire crew. ATC used an Aldis lamp to signal clearance to take off or land (green) or not to do so (red). A white signal was used to recall an aircraft. Croydon was not immune from complaints from those who had chosen to live near the airport and then complain about the noise of aeroplanes. In an effort to relieve this "suffering" it was decided to introduce periods of right-hand circuit flying as opposed to the standard left-hand circuits. This introduced the red and yellow diagonal striped arrow around one corner of the signal square, which meant that pilots had to observe it when joining the circuit. Many didn't, and as most operated without radio an entertaining mix of left- and right-hand circuits could be observed. The idea was to change the direction perhaps two or three times a day, but the ensuing chaos soon put paid to the scheme.

By October 1954 I had accumulated enough hours to apply for upgrading to Full Instructor's Rating and I flew the test with Len Wenman, Chairman of the Panel of Examiners and CFI of the Airways Aero Association. This was successful and I received my Full Rating on the 7th of November. I could now send my pupils on their first solo flights and this first occurred on the 30th April 1955 in the EFG "Maggie" G-AITN which had replaced G-AMBM (written off in a crash in France). The pupil had had the chance to fly solo before that date but when I vacated the "Maggie" and told him to fly one circuit on his own he flatly refused to go! After a few more hours dual I tried again and, having learned a useful lesson, just told him to do a circuit on his own and walked off before he had a chance to argue; his flight was completely successful.

One of the aeroplanes I flew quite a lot in those days was the Proctor 4 G-ANYC. Operated by the Vendair Flying Club it was the first aeroplane I came upon that had a radio. This was one of the four-channel variety where the frequencies could be changed by means of 'crystals.' A box of these could be carried if a wide variety of frequencies was required, with the idea of changing in flight any one of the three frequencies already installed in the radio (the fourth was normally 121.5 for emergency use and was therefore left *in situ*. However, I never found the need actually to change any in flight and left the radio operating on Croydon's 122.7. 'NYC had a vicious wing-tip stall and when I checked some pilots out on it they could be thoroughly put off by this. One day someone took it to Amsterdam and got lost in rapidly-approaching dusk on the return trip, finishing up in a field close by Gatwick, which was by then closed for its modernisation. The forced landing removed 'YC's undercarriage, which in turn damaged the centre section beyond repair. However, it was decided that the rest of the aeroplane could be restored and I recall a brand-new centre section turning up at Croydon on a lorry. This was duly installed, the rest of the Proctor repaired where necessary, and it flew again. Thereafter it stalled in a perfectly docile manner with never a hint of roll; the crash had done it a power of good!

Another activity which began for me in the Croydon days was the test flight for renewal of a Certificate of Airworthiness, the first subject being the Auster V G-ANIF. Additionally, more pre-war types became available including Miles Hawk Major G-ADWT, Leopard Moth G-ACMA (re-equipped with a 145 hp Gipsy Major 1C in place of the 130 hp Major 1), DH.60 Moth G-ABJJ, Puss Moth G-AHLO, Hornet Moth G-ADUR and Monarch G-AFJU. The Vega Gull G-AHET turned up at Croydon in June 1957 with its new owner Mike Hawthorn, the racing driver; he wanted an instructor to check him out on it so, being available, I flew a session of circuits with him, noting the livelier lighter airframe of the Gull compared with its development, the Proctor. A few foreign designs also became available including Aeronca Champion G-AOEH, Klemm L.25 G-AAXK, Jodel D.117 G-APOZ, Tipsy Nipper OO-NIF and, at the second PFA Rally at Sywell in September 1957, the Béarn Minicab F-PHUC. John Blake said that he couldn't help drawing the attention of the Minicab's owner to the unfortunate choice of registration letters and their pronunciation and meaning in English; this was by way of a joke but the Frenchman took it to heart and attended the third Rally in the same aeroplane which by then wore a different registration!

One Club which formed at Croydon in 1958 was the 600 Squadron RAuxAF Flying Group. This was an attempt by the former squadron's members to keep flying after the government closed down RAuxAF flying activities. An odd assortment of aeroplanes appeared at first, noteworthy among these being the DH Dragon Rapide G-ACPP. Some of the Club's members were ex-Meteor pilots and therefore were experienced in multi-engined equipment; they asked me to check them out in the Rapide and thus enable them to have a Group 'B' Rating on their PPLs.

I said I hadn't flown a Rapide.

"Then you'd better go and fly it," was the reply.

So I got into the solo cockpit and flew a few circuits in what impressed me as a thoroughly enjoyable aeroplane. I then loaded the Meteor pilots, one at a time, sitting behind them while they demonstrated their skills at asymmetric approaches and so on, being aware that there was little I could do if anything went wrong. Later I was able to fly another pre-war Rapide, G-AFFB, and the ex-RAF Dominie G-AKJZ, the latter to Nancy and back to retrieve equipment salvaged from a Luxembourg Airlines Curtis C-46 which had come to grief. That flight, terminating at Croydon, was the last time I landed at the airport.

January 1959 saw the commencement of civil flying at Biggin Hill, with all the Club aircraft and some private owners based there by mid-February. The almost totally free atmosphere at the former RAF base was such that few EFG members actually missed flying at Croydon. Comfortably clear to the east of the London CTR boundaries we could come and go as we liked. ATC consisted of a smallish box, glazed in its upper part, painted in orange and white chequers and mounted on an old bomb trolley. We landed on either of the two short runways (05/23 & 11/29) or on the grass between them. If the wind was across either of these we landed into wind on the grass, a NW or SE wind particularly calling for this. Later, grass strips were marked out alongside each of the tarmac runways and the rest of the grass area banned for everything except taxying.

Later, an unofficial scheme prevailed whereby radio-equipped aircraft landed on the tarmac, non-radio on the grass. Landings and take-offs thus took place side by side at times. Sometimes non-radio aircraft would land on either and I often wondered if the situation ever arose where two first-solo pupils landed beside one another, neither knowing about the 'expertise' of the other. The point is that today there would be tremendous wailing and gnashing of teeth if such an event occurred or was even planned!

A popular evening pastime for onlookers, particularly on a Sunday, was to watch gaggles of aircraft approaching to land on 29 grass and tarmac, looking like a swarm of bees that couldn't possibly all get down. Surprisingly they did with very few overshoots. I can recall a lady controller saying over the radio: "It's fifteen minutes to closing time and there's twenty-seven of you up there!" Most of them wouldn't have heard her but they all landed comfortably within time.

In June 1959 I flew to Rhoose Aerodrome, Cardiff, to attend the Welsh International Flying Rally. The aeroplane I used was our "Maggie" G-AKAS and it was a symbol of the march of time that it was awarded the prize for the oldest aircraft attending. In fact, she had little more than a year of life left in her due to a shortage of spares.

And so we moved out of the 1950s, comfortably settled in at Biggin Hill and re-equipping EFG first with Austers and then our first radio-equipped aeroplane, Tripacer G-ARDP. Three more decades have come and gone and a fourth will soon terminate, but the flying still goes on.

CHAPTER 12

FLYING TUDORS & ARGONAUTS

by

Archie Jackson

The outbreak of war in 1939 thwarted any hopes that Imperial Airways might have entertained of obtaining a British-manufactured aeroplane to replace its ageing Handley Page HP.42s. The armed struggle was still continuing when, in 1944, the Air Ministry presented A.V. Roe & Co Ltd with a specification for an airliner able to carry 60 passengers at 235 mph and 25,000 ft across the Atlantic. Avro had built the highly regarded Lancaster bomber, and Roy Chadwick, its designer, was given the task of producing a successful airliner. In November 1944 the Ministry of Supply ordered 12 Tudor 1s, and the prototype made its first flight in June 1945 (see "AEROPLANE MONTHLY," December 1993, 'Post-War Propliners'). Yet BOAC, as the airline had by then become via its merger with British Airways, was never consulted about its own requirements with regard to range and payload, and Avro was instructed by the Ministry not to deal directly with its intended customer when it was realised that the Tudor would be able to carry only 12 passengers across the Atlantic. Avro agreed to extend the fuselage by 6 ft and to provide accommodation for 28 passengers. Meanwhile Lockheed was receiving orders for the proven Constellation L-049 and Douglas was not far behind with its DC-6.

In March 1946 the stretched Tudor made its maiden flight, but the tropical trials conducted in Nairobi later that year convinced BOAC that the aircraft was totally unsuitable for the airline's African and Indian routes, let alone the North Atlantic. Both Qantas and South African Airways also lost interest and bought American airliners. Avro's problems were further compounded when Roy Chadwick and company test pilot Bill Thorn were killed testing a Tudor.

Meanwhile, British South American Airways (BSAA) was operating 'stop-gap' military derivatives – Avro Lancastrians and Yorks. Its chief executive was Air Vice-Marshal Don Bennett, who had led Bomber Command's Path Finder Force. He was determined to operate British-built aircraft, and subject to the outcome of tropical trials conducted by himself, and a greatly reduced price, he was prepared to consider the Tudor 4, powered by Rolls Royce Merlin 623 engines. A deal was done, and in August 1947 Bennett set off for Jamaica, with a refuelling stop at Gander. Over the Atlantic a fuel feed problem developed, presenting the possibility that the aircraft might have to be ditched. An emergency was declared and rescue services alerted, but fortunately the engines kept running and Gander was reached. On landing it was discovered that a fuel service cock, inaccessible in flight, had been left in the 'shut' position. The tropical trials were completed to Bennett's satisfaction, and he declared the Tudor to be a better aircraft than the Constellation. A number of the rejected Tudor 1s were required for crew training pending deliveries of the Tudor 4. Although this was their first experience of a pressurised airliner, BSAA's pilots were not greatly impressed by its handling or performance.

The manufacturer had not fitted a tricycle undercarriage. The massive tail made it difficult for the pilot to keep the aircraft on the runway in gusty crosswind conditions, particularly if the runway surface was covered with a layer of ice or compacted snow. The cabin heater often failed in flight, requiring a swift descent to avoid freezing everyone on board. This procedure often brought the aircraft into cloud, whereupon ice formed on the wings. When stars were visible in the night sky, the lack of an astrodome was unhelpful to navigation. Notwithstanding these inconveniences, a Tudor carried commercial passengers for the first time in September 1947. Its destination was Chile, and the following month witnessed the inaugural service of the aircraft to the Caribbean.

On January 27th 1948 Tudor Mk.4 G-AHNP "Star Tiger" left Heathrow for Bermuda via Lisbon and the Azores. Problems were encountered early on when the heater failed at 21,000 ft. Compass trouble and an engine snag were remedied at Lisbon, but the heater failed again en route to the Azores. "Star Tiger" reported nothing untoward on the long flight to Bermuda, its crew having chosen to cruise at 2,000 ft to avoid strong headwinds at higher altitudes. The last radio message from the aircraft was received when it was within 200 miles of the island. Thereafter repeated calls from Bermuda were not answered. Searching aircraft found no trace of wreckage, and the cause of the sudden disaster could not be determined.

In England the response of the Air Registration Board (ARB) was to advise the Minister of Civil Aviation, Lord Nathan, to ground the Tudor, pending an investigation. Bennett protested that there "was not a shred of evidence to suggest that the aircraft was unsafe to fly." A boardroom row erupted and he left the company, but very shortly afterwards events brought Bennett and the Tudor together again. The Russians imposed a land blockade on Berlin, and the Western Allies responded with an airlift using every transport aeroplane they could muster, including civilian machines. Bennett bought two Tudors from Avro and founded his own company, Airflight. The ARB certificated these aircraft to fly as freighters, unpressurised, and in any case the air corridors into Berlin were flown at low level. The first load, which Bennett himself flew, was ten tons of potatoes. Initially, Airflight's one other pilot was licensed only for daylight flying, so Bennett flew three round trips to Berlin every night. In October 1948 his two Tudors were converted to carry almost ten tons of diesel oil.

The investigation into the airworthiness of the Tudor had found no dangerous characteristics, and BSAA had resumed passenger services. Two Tudors were employed on the airlift, converted into tankers. But in January 1949, in circumstances as mysterious as before, G-AGRE *"Star Ariel"* disappeared without trace. No warning of trouble had been transmitted since the aircraft had departed Bermuda, and it was cruising towards Nassau in daylight and in perfect weather. Once again BSAA was obliged to withdraw its fleet from passenger service.

These two disasters effectively ended the existence of the company, but Bennett refused to accept that the Tudor possessed any serious defect, attributing the losses to sabotage. His own company had made 977 return flights to Berlin and earned substantial profits. When the Soviets lifted the blockade of Berlin in August 1949, Bennett's Tudors were converted to carry passengers and various modifications recommended by the ARB were carried out. The aircraft were then certificated to carry up to 78 passengers, and Bennett continued operations under the new company name, Fairflight. The first charter, to carry apprentices to England, was obtained from the Government of Pakistan. Other contracts followed; to Johannesburg, to Japan, and 25 round trips between Aden and Israel.

Then Bennett's company suffered a tragic accident, although the probable cause was less mysterious than those of the earlier disappearances. Tudor 5 G-AKBY, bringing rugby football supporters back from Dublin to a small airfield in Wales, crashed on final approach and 75 passengers and five crew members were killed. It was known that the pilot had expressed unease about the shortness of the runway, and witnesses described what appeared to be a stall as the aircraft was about to land.

Bennett continued to obtain contracts for the remaining Tudor. Flights to supply stores to the British troops in Korea were followed by freight services between Hamburg and Berlin.

In November 1951 he sold Fairflight to another entrepreneur who clearly shared his confidence in the Tudor. Freddie Laker had founded Air Charter Ltd in 1947, and conducted *ad hoc* operations from Croydon. By taking over Fairflight he inherited the contract to carry freight from Berlin. Recognising the great capacity of the Tudor, he bought all that remained on the market – four Tudor 1s, two Mk.3s and four Mk.4s. A very thorough conversion programme was carried out, including the installation of a huge freight door.

Renamed the Supertrader, the aircraft was granted a full C. of A. in February 1954, and the maximum all-up weight was increased to 83,600 lb. In a test identical to that undertaken by the ARB in 1946, the aircraft was found to perform far better. Laker's Supertraders were engaged in trooping to the Middle and Far East, and a Colonial Coach service to Libya and Nigeria was also operated. In addition, freight services were flown to the Woomera rocket range in Australia for the British government. In every configuration the Supertraders performed extremely well, and were not withdrawn from service until 1959.

If BOAC had been involved in the Tudor's development from the outset, and if the two disasters over the western Atlantic had not taken place, could the Tudor have become a more successful airliner? One handicap was the failure to provide the aircraft with a tricycle undercarriage. In the wartime years, when he designed the airliner, Chadwick had given it the wings and undercarriage of the Lincoln, the Lancaster's successor. Four-engined airliners with tailwheels no longer featured in the products of the major American manufacturers.

At home, Vickers was the first to produce a turbine-powered airliner, the Viscount, and de Havilland led the world with the first pure-jet airliner, the Comet. A new era had been ushered in by the rapid advance of technology as a consequence of wartime priorities.

But to return to 1949: when a second Avro Tudor disappeared without trace over the South Atlantic in that year, those of us flying for British South American Airways realised that our company's days were numbered. Before long the airline was taken over by BOAC. Most of the pilots were re-trained to fly Argonauts, 22 of which had been ordered by BOAC to replace the flying boats and bomber conversions. These aircraft were built in Canada, using the airframe of the Douglas DC-4, but they were pressurised and powered by Rolls Royce Merlin engines instead of Pratt & Whitney R-2000s.

At a time when the government possessed insufficient dollars to spend freely on imports, the choice of the Argonauts owed much to their use of British engines and the willingness of the manufacturer, Canadair, to allow BOAC to pay for them in installments as revenue was earned. The order had been placed in 1948 when Sir Harold Hartley was chairman and Whitney Straight his deputy.

The only other carrier to operate Argonauts at that time was Trans Canada Airlines, which called them North Stars. This was the first airliner with a tricycle undercarriage that most of us had flown and we found its handling qualities to be a great improvement on the Tudor. The operating crew comprised two pilots, a navigator and a wireless operator. A steward and a stewardess looked after 40 passengers in the original one-class configuration. BOAC were satisfied with the aircraft for its general reliability and economics, but passengers complained to us about the noise from the Merlin engines. We were disappointed that the Argonaut was slower than both the Douglas DC-6 and the Lockheed Constellation. One or other of these types was being operated by our competitors, and it was galling to watch them fly past us on every sector of our routes!

Radio communication, other than VHF contact with local airports, was still conducted in Morse code whilst the navigator depended on his sextant to fix the aircraft's position over the oceans and deserts. He had to take on board an air almanac, many volumes of aeronautical tables and an astro-compass. The aircraft was fitted with a drift sight, and other items stowed in the cockpit included an Aldis lamp, a Very pistol with cartridges and numerous national flags.

The Argonaut was flown to many destinations, westward over the South Atlantic to Brazil and Argentina, thence across the Andes mountains to Santiago, Chile. Eastward an Argonaut had inaugurated the first all-landplane service to Hong Kong, reducing the travel time from five to three days. Soon afterwards Argonauts took over the route to Tokyo and Singapore.

Today most mainline airports have an instrument landing system. In the fifties we were lucky to find a non-directional beacon somewhere near the airport, and it did not follow that it was sited in line with a runway. BOAC had equipped certain aerodromes with a relic from WW II, Eureka Rebecca. The navigator could interrogate this and obtain on his screen an indication of the aircraft's distance from the airport, up to a maximum of 90 miles. It was rare to find high intensity approach lighting to a runway and a few airports did not even *have* a runway. In Kuwait we landed on an area of hard sand marked by black oil slicks. A tent was provided for passengers waiting to embark. Horsemen with bandoliers of cartridges across their chest, clutching ancient rifles, provided an escort for Arab traders awaiting a consignment of gold or silver.

One piece of equipment that the Argonaut never came to have was storm-warning radar. Such equipment was still in the the development stage when the aircraft were ordered, but within a few years manufacturers were able to deliver airliners with this facility. Argonaut pilots had to fly through the monsoons of India and Africa and fearsome storms over the plains of Argentina. At night when the horizon was brilliantly illuminated by flashes of lightning we had a momentary glimpse of huge banks of storm clouds but no means of knowing which course to steer to avoid the worst turbulence. Once in a storm one tried to maintain a level altitude by reference to the artificial horizon and to ignore the wild and often contradictory fluctuations of the airspeed indicator. The noise of the rain and hail on the windscreen was accompanied by the screech of static over the earphones. The propeller tips were illuminated like Catherine wheels and little blue flames of St. Elmo's fire played about the windscreen.

In 1952 BOAC introduced tourist class and seating on the Argonaut was increased to 56 passengers. This may have been a boon to holiday-makers able to afford the reduced fare, but it infuriated the great number of expatriates in Africa and elsewhere who were entitled to home leave. Many employers booked their staff at tourist rates. The following year, when the Handley Page Hermes was being progressively withdrawn from African routes, our passengers were swift to note that they had even less space because the fuselage of the Argonaut was not as wide as that of the Hermes.

In 1954 the crash of the Comet at Elba, followed by another crash in the Mediterranean some months later, resulted in the grounding of the aircraft. Even the despised Hermes had been brought back into service. Whilst BOAC searched for second-hand Constellations to carry an increasing number of passengers, the South American route, the least profitable revenue-earner, was abandoned and not resumed until 1960. Those of us flying Argonauts could look forward to several more years before we could expect to transfer to a more modern aircraft.

Comet crews had been at the top of the pecking order as far as prestige was concerned amongst the crews. Now this mantle was resumed by those flying the Boeing Stratocruiser over the North Atlantic. Many of them liked to boast that they had never had to fly to the east of the Greenwich meridian. Dubbed the 'Atlantic Barons' they were envied for the extra pay that they received for having to combat the rigours of the winter weather, both en route and at the Canadian aerodromes. The improved and faster Lockheed Constellation 749As not only flew across the Atlantic and to Caribbean destinations, but also to Australia and South Africa. Their crews too ranked themselves as superior to those of us flying our slower noisy beasts.

In 1955 an Argonaut was involved in a serious accident for the first time. *"Altair"* arrived over the airfield near Tripoli, Libya, after the scheduled seven hour flight from Nigeria. The former Italian airforce base, Castel Benito, was little changed from its wartime condition, and the hangars still had the scars of bombing. There was no instrument landing system nor approach lighting to the runway, and at certain times of the year fog sometimes formed during the night and did not clear until after sunrise. The alternative airport, Malta, was close enough to suffer fog at the same time, and it was in such conditions that *"Altair"* crashed as the captain attempted to land.

The following year *"Argo"* crashed on take-off from Kano in northern Nigeria. It was the rainy season and the captain would have expected to encounter storms and turbulence in the course of his flight. We had asked for storm warning radar to be fitted to the Argonauts in view of their extended life on our routes, but were told that the expense was not justified owing to the limited period that Argonauts would remain in service.

The captain could not have expected any immediate problem as he began his take-off run. No cloud formation was visible directly before him, but as *"Argo"* climbed through the first 100 feet it passed though a thunderstorm cell developing invisibly in its path. It encountered a sudden dramatic reversal of wind direction and losing all lift mushed back at full power into the ground. There were very few survivors among the passengers and crew. Like the Argonaut, the airport was not equipped with weather radar. In due course the enquiry cleared both the captain and airport controllers of any responsibility for the accident.

I had completed 5,500 hours on Argonauts when I landed one at London Airport for the last time in May 1958. Shortly thereafter I began the course on the long-delayed Britannia 312. Others were not so lucky, because the last Argonaut was not withdrawn from service until April 1960 after 11 years service. By then they had flown 107 million miles and carried 870,000 passengers.

On a lighter note the Argonaut crews enjoyed one final moment of amused gratification. When BOAC put all ten of their new Douglas DC-7s on the North Atlantic service, the Stratocruisers were deployed on other routes. Where else but to Nigeria and Ghana? The dismay and distaste on the faces of their crews at their first encounter with the conditions of life in West Africa was pitiful to observe!

CHAPTER 13

THE RAF REVIEW AT ODIHAM

(AND OTHER EXCURSIONS)

by Mike Stroud

[NOTES ON THE AUTHOR: After being educated in London during the war, Mike Stroud initially worked in the Sales Department of Miles Aircraft, and then went on to Bristols and the Hawker Siddeley Group. He has also dedicated a great deal of time and effort over the years to writing articles for a number of magazines such as "AIRCRAFT ILLUS-TRATED." Since 1995 he has taken on the task of integrating the photograph library at Aerospace Publishing. As a freelance writer and photographer he has also contributed to several Airline & Helicopter Directories, and in 1990 co-authored with Lindsey Hart the publication "Hurricane – Clouded by Legend." He is an active member of a number of organisations including Air-Britain, the Brooklands Museum Trust, the Croydon Airport Society, the Handley Page Association and the Miles Aircraft Collection.]

In 1953, following my two-year National Service stint (in the Army, of course – I knew far too much about aeroplanes to be in the RAF!) and a period of recovery from government-inspired ill health, I began looking for a way back into earning my keep in aviation. Of course, going to air shows was very important, and although they were much less frequent than now, it was vital to one's credibility to be there, by whatever means, legal or otherwise.

In the spring of 1953 it was announced that after the Coronation there would be a Royal Review of the RAF at Odiham in July. Word got around on the grapevine that there would be no, or at best very limited, public access to the event, and some of us felt that we owed it to posterity (and to our fellow spotters) to find a way of recording the aircraft taking part, both those in the flypast and those ranged on the ground.

One of my particular friends at that time was the inimitable Tom Pharo, a carpenter by trade, but keen as mustard on anything to do with aviation and who, more importantly, was the owner of transport, namely a motor bike. We were both members of the Royal Observer Corps, with Tom on the Hounslow post (Dog 1) and myself at the Watford centre.

So on the appointed day we biked down from London, both somewhat apprehensive, and more and more wondering why we had ever agreed to do this mad thing in the first place, but desperately hoping that fortune would smile on us; after all, we were doing this not for ourselves but others in the spotting fraternity. Wearing our RAF-like ROC uniforms, we drove through the main gate unchallenged, and because Royalty was on the premises Odiham was teeming with RAF Special Police. There seemed to be thousands of them, making us even more nervous. We pressed on even deeper into the base until we could get no further without 'exposing' ourselves unduly. The motor-bike was parked up and we took to our heels, slipping from building to building a bit like Felix the cat, until we were on the very edge of the open grass areas, where we more or less ran out of ideas!

We took a breather and, loitering near a Nissen hut, wondered how we were going to get any further. Then, amazingly, the door of the hut was flung open and an RAF Flight Sergeant emerged, shepherding a flock of reporters and photographers, exhorting them to follow him across the airfield to where the aircraft (and the Royal dais) were situated. Without a moment's hesitation Tom and I joined on the end of the file, but quickly found it somewhat nerve-wracking and dropped out as we passed under the tail of one of four Neptunes. We were aware that the crew were looking at us somewhat suspiciously, so we decided not to push our luck any further and spent the next few hours trying to be as inconspicuous as possible. Many years later I met the pilot of the Neptune, who vaguely remembered us; he was Peter Howard, an expert on Neptunes and Shackletons (whom later I persuaded to author the 'Profiles' on those aircraft), who ultimately became a senior Captain with BEA & BA.

As we dared not move out from under the Neptune, Tom and I spent the next few hours nervously taking down as many serials and code letters as we could get, both from the 300-plus aircraft on the ground and the 700 others in the flypast, which was reported to be more than 30 miles long at one time. Of course, our records were far from complete, but once we had relaxed a bit and worked out a *modus operandi*, we began to realise what a historic day it was. For me, it was the last time I saw more than 1,000 aircraft in a single day, although this had been commonplace while on my way to school in London in 1943 & '44.

After the flypast the Queen left Odiham; things quietened down a bit, and Tom and I began to congratulate ourselves on achieving something. Then came the announcement over the Tannoy system that the airfield barriers would be taken down at 4 pm so that the public could wander around the aircraft. You can imagine how deflated we felt after all we had gone through, but of course we realised it meant that a proper listing would be made, and I have a faint recollection of seeing 'real aviation historians' like Mike Bowyer and John Rawlings with their notebooks in overdrive. Mike later 'saved the day,' so to speak, with a ten-year anniversary report published in Air-Britain's Military Aviation News for July 1963, and Mike Hardy followed thirty-five years later with a wonderfully nostalgic two-part feature in the September/October 1988 issue of "AEROPLANE MONTHLY." In June 1993 the 40th anniversary was celebrated by Mike Bowyer with a fine report in "AVIATION NEWS."

Nevertheless I felt for many years that nobody would ever publish a complete list of the aircraft which took part in the Coronation Review. However I ultimately fell in with someone who has spent years, if not decades, meticulously working on a substantial and definitive account of that glorious day. And as I write these final words on the subject, news has filtered through that 'the book' is about to appear. So, well done, Eric, I can't wait to devour it!

*   *   *

THE PANSHANGER PROCTORS

In *"Tails of the Fifties"* Rex Nicholls referred to a batch of Proctors ferried from Cosford to Panshanger in the early 1950s, and I can remember watching them steadily deteriorate over the years in the blister hangar there. The majority were registered from G-AOAP to G-AOBE, and I photographed the unconverted survivors in 1956, by which time they were down to a dozen or so.

Seemingly unconnected with all this, in September 1958 I took a £12 return Skyways Coach Air flight to Paris (Dakota G-AMWW out and G-AGYZ back) for a few days relaxation. Prompted by reports by my contemporaries of rich pickings to be seen on the airfields around Paris, I took the SNCF train to Versailles and a local bus to the airfield at Toussus-le-Noble. It was a long way to travel for nothing, and therefore I considered it prudent to check in and get permission to look around. This was readily granted by a man I understood to be the airfield commandant, whom I remember as a tall, dapper and most charming Frenchman, clearly a serious Anglophile. He spoke English without any trace of an accent, was impeccably dressed in a houndstooth check suit embellished with a red rose buttonhole, smoked Benson & Hedges rather than Gauloises, and drove a big Jaguar saloon.

The airfield itself housed much exotica, such as the EP.9 F-BEIG, Bristol Freighter F-BFUO, Mallard N2966, SIPA Coccinelle F-BHHL, a host of Boisavia Mercureys including F-BILA and F-OBRF, the unmarked B.260 Anjou prototype and the Proctor F-BEAK.

I had agreed to check out formally when finished, and was pleasantly surprised when my new-found friend offered me a lift back to Paris in his car. On the way we chatted about aviation matters and somehow the conversation turned to Proctors, whereupon he announced that he was the part-owner of a fleet of derelict Proctors somewhere in southern

England. What was more, having stripped out the useful parts such as engines, radios etc., they were of no further interest to him and his partners, and he made me a present of the whole lot, there and then!

We quickly established that they were indeed the Panshanger machines, but I never took up the offer seriously, other than regarding them subsequently as *my* Proctors, and of course the only aeroplanes I ever 'owned.' Alas, it was not to be, as my Frenchman was obviously unaware that they had already been burned at Panshanger on the 5th of November 1957 during what must have been a truly grand Bonfire Night party.

* * *

GOING TO FARNBOROUGH

During the 1950s so-called ordinary folk could get into the Farnborough Air Show at the weekends by paying, but it soon became apparent to the enthusiasts of the day that taking notes and photographs and watching the flying display more closely was obviously more pleasurable and productive if one could get in during the week on so-called 'trade days.'

Thus it became a point of honour (or more accurately dishonour) to achieve entry on those days, and it began to exercise the minds of 'dispossessed' people like me as to how to bring this about. The completely insatiable demand for trade day tickets, which was never satisfactorily solved during my time in the aircraft industry, brought its own folklore. Young people such as apprentices and those who had not achieved managerial status were somehow deemed ineligible. If you worked for a manufacturing company, obviously the senior management, heads of departments and senior section leaders were required to attend the Air Show, ostensibly to study the technology of the other exhibitors, and were duly issued with tickets. However, when it came to the 'erks' in the drawing office, on the factory floor, or other ancillary workers, a day out of the office was positively not encouraged, and the handful of tickets allocated to these areas were usually the subject of a selective draw, or sometimes even an auction.

It is known that apprentices were smuggled in in the boots of cars and sometimes resorted to hiding in the back of company support vehicles. Other friends of mine resorted to going over the fence using a home-made rope ladder. Students of Farnborough ticket design like me soon realised that the basic black and white paper discs issued in 1948 and 1949 were steadily giving way to ever-more-complex multi-hued designs, presumably in an attempt to defeat forgers, and by the sixties these culminated in what were virtually multi-coloured tickets not dissimilar to the Royal Stewart Clan tartan.

Within the companies, internal distribution of the prized Farnborough tickets was purposely left until the last minute to keep people guessing.

My own involvement in these intrigues came in the mid-fifties, by which time I was a junior administrator in a design office, one of my duties being to open the mail. My immediate boss was the Chief Draughtsman, whose Monday trade day ticket fell into my hands on the preceding Thursday. As I would have to turn it over to him the next day it was obvious that we would have to move quickly, as we had only about fifteen hours to do what was required. A phone call to my 'customers' to assemble at my house that evening was followed by another to my mother to secure sole use of the kitchen, an absolute 'must.' We photographed both sides of the circular ticket, developed the film, made 'real size' prints and cut them out. The tricky part was colouring them with photo-tints, which were very reluctant to dry. The two sides were then glued together and a small hole was punched at the top, through which a double length of fine silk was threaded to complete the illusion. Actually the silk string gave us the most trouble; the only place we could buy it turned out to be a very posh and expensive sewing shop in Regent Street. We usually made about six fakes which were not altogether convincing and were most unlikely to bear any form of close scrutiny.

Nevertheless, together with my 'customers' (some of whom were later to achieve quite senior positions in the aviation business) we set off for Farnborough on this particular Monday morning with great trepidation. Just as in the movies, we divided ourselves into three separate groups and did not attempt to go in together. I was on the back of a scooter and as we approached the official entrance near the Queen's Hotel it began pouring with rain so hard that we had to stop and quickly don our plastic macs (all the rage at the time).

Imagine our amazement, therefore, when as we approached the ticket checker in the teeming rain, he shouted: "OK, I can see your ticket under your mac" and waved us straight through!

We could never have planned this in a million years and it surely provokes the thought that God helps those who help themselves!

*   *   *

ON BEING ARRESTED IN SECRET PLACES

By 1957 I had grown weary of the hit-and-miss approach which came from engineering Farnborough trade day tickets and in any case by that time my writing career had begun and I thus acquired my first Press Ticket quite legally. This was a staggering advance in all sorts of ways, and some things made a lasting impression on me, such as rubbing shoulders with the press giants of those days, the air correspondents of the national papers, all imposing figures and very famous names in aviation. In those days the Press Tent opened for business at 9 am and the aforementioned reporters made sure they got there on time, primarily in order to avail themselves of the free bar and refreshments which were on tap all day long. You can imagine how accurate their reporting was by the end of the day!

One of the perks that came with a Press Ticket was being allowed to travel to Farnborough on a special bus from outside the SBAC office in Central London. The coach was used by both press and VIPs and I can remember with much pleasure sharing seats and spending time in conversation with a number of legendary aviation people going to and from the show. The coach was scheduled to return to London at 7 pm from a point near the Comet water-test tank, and one year, while killing time waiting for the bus and with only two pictures to go, I decided to finish off the film in my camera. The area around the test tank had long been a mystery to the inquisitive, and few seemed to know quite what went on there. A number of old test airframes could be seen scattered around the area (including quite a few dismantled Provosts and a large number of WP-serialled Hunter wings) and I chose to photograph a tatty but complete Meteor NF.11 that had been there for years. No sooner had I taken the pictures but a hand descended on my shoulder in true Scotland Yard fashion, and I was told that I was under arrest for photographing a secret jet plane in a secret place!

In those days security was in the hands of the Air Ministry Constabulary, which seemed to consist of men around the 60-70 mark, and my apprehender was certainly no younger. Remarkably, he insisted on taking me into the forbidden area and up to an office on the first floor of the tank block, where he phoned up his superior officer for further guidance. Having informed the boss of my misdemeanour, my policeman was rewarded with a truly tremendous rollicking, mostly in what one could call the vernacular, and all clearly audible to me. It appeared that his chief was virtually beside himself dealing with an old-style Farnborough traffic jam, which in those days normally encompassed all the surrounding counties, and was thus in no mood to deal with such a trifling matter. Unaware that I had heard what had transpired, and with considerable aplomb, my trusty guard delivered a serious warning about my doubtful activities and I was let go on the basis that the next time it would be a firing squad job. By the time I was released it was past seven o'clock, but fortunately the bus had been delayed and I scrambled aboard for my trip back to London.

*　　*　　*

ON BEING ARRESTED IN SECRET PLACES II

Some years later, seduced by their advanced features at what seemed rock-bottom prices, I bought a Russian camera. This was a two-and-a-quarter-square Rollieflex look-alike called the Lobitel, and, price aside, its great appeal to me was the ability to take 35 mm negatives on a 120 size film via an internally mounted masking frame (which I later found

136

resulted in hideous picture composition problems owing to the parallax effect).

One Good Friday, keen to try out the new camera, I set off with Mike Hooks and some other friends for a day by the Kent coast. We were actually headed for Ramsgate airfield which in those days was home to the Chrisair joyriding fleet of Dragon G-ADDI, Leopard Moth G-AIYS and Proctor G-AHGJ, all of which are remembered for their uniform scarlet red paint jobs finished off with silver 'Sellotape' trim. (The airfield finally closed in 1968 and is now the inevitable industrial estate.)

On the way to Ramsgate we had to pass Manston and it was decided that we would pop in and see what was there. In those days it was an active RAF station and had a Spitfire as a gate guardian, and it was this that caught my attention. The aircraft was in a little chained-off enclosure more or less outside the Guardroom and therefore not strictly inside the airfield. So we stopped and I alone got out of the car to take my first Lobitel picture.

Readers familiar with the Rollieflex will know that the camera had to be held at waist height and the photograph composed through the viewing lens, and in order to take parallax into account the aircraft had to be in the top half of the picture. I had framed the Spitfire nicely, looking only into the viewfinder, and was about to take the shot when an RAF Land Rover drove right into my picture, completely blotting out the aircraft. I looked up and again experienced the feeling I was in big trouble with the now familiar approach of yet another Air Ministry constable. Once again I was told that I had photographed a sensitive military aeroplane in a Ministry establishment and I was persuaded to accompany my interrogator into the Guardroom.

Any protestations about the so-called 'sensitivity' of the Spitfire and the well-publicised ending of the war fifteen or more years earlier fell on deaf ears and to make matters worse, when I looked for support from my fellow travellers, all they could do was to jeer about my predicament and egg on my apprehender from the safety of the car.

Once inside the Guardroom, my keeper rang up the Station Commander, who I imagine had just got in from morning church (or perhaps a round of golf), and was not at all happy about having his Good Friday morning spoiled. Once again I could hear what could well have been expletives and then the phone went down. Once again I was warned about my seditious behaviour which if continued would no doubt ultimately lead to my downfall. However on this occasion, it being Good Friday, and owing to the total unavailability of anyone to lock me up, I would not be detained any further. Working on the basis that I was beginning to win, I then had the temerity to ask if I could continue with my photographic sortie, which somewhat surprisingly was approved.

And that is how I got my original picture of Spitfire LF.16 TB752, which I photographed again many decades later alongside the Hurricane LF751, now joint centrepieces of the Memorial Pavilion at, wait for it . . . Manston. Perhaps I should have waited!

CHAPTER 14

MEMORY IS A CORRIDOR

(LINED WITH DISTORTING MIRRORS)

by

Ranald Porteous

Having been born in the drone of Zeppelin engines, one of my first recollections is of a great longing to take off and soar upwards until I could see over the Ochil Hills which loomed close and steep behind the small town of Alva, where we lived. Some twenty-two years were to pass before I actually took off in the little Chilton from a farm field there and fulfilled this ambition but the seeds of a lifelong love of 'personal' flying were surely sown then.

Memory is a corridor lined with distorting mirrors. Long ago strawberries were sweeter and the sun shone warmer and oftener. Not so, of course, but here lies the trap into which the ageing fall, of thinking that things were different and better in their day. I must therefore beware.

I have always loved flying. It has, in sum, given me immense pleasure, both of itself and in the less creditable context of good old-fashioned vanity. Praise for a display well given can be as heartwarming as for a poem well written, or a song well sung. Anyone claiming otherwise is a hypocrite.

The beauty of flying in the grotesque grandeur of sunlit cumulus cloudscapes never palled, nor did the wonder of bursting through heavy winter stratus into the dazzling blue-and-white world above. In a suitable aircraft, one could write poems of harmonized motion among the clouds, and the thrill of a perfect landing at the end of a flight never diminished. To those who are able occasionally to sample these experiences, surely the air is a segment of Paradise with its roof the very ceiling of the sky.

Practical introduction to aviation came in 1934. I had won a place at London University but, on an irresistible impulse, forsook it for the de Havilland Aeronautical Technical School, then at Stag Lane, the sooner to be among real aeroplanes. Thus a rather naïve schoolboy of eighteen was blooded and friendships were formed there which influenced his life greatly in later years.

Among my student friends at de Havillands were Andrew Dalrymple and Reggie Ward. This pair of clever, witty and iconoclastic Etonians were the John Britten and Desmond Norman of their day and were determined to enter the light aircraft market, efficiently and profitably. That, had peace continued, they would have succeeded spectacularly I have never doubted. They combined the vision, the business sense and the technical ability with the resources initially necessary. Such Chilton DW.1 light monoplanes as still survive are a monument to these. This fabulous little machine, which took its name from Ward's home near Hungerford where it was built, was designed by them in the Tech. School, under the watchful eye of Marcus Langley, as a kind of freelance exercise, and I dare to say that no comparable ultralight aircraft yet built has matched the Chilton for integrity and performance, both quantitative and qualitative.

Dalrymple, who was tragically killed on Christmas Day 1945 in a captured Fieseler Storch, his first flight since before the war, was, without exception, the most intelligent pilot I have ever known. His grasp of principles was instant and complete, and enabled him to put up a stirring exhibition of low-level aerobatics at an air display, with minimal experience and virtually no practice. On this occasion, shortly before the war, I had promised to do this, but was unavoidably prevented at the last moment. Determined not to allow the Chilton a "no-show," Dalrymple spent the previous evening with me, carefully mulling over all the factors involved in each manoeuvre. I read and heard later that his performance was faultless – and this on an aircraft with the characteristics of a baby Spitfire.

At de Havillands the workshop and lecture room were happily complemented by Clem Pike's Reserve Flying School and by the London Aeroplane Club, where by special arrangement students could fly for one pound an hour! Needless to say, I took every advantage of this and, having obtained a private pilot's licence, wheedled my way into the cockpit of every light (and ultralight) aircraft on offer. Looking back, I am amazed how trusting their owners were.

Reminiscing across a gap of some sixty years, I can recall only brief snapshots of each of these machines. Perhaps the simplest of all was Lowe Wylde's and Robert Kronfeld's Drone, virtually a glider with a motorcycle engine, a Douglas twin. Kronfeld occasionally let me fly one of them at weekends to some club or other to 'show the flag' and I do not recall an anxious moment beyond worry lest the wind should increase and prevent me from getting home. I clearly remember hovering stationary, headed into a moderate breeze and saying to myself as I looked down on the earthlings: "I may not be getting anywhere, but I *am* flying – and enjoying every minute of it!"

An acquaintance at Hatfield acquired one of these machines, which he kindly lent to me one weekend for the avowed purpose of visiting friends at Bourne End, where there was a small grass landing-field just behind the Quarry Hotel. This journey of some twenty-five miles was completed in just under an hour and the Drone was duly tethered down for the night before my host (an old rowing Blue) ferried me across the river. Next day we were horrified to find that cows, of whose presence I had been unaware, had chewed great lumps out of the Drone's tail. An engineer from White Waltham performed miracles and the Drone's owner was unexpectedly forgiving.

A young naval friend, Dawson Paul, occasionally lent me his Dart Kitten. This was an orthodox, low-wing monoplane, well-built by two immigrant engineers, Zander and Weyl. It was stable and solid, if perhaps a trifle underpowered by its Aeronca-JAP engine of 42 hp which for some reason I cannot recall was often most reluctant to start. Dawson Paul later became the first owner of the third Carden-engined Chilton, G-AFGI, which I vividly remember delivering to him at Broxbourne from Marlborough. He was delighted with it, appreciating its much higher cruising speed, greater range and far crisper handling – not to mention its powerful flaps.

After the war I acquired my original favourite, G-AFGH, the second Chilton and always, for some reason, the nicest to handle. This was professionally reconditioned by Air Schools Ltd of Derby, where I was doing a stint as CFI of the Aero Club. The Carden engine, based on a Ford 10, went simultaneously through the workshops of a local Ford agent, one Len Astle, who was a keen member of the Aero Club, which no doubt helped as 'GH served me well until, about a year later, my new position at Austers forced me sadly to say farewell to her.

I had done all the original flying of the Chilton at Witney in 1937 and, in the 300-odd flying hours I had accumulated in this little craft, had suffered only one mechanical disaster, which was of our own making. We had skimmed the alloy cylinder head of the Carden engine excessively in preparation for some race or other. I was in transit across London, between Gatwick and Luton, at about two thousand feet on a fine, clear evening (imagine this nowadays!) when there was a loud bang, with oil and steam – and a limply windmilling propeller. A.P. Herbert later wrote:

"London is a funny place;
Nine-tenths of it is open space . . ."

Luckily for me there was some truth in this. The open space which beckoned was Hurst Park racecourse and a few 'S'-turns brought me gently down on to firm, smooth ground between various bushes in the no-man's land inside the race track itself.

End of story? Not a bit of it. My problem was yet to come. Off season, the racecourse was closed and totally deserted. I plodded wearily around inside various fences and barriers for what seemed an age, quite unable to find a way out or indeed to detect signs of human life. Apparently nobody had seen the Chilton land, or had attached any significance to it. I recall a growing sense of panic and even visions of news headlines: "Promising young aviator starves to death in London wilderness!" But this was not to be. Eventually I found an opening which led to the back garden of a suburban house, complete with owner and telephone. A replacement engine was brought in next day and the little Chilton had no difficulty in clearing the surrounding trees – so all was well.

After the war, when I had in effect two Chiltons, one ('GH) mine, the other the Train-engined 'SV, lent to me by Reggie Ward for safe keeping and 'flag-flying,' I had a great tussle with the authorities over the question of reviving the pre-war ultralight permit-to-fly and recall passionately importuning the Minister, Lord Pakenham, at an air display. He took this in good part, seemed interested and promised to examine the matter. It apparently worked, as permits were shortly granted and the two Chiltons flew officially once more, spinners held high. I remain under the impression that these were the first post-war permits but will gladly stand correction if the record shows otherwise.

Prior to the first flights of the Chilton in 1937 I had become involved with Luton Aircraft (C.H. Latimer-Needham) and had undertaken to fly their Buzzard around flying clubs etc. at weekends. Like Kronfeld's Drone, this machine had glider ancestry but was of low-wing, semi-cantilever layout with a much more sophisticated monocoque wooden fuselage design and spatted undercarriage. The engine was a V-twin Anzani, of Morgan three-wheeler ancestry, delivering (well, sometimes) about 34 horsepower. Its carburettor was fed by gravity from an "Autovac" culled from an old Buick car and drawing its petrol from a 5-gallon drum mounted vertically in the fuselage below.

For the benefit of the Very Young (i.e. below about sixty-five), the "Autovac" was a small cylindrical tank, usually mounted on the bulkhead behind a car's engine and connected to the induction manifold, whose suction it used to lift petrol up into its reservoir, whence it could flow by gravity to the carburettor. In practice this crude system worked reliably on the Buzzard (as indeed did the "Autovac" in cars of the time), in sharp contrast to the rest of the power plant, which suffered endless failures, usually due to valves overheating, sticking, seizing and breaking their springs. On my last flight in this machine, from Hatfield to Christchurch, I suffered four engine failures! The first three forced landings were simple but the fourth failure, on a test flight in windy, rainy weather, after alleged repairs at Somerford, connected me somewhat violently with an oak tree on the edge of the airfield, of which I was just out of reach. In view of its known unreliability, I was an idiot to have been flying the machine at all in such conditions, let alone to be doing a low circuit in a hurry. I believe it taught me a lesson and that, after a spell in hospital with various painful fractures (including five vertebrae), I emerged as a much more cautious pilot.

Latimer-Needham developed another ultralight single-seater, the Luton Minor, a braced parasol tractor monoplane, owing nothing to the Buzzard or its sailplane derivation. It also used the Anzani V-twin, replaced in its later versions mainly by the much more reliable Aeronca-JAP horizontally-opposed twin of some 40 hp. I recall that, some four months after my disaster in the Buzzard, Latimer-Needham invited me to fly the Minor prototype (G-AEPD) at Hanworth to pose it for photographs by "SHELL AVIATION NEWS." I felt that this might be a gesture to indicate that he did not blame me for the Buzzard crash. This time the Anzani ran for thirty minutes without failure and the experience was enjoyable, despite an unusually windy cockpit and marginal stabilities.

The tiny machine had a simple undercarriage consisting of a straight-through axle trussed by bungees. This was derived from Henri Mignet's Pou-du-Ciel and allowed the fuselage almost to slither along the grass, so low was it and so small the angle of attack. Whoever invented the term "ducks' disease" must have had the early Minor in mind. All this had a fascinating effect upon the take-off characteristics, as I recall them. On an average grass surface the little machine, lacking the ground-effect benefits enjoyed by the Buzzard, would rush forward eagerly but was unable to attain anything near to a take-off angle of attack until the front was bumped upwards by some unevenness of the ground, whereupon it would leap up quite startlingly, giving a false impression of a healthy rate of climb. Forewarned by experience, one had then to nurse it through a transition period, slowly increasing speed until a modest climb could be sustained. I recall standing next to the great and good C.G. Grey at the Royal Aeronautical Society garden party at Heathrow (then a grass flying field!) in 1938. We were watching the Minor being demonstrated when he suddenly exclaimed: "See, it loses height in a climbing turn!" Such, indeed, seemed to be the case and it released a diatribe by "C.G.G." against ultralights in general, to which he was fanatically opposed, referring to them in "THE AEROPLANE," of which he was Editor, as "silly pop-bottles."

The Minor was later developed in much more satisfactory form by Arthur Ord-Hume (as Phoenix Aircraft), mainly in home-build kit form. One of the first and most obvious improvements was an orthodox undercarriage with compression struts and reasonably-sized wheels, giving the machine an adequate ground angle for normal take-offs.

Later in the same programme I had the unnerving experience of seeing Robert Kronfeld crash "my" Luton Buzzard, rebuilt laboriously since the disaster of some eighteen months before. C.G.G.'s only laconic comment was: "What did I say . . . ?" This time the Anzani engine could not be blamed. As far as I could see Kronfeld merely misjudged some spectacular crazy-flying and inadvertently dug a wing into the ground, causing the machine to slew round violently, snapping the fuselage clean off just aft of the engine pylon. The two parts came to rest at an angle of some forty-five degrees to each other, the cockpit, deprived of support, canted steeply backwards, with poor Kronfeld sitting there and the Anzani still ticking over. I really felt for Kronfeld then and imagine his face to be as red as his dark-tanned Southern European complexion would allow. I always liked him immensely and heard with real sadness of his death a few years later test-flying an Armstrong Whitworth tailless prototype.

Other memorable ultralight single-seaters which I recall flying at about this time include the Belgian Tipsy 'S' and the Currie Wot. The former, a very clean, low-wing monoplane, was underpowered by its 600 cc motorcycle-derived Douglas engine and lacked flaps, which it sorely needed. Nevertheless it handled beautifully and, had it had flaps and more power, it would have become . . . well, a Chilton. The Wot, by contrast, was a neat little biplane, resembling nothing so much as a half-scale model of the DH Technical School's TK.1, or indeed a Moth. Its Aeronca-JAP engine powered it adequately and the controls and stabilities were normal and typical of its layout. I remember feeling exceptionally safe in this little machine, regretting only its rather high drag, which limited progress. Flapless, its glide angle approximated to that of the Chilton, its very effective split flaps fully down!

*   *   *

In 1937 I enjoyed a spell of Service training at Montrose and Driffield in an odd little cell of the RAF labelled "The Reserve of Air Force Officers – Class 'A'" (somewhere between the Volunteer Reserve and a Short Service Commission). This was mainly on Harts and Harrows, which latter huge and heavy bomber I recall treating as an outsize light aircraft – and enjoying it.

The Hart phase was marred by the death of my closest friend and co-pilot, Henry Peacock. For training purposes we were paired for the duration of the course and, for the first, last and only time Henry was flying with another pilot, I being unserviceable with 'flu. We used to alternate, pilot or observer, and this time Henry was in the rear observer's cockpit, being flown on what seems to have been a low beat-up of some boats in Montrose basin. I remain convinced that there would have been no crash if Henry had been flying the aircraft.

My instructor at Montrose was an extremely tough and jovial NCO named Heath who, I quickly and perhaps luckily sensed, was bent on catching me out. I had of course by this time done rather more flying than the other trainees, which made me easy game for "taking down a peg." He would surreptitiously move the trim-wheel or petrol cock just before take-off, claiming that I hadn't done my checks properly. This was perfectly legitimate, as it trained one to be on double-alert. Nevertheless, I eventually counter-attacked by closing the throttle just after we had started our take-off run, claiming that the aircraft was unserviceable.

"Why?" he asked.

"The trim-wheel moves of its own accord as one opens the throttle. There must be a fault," I replied.

He saw the joke, laid off thereafter and we got on famously.

After this (to me) exciting RAFO interlude, with its undertones of a rewarding social nature, Geoffrey Alington, another friend from DH days, invited me to join him and "Bunny" Spratt in their new venture Air Touring at Gatwick, which in those days was still a grass airfield, though increasingly busy, being blessed uniquely with its own station on the Brighton line and with customs facilities. Our aircraft comprised Geoffrey's luxurious 6-seat Short Scion, with its two Pobjoy Niagara engines and busy reduction gears, his Desoutter high-wing three-seater and Bunny Spratt's four-seat Miles Falcon Major. Halcyon days indeed, enlivened by many enjoyable expeditions, including a quick return trip to Le Touquet carrying five Etonians who had a bet with their chums that they could visit France after lunch and be back by "bell" (or whatever it was called) with the evidence. They carried no passports but the Le Touquet authorities knew me well by now and accepted my explanation of the jape with much good-nature and wishes of *"bonne chance!"* We were back at White Waltham, via Lympne, in good time and the party left for Eton armed with date-stamped slips of paper headed "Le Touquet." With such a grounding they must have graduated later into MI6, justifying the revised claim that the war was to be won on the landing-fields of Eton!

An exciting and profitable sideshow to this Gatwick interlude was the opportunity to 'moonlight' (literally!) with Air Dispatch at Croydon, owned and run by Mrs Victor Bruce, a most charming person, famous in her day as a racing driver at Brooklands. They held contracts to provide night-flying aircraft for the training of the Observer Corps (as it became) and other Army anti-aircraft units, embracing guns and searchlights. On receipt of a telephone call we would rush up to Croydon, report to "Mrs V.B." or her lieutenant, Eric Noddings, and be assigned to a (usually) triangular route, sometimes with an overnight base, as often as not Church Fenton.

On one such jaunt, on an exceptionally clear fine night, I found myself in the wee hours droning back south towards the still bright lights of London, heading for Croydon. The DH Dragon offered its pilot exceptionally good visibility and from quite a distance away I was able to identify most of the main roads radiating from the metropolis. When over the northern suburbs I clearly saw Piccadilly Circus, with Regent Street's hockey stick curving left into it. This, I thought, was too good a chance to miss and followed a gentle slope down towards the main north/south line of Regent Street, along which I flew at a few hundred feet, following the curve leftward into Piccadilly. From the comparative safety of the Dragon's cockpit, I could clearly see the colourful and immaculately dressed ladies of the night who still adorned the corners around Regent Street, Piccadilly and Shaftesbury Avenue, some equipped with frisky small dogs on leads.

A modicum of discretion then reasserting itself, I climbed gently away to the right and flew sedately down to Croydon at a respectable height. In those days one 'reported in' in person and I rather expected to hear telephones ringing and to find myself the object of quizzical looks. But no; not a bit of it and I never heard a word thereafter, though there was some small mention of it in the press . . . "mystery plane," "German spy . . . ?", etc. I hope the file is closed long since and can only say: "No, I wasn't a spy – just a young idiot enjoying himself!"

This altogether pleasant spell at Air Touring was made even more so by the use of Chilton 'GH, in which I 'showed the flag' whenever possible at nearby aero clubs such as Redhill and Shoreham. It was at the latter, one warm summer evening, that I first encountered the Miles brothers, whose home territory it was. They were joined in the club bar by Charles Lindbergh, who had just flown in from Germany in his immaculate black Nighthawk, which they had built to his specification. He seemed to be in serious mood and I listened intently to what he was saying. He had been lionised by the Nazis and had been shown round their hugely developed aircraft industry, with which he was mightily impressed – as well he might be, and as they had intended. I gained the impression that he was not fundamentally anti-British, indeed that he wished us well but was exasperated by our government's lack of comprehension of the danger in which we stood and the unwillingness of Whitehall to listen to the warnings which he had repeatedly tried to convey.

Among our aircraft at this time was Geoffrey Alington's Desoutter monoplane, a boxy wooden three-seater with a Hermes engine and a reassuringly thick high wing. I believe that its original design stemmed from Koolhoven in Holland. It flew quite well, but lacked flaps and was only just adequately powered when three-up. Flecks of oil used to accumulate on the windscreen and the flat-sided cabin drummed incessantly. It had, however, one endearing feature, namely a large, hinged skylight or trapdoor in the cabin roof, between the spars of the centre section.

I doubt whether there are many people around nowadays who remember the rumbustious comedy pair Lucan and McShane. They were at that time filming an uproarious sequence in *"Old Mother Riley in Paris."* They were supposed to have panicked on a cross-channel flight, donned parachutes and jumped out of the Dragon which served as an 'airliner' and was, I believe, provided by Hillman Airways. This led inevitably to a scene where "Kitty" McShane was blown along the ground, gesticulating and struggling, parachute still fastened and canopy billowing, by a Very Strong Wind. I claim proudly to have been that VSW. We had chocked the Desoutter's wheels and lashed its tail to the ground, my part in the operation being to kneel on the rear cabin seat-back, head protruding aft through the open trapdoor and working the throttle with the toes of my right foot, at full stretch. All went well, the VSW waxing and waning in accordance with signals made to me by the director, until at the height of a gale the catch on the forward-hinged trapdoor failed, allowing the not-insubstantial contraption to whip over and catch me plumb on the top of my head, with consequences which I do not clearly remember. I saw the film many years later, laughed a lot and could detect no hitch, so all must have been well. Thus ended my career in movies.

A chance arose to join the Miles organisation, starting as assistant to the famous, great and good (all three, in generous measure) Tommy Rose, who at that time ran the Reading Aero Club at Woodley. There was talk of occasional test-flying etc. within the firm so, brandishing my recently-acquired instructor's licence, I bade fond farewell to Geoffrey and Bunny and to the recently recruited Tom Brooke-Smith, later to distinguish himself with Shorts and the GAPAN. It had been a fun time but Woodley was a more serious challenge.

Tommy Rose was beyond all praise. Bluff, jovial, kindly and extrovert, he was nevertheless shrewd in matters of human nature. His considerable fame and seniority rested lightly on his shoulders and to me, a relative whippersnapper, he combined the functions of benevolent boss, father-confessor and merry uncle. He had, to an exceptional degree, the rare gift of giving one a feeling of his real interest and genuine concern. He had lost none of this when I stayed with him many years later in Alderney.

The club aircraft, all very modern for their day, consisted of two Miles Hawk Majors, one Hawk fitted with a Menasco engine of power (130 hp) and characteristics similar to the Gipsy Major, and one Miles Whitney Straight, a most civilised and roomy side-by-side cabin two-seater, developed for the eponymous Anglo-American millionaire, famed from his Brooklands motor-racing era and now proprietor of a string of flying schools, shrewdly set up in advance of the now seemingly inevitable war.

All these Miles aircraft and their stablemates flew beautifully, due to exceptionally efficient wing design, coupled with simple and reliable split flaps which gave just about the ideal degree of increased drag without unduly disturbing longitudinal trim. The Menasco engine, being American, rotated in the 'wrong' direction, which confused some novices no end as they experienced yaw and torque effects the reverse of what they had come to expect. In this regard it served as an excellent training tool.

I cannot look back on this very positive period, when I felt that I was learning so much (not all of it in the cockpit!), without remembering with horror one very nasty narrow squeak which may well (like the Buzzard incident) have frightened me out of any drift towards over-confidence. I was nearing Woodley in one of the Hawk Majors with a charming, youngish woman as pupil, after a routine training flight. Her progress had been excellent so far and her aptitude markedly above the average. As we began our final approach she remarked to me through the Gosport tube that we were a trifle high and should she go round again or sideslip some of the height off? We had been practising sideslips during the previous week and she had become quite expert, so I agreed to the latter, whereupon, in a split second, she violently applied full rudder and opposite aileron with a considerable amount of up-elevator . . . and we had executed a half-flick-roll at what cannot have been more than about four hundred feet. Emitting what must have been a startled yelp, I managed to seize everything and nurse the Hawk downwards through its half-loop, steering at high speed between two rows of suburban houses on the edge of Sonning at below roof-top height. It was all very scary, not least to the lady in question, and I can only claim that, in thousands of hours instructing, nothing similar was ever allowed to happen again – thank God!

A favourite club member, with whom I greatly enjoyed flying, was Veronica Innes, lately 'Queen of Beauty' at the Runnymede Pageant. She had a charmingly insouciant way of tackling things, as I shall show. When war came she quickly graduated from the Civil Air Guard (which the club had served) into the Air Transport Auxiliary, in which she flew almost every type of RAF aircraft, from Spitfires to Mosquitos and Lancasters. Her vivid air-focussed book *"The Sky and I"* by Veronica Volkerz (her married name) makes wonderful reading even today; in fact, perhaps more so by having acquired historical significance. It makes a splendid lens through which to view from a distance many fascinating aspects of the war period and embodies the full story of the Air Transport Auxiliary.

I have mentioned Veronica's 'insouciance' and can only relate the following. In her Civil Air Guard days at Woodley she was largely my responsibility – no hardship to me. One late afternoon she was authorised to do a triangular cross-country navigation exercise which, as far as I can remember, should have taken her to Suffolk, Cambridgeshire and home after about an hour and a half. When she was more than an hour overdue and a thickening haze warned of the approach of evening we were all decidedly anxious, the famous furrows on Tommy Rose's forehead being much in evidence.

Just as we were on the point of initiating all sorts of emergency procedures by telephone, the Hawk's engine was heard and the aircraft appeared through the haze, clearly identifiable. My feeling of relief cannot be described. Apart from the responsibility, I was really fond of Veronica, who by now had landed and was taxying in to a clamorous reception embracing: "Where the HELL have you been?", "What went wrong?", "Thank God you're back!", "Join us in the bar."

Veronica's reply to all this was calm and clear. "The visibility was very poor and I'm afraid I got lost for a while, but I found myself among some barrage balloons, so I knew it was Cardington and remembered a friend who farms near there, so landed in one of his fields for a chat." . . . Bless her!

At about this time I was, to my delight, entrusted with the prototype Miles Monarch (G-AFCR) for a demonstration to the French civil aviation authority at Le Bourget. The Monarch was a quiet and comfortable three-seater, somewhere between the four-seat Falcon and the two-seat Whitney Straight, which it resembled most closely. To my way of thinking, the controls and stabilities were perfectly harmonised and the machine was a pleasure to fly. My contacts at Le Bourget turned out to be a couple of gravely important Garlic-and-Gauloises gentlemen in blue pin-stripes and wearing Homburg hats. They spoke (or pretended to speak) no English so my halting schoolboy French was stretched to its limit. Having taken off into a smoggy autumn haze which, at two thousand feet, prevented one from seeing anything of the ground save vertically downwards, they proceeded to perform a series of lurching gyrations, timing various recoveries with a stopwatch. Sitting there helplessly in this grey horizonless void I suddenly felt an increasing panic lest I should be airsick for the first time in my life, thus disgracing myself, Miles Aircraft, King and Country . . . in that order. Great was my relief when Mafia Boss No.1 gestured to me to take over and return to Le Bourget, which I found in the murk more or less by luck. In reply to my innocent query as to their opinion of the aircraft, their only comment was *"Ce n'est pas assez stable transversellement . . ."* This, I remain convinced, was *"une charretée de savetiers"* – to coin a phrase.

I returned to Woodley feeling that I should have done better but George Miles generously dispelled this and explained that the exercise had been something of a "long shot" anyway.

Some months before the war I was transferred from the club to the Flying Training School (No.8 EFTS). The training of pilots had by now become desperately urgent and we flew our Magisters, Hawks and even a Hart or two in all weathers for long hours. Our particular version of the Hawk Trainer had one noteworthy failing: its carburettor float tended to stick when subjected to negative *g*, as in a slow roll, thus cutting off the petrol from the jet. Sometimes it could be shaken loose by violent 'jinking,' but more often one had to execute a model forced landing, with full "patter" as a matter of honour! Consequently each instructor had to choose his field or area, over which alone he could teach aerobatics. There were plenty of good fields within range of Woodley. My chosen plot was on a hillside between Henley and Wargrave. The surface was concave, the slope increasing markedly as one went uphill, rather like a ski-jump in reverse. In all but extreme winds, therefore, one landed uphill. The ensuing take-off downhill was always fun. Meanwhile life was restored to the Gipsy Major by opening its cowling and striking the carburettor sharply with a stone or, failing that, with one of the easily removable control sticks. This resulted in an audible metallic 'clink' as the errant float dropped down into its proper position. This was scarcely high technology but I recall one training course during which no less than 91 dead-stick forced landings were recorded without any aircraft suffering so much as a scratch.

"Spinning" was of course an important item in the training syllabus of those days and the pressure of events forced us sometimes to carry on with this in appallingly unsuitable weather. Accordingly, to help us and our charges to keep track of the number of turns completed, we were in the habit of counting aloud: "Reading one – Reading two – Reading three . . ." as the brick-red blur on an otherwise green landscape flashed by. A story which my wife picked up many years later has it that on one such occasion my patter ran: "Reading one – Reading two – Reading three – recover . . . Bloody Hell; it's Basingstoke!" I vaguely remember this but had no idea that it would survive as folklore. *Sic transit Gloria* . . . whoever she may be.

During my spell in hospital after the Buzzard disaster I had read *"Sagittarius Rising"* by Cecil Lewis. It was and is a truly marvellous book and Cecil Lewis instantly became – and remains – my literary hero. There is a charming section late in the book in which Lewis vividly depicts his time in China after the First World War, charged with training their embryonic air force – initially with no aeroplanes! His social life in Peking and Shanghai seems to have been idyllic and in one passage he describes how, after a movingly romantic encounter of almost supernatural intensity, he later muses: "On what white pillow lay that head? So close, so far away, so dear, yet so estranged by one brief step of time." When I read this I sat up in bed with such alacrity as my painful back would allow. It remains the most perfect gem of poetic prose (save perhaps for David's lament for Jonathan) I have ever read and it seared its impression instantly in my mind and memory.

This leads me to relate that, George Miles having kindly suggested that I join him, Tommy Rose and one or two others for a drink in the White Hart at Sonning, I found myself at the bar there enjoying a preprandial gin in this august company, which included Victor Burnett of the "DAILY EXPRESS." Suddenly the door opened and in it stooped a massively tall, impressive figure in an astrakhan-collared greatcoat.

"Come in and join us, Cecil," said George Miles; "I think you know everyone here . . ." Then, looking round, he added, "Oh! this is Ranald Porteous: Cecil Lewis." I don't think the word "gobsmacked" had yet been coined, but that is exactly what I was. My literary hero . . . himself . . . in the flesh . . . I took refuge in another large gin.

After two or three further such fortifiers, my courage welled up and, having caught Cecil Lewis' eye, I solemnly intoned: "On what white pillow lay that head? So close, so far away, so dear, yet so estranged by one brief step of time."

For a moment he looked like a (very large) shot rabbit . . . then: "I wrote that!" he exclaimed.

"I know. *'Sagittarius Rising',*" I replied. For a few seconds he said nothing, then a slow smile spread across his face: " . . . bloody good, wasn't it?" . . . It was.

Lewis died not long ago, within a year or so of his century. He had become a revered religious and philosophical guru, holding court at his exotic villa in the Aegean and his sonorous voice on the BBC's *"Thought for the Day"* programme some years ago was most impressive. He must then have been well into his eighties.

*　　*　　*

After the war, mainly spent most unheroically instructing in the UK and Rhodesia, I intended to rejoin Dalrymple and Ward at Chilton, initially to set up a sales structure. Dalrymple's sad death, which I have mentioned earlier, put paid to this and I found myself in urgent need of a niche to fill while seeking an alternative opening in the aircraft industry. The Miles company was already running into trouble and Auster had filled its sales and test-flying slots. Nevertheless, George Miles remained as helpful as ever and gave me the use of a Sparrowhawk and of the M.18 prototype to help me remake my contacts here and there.

After a brief and unhappy spell with an embryonic charter company at Kenley, near Croydon, including a horrendous flight, seven aboard, from Croydon to Johannesburg in a heavily-laden Consul (civil Oxford), completed in 3 days and 23 hours (!), I engaged myself with voice recording (having done a certain amount of concert and radio singing in Rhodesia), setting up Vox Recordists at Wargrave, firstly with equipment which I had brought from South Africa. This soon brought me into renewed contact with Stephen Appleby, whom I had got to know at Heston before the war when he was involved with Henri Mignet's Flying Flea. Appleby, who had changed not at all, ran a much more sophisticated recording business just off Piccadilly and was a tower of strength.

Eventually the grapevine signalled an opening as CFI of the Derby Aero Club at Burnaston. At least this was a chance to get into the air again, so I boarded the Sparrowhawk, flew up to Burnaston – and the job was mine.

The Derby club's aircraft included a Miles Messenger 4-seater, an aerodynamic marvel and a monument to George Miles' wing design, 'my' old Monarch, G-AFCR, still presumably *"pas assez stable transverselle-ment,"* and three Auster Autocrats, which I found tiring to instruct in and lacking control finesse, though one had to admire their impeccable serviceability.

My (then) wife, Elaine, had meanwhile acquired the closed-cockpit M.18, G-AHOA, which had been designed as a Chipmunk competitor and was a truly splendid aircraft, in my view a far better trainer than the Chipmunk in all but one respect, over-docility at the stall. This was, of course, a plus feature in a private aircraft, but not in a serious trainer. Its roomy cockpit and layout were far nearer to those of 'grown-up' machines, as were its performance and general handling, which enabled me to give fairly effortless aerobatic displays at various airshows.

Its arrival at Burnaston caused quite a stir, for the wrong reasons. I had ferried it up from Woodley and, full of enthusiasm, took Elaine up for her initial flight in it. Halfway round our first circuit the engine (a Cirrus Major III of 155 hp) slowly died, leaving us with a windmilling propeller and no 'feel' to the throttle, whose linkage had in fact become disconnected.

Luckily, although downwind, we were within gliding distance of the airfield, on which I landed crosswind with no difficulty, trying hard to convey that such trifling inconveniences were part of the routine lives of competent, masterful flying instructors. G-AHOA, overhauled and glamourously painted by the folk at Derby, never again gave cause for anxiety and was the source of great enjoyment. Eventually she was sold to Tom Hayhow, later of inter-city record fame, who crashed her terminally into a cloud-covered Pennine hillside, escaping with little more than a broken ankle and confirming my long-held view that, if you *must* crash, it is best to choose a wooden aircraft!

Only two M.18s were built: G-AHKY became the property of Brian Iles, an old pupil of mine, who became air-racing champion with her. She had Magister-like open cockpits, whereas G-AHOA was blessed with a really splendid sliding canopy, resembling that of a Harvard.

The Sparrowhawk, which I was still enabled to use from time to time for aerobatic displays, was a joy. It was immensely clean, with crisp controls and stabilities perfectly harmonised, cutting through turbulent air as straight as an arrow, without the slightest trace of 'jinking,' yaw or dutch-roll. It seemed to obey one's thoughts, always with effortless accuracy, and was by far the best and most enjoyable light aircraft I have ever known in the context of low-level aerobatic display flying. With most light aircraft one had to employ a certain amount of skill and downright cunning to achieve continuity while maintaining height during such displays, but in the Sparrowhawk the problem was to avoid accumulating more and more height as one's programme progressed!

In the Sparrowhawk I devised a pattern which suited its merits and which I called a "four-leaf clover." This required a display crowd arranged in 'L' form, which was quite usual. The Sparrowhawk would be flown very fast and low just inside one arm of the 'L,' parallel to the spectators, then brought up into an absolutely vertical climb, aileron-rolled through precisely 90 degrees, the loop then being completed to bring the aircraft down just inside the second arm of the 'L' . . . and so on, four times. Simple stuff, but easy for the Sparrowhawk and I was told that it "looked artistic"! Sadly, this gem of an aircraft ended its life when a Rolls Royce test pilot took off with the fuel tap wrongly set.

In the summer of 1948 the "DAILY EXPRESS" set out to organise at Gatwick the first major post-war international air display in this country. Victor Burnett was naturally at the hub of this and there were big names on his provisional menu.

I had promised to be there with both the Chilton-Train and the M.18, as a flexible aerobatic slot-filler, and to see him in London to discuss other ways in which I might be able to help. On arrival at his office I quickly saw the need for this. As in American movies of the time, the scene was phrenetic. Phones were ringing all over the place and aides (with or without visitors) kept popping in unannounced every minute or so. Victor found time to confide that the mighty Women's World Aerobatic Champion, Betty Skelton from Tampa, Florida, had arrived early at Southampton and was due at any moment. Would I *please* take her off his hands, for lunch and longer if possible, as he was desperately busy and quite unable to cope with a leathery he-woman, as I think we both envisaged her.

Just then, through the open door, there wafted the most delightful vision of sunlit sea-spray in the shape of a demurely pretty, chic and graceful young and slender woman, who announced in the most charming Southern drawl: "I'm Betty Skelton. I guess you're expecting me."

I can't actually remember being given smelling salts and helped off the floor but it must have been fairly near to that. Burnett, too, was clearly impressed and I recall a moment of dread lest he should renege on the take-her-out-to-lunch arrangement!

Betty Skelton seemed to like the idea of lunch in the Royal Aero Club, whither we repaired by taxi. During our meal the conversation naturally tended towards aerobatics and she seemed to be baffled by my use of the term "flick roll," asking me to explain it, whereupon she exclaimed: "Oh!

you mean *snap* rolls!" . . . Then, musing: "Flick rolls . . . gee, that's a cute little British expression. I must remember that!"

Betty Skelton described to me her own various routines with what, when I came later to see them, I recognised as truly charming modesty. Her display was terrific, involving poles, streamers and multiple flick (sorry, snap) rolls and everything else in (and out of) the book – everything being flown very low and with almost unbelievable accuracy. I understood how she had become World Champion. Her background was interesting in that her nursery had been the highly-professional family flying school run by her father and embracing display flying as a speciality. Her aircraft *"Little Stinker"* had been designed to her specification and I believe that the later Pitts Special, which closely resembled it, was a direct offspring. To my diffident enquiry as to whether I just might be trusted with *"Little Stinker"* for a quarter of an hour or so, the reply, soothingly delivered, was: "I guess even my Pap ain't allowed to fly that one!"

She later held the Women's World Land Speed Record. I'll wager that she was as charming and modest about that as well . . . bless her!

The "DAILY EXPRESS" had mustered an impressive array of interesting aircraft for this display, including a "flying motor-car" (never a successful formula – and never likely to be) and "The World's Smallest Piloted Airplane." This was a tiny metal monoplane, about half the size of a Chilton or Tipsy 'S,' along the top of whose minuscule fuselage the pilot lay strapped prone, separated from the ground by a midget tricycle undercarriage. I can't recall any technical details – or even the machine's name or (American) origin, save that the engine was a horizontally-opposed twin two-stroke, probably of about 20 hp. The contraption flew – quite well, in fact – but, no, I didn't beg a ride!

Air racing, in its pure and immensely spectacular form, faded in this country with the demise of the Schneider Trophy events. At that time I was lucky enough to be at a prep-school not far from the Solent, where we could see the Supermarines, and others, practising out of Calshot and could argue (with zeal but almost total ignorance) about the relative skills of such as Waghorn, Webster, Orlebar, Atcherley, Kinkead and d'Arcy Grieg. Kinkead's tragic death is etched on my memory. Some of us had been watching events from a point of vantage on the edge of the school grounds but had repaired indoors for our weekly "house singing" ("Forty Years On," "Tom Bowling" etc. etc.) under our admirable music mistress. It was a still, warm evening and the penetrating yowl of the racing engines and their propellers (which must have been supersonic) intruded from time to time and was sweeter music to our philistine ears than the pallid tinklings of the piano. To our horror, however, one such yowl ended abruptly at its peak with a horrible "tunk" – then complete silence.

The music mistress rose slowly to her feet, closed the lid of the piano and said softly: "That will be all. Please go quietly." We did, many in tears, as it was clear to all what had happened. In due course we learned that Flight Lieutenant Kinkead had flown straight into the glassy surface of the water on a very high-speed run.

A totally glassy surface, devoid of even vestigial ripples, is a rarity but on one or two occasions in later life, when one has offered itself, I have experimented close to it, with Kinkead in mind. It is very, very dangerous.

Long-distance air races, such as the MacRobertson race from Mildenhall to Melbourne and the later Portsmouth to Johannesburg race, both in the mid-to-late thirties, were, of course, a completely different matter. They could be of great news value but their spectator appeal was limited to a few *aficionados* at the start and perhaps a sizeable crowd at the finish, far away.

I was at the early-morning start of both these events, highly motivated as a de Havilland student who had watched the Comet take shape in the first case and by my friendship with Geoffrey Alington in the second. I shall never forget the sight of Geoffrey's indomitable mother, heroine of an unscheduled parachute jump at Brooklands, calmly polishing the leading edges of Geoffrey's BA Eagle while everyone else seemed to be rushing about in a panic. If anyone ever slotted comfortably into Kipling's "*If*," it was she.

Air racing as typified by the King's Cup, which was big and lively news in the thirties is, to the logical and disinterested mind, quite the silliest and most pointless sport ever devised. The same group of private (or semi-private) owners congregated to fly at full throttle round a cross-country course which was, as often as not, largely beyond the view of such spectators as may have gathered. The aircraft were lined up and flagged off one at a time in accordance with calculations made by a team of expert handicappers, whose object was to ensure that, given equal piloting skill, all the competitors arrived at the finish dead level. In the event the handicappers usually proved more fallible than the pilots, whose relative skills were marginally significant, as between the best and the worst, though little would have separated the best few, one from another. This being said, air racing of this nature was a marvellous sport for its participants, a splendid bunch of enthusiastic and expert people, always a tonic to be with. I became hooked on it well before the war, being blooded in the little Chilton, entered for the Isle of Man and Tynwald races in June 1938.

Having left Hatfield as limit man, I recall flying my busy 32 horsepower with desperate accuracy and at almost zero height all the way to Speke (Liverpool) where I landed, still in the lead but closely followed by a gaggle of orthodox biplanes with four times the power, who were slowly but steadily catching me up. I remember also arriving at the refuelling Bowsers among these aircraft, whose vastly more experienced pilots were well-positioned and calling loudly for "Twenty-five gallons of Shell" . . . "Twenty gallons . . . etc. etc." My own timid request for "two and three-quarter gallons of National Benzole Mixture and a little Redex, please" caused some amusement and rings in my ears today.

For this event the Chilton had been fitted with a new propeller, of 'racing' design, i.e. of smaller diameter and coarser pitch, which certainly gave one or two extra miles per hour flat out, despite being a trifle sluggish in acceleration and climb. This was as expected. It had been completed just before the race and there had been no time to fit the usual metal leading-edges, essential to protect the wooden laminations against onslaught by rain, hail or grit. All was well at Speke. There had been no rain and the propeller was in pristine condition.

The second half of the race, to Ronaldsway via St Bees Head in Cumberland started well. The weather remained clear and dry and the little Carden-Ford engine hummed contentedly as we rounded the white lighthouse on St Bees Head, still in the lead.

Ominously, however, the Isle of Man was not visible and, after what seemed to be a long time flying low across the water on a compass course, spots of rain started to strike the Chilton's tiny windscreen, increasing rapidly. To my alarm the engine revs and the airspeed both fell noticeably and I began to ponder the aircraft's ditching characteristics, the best way of inflating the old inner tube which was my sole survival kit, and the likelihood of being picked up at all. In short, I began to wish I were elsewhere.

By now the rain was quite heavy beneath a lowering cloud-base but I drew a trace of comfort from the proximity of other competitors who were now looming out of the murk and passing me on either side, one with a cheery wave. At least I must be on the right track.

Great was my relief when land appeared dimly, straight ahead and quite close. The little aircraft's battered propeller was just able to lift me over the promontory before Ronaldsway and so my first race ended with my being placed tenth, about halfway down the field. The propeller was a horrible sight, both leading-edges looking as though bashed with a meat hammer, so it was quickly removed in favour of a standard 'touring' one, which was probably a blessing since we had entered the Chilton for the Tynwald race later in the weekend. The triangular course for this was somewhat hilly and there is little doubt that the greater diameter and finer pitch of this propeller gained more on the long uphill stretches than it may have lost downhill. Anyway, despite the handicappers having reassessed the Chilton's speed in view of its performance as far as Speke and St Bees Head, it acquitted itself well in the Tynwald, coming third and confirming me as "hooked on racing."

I have mentioned the relatively small part which pure pilot skill plays in such races, at least in comparison with the whims and vagaries of the handicappers. This does not imply that it is negligible. The three Carden-engined Chiltons were later joined by the Train-engined version, boasting 44 horsepower and a much more streamlined nose. During my sojourn as an instructor at Woodley, I surreptitiously "borrowed" our approved low-flying area after hours and, armed with a stopwatch, used the Chilton (and occasionally other aircraft as well) to experiment with different cornering techniques. I remember many conflicting views offered by "experts" at the time of the Schneider Trophy races and had watched spellbound the varying styles of the pilots during the races themselves.

To understand the main facets of the problem one needs a little knowledge of aerodynamics, specifically 'induced drag,' 'profile drag' and 'power loading.' The first is highest under g loading in aircraft with short, squarish wings (low aspect-ratio) and minimal in the case of long, finely-tapered wings (high ditto). The second is a straightforward measure of the aircraft's 'cleanness' or slim, streamlined form. Thus one may have aircraft at opposite ends of the spectrum in the same race, typified by, say, the Chilton-Train, very slippery and free of profile drag, with finely-tapered high aspect-ratio wings, giving low drag under g loading, but with very limited power, *ergo* thrust for acceleration or climb. At the opposite end was, say, an Auster AOP Mark 11, with huge drag, both 'induced' and 'profile' but with lots of power and thrust. With the former the important thing was to nurse the speed round (and especially out of) the turn, avoiding any coarse or inaccurate control movements or excessive loading which might reduce airspeed unnecessarily.

With the Chilton-Train my stopwatch convinced me that, in the absence of external governing factors such as a marked wind-gradient, the best technique involved a very slight increase in height before a meticulously smooth, gradual entry to the turn, which itself could be of fairly high 'g,' followed by an equally gradual recovery, slightly downhill at first, to help the aircraft to regain speed and re-establish its optimal high-speed airflow or, colloquially, to "get back on the step." The 'draggy,' higher-powered aircraft could, by contrast, be hurled quite coarsely into and out of the turn and benefited hardly at all from that little bit of extra height for a dive-out.

These principles could be projected right through the spectrum of possible racers, from jets through Spitfires and the Mew Gull to (God forbid!) the 260 hp Auster AOP Mark 11. They are, however, of relatively little account if the pilot does not follow an optimal track round the (always visible) turning markers. Generally this is approximately parabolic and the marker should lie just (and only just) within the apogee of the parabola. This calls for a good eye and much practice which, we tell ourselves, makes perfect. As a spectator I was often dismayed to see some competitors cornering with the marker more or less in the centre of their turn. A simple diagram will show that they must have lost a distance approximately equal to the diameter of their turn on each such occasion. But at least they avoided disqualification! High-speed racing round short pylon circuits seems nowadays to have survived only at Reno – and thrilling it must be to watch. From the evidence of a recent TV film it seems that the best of the pilots there adhere to the precepts outlined above.

The handicappers were splendid people and the even-handedness of their fallibility can be illustrated by my results: one up, one down! In the first case the race, sponsored by Butlins, was over three or four laps of a triangular course inland from the North Yorkshire coast. I had promised a ride to three keen members of the Derby Aero Club, so accordingly we entered our rather smart 4-seat Miles Messenger (G-AILL) for the event. The Messenger had almost certainly not been raced before and without doubt the handicappers had dismissed it in their minds as a tubby, flappy dragbox, only just able to lug its four occupants round the course. In fact, the Messenger, despite its remarkable designed-in low-speed capability, was surprisingly 'clean' and, when the handicaps were posted, I was amazed to find G-AILL seeded among various types which I was sure it could easily outstrip, four-up or no. Such proved to be the case. By the end of the first lap we had passed all the aircraft ahead of us and we continued to sail effortlessly round the course to win by roughly half a county. I am tempted to imagine that we were all in the bar, enjoying our second drink, when the next competitor arrived!

Alas! I never actually won another race, though as often as not I was placed among the first four. This leads me back to the handicappers and the (still) prestigious King's Cup. In 1963, some time after Auster had merged with Miles to become Beagle, I was entered in the King's Cup to fly our shiny new Airedale four-seater, developed from the Atlantic concept. My young wife, Susan, had already flown with me in this aircraft through Spain, Portugal and Morocco on various hot-weather development trials and business visits. She was delighted, therefore, to have the chance of riding shotgun in the King's Cup – no less. However, I soon discovered that having us both in the front seats resulted in a degree or two of up-elevator, which inevitably must have caused an imperceptible amount of drag. Susan was therefore banished to the quite comfortable rear seat, a demotion which she accepted with charm and grace, once we had verified that the elevator was now precisely in line with the tailplane and (was it imagination?) the airspeed indicator seemed to settle down at a bare needle's thickness higher reading. As none of the aircraft's services would be needed in the race and having previously ascertained that no harm would result, I planned to switch off the alternator after starting, in order to relieve the engine of most of its electromagnetic drag. This gave us another needle's-width of indicated speed, the two aggregating perhaps to one mile per hour, or a gain of about a thousand yards at the finishing line. With the close finishes that by this time the handicappers were achieving, a thousand yards could mean the difference between first and sixth!

The race, which was over an angular course starting and finishing at Coventry, progressed well. Susan, who had been given the title of "Official-Lookout-Astern-on-Both-Sides," continued to report no over-taking aircraft, while we gleefully ticked off the various slower machines as we passed them. These, to my delight, included my friend and colleague, the late Vyrell Mitchell, passed inside on a turn with an advantage of about a hundred yards.

At last, the final leg of the last lap. Susan was by now excitedly identifying various faster aircraft as they approached from behind, while I scanned the clear, empty air ahead, satisfying myself that we had passed everything there was to pass. Finally, the long, straight belt low across the airfield to the finishing line – and our excited yelps: "We've won! We've won!!" Alas . . . the handicappers (may their slide-rules shrivel) had massively underestimated a little Tipsy Nipper, the limit man, who must have finished about three miles ahead of us all, as he was never in sight. Oh! well . . . second in the King's Cup was worth a brownie-point or two; but it would have been nice to have won!

One other race which remains vividly in my memory was the Folkestone Trophy in 1947. Reggie Ward had entered the Chilton-Train, G-AFSV, for me to fly and it had been arranged that I should put in an extra lap which, with the three of the race itself, would qualify as an attempt on the "International 100 km Closed Circuit Speed Record – Class 'A'," this being for engines of less than two litres capacity. The little French Train engine just fell within this limit, by the skin of its piston-rings.

It was August, fine and warm, if a trifle bumpy. 'SV ran beautifully, won its heat and was third in the final, following which I began my last 'solo' lap through the now empty air. I recall a strange feeling, almost of loneliness, as we sped on. This soon changed to anxiety as flecks of oil began to appear on the windscreen and a warm smell to permeate the cockpit. However, the lap passed quickly and I landed to find myself the possessor of an International Record and very little oil!

Some time later the FIA (or whoever) abolished Class 'A' – and, presumably, me with it – but I was delighted a few years ago to see my name in some reference book, recorded as the final holder. Immortality? Well, not quite; but it gave my flagging ego a welcome boost!

*   *   *

Late in 1948 I learned that Lester Pendleton, Auster's Sales Manager, was probably leaving, so I quickly renewed my contacts there. It was he who had brought the horrible Avis prototype over to Derby for us to evaluate. This had evoked some rude comments, verbally and in writing, so I rather feared that my chances of landing a job with Austers might be slim. I believe that my letter contained phrases such as "an insult to the British private owner"!

However, to my great delight I was accepted, assuming also the responsibilities of Chief Test Pilot as the incumbent, George Snarey, had also decided to leave. Years later, when I had become a Director, I tried unsuccessfully to trace my provocative letter, so doubtless it had found its way straight into the bin!

It was my good fortune later to work in the environment of my own choice, concerned with the development and marketing of light aircraft. It is a fascinating business, in which Britain formerly held a proud place. That we lost this was tragic and totally unnecessary and is traceable to one or two wrong decisions made in the post-war years by people whose lack of the very necessary 'feel' for the business should have disqualified them from making these at all.

There are great misconceptions as to how aircraft are marketed and what a selling organization comprises – and how it is built up. I have used the term "marketed" rather than "sold," as the design and development of a machine, with control of its costs, are just as much a part of the "marketing" process as is the final putting of signatures to a contract of sale. Indeed, it is in just those facets that so many projects (and the companies which nursed them) failed.

Speaking as a former design student and with great diffidence and affection towards many good friends who were designers, I will say that they generally were the last people who should have decided *what* to design. Save in the military context (and even then, sometimes) such decisions should have been purely commercial. There were great and illustrious exceptions to this rule but, alas, not in the general run of things.

The marketing of aircraft, large or small, involved (and still involves) a degree of 'vision' not derived entirely from statistics. It was necessary to build up a network of contacts in all relevant parts of the world. In the context of light aircraft, these might vary from listening posts to fully-appointed distributors. They had to have two things in common, namely a material motive for furthering one's sales and roots in the market throughout their territory.

Once this had been done, market research of one's own became possible, quite independent of the many and excellent sources of statistical information available to industry "through the usual channels." Experience gave me a firm belief in this more direct method and I doubt whether there is any other industry in which block statistics are more capable of misinterpretation.

The small aircraft market in different countries has always fluctuated, sometimes in phase with saturation, obsolescence and changes in design, and sometimes under the influence of trade balances and exchange control. Some knowledge of these shifting sands had, therefore, to be maintained. Suitable agents and correspondents had to be found and terms agreed. Contact had to be established at Service, commercial and, if possible, diplomatic levels at the embassies, in order of potential, and these had constantly to be fostered. This naturally involved a great deal of travelling abroad and an alert ear to the ground in London. This *modus operandi* may suggest elegant life in exotic climates and such interludes did (thank God) happen. But they were the cream on the jelly, most of which consisted of hard, continuous and dedicated office work.

One day during the early 1950s I found myself en route to Tokyo in connection with the possible sale of a number of aircraft to a prominent newspaper there. Our agent had been doing his spade-work excellently and had himself recently acquired a new Aiglet Trainer. I was warned that I might be expected to fly it in an air display and had agreed to do this.

On arrival I found that the display was scheduled for the following weekend at an airfield named Tamagawa, which bore roughly the same relationship to Tokyo as did Biggin Hill and Elstree to London. When the day came and I found myself at Tamagawa I naturally began to make enquiries as to the nature of the programme and my slot in it. My Japanese hosts looked surprised. "The programme?" they said, "Why, *you* are the programme . . ." I found to my utter horror that this was literally true and that, apart from a flypast by a few local Cessnas etc., I was expected to entertain the crowd, estimated at about twenty thousand, for about an hour and a half with only a short break in the middle for the aforementioned flypast! It should be mentioned that one's slot at Farnborough, Paris or any comparable Western air display was usually about three or four minutes.

Accordingly, with no option, I gritted my teeth and in due course took off, maintaining a flow of absolutely non-stop low-level aerobatics until I was utterly exhausted. I think it must have been over half an hour and I remember that, on landing, I was just able to totter out of the aircraft and lie flat on my back in the grass, panting and sweating like an overweight marathon runner. My hosts said, in effect: "That was very nice and we look forward to the second half of your programme." The Cessnas etc. meanwhile droned steadily overhead, dropping leaflets and what looked like flour bombs, to my intense relief taking rather longer than I had been led to expect. Nevertheless I had to remount and do my thing all over again, following which I was asked to lead the procession of light aircraft over the centre of Tokyo in honour of Crown Prince Akihito's coming of age.

This was the last straw, but I had no option and again took off for the centre of the vast city of whose topography I had only scant knowledge. This time I was at the head of a motley and straggling squadron and the arrangement was that I would break off over the centre of the city and perform some more aerobatics. By this time I was totally punch-drunk and was in no state to care much what befell me. I am a timid fellow and the vast concrete jungle of Tokyo did not look to me at all a suitable place over which to perform low-level aerobatics in a single-engine aircraft, no matter how good or reliable it be. I remember, however, being just capable of a flicker of interest when my doubtless bloodshot eyes lit upon the Imperial Palace, which I recall as being a hollow-shaped (pentagonal?) building set upon a mound surrounded by a trough or moat. The courtyard occupying the centre of the building was spacious and I examined it, as carefully as I could, for obstructions such as electrical cable, but could see none.

The temptation was too great! Casting my last shred of sanity to the winds, I dived upon the building and arranged matters so that the bottom of my dives and loops were in fact virtually within the space enclosed by the palace walls.

Feeling that honour had been satisfied and by now caring little for my fate, I staggered wearily back to Tamagawa, which I was relieved to find, having no map. As I taxied in I was nevertheless horrified to see two frock-coated, top-hatted officials walking towards me. Although I mentally christened them "Tweedledum and Tweedledee," I felt that they must be harbingers of doom. What *had* I done? It must be unforgivable. Tweedledum advanced to me and bowed. "His Imperial Majesty . . . sssss . . . ," he said, "has commanded us . . . sssss . . . to thank you for an excellent . . . sssss . . . performance . . ."

All had ended well. They made me an honorary member of the Japanese Pilots' Brotherhood (the "Otori Kai," whose only other Western member was said to be General Douglas Macarthur) and our customer confirmed his order for a substantial number of aircraft. So it was all worth it – well, I suppose so!

*   *   *

When we introduced the aerobatic Auster Aiglet Trainer at Farnborough, its gyrations were noticed by a visiting team from Persia (Iran) who saw in it a plane suitable for their government training scheme. After the necessary preliminaries in England I soon found myself out in Persia negotiating single-handed, with our excellent agent as interpreter, a contract for a sizeable number of aircraft, with spares. Daily sessions were held with the Persian team of specialists, each eager to score a point

UPPER: World Aerobatic Champion Betty Skelton with her biplane *"Little Stinker,"* seen at Gatwick in 1948.
LOWER: Enthusiastic Japanese youngsters help to push out Ranald Porteous' Auster prior to his aerobatic display at Tamagawa, Tokyo, 1952.
Photos: via Ranald Porteous.

THREE SOMEWHAT UNUSUAL ATTITUDES SHOWN BY
RANALD PORTEOUS' AEROPLANES!
UPPER: Taxying (?) the Chilton-Train G-AFSV at Derby, c.1947.
Photo: via Ranald Porteous.
CENTRE: Brushing the grass at a Derby Aero Club display in 1948 in
Messenger 2A G-AILL. Photo: via Ranald Porteous.
LOWER: Doing his famous one-wheel landing at the 1952 Farnborough
display in Aiglet Trainer G-AMMS. Photo: Richard Riding.

UPPER: "Magical moments" in Harvard 2B KF269 of No.3 FTS, Feltwell, 1953.
LOWER: National Service pilots Ambrose Barber and John Crabb with 208 AFS Vampire FB5 VZ279 at Merryfield, 1954.
Photos: via Ambrose Barber.

UPPER: Arthur Ord-Hume's first Luton Minor, G-AFIR (seen here in its third reincarnation), on September 22nd 1956.
Photo: Charles E. Brown via Arthur Ord-Hume.
BELOW: Arthur's second Luton Minor, G-ASAA, built at his I.O.W. home and here pictured at Sandown c.1962. Photo: Arthur Ord-Hume.

UPPER: The scene that confronted Arthur as he arrived to join Britten-Norman on the I.O.W. in 1956. It seems that manipulating a Tiger Moth fuselage through the doorway was a fairly regular occurrence.
BELOW: Druine Turbi G-APFA, completed by Arthur, on roll-out day at Bembridge, I.O.W. during summer 1957.
Photos: Arthur Ord-Hume.

UPPER: Chris Dearden (in rear cockpit) prepares for a lunchtime flight from Redhill in Tiger Moth G-AMNN during 1957.
LOWER: A view from G-AMNN of the new Gatwick Airport under construction, summer 1957.
Photos: Peter Amos.

before the others. One dealt with specifications, another with performance, one with shipping, one with contract terms, and so on. The British Embassy was gloomy. Ten weeks, they said, was the average for seeing this whole rigmarole through.

I had by then some experience in the East and knew the charade of market-place bargaining through which one was expected to go, and in which the Westerner is invariably outplayed and outsmarted. I thought I knew a better way.

"Gentlemen," I said, "I know that in your country much store is set by the give-and-take of bargaining. Clever people from big companies are accustomed to it and will come here with margins in their prices and delivery estimates, from which they can yield concessions. But we are a small company, simple country folk, who are not well versed in these things; the prices I have given you are real ones and contain no hidden margins which we can concede. Also, our delivery estimate is what we honestly think we can do. Sixteen weeks means sixteen weeks, not twelve or ten. Nothing on earth, even the risk of losing your valued order, will make me promise less, when I know we cannot achieve it. Surely you would think the less of me if I were to do so?"

This *naïveté* seemed to baffle the Persians, who retired for a couple of days apparently into a council of war. When next summoned I was asked whether I would accept a penalty clause on sixteen weeks. I replied: "No," but I would on twenty weeks, provided that it worked both ways. Late: penalty. Early: bonus.

When this odd proposal was explained, a gust of gold-toothed laughter went round the room and, to my surprise, the grotesque wager was accepted, with much hand-shaking.

Within a week the contract was completed bilingually and cross-vetted clause by clause at the embassy, who threw a party to celebrate this tiny triumph. Some of the clauses, including the sporting two-way penalty agreement, were "way out" and I felt some anxiety as I mailed the finished product home and departed for other lands. However, the cable of congratulation which shortly intercepted me rapidly dispelled this and gave me pleasure out of all proportion to the efforts involved. Such things did not come easily. In the commercial sense, Auster was a hard and an excellent school.

As a sequel to this, after all the aircraft were delivered, correctly and on time, I was invited back to Persia as a guest of the government to tour the country and see for myself how our machines were operated there. They told me frankly that it was more in the nature of a holiday, as a reward for straight dealing. I toured the whole of the country by car and airliner in fine state for a fortnight. The drive over the mountains from Tehran to the Caspian is one of the scenic wonders of the world and the long, rich coastal belt past Ramsar to Pahlevi is a Shangri-La little known to the ordinary tourist. My guide and mentor on this marathon turned out to be none other than the brother of Billy Sharvin, known to thousands of teenagers at that time as the proprietor of "Whisky-a-Gogo" in Wardour Street.

While in Tehran I was happy to remember my good friend the late Ian Reid, Sales Manager of Scottish Aviation in Pioneer days. At that time I held a similar position with Auster Aircraft and we very successfully worked a mutual assistance pact, conceived at the Long Bar of the Park Hotel. We shared the same agent, who was misguided enough to try to keep the presence of each secret from the other, imagining for some reason that we must be deadly rivals! In the event we were both successful. I recall well the look of horror on our agent's face when Ian and I, by previous conspiracy, walked arm in arm into his office one morning.

On another occasion, during a visit to India, I found to my consternation that our agent there had entered his private Aiglet in the "Crazy-Flying Championship of All India" at a big national flying event due to be held at Kanpur. He had put me down to fly it and I protested in vain that I had done little of this kind of thing for quite a while. Secretly, I was decidedly scared. "Crazy-flying" is a delicate art, involving some fairly marginal judgement near the ground, and it seemed risky to introduce a free-for-all element of competition, especially in such hot-blooded surroundings.

The tragi-comedy unfolded in due course. The sun beat down mercilessly upon a packed crowd of about sixty thousand and the Tannoy system whipped up a great deal of interest and anticipation. I gathered that I was being cracked up as something of a visiting celebrity, which made me lament even more bitterly my lack of practice. However, the little Aiglet responded nobly. It lent itself remarkably well to this kind of display, having a self-aligning undercarriage which enabled it to be waltzed sideways from wheel to wheel, and its controls and characteristics generally were excellent, quite devoid of the sudden trim changes with yaw which were such a trap for the unwary in many other aircraft. The huge Indian crowd seemed to appreciate its antics and their applause was generous. I was eventually adjudged the winner, meriting (*inter alia*) an introduction to President Nehru, who had been at school with my brother.

The inevitable soon happened, however, and the next competitor stalled his aircraft and spun a half-turn straight into the ground. At this shocking moment, before the dust had settled and while ambulances and fire-tenders rushed across the parched earth to the smashed machine, an excited voice came stridently through the public-address speakers: "Ladies and gentlemen, you have just witnessed a terrible accident. We do not know whether the pilot is dead. Joyriding will now commence."

Austers of early post-war origin were derived from the wartime Mk.V. Although they were staunchly reliable and generously forgiving, they were characterless and wishy-washy in their handling. The Gipsy-engined AOP.Mk.6 and T.Mk.7 of this period were downright nasty, with gross trim changes and some less-forgiving characteristics. These vices were only partly alleviated much, much later, in the AOP's civil derivative, the Terrier.

The later J-series Austers were, however, steadily developed to a point where their control effectiveness and harmonisation were really excellent: well ahead of US contemporaries.

One of Auster's most interesting facets was the wide range of uses to which its aircraft were put and thereby the broad spectrum of interesting people whom one met. Spells with the Army Air Corps on Salisbury Plain and in Malaya were especially rewarding, as were the Flying Club and air racing fraternities at home.

I recall having to arrange a flying-and-buns hospitality day at Rearsby for a horde of invited journalists covering the introduction of a new "sky-shouting" ("aerial address" to the dignified) set-up which we had developed and were promoting. At the end of a day given to various demonstrations, photography etc, most of the journalists seemed satisfied and began to disperse, only the duo from the "DAILY MIRROR" remaining and keenly requesting further flights, demonstrations, poses etc. Pleased by this show of intelligent interest, my colleagues and I complied willingly with everything they asked and eventually bade them a cordial farewell, feeling that some helpful publicity might well result.

Sure enough, next morning the front page of the "MIRROR" showed my manly features, I being seated in the aircraft holding a microphone and presumably flying the machine. So far, so good; but underneath was a bold headline: "Sky-Barker Porteous shouts at Britain," with adjacent editorial whose gist was: "New Menace from the Skies" – "Should this be allowed?" and so on. Oh! well . . . in such matters *any* publicity is better than none. We all had a good laugh.

One sometimes hears *aficionados* arguing as to which was the best (or worst, or fastest, or slowest, or noisiest, or nastiest) of the Austers and, as I was lucky enough at one time or another to fly all of them, a trimmed patchwork of reminiscences may at least be provocative.

The fastest? Certainly the J/5E. This was prepared for air-racing, in the days when these events carried some commercial prestige. It was basically a J/5G Autocar fuselage with a Cirrus Major 3 engine (nicely polished internally), flapless J/4 wings – cut down to a total span of only 30ft – and an Arrow undercarriage neatly faired to the fuselage. It did about 165 mph and I remember clearly the startled faces of the pilots of various Proctors, Geminis and the like which I passed with ease somewhere near Littlehampton in an air race which started at Bournemouth. Alas, the thrust-race housing bolts took a dislike to these un-Auster-like capers and the J/5E ended its brief but glorious dash by the skin of its tyres on Lympne airfield in a cloud of very expensive blue smoke, having frightened me quite badly below the level of Beachy Head.

The slowest? Without a doubt the J/2 Arrow. This flapless little aircraft, with its 75 hp Continental engine, was in many ways rather appealing, provided that one's destination was either downwind or within ten miles.

The best? Unhesitatingly the Atlantic. This delightful and beautifully furnished tricycle four-seater was an infinitely better aeroplane in every way than the later Beagle Airedale, which was both much costlier and heavier. The Atlantic, which flew about 10 hours in prototype form, was well ahead of the contemporary Tripacer. We had a market for a goodly number of these ready and waiting, had the disastrous Agricola decision not supervened.

The worst? Here I am beset with indecision between the Avis, a civil four-seater prototype which both taxied and flew like an inebriated porpoise, and the A2/45, a military prototype with a Gipsy Queen (or Six) engine, which looked like a Fieseler Storch but flew like a jellyfish in a vat of vodka.

The most interesting? Probably the Agricola. This low-wing specialist agricultural aircraft, after an inauspicious beginning, was developed into an excellent flying machine. It was well suited to its principal duty of top-dressing in New Zealand but was, however, a commercial white elephant, based on marketing misconceptions which should never have prevailed.

The formula for the Aiglet Trainer resulted from a distillation of requirements found during a trip which I made through the Middle and Far East during 1950. The prototype first flew in mid-1951 and appeared at Farnborough that year. The Avalanche was concocted for its second year.

The origin of the Avalanche was amusing. Realising that Farnborough was approaching and having done little flying since the previous year, I took our demonstrator Aiglet Trainer up to see whether I could string an improved programme together, being reluctant to dish up "the mixture as before." After some experimentation, it occurred to me that a flick roll from inverted to inverted at the top of a loop would look spectacular from the ground and might help attract the attention of wandering overseas customers which, in the event, it did. The Aiglet's flick/spin recovery characteristics were crisp and consistent and, after a little practice, I found that this manoeuvre could be done accurately and without undue stress, the entry speed corresponding nicely to what was attainable at the top of a slightly fast loop.

After some further practice at a discreet height, I returned overhead Rearsby aerodrome and noticed that the workforce was trooping over to the canteen for lunch. It seemed a good opportunity to try out my new programme on these captive but willing spectators. At the end of this rehearsal I landed and taxied towards the canteen, feeling that lunch had been at least mildly deserved. Upon dismounting I noticed that our Managing Director, Frank Bates, was himself heading for lunch on a converging path, so I joined him and, reminding him about Farnborough, asked whether he had by any chance seen what I had been doing overhead. He paused in his stride and then looked at me quizzically, saying: "Are you trying to tell me that that was intentional?" . . . Oh well!

Incidentally, I dreamt up the name "Avalanche" on the spur of the moment and without any special significance, save that I suppose the manoeuvre reminded me somewhat of a lump of snow tumbling head-over-heels down an Alp. I remember having my leg pulled at the time, it being alleged that the name stemmed from the fact that we were about to "'ave lunch."

The Avalanche, incidentally, found its way into the RAF training manuals under the title "The Porteous Loop." I knew nothing about this until, years later, Charles Masefield strolled cheerily into my office in flying suit to tell me that he had been practising "Porteous Loops" in a Chipmunk. "Practising *what*?" I asked. He explained and seemed amazed that I did not know.

*   *   *

The SBAC display was, in those days, held annually at Farnborough and was the lynch-pin of most of our activities. Indeed, the aircraft industry's calendar was once designated: Jan., Feb., Mar., Apr., May, June, July, Aug., Farn., Oct., Nov., Dec.! For those involved it was immensely exciting and interesting, doubly so for myself, perhaps, as my responsibilities embraced both the sales efforts and flying – the latter being part of the former really. It involved me in some heroic, if futile, efforts to be in four places at once; the exhibition stand, the company 'chalet,' our static aircraft exhibits and the test-pilots' briefings as well as the flying programme – not to mention the lavish buffet lunches! I was glad occasionally to take refuge there from the madhouse of the exhibition.

For some years I enjoyed my status as a kind of faithful "Tail-end-Charlie" and I was for a while the only pilot allowed to fly in the display without a radio, an indirect compliment which was much appreciated. I remember one day (a Saturday, I think, as there was a large crowd assembled) when the weather deteriorated to such an extent that the whole flying programme had to be shelved. There was a misty drizzle falling from a very low, amorphous cloud-base. I was summoned and asked if I could do my best to entertain the disappointed spectators for as long as possible . . . "carte blanche, but don't kill yourself!" Accordingly I took off in the Aiglet Trainer and cavorted around in the rain, low down and mainly between the spectators and the runway. It was soon evident that, while the cloudbase allowed horizontal, straight rolls, attempting anything in the vertical plane, even simple loops, took one rapidly into the cloud, too near the ground for comfort. Nevertheless, donning my ill-fitting hero's cloak, I persevered, carrying out various rolls-off-the-top etc. more or less by memory, emerging in each case dead on line. Just as I was beginning to feel smug about all this, I entered another such antic to find the cloud lower and thicker than before – and the rain heavier. Memory was increasingly stretched during this prolonged obliteration and I felt relieved when the runway appeared dimly, straight ahead, allowing me to do a couple of rolls carefully aligned with it, followed by a vertical reverse, which took me into the murk again for a short while.

As I dived back along the line it seemed to me that the crowd of spectators was larger than I remembered and, peering through the rain-streaked perspex, I was mortified to see dimly that this 'crowd' was in fact a line of large military aircraft. I had in fact come out of the cloud at the runway intersection and had picked up the wrong runway! As I rather prided myself on meticulous placing and alignment, this was a matter for suicide or at least running away to sea. But worse was to follow. After landing I was thanked profusely and it soon became apparent that nobody, but *nobody*, had noticed!

The flying displays at Farnborough were run on a firm but loose rein, relying on the intelligence and absolute integrity of all concerned who were, after all, people of high calibre and standing. Time-keeping was immaculate and the very nature of it all allowed of some flexibility and rapid improvisation, should a hitch occur. Paris, on the other hand, was ludicrously over-organised and therefore inflexible. I once had the pleasure of persuading the RAF officer who had controlled the previous Farnborough to come with me to the pilots' briefing meeting, lasting some two hours, as against Farnborough's usual 15-20 minutes. He nearly died of laughing!

My only flippant memory of flying at Paris was of being told on my radio, halfway round a loop, to land *immediately* as the American Hustler was due. I complied by letting the Aiglet hurtle towards the runway in a series of flick rolls, sandwiched between the fronds of a "falling leaf," proclaiming to the controller as I did so: " . . . X-ray Charlie on finals," to which the reply came up: "Such a finals 'ave I nevair seen . . . nevair!"

There was truly wonderful flying to be seen at these displays and, even now, I am sometimes asked which of the pilots or aircraft gave me the most pleasure to watch. Without hesitation I must name the late Bill Bedford in the Hawker Hunter. It was consummate artistry, real poetry in motion. Bill did nothing that the others did not and his perfect positioning was equalled by at least some of them, but it was the way he did it all. Any attempt to describe this tiny margin of super-excellence would involve hackneyed terms such as "harmony," "flow" and "smoothness" – so I shall make no such attempt.

I deny being influenced in this by the apocryphal (?) tale of the commentator who, in tones of rising excitement, proclaimed: "Look to the left . . . towards Laffan's Plain . . . he's coming in very low . . . very fast . . . here comes Bill Bunter in his Bedford!"

Two others whom I must mention were Duncan Mackintosh in the Miles Student jet trainer, whose performance was always of Bedfordian quality in grace and accuracy, and (surprisingly perhaps) a certain Flight Sergeant Harrison (I think, though I have no record of it) who gave an impeccable and comprehensive show of continuous aerobatics, perfectly placed over the runway in front of the crowd in, of all things, a Vulcan jet bomber. His whole performance was thoughtful and controlled, so that the huge machine stayed in the low-to-medium segment of its speed range and seemed never to come near to an excessive g-loading. Never mind that it may have been unauthorised and illegal. I have no idea what became of this chap, though I heard that there was a court-martial in the wind.

I can only hope that the RAF, whatever rap they may have administered to his knuckles, did not curtail his flying career. Failing this, my advice to him would be to ensure that, when he finally sets course for St Peter's arrival desk, he goes armed with a video tape of his performance at Le Bourget. It should qualify him for immediate admission to The Great Flying School Beyond the Clouds.

*　　*　　*

"There I was . . ." stories have always been a big yawn . . . and best avoided. Nevertheless since, after much of a lifetime spent in 'personal' flying, I am sometimes asked for tales of fright, one or two alarming reminiscences may be in order, even though dredging them up may be blamed for my likely nervous breakdown. 'Personal' flying, as I define it, includes all peacetime flying in small aircraft: private, sporting, testing, demonstrating, instructing and the like.

The Luton Buzzard disaster of student days happened so quickly that I can't recall having time for fear. The same can be said of the very narrow squeak with the half-flick-rolling pupil at Reading, though this shook me badly for a while afterwards. The wooden propeller of some Auster variant (I forget which) disintegrated on the top of a low loop during a display rehearsal at Rearsby. I was over the airfield anyway (albeit low) and nothing seemed more natural than a downward half-roll out followed by a gently curving arrival on the grass. All very dull so far: terror – nil.

Ah! but I do recall one bad fright during my spell at Auster. I was carrying out spinning trials, CG aft, on the prototype of the (then) new AOP Mark 9. This was equipped with a tail parachute which could be relied upon to check any spin which 'went flat' or otherwise proved uncontrollable. Sure enough, the first spin of any length which I attempted flattened dramatically and resisted every recovery action in the book – or in my head. Eventually I reached up to the overhead lever which was connected to the parachute release mechanism and began to push it forward. Just then there was a loud 'bang' and the seat structure collapsed, whereupon I found myself sprawling on the floor, firmly centrifuged into the rear of the cabin, well out of reach of any controls and quite unable to move towards them. Worst of all, I did not know whether my efforts with the lever had succeeded. Certainly nothing had happened after what seemed an age, though it was probably only a few seconds.

Suddenly the rotation stopped and I was catapulted (seat wreckage and all) forwards, feet firmly on the instrument panel. Between them and past the nose I could see the United Kingdom, directly ahead and approaching quite rapidly. I had to struggle hard to reestablish myself at (or near) the controls. Again, this seemed to take an age – far longer than it can really have done – but I eventually found myself, at floor level and therefore quite unable to see ahead, easing the aircraft out of its dive, squinting sideways past the bottom of the cabin window panel. The flap control was out of reach, as was the tail parachute lever, which did not matter since the parachute had gone, probably released involuntarily by me during my struggles to get forward. Levering myself up awkwardly on the edge of the flattened seat-frame enabled me to see through the corner of the windscreen just enough to guide the aircraft back to Rearsby and to do a flapless landing, completed to my immeasurable relief. The nature of my predicament had meanwhile filtered down to Rearsby via the radio and there was something of a reception committee waiting on the tarmac. From its ranks there emerged my charming young secretary, bearing towards me a glass of sherry on a tray! This almost made the whole thing worthwhile . . . . bless her! The cause of all this was found to be a missing securing-pin, overlooked during assembly. This had concentrated all the stress on the opposite pin and seat leg, which failed comprehensively.

My worst scares were suffered during flying of a quite different nature. Firstly, my 3 days 23 hours flight from Croydon to Johannesburg, seven-up in a Consul, found me at night over the vast North African desert and heading in a dramatically wrong direction, due to spurious bearings being received from Wadi Halfa on an ancient W/T set. Our bacon was only saved by their letting off a massive display of pyrotechnics at our request. These we saw as a tiny pinprick of light some eighty miles away and almost at right angles to our instructed heading, which would have taken us right into the heart of the desert, where our chances of a safe landing or of rescue would have been nil. On landing I blew my top to the 'Gonio' operator, an African corporal, whose grinning reply was: "Yes, baas, there's something very funny about the bearings from here. We lost a Dakota last week!"

Later on the same trip, at Kasama in the north of what is now Zambia, we suffered an undetected fracture of the Bowden cable operating the engines' hot/cold air selectors. This resulted in a take-off in very hot conditions, some distance above sea level, with the air intakes effectively at 'hot,' though set for 'cold.' We were well past the point of no return on the 1,000 yard runway when I began to realise that the loss of power from both engines was due to something other than the extreme heat. As we were by now just airborne there was no option but to continue. With hundreds of hours instructing experience on Oxfords in comparable conditions in neighbouring Rhodesia, I trusted to my 'feel' and it paid off, but only just. The terrain sloped slightly upwards as we went and at no time for the first two miles or so were we ever more than about 20 feet from the rocks and bushes. One mile an hour too slow and we would have sunk into them; one too fast and we would have flown in. I wished I had gone fishing.

Later, in Rhodesia, where there were identifiable landmarks, I found that, once again, we were heading in a vastly wrong direction, due this time to our magnetic compass having suddenly developed a huge deviation, over 50° as I discovered later. This was apparently caused by the reversal of the Earth's magnetic dip as we moved into the Southern Hemisphere, allowing the fairly massive built-in corrections to take charge. As I knew the country and as the weather was clear, the whole of the rest of the trip (some 700 miles) was flown by map-reading, setting the directional gyros by landmarks such as roads or distant hills.

Lastly, on the subject of 'frighteners,' I must give pride of place to the Beagle 206(S) which I took from Shoreham to Buenos Aires in 1966. My route took me via Prestwick, Iceland, Greenland and Baffin Island and it was a very scary experience. First of all, over the sea between Scotland and Iceland, our HF radio packed up. This did not worry me unduly, as I believed that someone would be found at Reykjavik who could replace or repair it and also that our dual VORs would serve us in the USAF-dominated Arctic. Both assumptions proved wrong. The HF lay dead until Florida while, more seriously, the Americans were found to have removed their network of VOR beacons from the arctic wastes, without any information about this having been fed to our civil authorities who had briefed me.

Trouble began over the Greenland ice cap, invisible because of cloud, interminable due to a massive headwind. The oil pressure gauges began to fluctuate, slightly at first then more noticeably. My very able companion and engineer on this trip, Ian Aslett, suggested that we increase power settings as he rightly suspected 'coring' (partial freezing) and believed that anything which might raise the temperature of the whole installation might help. It seemed right to do so since the oil pressure remained reasonable, though not yet entirely stable. At last, to my great relief, we came out of cloud almost within sight of Sondreström Fjord and found the airstrip, tucked into the head of this great cleft, with the aid of their VOR.

After some minor modifications suggested by cable from Shoreham, test flights seemed to indicate that our oil coring problem was solved and we took off a few days later for Frobisher on Baffin Island, Canada's frozen, treeless wilderness of rock, ice – and mountains.

Our track to the first waypoint, an ADF beacon on the Baffin Island coast which "might or might not be operating as it is believed to be smothered in snow," took us over an area of rocky mountains, some 9,000 feet high and about 90 miles away. Accordingly I climbed to 14,000 feet and set course on a VOR back-track, still in a milky-grey cloud with zero visibility and no variations of texture or light and shade. After half an hour or so we estimated that we must be over the mountains but, as warned, had so far failed to pick up the Baffin Island coast beacon, now some fifty miles ahead. All, otherwise, seemed to be going well when our relative serenity was suddenly shattered by coughs and hesitations, first in one engine then the other. No amount of jugglery with the various engine and propeller controls had the slightest effect and within a few minutes we were reduced to a powerless glide, with no more than an occasional weak "chuff" from either engine. I turned immediately left on to a course at roughly right-angles to the line cut by Sondreström Fjord, which I guessed to be some twenty miles away, and continued the nightmare glide. Eleven, ten, nine thousand feet . . . we must now be level with the mountain tops . . . eight, seven, six . . . now the milky void around us began to darken, first on one side then the other as we presumably passed perilously close to rocky mountain faces . . . five, four, three, two . . . and I thought I caught a momentary glimpse of rocky terrain passing beneath us . . . fifteen hundred feet and – bingo! – we emerged into clear air, over the water, well towards the middle of the fjord. Both engines immediately began to pick up and within a minute we were humming evenly back up the long fjord to the airstrip, mightily relieved. They told us there that our weak transmission faded and we disappeared from their radar when we descended into the mountains and that they had mentally written us off. I suppose the chances of threading 'blind' down through those mountains must have been about 1:6, so Someone had been good to us. I gave thanks where due.

Ian Aslett, normally good-humoured and possessed of a refreshingly caustic wit, went ballistic on receipt of some rather unimaginative advice by cable from Shoreham and we agreed that progress thereafter would be slow and cautious. The truth of it all was that not nearly enough research had been done on flight in low-temperature dry-ice cloud as it affected the big Continental TSIO 540 engines supplied by Rolls-Royce and installed by Beagle. The air induction trunk incorporated a 180° U-bend, before which the air had to pass hot regions of the engine, warm enough in fact to liquefy instantly the microscopic grains of dry ice ingested. When these tiny droplets reached the U-bend, itself very cold, they naturally tended by inertia to travel straight on, refreezing instantly on the wall of the bending trunk. This ice accretion could build up rapidly, with results as described. Foreseeable? It can be made to sound so but the real problem had probably been that ultra-cold dry-ice cloud conditions are seldom found in Britain.

During our penultimate stop, in Uruguay, Ian received disquieting news of family illness and had to abandon ship and jet home. He was much missed on the last leg to Buenos Aires. Ian, a most talented engineer, later went to Japan and I believe was largely responsible for the design of the much-admired Mazda 2-seater sports car, no stranger to our roads. He died in 1994.

* * *

Following this monumental excursion, which had included a great deal of flying about the USA and the 'netting' of a good agent with a substantial order, my long and enjoyable years of 'personal' flying drew gradually to a close, to be superseded by a great deal of jetting around the world on company business, I having become Director of Marketing at Scottish Aviation, whose motto (well justified) was "The World O'er" . . . I recall more than once sitting back in the luxury of a 747, aperitif in hand, surveying the vast premises around me and thinking: "This thing is an aeoplane and we're actually flying – I can't believe it!", following which my mind would inevitably travel back to my little Chilton.

Now, in total retirement, I pilot our small motor cabin cruiser about a loch in Galloway, seeing some strange relationship between curving gently in to a smooth arrival at the marina jetty and a well-judged approach and landing in a small aircraft. Indeed an African General, basically a pilot who had become C. in C. of his country's defence force, remarked when put in charge of the wheel: "My goodness! It's just like flying an aircraft, isn't it?" Well . . . at six knots . . . not quite!

Shining a lamp back along the corridor of memory has been fun. Its beam has inevitably been very narrow, concentrated by the lens of my love of 'personal' flying. I hope that, in picking out a few of the images which it has illuminated most brightly, I have avoided most of the distorting mirrors.

My wife, Susan, won't let the urge to fly quite extinguish itself. Every year, on my birthday, she has presented me with a neat little green ticket

173

from the local flying school entitling me to a *"30-minute Trial Flying Lesson with a fully-qualified instructor, during which you will be allowed to handle the controls."* As in the King's Cup she comes along in the rear seat of the Grumman Cheetah, but nowadays armed with a video camera.

So far I have not disgraced myself but, at 82, who knows?

CHAPTER 16

THREE WEEKS IN THE LIFE . . .

by

Peter Campbell

Hopefully you'll forgive me if you recognise some of the details at the beginning of this chapter; they may have been mentioned before in *"The Fifties Revisited"* and in *"Tails of the Fifties."*

My interest in aircraft had blossomed from 1952 onwards due to my being at boarding school at Lancing College in Sussex, which conveniently overlooked Shoreham Airport, and to my being encouraged by a fellow pupil, Tim Foster. Indeed most of my spare time throughout each term seemed to be spent, if not actually *on* the aerodrome (which was of course 'out of bounds' to school pupils), at the top of a grassy bank overlooking it. Of course I was not the first, nor the last, to be fascinated by the place.

After 'A' Level examinations were finished near the end of the summer term it was common for pupils to get some work experience of one kind or another; my turn came in 1955, and early that year I resolved that I would somehow arrange to get some work experience with F.G. Miles Ltd on the Airport. However this proved a lot more difficult than I had thought; in fact there was a lot of opposition at first to the idea, not from George Miles, who was most cooperative all the way through, but from both my parents and also the school's Headmaster.

I still have two letters that were written on the subject to my father in early June 1955, which show that I must have been considered as something of a problem case! The first was from the Headmaster, John Dancy, and the second from my housemaster, Sam Jagger, who was not only a brilliant squash player in his day and latterly an excellent coach, but who, fortunately for me, was also a pretty understanding sort of chap.

The first letter read as follows:

"Dear Mr Campbell,
Thank you for writing about your son. I am glad to see that you feel as I do about the matter in general.
We do not, as a matter of fact, normally allow boys to work outside the school, and I have told Peter that his case is not similar to that of other boys who are being allowed to go on courses of educational value, some of which are with industrial firms and others not. However, in view of his immense

keenness for this subject I told him I would consider it as a special case, even though I do not myself share his tastes any more than you do.

I have now asked Mr Jagger if he will go down to see the Manager of the airport and ensure that Peter will be given work to do which is both sufficient and useful to himself and to the Aerodrome authorities. Provided that may be arranged I am prepared to allow him to go. I will see that you are informed when the final decision is taken.

Yours sincerely etc."

The follow-up, from my Housemaster, read thus:

"Dear Mr Campbell,

I have today been down to see Mr Miles at Shoreham Airport. He and I have arranged that, with your permission, Peter will do three weeks in the Assembly Sheds there. This will entail a full six-day week from 8.30 to 5 and he will be the mate of a fitter on constructing aircraft there. He can have two days finally on the Coding Systems and the Landing Control of aircraft.

I have spoken to the Headmaster and he is now quite agreeable to Peter going there. Previously he was doubtful because he did not want him to slack about for three weeks after his 'A' Level exams and in this I quite agreed with him. I too am now in favour of the project.

Mr Miles is impressed with Peter and he should get a good report on him from his foreman after the three weeks; he says that he would be quite willing to recommend him to de Havillands for a place in the experimental and technical training establishment at Farnborough.

Kindest regards etc."

When the time finally came, I actually spent a whole week in Air Traffic Control, and all the lunchtime breaks during the next two weeks were also spent there! These weeks I remember with great pleasure and the period was without doubt the most fulfilling of my young life up until then.

A few years ago I learned from Phil Ansell (whom I had known since those early days when I used to meet him on the airfield occasionally) that all the old Aircraft Movements Books from Shoreham covering the 1950s were to be thrown out (quite unbelievable!), and fortunately I managed to acquire a selection of them. The oldest ones still in existence proved to date from the autumn of 1954 onwards, but that meant that the book covering July 1955, when I was working at Shoreham, should be amongst them. Imagine my feelings of nostalgia then, when opening up the book in question some forty years on, to find several pages of entries all – or in part – in my (still recognisable) handwriting! Two of these I am reproducing here, to give an idea of what a typical summer day's movements were like at Shoreham back then.

East Anglian Flying Services, who at the time flew between Ipswich, Rochester, Southend, Shoreham, Portsmouth, Paris (Le Bourget), Jersey

& Guernsey, operated regular scheduled services (except in the winter months) with Dragon Rapides G-AEMH, G-AKJZ, G-AKRN & G-AKSC, and in 1955 were just starting to introduce Doves as well (G-ANVU, G-AOBZ & G-AOCE). The Southern Aero Club had two Tiger Moths (acquired from the Midland Flying Club at Elmdon), G-AKXO & G-ALVP, and two Hawk Trainers, G-AITS & G-AIZK. There were several other active resident aircraft including F.G. Miles Ltd's Gemini G-AKEL, H.B. Pursey's Gemini G-AJOJ, T. Carlyle's Messenger G-AIBD, E.W. Westbrook's Messenger G-AJDM and Meridian Airmaps' Autocrat G-AGXU and Aerovan G-AJKP.

During the mid-fifties a number of Flying Clubs used Shoreham fairly regularly as a cross-country destination, the most common aircraft seen being either Auster variants, Tiger Moths or Hawk Trainers, with the occasional Hornet Moth. Amongst these Clubs were Airways Aero Associations, Christchurch Aero Club, Croydon Flying Club, Experimental Flying Group, Ford RNVR Flying Group, Hampshire Flying Club, Hookwood Flying Group, London Aero Club, Nightscale Flying Services, Penguin Flying Club, Royal Artillery Aero Club, Royal Naval Flying Club, Short Bros & Harland Flying Club, Southern Flying Schools, Surrey Aviation, Universal Flying Services and Wiltshire School of Flying. Most if not all of those names are with us no longer, but their mention will doubtless stir up some memories for any reader who was involved with club flying at that time.

Other regular movements involved the Dragon Rapides of Don Everall Aviation and Marshall's Flying Services, together with the Gemini of Flightways; these were used to ferry jockeys, trainers etc. to and from the regular race meetings at Brighton Racecourse.

My first day working at Shoreham should have been Monday July 4th, but such was my keenness that I unofficially started on Sunday 3rd. I was apprenticed to a vivacious red-haired lady air traffic controller (after racking my brains for some time I recall that her name was Yvonne Mitchell – I think!); she was very patient with her new charge, who wanted to be doing absolutely everything connected with ATC without any previous experience!

The first movement of that day was a placement flight in an East Anglian Dove by Capt. Whellem from Southend at 08.00, which then left for Guernsey with passengers at 08.33. Cecil Pashley checked the weather prospects in Hawk Trainer G-AIZK, and from then on the day became quite busy. Several Army Austers arrived for the start of a summer camp, which lasted some ten days, with a variety of aircraft coming and going during that period. Also Flt. Lt. Woods, a regular visitor, brought in Harvard KF729 from White Waltham, on this occasion staying overnight and leaving at 07.30 the next morning.

3rd July 1955

INBOUND

Type of Flight	Type of Aircraft	Regis. Letters	Captain	From	A.T.D.	E.T.A.	A.T.A.
S	DOVE	G-ANVU	WHELLEM	SOUTHEND			0800
PC	MAGISTER	G-AIZK	PASHLEY	LOCAL			0925
S	DOVE	G-AOBZ	BURGESS	SOUTHEND			0930
PC	AUSTER	G-AGXP	WILLMOTT	PORTSMOUTH			1002
PC	MAGISTER	GAITS	PASHLEY	LOCAL			1013
PC	GEMINI	G-AKEL	BRUNICARDI	LOCAL			1025
M	AUSTER 6	VF-581	CAPT HALL	HENLOW			1116
M	CHIPMUNK	WP905	CAPT DUNN	HENLOW			1117
PC	MAGISTER	G-AIZK	ATKINS	LOCAL			1118
S	DOVE	G-ANVU	WHELLEM	JERSEY			1119
PC	MAGISTER	G-AITS	FRY	LOCAL			1121
PC	T.MOTH	G-ALVP	PASHLEY	LOCAL			1133
PC	GEMINI	G-AKEL	BRUNICARDI	LOCAL			1120
PC	MAGISTER	G-AIZK	SWALOR	LOCAL			1154
PC	TIGERMOTH	G-ALVP	WHEELE	LOCAL			1157
M	AUSTER 6	VX110	JONES	HUCKNALL			1239
PC	TMOTH	G-ALVP	WHEELE	LOCAL			1240
PC	AUSTER	G-AGXP	WILLMOTT	PORTSMOUTH			1308
PC	T.MOTH	G-ALVP	WHEELE	LOCAL			1312
M	AUSTER 6	VF581	JONES	LOCAL			1320
S	DOVE	G-AOBZ	BURGESS	LE BOURGET			1359
PC	T.MOTH	G-ALVP	MOCKETT	LOCAL			1405
PC	GEMINI	G-AKEL	BRUNICARDI	LOCAL			1423
PC	MAGISTER	G-AIZK	PASHLEY	LOCAL			1440
M	HARVARD	KF729	F/F WOODS	WHITE WALTHAM			1500
PC	MAGISTER	G-AIZK	PASHLEY	LOCAL			1523
PC	T.MOTH	G-ALVP	WHEELE	LOCAL			1610
PC	GEMINI	G-AKEL	BRUNICARDI	LOCAL			1630
S	RAPIDE	G-AKRN	PASCOE	JERSEY			1638
PC	AUSTER 5	G-ANHS	HENRY	BEMBRIDGE			1720

178

3rd July 1955

OUTBOUND

Type of Flight	Type of Aircraft	Regis. Letters	Captain	TO ~~From~~	E.T.D.	A.T.D.	A.T.A.
S	DOVE	G-ANVU	WHELLEM	GUERNSEY		0833	
PC	MAGISTER	G-AIZK	PASHLEY	LOCAL		0920	
PC	GEMINI	G-AKEL	BRUNICARDI	LOCAL		1000	
S	DOVE	G-AOBZ	BURGESS	LE BOURGET		1007	
PC	MAGISTER	G-AIIS	PASHLEY	LOCAL		1010	
PC	AUTOCRAT	G-AGXP	WILLMOTT	PORTSMOUTH		1016	
PC	MAGISTER	G-AIIS	FRY	LOCAL		1040	
PC	T.MOTH	G-ALVP	PASHLEY	LOCAL		1042	
PC	MAGISTER	G-AIZK	ATKINS	LOCAL		1043	
S	DOVE	G-ANVU	WHELLEM	JERSEY		1142	
PC	GEMINI	G-AKEL	BRUNICARDI	LOCAL		1110	
PC	T.MOTH	G-ALVP	WHEELE	LOCAL		1110	
PC	MAGISTER	G-AIZK	SHAILER	LOCAL		1120	
PC	T.MOTH	G-ALVP	WHEELE	LOCAL		1212	
PC	T.MOTH	G-ALVP	WHEELE	LOCAL		1252	
M	AUSTER 6	VF-581	CAPT JONES	LOCAL		1314	
M	AUSTER 6	VX 110		LOCAL		1330	
PC	T.MOTH	G-ALVP	MOCKETT	LOCAL		1332	
PC	MAGISTER	G-AIZK	PASHLEY	LOCAL		1349	
PC	GEMINI	G-AKEL	BRUNICARDI	LOCAL		1405	
PC	AUTOCRAT	G-AGXP	WILLMOTT	BEMBRIDGE		1440	
PC	MAGISTER	G-AIZK	PASHLEY	WHITE WALTHAM		1440	
S	DOVE	G-AOBZ	BURGESS	SOUTHEND		1455	
PC	GEMINI	G-AKEL	BRUNICARDI	LOCAL		1555	
PC	GEMINI	G-AKEL	BRUNICARDI	LOCAL		1623	
S	RAPIDE	G-AKRN	PASCOE	SOUTHEND		1653	

179

Mondays were usually very quiet as the Southern Aero Club did not operate on that day, but on this particular Monday, July the 4th, there was a wide selection of visiting aircraft, as it was very hot and sunny. Unusual was the Anson G-ANWW of Fairey's, and there was also the first visit of a new type, an Auster AOP.9 from Middle Wallop, flown by Major Warburton – I remember marshalling the aircraft to the parking area and commenting as much to him as he exited the cockpit. The day also produced the inevitable crop of visitors from Croydon, and I well remember "Tiny" Marshall, one of the Surrey Flying Club instructors, who was with a student on a cross-country flight; he was, as his nickname implied, a largish individual, and being encased in the Sidcot suit obligatory for Tiger Moth flying all the year round made him look several sizes larger still. I can recall him complaining that his hayfever was really bad that day.

On Tuesday the 5th, two of the ubiquitous Aiglet Trainers operated by Airways Aero Associations paid a visit, and more service aircraft, both Chipmunks and Austers, joined the summer camp. On Wednesday the 6th, yet another Auster joined them and a Mr Barber (to whom I shall refer again later) flew in Dragon Rapide G-AHPU from Usworth for a stay of several days. An unusual visiting aircraft on Thursday the 7th was the Auster 5 G-AKOT from Denham. On Friday the 8th two individualized Hawk Trainers arrived, the red and spatted G-AIDF from Denham, and J.R. Johnston's coupé version, G-AJRT, from Fair Oaks.

On Saturday the 9th East Anglian were so busy that their Autocrat G-AGXP was pressed into service to ferry passengers between Shoreham and Portsmouth (can you imagine that being tolerated today?!). Mr Barber was due to fly his Rapide back to Usworth, but I remember him saying before he left that he didn't feel at all well. Nevertheless he took off on his long flight quite alone, and naturally we were somewhat concerned for him, although he had of course filed a flight plan. Later that afternoon we heard on the phone that he had had to make a forced landing at RAF Dishforth, after which he had collapsed at the controls; so he was really very fortunate still to be alive.

On Sunday the 10th, Capt. McDonnell, who had left for Le Bourget at 10.00 in EAFS Dove G-AOBZ, had to return shortly afterwards as one of the engines had had to be shut down in an emergency. This change of plan necessitated some quick thinking, but fortunately Dove G-AOCE had arrived from Jersey only two minutes before the emergency landing, so this was hastily turned round and eventually took over the Paris service only just over half an hour behind schedule – not bad going! But this technical problem and the resulting aircraft shortage had ramifications in all directions, and as a result the EAFS Proctor G-ANGM (something of a *rara avis*) was then used to ferry passengers in from Ipswich.

On Monday the 11th I began two weeks work in the assembly hangars, and under the tuition of Bernie Fieldwick learned how to cut, drill and shape metal. Amongst other things I recall making a couple of brackets for the engines of the Aries G-AOGA which was then nearing the final stages of construction. Also on that day Test Pilot Ian Forbes brought in Douglas Bader's Gemini G-AMGF from Croydon for a number of modifications to be carried out by F.G. Miles Ltd (which Ron Paine discussed in more detail in *"Tails of the Fifties"*), and Mr Atherton paid one of his regular visits in Cub Coupé G-AFSZ from his strip near Dorking (on Ranmore Common, I believe). On Tuesday the 12th Mr Cooper's Hornet Moth G-AEET passed through en route from Le Havre to Southend.

Wednesday the 13th produced a marvellous sight early in the morning, namely four Ansons arriving in formation from Aston Down. I remember being at work in the main hangar and dashing out to see what all the noise was about! With another Anson arriving from Manston at lunchtime, this made an unforgettable line-up of no less than five of the type parked up together. Friday the 15th produced "Buster" Paine's famous red Proctor G-AHNA, which came in from Blackbushe at 19.50 and stayed over until the 17th. That day also saw the arrival by road of Meteor FR.9 VZ608 for top-secret modifications (discussed in more detail in *"Tails of the Fifties"*).

That weekend saw me back in ATC, quite voluntarily, after my first stint in the hangars, and Saturday the 16th produced a Naval Dominie from Lee on Solent, NF871. Other visitors of note that day were Vivien Varcoe in his familiar Messenger G-AKKG, a Gemini, G-AMME, ferried in by Company Pilot Mr Brunicardi for minor work (and returning to Derby on the 18th), and Chipmunk WP861 from White Waltham with Flt. Lt. Woods; I remember being told at the time that this was the aircraft in which the Duke of Edinburgh had had lessons, but I have not seen this confirmed in other publications on the Chipmunk.

Sunday the 17th was another gorgeous day, and saw a fairly regular visitor, Dove G-AMFU from Leicester; we also had the first recorded visit by an aircraft unique both then and even today, the Spartan Arrow G-ABWP, which had been flown in from Denham. I remember going out to greet the crew, Mr Dennison and his lady companion, and they agreed to let me photograph them in front of the aircraft.

On Monday the 18th, Mr Pearse-Smith arrived in Auster 5 G-AJAK from Elstree to carry out some banner-towing along the local beaches. This was a fairly regular occurrence during the summer months, and on one occasion I remember seeing the message *"Right Monkey"* being borne over my head in bright red lettering, and wondering what it meant; it was only later that I found out it was the catchphrase of the comedian Al Read, who was doing a summer show in Brighton at the time. On

Wednesday the 20th the de Havilland Company's Beaver G-AMVU paid a visit from Hatfield, flown by a Mr Lucas; George Miles, who always enjoyed the opportunity of adding new types to his logbook, took it up during the afternoon for a twenty-minute flight. Also on that day the Sparrowjet G-ADNL was flown up to Elmdon by Ian Forbes.

Friday the 22nd brought another regular visitor, Mr Martin's Prince G-AMLZ (normally based at Leicester but flown in on this occasion by a Mr Clark from Hendon), and another rarity, John Reid's DH.60 Moth G-AAWO from Tarrant Rushton. Saturday the 23rd saw Fox's Glacier Mints' Rapide G-AIDL and Mr Challis' Aerovan G-AISF, inbound from its base at Eastleigh and outbound to Cardiff (Rhoose). Sunday the 24th brought another formation, this time of three Proctors from Croydon, led by the redoubtable Mike Conry in G-AKDZ (some of whose exploits were recounted by Eric Bell and Lewis Benjamin in *"Tails of the Fifties"*); the other two pilots were Messrs Speechly and McDonald in G-AIKJ and G-AKXK respectively.

The following day, Monday the 25th, was the last day of the school term, but looking through the Movements Book I see that I must have paid a final visit to the aerodrome, as my handwriting records the booking in of Hornet Moth G-ADKC from Eastleigh at 10.25! On reflection I think that this visit must have been primarily to see George Miles to thank him for allowing me to work on the airfield for the previous three weeks. I can remember that, although nothing had ever been said about my being paid, he presented me with a 'gift' of £6, not an inconsiderable sum in those days.

So ended three of the most enjoyable and unforgettable weeks of my life. When I met up with George Miles again a few years ago, he did actually remember me, which was not bad considering that almost forty years had passed and neither of us had got any younger.

So perhaps now is an appropriate time to say in my own small way: "Thank you, George, for everything that you, your brother 'F.G.' and the entire team achieved over many years which contributed so much to the development aviation in this country."

ADVENTUROUS FIFTIES

by

John Pothecary

As the decade opened I was living at Thruxton (in the haunted control tower), and had the ultimate ambition of becoming an airline pilot. I had recently converted my pilot's 'A' licence to the then new PPL format. The previous year I had completed an RAF fitter's course on big piston and turbine engines, having been made redundant from an early post-war aircrew course. Memories fade faster than the ink in one's log books, so I'll take you on a trip through these and a recount of highlights of my flying in the fifties.

Early in the year of 1950 I was checked out on glider-towing with Autocrat G-AJAE, at that time owned by the Royal Artillery Aero Club. Eighteen years later I was to become her second owner. My towing effort at this time was largely confined to getting Laurie Jennings airborne in his Olympia sailplane – on one occasion he resisted by inadvertently leaving the airbrakes open – but the Autocrat did manage to get airborne. Laurie later checked me out on Moth Minor G-AFPH and Swallow G-AFCL, both of which retained their pre-war paint; he was a superb instructor who had flown and crashed Fleas pre-war and Mosquitoes during the war. He was later to achieve some fame as the pilot who was *not* in the Olympia when it was towed off Lympne by the Newbury Eon. Towards the end of the year I was allowed to fly Moth G-AAWO, then still in her Highland Airways colours of silver and turquoise.

1951 saw me put in fifty hours on 'WO towards my CPL, as well as getting experience on Heath Parasol G-AJCK and Puss Moth G-AAZP. That year was the second of the "DAILY EXPRESS" round-the-coast air races. In 1950 I had attended the Wolverhampton air races as mechanic for Geoffrey Marler who raced his Messenger G-AGOY. Now twelve months later the venue was Shoreham. He was to have raced Tiger Moth G-AMMP but sea mist prevented the August race and it was postponed to September. In each case it gave myself and companion some cross-country time in the Tiger between Thruxton and Shoreham.

The most significant happening in 1951 was that I transferred from my RAF reserve to the RAFVR and once again became a cadet pilot, this time at 19 RFS at Hamble. Chipmunks were well-established in the Reserve schools by this time; young and sprightly they were in those days, with a higher VNE than nowadays – it was possible to do two upward rolls following a maximum speed dive.

Tiger Moths were still on strength however, and I had to be checked out once again. Even in those days I thought I knew all there was to know about the DH.82 but was soon put to rights by the chain-smoking CFI Squadron Leader "Tubby" Helyer. Among the tricks this old dog imparted to me was how to taxi a Tiger downwind. I was to make use of this technique many years later when 'sailing' a Piper Cub across the Florida Lakes.

During 1951 I had obtained my first engineer's licence. The exams were taken at the ARB office in a small wooden shed on Southampton Airport. The surveyors at that time were Johnny Johnson, who became Technical Director of East African Airlines, and Tommy Dance, who retired as a senior CAA surveyor.

Early in 1952 I gave up my job as a licensed aircraft engineer. I had been accepted by Southampton University for the CPL course at their School of Navigation. In my spare time I flew with the VR and utilised the free services of my instructors towards my Assistant Flying Instructor's rating; this I obtained at the hands of Flight Lieutenant Paddy Kinnon in a VR Tiger Moth.

I was still short on night-flying for my CPL and this was completed at Thruxton during the short nights of June. We flew from the grass between the runways. The flarepath was just that, the flares being domestic kettles filled with paraffin and fitted with wicks in their spouts. A double flare marked the threshold and there were about four laid out, one hoped into wind. The ARB had insisted on a landing light being fitted, so the ingenious James Doran Webb had a car headlight fitted under the centre fuselage – quickly to be covered in black oil, rendering it useless but satisfying 'The Board.' The duty pilot had an Aldis lamp and a Very pistol, request to land being made on the downward ident. light of the Tiger, and duly acknowledged by the shivering duty pilot.

As the junior on the unit it was my job to run up and down the flare path topping up the kettles with paraffin; I was also the duty prop-swinger and refueller. Now at Thruxton we had a 14.9 hp Ford 'B' shooting brake, whose nocturnal duties usually consisted of touring the local pubs and at weekends conveying staff to the fleshpots of Salisbury. By day it carried water in churns to the local residents as we had no mains water, only a well. It also towed the bowser, another of my duties being to do the night refuelling. On one memorable occasion the bowser broke loose as I was going downhill on Runway 13 and overtook me with sparks showering from its dangling tow-bar.

Far more memorable however was the flying. Up to ten thousand feet over Salisbury Plain on a starlit night, looping and spinning back into the circuit, still brings nostalgic tears to my eyes. All my hard work paid off and I became employed for the summer by the Wiltshire School of Flying as an assistant instructor. De Havillands had just started a flying scheme whereby their employees could fly for ten shillings an hour – the normal rate for Austers, Tigers and "Maggies" was £3 an hour.

That summer was hard work. Instructors were on duty from 8.00 am to sunset plus 30, six days a week, and a target of eight or nine sorties a day was quite usual. I managed to find time to complete my CPL test at Stansted on Gemini G-AKDD, Chipmunk G-AMMA and Oxford G-AJXH. The Ministry of Civil Aviation also used Auster G-AGLK with which I was later to do a television series and Tiger G-AGRA which I ferried away to Thruxton in 1952.

I now had the experience for upgrade to a Full Instructor's rating, again courtesy of Paddy Kinnin at AST Hamble. Christchurch Aero Club had recently started up and I accepted the post of CFI. We had de Havilland employees flying for ten shillings an hour and those from Flight Refuelling flying for a pound per hour. Sir Alan Cobham took a keen interest in his flying employees; he had been a co-founder of the original Bournemouth Airport Company as Christchurch (Somerfield) aerodrome was known pre-war. I taught his sons Geoffrey and Michael to fly up to PPL status. Another help to club finances was the 'petrol rebate' whereby fuel tax was refunded to us by a grateful Labour government.

The next three years were a hard slog, 9.00 am to dusk, six days a week. Some of the routine flights would be quite unique nowadays – Christchurch to Gatwick in Ben Heron's Monarch G-AIDE to collect Stinson Reliant G-AFVR for example. There was also a winter 'charter' flight by Autocrat to Luton – no radio, no PPR. Most of southern England was covered in snow and on arrival and booking in I was told the aerodrome was closed. How was I to know? The signals area was covered in six inches of snow!

Having passed the commissioning board in the RAFVR and with my current flying experience, I could have gone back to the RAF, but I was just beginning to carve myself a career in civil aviation.

George Errington (Chief Test Pilot) of nearby de Havillands was kind enough to take me along on Ambassador test flights and to let me 'have a go.' His colleague Ron Clear, who had been a Wiltshire School of Flying apprentice a decade before myself, allowed me to fly his Comper Swift G-ACTF, and later on gave me a taste of supersonic flight in a Sea Vixen! Flights such as these gave relief to the tedium of club instructing.

An annual highlight of the year was the Royal Aero Club rally at Deauville – invitation only, cost £5. Within three hours of landing the weekend usually sank into an alcoholic haze. We took the Auster with a long-range tank, and I do remember the fuel being turned 'off' in mid-channel! The shock was such that I've not crossed the channel on one engine since!

An even greater shock was a complete engine failure in an Autocrat at about 100 feet after take-off over a housing estate. A rapid check of the mags showed that the engine would run on one mag only as the gearing had stripped and slipped on the other – I didn't see that student ever again!

In May '54 I had a charter (air taxi) flight to Pershore in the morning with a pick-up at Wolverhampton late afternoon. "Fine," I thought, "I can visit my pretty cousin at Seighford." Ben Gunn the Chief Test Pilot had given me his permission earlier.

I alerted my relative by flying low around her house, closing the throttle and shouting out of the window: "Pick me up at Seighford." Unfortunately it was the police who picked me up, and that resulted in a £20 fine in Stafford Magistrates Court. It would have been more I'm sure but for my fine defence speech. "Who wrote it?" asked the Ministry of Civil Aviation prosecutor. I could not tell him because it was my star pupil, Michael Cobham QC.

A few days later I was low-flying again on a "BOURNEMOUTH TIMES" photo sortie, around the *Britannia* on her maiden outing – but this time I had MCA permission.

As we reach the mid-point of the decade, Auster and Tiger Moth instructing, pleasure flying and air taxi were all in the day's work. I had made a lot of friends and sent many first solos, and renewed pilot's licences for at least three who had been in the 1914-18 war. It was indeed a privilege to 'check out' Sir Alan Cobham in a Tiger Moth, and also Louis Strange, whose claim to fame was that he had fallen out of his SE.5A whilst struggling to change a Lewis drum of ammunition; he held onto the gun and hauled himself back in again!

Our Auster Autocrats had been re-engined with Gipsy Majors, and as Tiger Moths came down in price, so we added to our fleet. Tiger Moths at £50 are often quoted, but as the market was flooded when Chipmunks replaced Tigers in Reserve schools, we were tendering £11-10s each – and getting them. But these well-used trainers could have hidden defects. One day after an aerobatic session including a falling leaf, I landed with the fin and rudder leaning over alarmingly – the fin post had cracked right across.

In the PPL syllabus in those days was 'action in the event of fire.' We turned off the fuel and ignition and flew down to the stall and stopped the engine. This led us neatly into the next exercise which was restarting the engine in flight. At this point the trick was to be high enough to do a couple of loops and a slow roll with the prop stationary – a very satisfying manoeuvre. Without power this was the only occasion when I managed unintentionally to tail-slide a Tiger.

To restart in flight one had to dive to near VNE to get the prop to rotate, and providing one had remembered to turn on fuel and switches the engine should restart. On this particular occasion we were at about 4,000 feet, just east of Hurn Airport, and following restart a terrific vibration occurred. I shut down again, made for Hurn and carried out a textbook forced landing on the grass to the right of Runway 35. The reason for the vibration was obvious, the outer 6 inches of prop leading edge and sheathing had departed. Incidentally, our arrival was not seen by anyone in the control tower!

For some time I had thought that this way of life was not sufficiently adventurous and had been trying to get a job in East Africa. In September 1955 I was taken on by Pest Control as a crop-spraying pilot in the Sudan for the forthcoming cotton-spraying season. I flew out to Khartoum as a passenger on Hunting Air Safari, a mode of travel almost as nostalgic as the lamented flying-boat service. An unpressurised Viking airliner gave good views of the countries overflown, together with the luxury of a night stop in the Phoenicia Hotel in Malta. The cotton-growing area in Sudan was an area between the Blue and the White Nile extending to two hundred miles south of Khartoum, and irrigated by a system of canals fed from the Sennar Dam. The fields were of a uniform 90-acre size and very flat, albeit 3,000 feet above sea level. This together with a temperature of 40-45°C meant an environment of ISA + 30-35°C.

The aeroplanes used for spraying were Auster J/5 Autocars with a Cirrus Major engine of 155 hp and carrying insecticide tanks of 75 gallons. This implied that most take-offs were at least 10% over all-up weight, and combined with ISA + 30-35°C temperatures performance was marginal to say the least. These limitations were demonstrated when in my first few days I attempted to climb a fully laden Autocar over telephone wires. I was flying downwind and, rather than climb, the aeroplane ploughed its way through the wires . . . Damage to aeroplane, one pitot head sliced off: damage to wires, Cairo to Cape communication severed: and to me, damage to my pride. But a lesson learned. Flying continuously 3 to 30 feet level provides material for lessons and demonstrates points regularly argued about in technical publications. But I know from my low-flying classroom that I can feel the difference between flying into wind and downwind: I am well aware of the gyroscopic qualities of my metal propeller and that the aeroplane loses speed in a level downwind turn.

I also learned about the dangers of chemicals used. Nicotine as an insecticide had been withdrawn in the early fifties and had been replaced as an universal antidote to white fly and aphis by DDT. We eradicated malaria from the lower Nile regions by spraying river banks and villages. Advances were made in the chemical world and organic phosphates were brought in to replace DDT. Parathion was banned but we used Malathion, only because it was more efficient and not for environmental reasons, as OPs were a derivation of wartime nerve gases and could still be as lethal. But, joy of joy, I was paid more for spraying with them, and I returned home after four months having earned more than I had in two years as a flying instructor.

My priority now was an instrument rating, and to acquire this I went back to Hamble and flew again with the instructors that I had known in the VR, being again re-acquainted with the Airspeed Oxford; this I had always regarded as being the best of twin-engined training aeroplanes.

One had to take the IR test on a DH Dove at Stansted and this I had trouble with at first as the Oxford and Dove are totally different aeroplanes, conceived twelve years apart, but who cared with IR tests at £20 a go? Later on I came to love the Dove/Devon as another delightful de Havilland type.

Jobs were not easy to find but I joined Hunting Air Surveys at Elstree as an 'Aerofilms' pilot. For the early summer of 1956 I roamed the length and breadth of Britain on contract and 'spec'-photography in their Autocar G-AOFM. All this fine-weather flying was not of great use to me and the Christchurch Aero Club called me back for the remainder of the season to fly their Gemini and Rapides on charter work.

There was of course lots of instructing and aerobatics in Tiger Moths. That year I entered the Lockheed Aerobatic competition and opened with a half roll and an inverted falling leaf – spectacular but expensive in height – followed by a Cuban 8 and ending with a four-point hesitation roll. But the Tigers were outclassed by the Stampes, Zlin and Jungmeister and the pilots by Biancotto and Aresti.

With the remains of my last winter's earnings I bought my first Tiger Moth, like this, outside the Christchurch Aero Club.

Him: "Would you like to buy my spare Tiger airframe?"
Me: "Yes."
Him: "What will you offer?"
Me: "Fifteen pounds."
Him: "I must tell you that one wing has a broken spar."
Me: "In that case twelve pounds ten."

Deal done! And this was duly delivered to our new blister hangar at Christchurch, frames of which had come from Warmwell and Bisterne.

This was the summer that we had the BA Drone at Christchurch, great fun it was. Read the previous *"Tails of the Fifties"*: several authors mention it. We also had the Reid & Sigrist Desford as a toy; the passenger ahead of the pilot (invariably female) had to lie prone!

Other odd types to come to me that summer were the Zaunkoenig (originally a low-speed research aircraft from Brunswick University and now in a German museum), the Hirtenberg (an Austrian parasol a bit like a grown-up Pietenpol), a Motor Tutor and a Dart Kitten.

Time again to think of earning a living, and so it was back to the Sudan in early October. My unit had worked its way along the cotton fields of the White Nile and came to Aba Island. This was a large island five miles by one mile set in the middle of the White Nile north of Kosti. It was the private estate of the Mahdi.

We were living in a rest house on his estate and as was Arabic custom, we were invited to dinner at his palace. A superb meal, the only time I have eaten from gold plates. I tried to persuade the Mahdi to come flying with me. Remember the British had cut off the head of his grandfather and thrown the body into the river. He politely declined, which was perhaps a good thing, as on my first take-off the following morning the port axle of my Auster failed and parted company from the leg with disastrous results. The heavily-laden machine emulating a cartwheel for a few seconds. The spare machine was wheeled out and the next three hundred (almost) hours were without incident.

I returned to the UK at Christmas-time and resumed my duties with the Christchurch Aero Club, accumulating valuable instructional hours. Time again to renew the Instrument Rating – that's why I have so many Dove hours!

Jobs were still not easy to find. Aquila was my desire, but I had to settle for Independent Air Travel, a small company operating Vikings and DC-4s out of Bournemouth and Blackbushe.

Those were the early days of inclusive tours (ITs). Flights to the Costa Brava terminated at Perpignan across the border. It was thought that the Viking was ideal as it had thirty-six seats, the same as a coach. The DC-4 had 70 and, apart from some IT work, it was used on military cargo flights to Malta and Cyprus.

During August of '58 I flew 140 hours, my best total for flying in the UK. But the MCA were becoming interested in the industry, and as a result of a terrible accident to a Viking, the Authority virtually closed the Company and introduced flight-time limitations much as we know them now.

1958 was also the year when I first flew my Tiger G-APJP. The slats and strakes were deleted and plywood leading edges added. It was placed second and third in the heats for the King's Cup and so qualified. However I was called back to work on the Big Day; Jimmy Denyer was thus allowed to compete – and he won!

Having my own aeroplane meant that I could experiment. I tried skywriting by attaching smoke flares to the interplane struts, but my efforts did not last very long. In an effort to reduce oil drips I connected the manifold drain to the oil tank vent and led them both to the bottom of the undercarriage leg. When the aircraft was inverted oil was sucked back into the engine. The subsequent smoke trail caused great consternation on the ground, but not as much as when I got out of the front cockpit and sat on the leading edge waving at the audience below!

At the end of the year I went back to Africa again for a rest but found myself hunting locusts. Two Auster Autocars were based in Kassala with a daily task of flying over the Eritrean mountains to the Red Sea and along the coast to Port Sudan, then to refuel and route back across the Nubian desert.

The range with two wing tanks was not quite good enough so in the back we each carried three 4-gallon cans of petrol and landed on the silver sand at the side of the Red Sea and refuelled. These cans blew up like footballs at nine to ten thousand feet over the Red Sea hills and invariably leaked. However we survived and even got to spraying locusts with an extremely heavy insecticide that was carried in the long-range tank. Those that were killed and cooked on impact with the engine cylinders were considered a delicacy by the natives. Yes, I did try them – after all St. John did.

Returning to the UK again, by now we had Rapides G-AKIF, 'FRK and 'GJG at Christchurch; their pedigrees were immaculate – Manx Airways, BEA and Island Airways at Heathrow respectively.

Lots of charter flights, parachute dropping and pleasure flights from such long-closed fields as Abingdon, Portsmouth, Hullavington and Merryfield. My last visits to Croydon were the early newspaper flights to the IOW on Saturday afternoons with the Football Special evening papers.

On one Saturday in 1959 I took six parachutists to displays at Andover and then on to Gaydon. On each occasion Sgt (now Squadron Leader) Jim "Paddy" McLoughlin managed to link hands with his team-mates, the first time that this had been done in the UK.

Many times I had taken the pre-war demonstration parachutist Gwynn Johns aloft in Tiger Moths. He was struggling towards his 90th descent when I introduced him to "Paddy" McLoughlin, who at that time was approaching nine hundred drops and was then engaged in proving the exit systems from Beverleys at Boscombe Down.

As the decade ended I went back to Africa, flying Super Cubs this time – magnificent flying.

The sixties would see me in command of something much heavier, seated in between a pair of 2,000 hp Hercules. But in the the final few days of the decade ('50s) I took delivery of the then 28-year-old Redwing. That will merit at least a chapter in the next book!

CHAPTER 17

A PROCTOR TO PARIS

by

Tim Foster

One day in 1956 I was at Croydon making myself generally useful and trying to scrounge the odd flight. I was hanging about at the hangars when a chap I had seen around a bit asked if I could help him push a Proctor out. (This is precisely why I would hang around the hangars. In fact that's why they're called hangars. Then I could say: "Are you going flying? Got a spare seat? OK if I come along?" The desired answers are yes, yes and yes, in that order: I got them!)

The next question, of course, is: "Where are you going?"

When he answered, it was one of those delightful surprises life seems to store up and dish out at random intervals. "Paris!"

"What, now?" I said. It was about 6.30 pm but, being August 11, it was still broad daylight.

"Yes. Soon, in fact."

Good job I always had my passport with me, just in case. I called home and told 'em what I was up to.

The man was Bill Brailsford, a former RAF Meteor pilot in his late 20s; a nice guy, but perhaps a bit dim. He had somehow talked an attractive young woman into flying off to Paris with him for the weekend. It had never dawned on me that I might be in the way – nor on Bill, apparently. She, being a well-bred young lady, treated me without animosity.

He got the Proctor fuelled up, filed a flight plan and finally we were ready to leave (for some reason we had to clear with Customs outbound before we left – I think it let us buy tax-free fuel, but it slowed us down). We departed at 19.20 and headed straight for Paris, which is 220 miles roughly south-south-east of Croydon. If you draw a straight line between Croydon and Paris, you leave the UK at Hastings and make landfall on the French coast at Le Tréport. That's an 80-mile water crossing – perhaps not the best idea at 1,000 feet in a single-engine aircraft, with no life jackets on board. But nothing was to stand in the way of our Bill. It only took about half an hour over the sea, anyway.

191

This Proctor, G-ANYV, had no radio or navigation aids. Nada. Fortunately, the weather was good, but shortly after crossing the French coast it got dark. I was ensconced in the back seat which was quite a long way from the two at the front. I had no controls and no intercom, so communication was by shouting. All I could do was watch and look at the map with a flashlight.

Paris was not difficult to find. It ain't called the City of Light for nuthin'. We flew right over it. There was the Eiffel Tower. Yes, definitely Paris. Now to find our destination: Toussus-le-Noble, a small field for private planes about ten miles west of Orly, the major international airport south of Paris. Orly was easy to see. There were all these lights and Stratocruisers, Super Connies and DC-7s coming and going. But off in the dark bit, to the west, we could not find Toussus. If Bill had done a bit more careful checking, he would have discovered that Toussus was, in fact, closed at night. Well we certainly did not want to go into Orly without radio, especially at night. So what to do?

Fortunately, there was another airport nearby, which we kept flying over in our search – God knows where. It was southish of Orly and dark, but we could see a long runway, and loads of Marcel-Dassault Flamants (a sort of frog-eating DC-3 equivalent) parked side-by-side on the ramp.

The third time we overflew it, still with no Toussus in sight, Bill announced that we would land at the mystery airport. He flew down the runway with the landing lights on, hoping someone would switch on the runway lights, but no-o-o-o. So he pulled it around and landed on the runway. No problem. But now someone acknowledged us. Like *trois camions des gendarmes* armed with great big machine guns. They came out to us on the runway and ordered us to *"suivez moi"* in no uncertain terms.

We had arrived at Bretigny sur Orge, a top-secret military air base, equivalent to Boscombe Down in the UK, or Edwards in California. After ascertaining that we had not come to take it over, we were treated most politely and taken to the nearby village, where we were put up at a pension and given a meal of *tête de veau* (calf's brains).

My passport of the time bears this inscription: *'Vu à l'arrivée, à 21H20 par la Brigade de Gendarmerie Nationale.'*

Being proper British types, on being told that there were only *deux chambres* available, one large and one small, the young lady took the single room and Bill and I lucked out with the double. It had a large four-poster bed, replete with a large doll in folk dress sitting on the duvet, and over to one side of the room, a bidet. As we prepared to go to bed, Bill pointed at the bidet and said: "What's that thing for?"

"I don't know, but I think it's something to do with honeymoons," I replied, ever as helpful as possible. Spending endless weekends at

Croydon Airport did nothing for one's sex life. I was yet a virgin (this was 1956!), so I knew little of which I spoke.

"Oh," he replied, a puzzled frown decorating his face. With stiff upper lips (and that's all), we climbed into bed and had a jolly good night's sleep (and that's all). Perhaps this was not what Bill had in mind when he set up this trip with the young lady. I think the Proctor was about £4-10s an hour, so it was costing over £20 on air transportation alone. A lot of money in those days. And he ends up with me!

The next day was beautiful. After a continental breakfast (what else?), we were picked up by l'Armée de l'Air and taken to our Proctor. When we were ready to start the engine, a very capable-looking man came up and stood by with a huge great fire extinguisher. Great service! Toussus was only about 12 miles-northwest and we were there in a few moments. We landed and cleared Customs properly this time.

Bill and friend departed for Paris while I pleaded the need to stay at Toussus. We agreed to meet there the next morning, Monday, at 6 am. I and the young lady both were due to go to work at our respective offices then. I figured I could make it in by about noon.

I started exploring the airport, which, this being early Sunday, was practically deserted of people, but heavily populated with hundreds of strange frog-eating *avions*, mostly in rows of T-hangars. There were *Norécrins et Noralphas et Druines et Jodels et Sipas et Nords et Morane-Saulniers et Broussards et Stampes et même un Potez ou deux.*

At noon, people started arriving and going to work on their aircraft. Weekend flyers. One was Jean-François Ripert, who had a Jodel D.111, F-BGLO, that he had built himself (there was a strong homebuilt movement in France). I got talking to him, and managed to negotiate a flight in the Jodel – 15 minutes for ten shillings: it was a sheer delight – very light on the controls and very responsive. We were on close final for landing and suddenly M. Ripert put the Jodel into a 90°-banked 360° steep turn. *"Traffique!"* he shrugged.

Later I went to the Commandant and asked, in my best schoolboy French, if I could spend the night. *"En votre avion, monsieur?"* he cut in.

"Mais non, actuellement, je désire de dormir dans votre Aeroport." He agreed. I spent the rest of the day exploring *les avions.* I was just about out of money and I managed to get the restaurant to cash me a cheque for £1-10s so I could get some food.

I slept in the terminal. It was so cold that in the middle of the night I went out to the Proctor and got a cockpit cover to use as a blanket.

Dawn arrived early and so did Bill and his date. But something else was present – low cloud. Not here, but on the English coast. The trouble was that we had to file a flight plan to leave; that had to be signed by the weather briefer and he wouldn't sign a VFR flight plan when there was low cloud on the coast. The reports from the French coast were little better. Le Touquet was, in fact just VFR. Croydon was marginal.

We waited for two hours or so for things to improve. They didn't, so Bill hit on the idea of filing a flight plan to Le Touquet. We got our signature and left, taking off at 09.40. Our destination was ideally Croydon, but we were officially aimed at Le Touquet. Of course, when we got there, Bill just kept on going (remember, no radio) and we crossed the Channel at about 200 feet to stay below the low cloud. Turn left at the White Cliffs of Dover, whose tops were obscured in a layer. Aim for Lympne, just down the coast a bit (I'm still in the back seat, helpless except as observer). We got on top of a layer of broken cloud, and there was Lympne, directly below us, visible through a hole in the cloud. Not possible to make an approach, so on to Lydd (known as Ferryfield), laid out on Romney Marsh to handle the Silver City car ferry flights that ran all day to France. One big advantage was that it was virtually at sea level, so when the clouds are low, it's easier to get in visually. One big disadvantage was that the airport was private and closed to non-Silver City aeroplanes.

Since when has any silly little rule like that stood in Bill's way? Certainly not today. We landed on the paved runway and taxied in. Bill got a severe bollocking from an airport official, who said he had to tell a Bristol Freighter to overshoot his landing to avoid crashing into us. I think he was bullshitting, actually, because he wasn't an air traffic controller. He asked us to leave, but of course, the low cloud was in the way. So we were grudgingly allowed to stay until the weather improved.

We moved to the coffee shop, with reluctant permission; we were treated like, and felt like, lepers. Bill's date was by now thoroughly unimpressed. She had not displayed enormous enthusiasm about the whole weekend when she arrived at Toussus that morning, except possibly for the idea of going home. I don't know what happened for her in Paris, but it probably didn't come up to expectations. Now here we were, on the south coast, just before noon, and she had to get to work. She chatted up a motorist for a lift to London and was out of there in ten minutes, never to be heard from again. I phoned my office and said I'd be in tomorrow.

Finally things improved and we got away at 16.40. At last I was up front in the right-hand seat. It was so good to be there after more than four flying hours all by myself in the back; it felt really high up, like sitting on a throne. The visibility was superb. And we were nipping along; it was a quick 40 minutes to Croydon, where the weather was at last fine. We landed, cleared Customs and put the aeroplane back in the hangar. I thanked Bill profusely and went home.

Three years later he disappeared, ferrying an Auster to Australia. After eight months the wreckage was found in the bottom of a lake in France. Bye, Bill. It was fun while it lasted.

CHAPTER 18

NATIONAL SERVICE PILOT

by

Ambrose Barber

[NOTES ON THE AUTHOR: Ambrose Barber was educated at Aldenham School, Herts, and the College of Aeronautical Engineering, Chelsea. After leaving the RAF he flew as a part-time flying instructor at Fair Oaks before finally going supersonic in 1957 while acting as a Hunter flight test observer with Hawkers. He subsequently had various managerial appointments with the company, was elected a Fellow of the Royal Aeronautical Society in 1984 and retired from BAe as a Divisional Director, Military Aircraft. A member of the Tiger Club's early display teams, he still enjoys 'three-pointing' with his friends in the Southdowns Auster Group.]

"It may be unfashionable but I loved my National Service. Of course, I was doing what I wanted to do. . . the RAF took a boy of seventeen and a half and turned out a man. Not always a very sensible or mature one; but somewhere, sometime, at the controls of a Vampire, I think we all crossed that threshold." – *the author Frederick Forsyth, quoted by his kind permission (and that of the publishers) from p.82 in "Per Ardua ad Acting Pilot Officer," a chapter in* "High Flyers" *(Greenhill Books 1993).*

We students were a mixed bag in 1950 and those of us who were straight from school found ourselves amongst both older students returned from the forces and many who had come to study from overseas. To appreciate our lifestyle one has to remember that for Britain the forties had ended much like an austerity version of the thirties. The second world war had left our economy impoverished and there was little spare cash about, least of all for full-time students. Food and petrol were still rationed and inessential activities had been slow to resume. Relatively few people could afford a motor car and fewer still had flown in civilian life, even as passengers. Wish as one might, the prospect of learning to fly seemed justifiably remote. Since 1945 the Services had had to concentrate more on shedding aircrew than training them. Then, in June 1950, misfortune befell a little-known country on the other side of the world when South Korea was attacked by North Korean communist forces.

Korea, a Buddhist state about the size of Britain, had been dominated by the Japanese since 1910. At the close of WW II the Japanese forces in northern Korea had surrendered to the Chinese and those in the south to the Americans. As loyalties polarised in the ensuing cold war the border dividing north and south had become part of the "bamboo curtain" between Communism and the West. In other circumstances, what followed the North's invasion might have been just a Korean civil war, but opposing ideologies ensured the United Nations' support for the South against the spread of totalitarian communism by force. By the end of 1950 the communist Chinese had joined in to support the North Koreans and contingents from nearly twenty nations were, in one way or another, supporting the South. The whole Korean peninsula had become the scene of a full-scale war.

Initially, the United Nations were predominantly flying piston-engined aircraft on ground-attack duties, but the arrival of transsonic MiG 15 jets in the hands of the Chinese seriously threatened UN air superiority. (While a piston-engined Hawker Sea Fury flown by Cmdr. Carmichael RN shot down one of these jet fighters, it was a rare achievement.) In response, the Americans and Australians converted many operational pilots in Korea to their first jets. If the international head of steam developing between the Communist countries and the West were to draw Russia into the conflict then we could again face war on an inter-continental scale. We all hoped for the best while the British Government now seemed to be preparing for the worst. Military training budgets must have been rapidly revised as the official foot was transferred from the brake to the accelerator.

Some WW II flying training facilities were hurriedly re-established both here and in the Commonwealth, the whole training machine gathering considerable momentum during 1951 so that by the time my course of studies was complete and I was due for call-up, the RAF was accepting increasing numbers of National Servicemen as aircrew trainees. I volunteered for all I was worth and in 1952 soloed in a Grading School Tiger Moth at RAF Kirton in Lindsey, Lincolnshire.

Kirton was a 'permanent' RAF station in substantial brick-built style and it was then the home of No.2 Initial Training School. Quartered in barracks, we cadets were marched up each morning in squads to the airfield where, lifting their tails to shoulder-level, we would push out the Grading School's Tigers onto the grass. These rows of inviting silver biplanes adorned with RAF roundels had all the appearance of a previous era. We donned our flying suits and strapped on our parachutes. How privileged we were!

The direction for take-off and landing was indicated by a single row of markers across the grass: take off to the left and land to the right, nothing could be simpler! It was quite usual to see three or four Tigers on final approach at the same time, and more than once I counted six or seven. Of course most aircraft had instructors aboard and we had no radio to distract our attention or that of the Aldis lamp controller in his caravan look-out.

The aircraft and Grading School were operated by Airwork Ltd using ex-RAF instructors wearing mufti. I was lucky with the two men who initiated me into aviating. The first, Mr Bailey, was a genial north-countryman who showed me my first spin and taught me how to land. Mr Duttson, who had gained his commission in the thirties "when the RAF was the best flying club in the world," carried on from there and treated me to my first loop. What was engaging about both men was that they seemed to enjoy their work, which is more than I can say for one or two of the RAF instructors I was to come across later.

Our 'transports of delight' among the Tigers lasted only a few days. At the end of our twelve hours of grading some cadets were relegated from further flying. As for the rest of us, it was back to the parade ground and classroom where we braced ourselves for the usual physical and mental exertions associated with being "licked into shape" – a routine familiar to countless thousands before and, no doubt, many since. Endless 'spit and polish,' extra 'bull' nights and punitive 'fatigues' were all absorbed as a price worth paying for the chance to fly again. However, our ITS training seemed to be run without much inspiration and the only humour around was of our own making. Any 'drop-outs' were immediately posted away to RAF Innsworth where they were officially categorised as "LMF" (lacking moral fibre), a threat which was to follow us throughout our training.

Our transfer in mid-term to No.1 ITS on the Isle of Man proved to be an enlightening experience. Here the syllabus was just the same but the atmosphere was noticeably different. RAF Jurby seemed, after our previous experience, to be a "happy ship." We were put through our paces in a disciplined but good-hearted way, down to the NCOs who drilled us before breakfast as the dawn rose over Snaefell mountain. We were commanded by a Sqn. Ldr. Lewis who combined his exacting standards with a gentlemanly style. As our tails rose so did our levels of attainment, in itself an enduring lesson in leadership. While most of his officers were pilots, Lewis himself wore the Navigator's brevet. Under him, our flight commander was none other than James Lacey DFM and bar, the RAF's highest-scoring pilot in the Battle of Britain. Eventually retiring as a Squadron Leader, "Ginger" Lacey had risen from Sgt. Pilot to acting Wg. Cdr. during his war and we held him in affectionate esteem. A quietly-spoken man with a mischievous smile, he took several of us up for our first flights in a glider. The station commander was Group Captain

Worthington and it is sad to record that he was killed the following winter when the Anson in which he was flying hit Snaefell in thick cloud.

Anxious moments and not a few departures accompanied the assessments of our exam results and "PQs" (personal qualities). We were a mixture of cadet pilots and navigators mostly trying for short-service commissions, with us national servicemen hanging on in there. Finally the longed-for Passing Out day came. Following this, Algy Allington, John "Jock" Crabb and myself (by now nicknamed "Ali") were amongst those posted to join No.3 Flying Training School at RAF Feltwell, Norfolk. All three of us were two-year national servicemen but it was a condition for our continued training that we would thereafter serve in the RAF Volunteer Reserve for five years – hardly a deterrent!

We arrived at Feltwell to meet several fresh faces with whom we were to make up the incoming No.9(P) course. We ranged in age from 18 to about 24. Algy, Jock and I were all 21, having had our call-up deferred for further education. The eldest, Kirk, was an RAF regular who had already served in Korea as ground crew. As Acting Pilot Officers we trainees were now allocated a room between two, but we did not aspire to the same Mess as was used by the 3 FTS staff.

No.3 FTS comprised three training squadrons, one equipped with the Percival Prentice basic trainer and a couple with the North American Harvard IIB advanced trainer. (Chipmunks, Oxfords and Balliols were also in use at some other UK flying schools.) Three other courses were already there under training at various stages ahead of us. We were to start 28 strong and were divided into two sections which alternated on mornings and afternoons between the ground school and the flight offices ("flights"). The course would last ten months, during which we could expect to fly 60 hours on the Prentice and 150 on the Harvard, and those successfully completing the course would be awarded their flying badge ("wings"). Our instructors seemed to be mostly about thirtyish and we could see from their medal ribbons that they had all had greater moments in their lives than we could now offer them. Most of them were commissioned but there were a few NCO and Master (warrant officer) Pilots among them – we called them all "Sir" just the same.

On our first visit to "flights" we were allocated a crew room and lockers. My first flight in a Prentice was with Sqn. Ldr. Robson, our CO. Having ascertained that I had soloed in a Tiger Moth he announced that I would do the first take-off. I found this rather startling but, with its nice wide undercarriage and (as single-engined tailwheel aircraft go) its good forward view, I needn't have worried! Beyond this, the cumbersome yet comfortable Prentice was altogether a strange aircraft to use as a basic pilot trainer. In addition to its unchallenging take-off and landing characteristics, its abysmal rate of climb made it a time-waster except in the circuit. However, for a mere 100 knot aeroplane its cockpit seemed so cluttered with complication that even circuit-bashing lost some of its shine. True, it was amiably aerobatic, but it was also capable of producing a potentially lethal flat spin, of which more anon. It was more in its element on sedate cross-country flying, trundling along behind its sweet-sounding 6-cylinder Gipsy Queen engine, but I was delighted at being taught to fly in anything!

Feltwell was, unusually for a former bomber station, an all-grass airfield. To the south lay RAF Lakenheath and Mildenhall, both by then used by the USAF. To the north lay our own diversion field of Methwold, where we practised cross-wind landings on its tarmac runways – not a favourite pastime when juggling with a Harvard! To the east lay Thetford Chase, but it was to the west that we flew to our sparsely-populated practice area between Downham Market, Wisbech and Ely. Here its low-lying farmland was traversed by a parallel canal system which made an excellent landmark, except when we saw the whole area flooded early in 1953. At this juncture we were trucked out to fill sandbags with mud where the River Ouse had burst its banks.

Flying was organised so that several of us were allocated to an instructor with whom we usually flew. Algy Allington and I had a sardonic Glaswegian whom I can best describe as "Flt. Lt. Dry." He had developed an intense and wary attitude to flying and was hard to please, which I found more difficult than did Algy, my more phlegmatic room-mate; but satisfied he had to be or we risked being 'chopped' off the course and I'm glad to say we stuck each other out! At no time was "Dry's" tetchiness more exposed than when we were practising getting the Prentice out of a spin. By the time I was released to repeat this exercise solo he had so infected me with his own tension that, in my inexperience, I determined to 'lay the bogey' by holding the spin for longer before taking recovery action. Quite suddenly the nose came up and the view in the windscreen changed from rotating fields to the horizon racing sideways. With no flying speed everything went deathly quiet while I taught myself that if you are ever to recover from a flat spin it requires brute force on the stick! At the same time I also learned what a cold sweat feels like! Later I gathered that in a similar incident a previous Feltwell trainee had not been so lucky.

A more comfortable character to fly with was Flt. Lt. Willmott DFM, our flight commander. A jovial survivor, he had learned in a hard school, arriving as a young Sgt. Pilot at his first squadron in 1940. On reporting, the Adjutant had asked him how many hours he had flown.

"Ninety, Sir."

"Yes, on *Spitfires*, Willmott, but how many altogether?"

"Ninety, Sir."

Sgt. Willmott first flew out to meet the enemy with just 99 hours total flying experience!

The sixty hours basic training on the Prentice covered a syllabus similar to the contemporary civil Private Pilot's Licence with the addition of aerobatics and some basic instrument- and night-flying. Both Prentice and Harvard trainers were equipped with a 4-channel radio, preset to 'circuit,' 'approach,' 'Flying Training Command common' and 'emergency' frequencies. Use of radio was restricted to concise essentials, but it could also receive Beam Approach signals to help us line up with the airfield in poor visibility. Flying discipline was strict and there was no such thing as a "wizard prang" even if there ever had been. In the past, Flying Training Command had lost too many pilots without a shot being fired, but now, under Grp. Cpt. Rump OBE, Feltwell enjoyed one of the best safety records of any RAF flying training school with a fatal accident rate of only one per year. No small contribution to this was made by the maintenance of our aircraft's reliability, which was always beyond reproach. Our ground schooling included the various subjects associated with leadership and airmanship, and practical training included, amongst other things, inflatable dinghy drill after 'baling out' from the top board at the swimming pool. This outing was enlivened with some stylish swallow dives by Dave Bromley, 9 Course's popular pianist.

In the fullness of time most of us progressed to the excitement of the Harvard. In 1939 No.3 FTS, then based at Grantham, had been the first RAF unit to receive Harvards. The pupil always sat in front, whether dual or solo, except for blind-flying practice under the hood in the rear cockpit, and the first thing we noticed through the windscreen was the impact on the field view of the cowled radial engine. From it emanated a powerful rumbling sound at modest revs, but with 550 horsepower in take-off pitch its propeller tips produced a notorious racket at a full 2,250 rpm. The cockpit was spacious (being American!) and amongst the levers was an important new one for raising and lowering the undercarriage. The Harvard had a business-like look about it and its responsiveness to the controls promised well, once we had cleared the hurdle of going solo. In this respect its landing behaviour in the hands of the unwary could be pretty unforgiving and one also needed to acquire the knack of keeping straight during take-off! Once mastered, we found the Harvard a reliable and friendly aeroplane and very satisfying to fly. At the time it was being used operationally in Korea, for artillery spotting by 4167 Sqdn USAF and by the RAF against Mau Mau insurgents in Kenya and Communist terrorists in Malaya. More significantly, we were conscious of joining the thousands of our predecessors who had trained on the AT-6 Harvard/Texan on both sides of the Atlantic during WW II, when some of the Feltwell Harvards had been built in Canada. Incidentally, I believe the last RAF pilot to gain his "wings" on Harvards graduated at Feltwell in 1955. After this, 3 FTS had Percival piston-Provosts, before becoming a jet school at Leeming.

Our Harvard training squadron was commanded by Sqn. Ldr. Bayley, and his team of instructors included two Poles who had escaped in 1939 to join the RAF, Flt. Lt. Wardzinski and Flt. Sgt. Antoniak. Eric Wardzinski took Algy and I under his wing and proved a good instructor. Unlike many of his colleagues, he had previously flown jets and would represent the Station with his solo aerobatic displays in the Harvard. Tall and good-looking, he was a gifted athlete and a natural pilot who rose to become our flight commander. His excellent command of English was occasionally impaired by a touch of aristocratic vagueness which kept us on our toes when he mixed up the words "left" and "right"! Above all, he often had a twinkle in his eye and so, for that matter, had Jock's instructor, Sgt. Wichall.

Life took on a satisfying routine in the early summer of 1953 as we learned to put the Harvard through its paces. In the warm weather we could slide the canopy aft and savour open-cockpit flying again. I particularly enjoyed solo aerobatics and formation-flying, in which we learned to keep increasingly closer station, aided by the Wasp radial's responsiveness to our gradually less hectic throttle movements. And then there was blind flying on instruments! During this, the very senses which add finesse to "seat of the pants" flying send out misleading signals once visual references have disappeared (as can be demonstrated when rotating blindfold on a swivel seat). These have to be fiercely ignored while concentrating instead on interpreting the movement of the pointers on the blind-flying panel. This process only comes with practice and, in this respect, it seemed I needed more practice than most!

Meanwhile, that far-off East-West conflict had mercifully been contained in the Korean peninsula where opposing sides had reached a stalemate close to the originally-disputed border. Forty-five years later there remains an uneasy truce with Korean unity as remote as ever. The spread of Communism by force had been successfully frustrated by the UN forces, but in three years of war the ghastly cost had been two million lives and the majority of these tragic victims were, I believe, the civilian inhabitants.

The Korean armistice was signed at the end of July 1953, by which time I had logged 155 hours by day and 3 hours night flying. If that was more than enough to have joined Willmott's Spitfire squadron thirteen years earlier, it was perhaps just as well for us too that the shooting had stopped! Thankfully, it is now two generations since a British citizen army has had to kill and be killed, but some national service soldiers had indeed seen action in Korea. It was not to be our destiny to discover how we would have acquitted ourselves in an air war. While I trust we would not have disgraced ourselves, what was of more pressing concern to us now was whether aircrew training would be curtailed as it had been in 1945. I therefore decided to apply for a Licence while the going was good to at least fly civilian light aircraft. In response to a signature from my squadron commander and swotting up Civil Air Law, the Ministry of Aviation granted me a "Private Pilot's Licence – FLYING MACHINES" (sic), issued in September 1953 and happily in use to this day. Soon there were indeed signs of the training machine reducing its intake and throughput. Pass marks were being raised and Airwork's Grading School instructors like Bailey and Duttson would become redundant. Right from the start the acceptance standards for mere two-year men had been understandably tighter, unless we were prepared to sign on for longer. Although it later transpired that lessons had been learned and NATO and the Second Tactical Air Force would continue to be strengthened, for the time being we continued on tenterhooks.

We now entered the final testing stages of our course to become Qualified Service Pilots. Most of the flying was now solo with longer cross-country flights and more formation flying culminating in tail-chasing our instructor, and there was night flying. Heading home from a night cross-country in the small hours, the powerful sodium runway lights from Lakenheath and Mildenhall would show up from miles away. We then had to find, somewhere in the night, two parallel lines of tiny paraffin gooseneck flares deployed across the invisible surface of our grass field. We then lowered ourselves gingerly into the black abyss between them, hoping like hell that something solid lay beneath us to catch our stalling craft!

In October the unbelievable arrived and it was graduation day for 9(P) Course. Two of our number had been dropped on Prentices and four more later on. There remained twenty-two of us, of whom seven were national service pilots: Allington, Barber, Crabb, Rymill, Shenton, Walley and Worley. Plt. Off. D. Bromley won the Flying Trophy and went on to become a Squadron Leader at 34. Much to my genuine surprise (and probably everyone else's!) I came out a close second. As our results came through we decked out No.2 Officers' Mess for our Graduation Dance, an occasion graced by pretty girl friends in their long evening dresses, my cousin Celia among them. It was a much more decorous affair than some of our Dining-In Nights had been!

On The Day our nearest and dearest came to see "wings" pinned on, my mother looking just right for the occasion, my father wearing his RAFVR tie, but I think that only Kirk yet had a wife to witness the proud moment. Years later I was to meet another former national service pilot, Norman Tebbit MP, during his opposition to the nationalisation of our aircraft industry. Writing about his own similar graduation at No.2 FTS, Lord Tebbit observes that for him, few if any of his subsequent distinctions were to compare with that. I think most recipients of this award would share his sentiment.

It was all such a vivid experience in our still formative years that it is little wonder that even now reflection yields up memories too numerous to elaborate on here. Recollections tumble out, such as Harvard-flying below the height of canal banks and also night-time aerobatics, both strictly dual only; an escape and evasion exercise to cross the Suffolk border after 24 hours on the run; the sound of *Sugar Bush* played repeatedly on the ante-room gramophone; sailing with my cousins on the Norfolk Broads in breaks from training; partying in the Mess, Algy and I a bit giggly, the ever-cheerful Jock a wee bit more so; visits by short courses from University Air Squadrons and the RAFVR with, interestingly for those far-off days, at least one woman Harvard pilot among them; mischievously duping an incoming course by greeting them with a profusion of spurious "casualties" wearing bandages, splints and crutches borrowed from the MO – supported by much invented detail, it proved hilariously convincing for the few hours it lasted.

Above all, there is a memory of magical moments at the controls of a Harvard, wandering on my own just above an undulating sea of horizontal cloud, the peaks and troughs across its surface picked out with shadows cast by the slanting autumn sun. They beckon me down to join them and, viewing the prospect with relish, I cast responsibility to the winds and willingly answer that call, swooping like some powerful bird in graceful abandon over their bright seductive dunes. In tempted wonder, I descend carefully between their soft celestial ramparts, here to feel transported into a secret world of tortuous shady lanes, unknown to earthlings, where lovely burgeoning shapes are there to be explored at will. Now easing back on the stick, I rise again to hurtle through the brilliant vaporous crests which flash harmlessly by my opened cockpit as I surf over my friend the cloud's mightly steaming rollers. Soaring higher still, I pause to look down and revel in this shining example of Nature's transient beauty, only to bank steeply in the golden sky before diving with eager heart back into her outstretched arms. And so my sunlit wings caress again those white resplendent contours as I weave my happy youthful way, winging reflectively towards Creation's next horizon! Wished I, like a lover, that the blissful carefree hour might never pass, but thus are cherished memories collected . . . Unless, of course, by some mischance you happen to meet another such amiable lunatic intoxicated with similar temptations and coming through the cloud tops from the opposite direction!

The Harvard was the nearest I got to piston-engined 'heavy metal' unless, of course, you count two flights I had as co-pilot of Mk.III Lancasters SW294 & SW295. I was then attached to a small Chain Home Radar Station, RAF Sennen, commanded by another national service officer, Norman Cuddeford. We in turn were under the command of Sqn. Ldr. Templeton-Rooke DSO, DFC & Bar, AFC, the CO of neighbouring

RAF Trerew, and a distinguished bomber pilot. "T-R" regularly flew Lancasters from St. Mawgan, the last RAF unit to operate them, and he kindly took me along. It is curious to reflect that my chance to fly this historic bomber was by courtesy of Coastal Command while I was actually serving in Fighter Command. But before Fighter Command would have me, I had first to become a 'jet jockey.'

* * *

Jock, Algy and I found we were deemed suitable fodder for Day Interceptor fighters and we all landed Vampire postings, Algy to RAF Valley in Anglesey and Jock and I to RAF Merryfield in Somerset. The alternatives were Gloster Meteors or, for those going on to 'heavies,' the Vickers Varsity. Merryfield was a wartime airfield with single-storey accommodation built for the Americans. Located between Yeovil and Taunton, it has in more recent years been used by the Royal Navy, but in 1953-4 it was the home of No.208 Advanced Flying School. Westland Aircraft also had a small presence there for testing their Wyverns but the daily bustle was provided by our DH Vampires with the characteristic banshee howl of their Goblin jet engines. The station was commanded by Grp. Cpt. Wood and our CO was Sqn. Ldr. Babbage DFC. Curiously, 208 AFS is omitted from some popular references, but it was the subject of a full-length feature in "FLIGHT" in 1953.

The jet conversion course was very different from flying school. Jet-flying was still comparatively new and its adoption by the post-war Great Powers continued to be a major undertaking for their air forces. Our instructors were able pilots although mostly young and without any great wealth of experience themselves. Many, perhaps most, RAF pilots serving then had yet to make this transition and the student intake was not confined to newly-qualified pilots. Courses were small and intermingled freely in both crew room and Mess. We therefore enjoyed the benefit of an interesting mix of previous backgrounds and experience. Jock and I were the only national service officers on No.45 course, the senior course member being Flg. Off. Brian Longworth, a genial product of Cranwell with a permanent commission. Anderson, Bywater, Dunbar and Ellis were all serving on short-service commissions. Other members of our crew room included Flg. Off. Vincent, who had been on a piston-engined fighter squadron, and a young Flt. Lt. who had recently won an AFC as a Hastings captain making supply drops in arctic conditions. The most senior man was a spry Wing Commander gamely making the big change!

Unlike the earliest participants in this revolutionary new jet era we had the enormous advantage of being introduced to it via a two-seater. Our first such flight was an eye-opener and was an essential introduction to the procedures we would have to grasp, and the necessity for them. The acceleration, smoothness, rate of climb and sheer speed escalated our flying into dimensions we had hitherto never experienced, yet today they are as commonplace as the holiday jet. The Goblin's banshee whine hardly penetrated the pressurised cockpit and the quietness almost amounted to a sense of silence after the Harvard. Flying the Vampire was going to be a big step from the Harvard and we realised that with a jet fighter the whole flight envelope had opened up and would require a fresh awareness and alertness. All solo flying was in the single-seater Vampire FB.5. First solo on type would no longer be a quick circuit but straight up to 10,000 feet, get your breath back, get the feel of her and, when comfortable, descend and rejoin the circuit for landing.

Small and agile, the Vampire's distinctive layout consisted of almost symmetrical wings centred on a miniscule fuselage housing the pilot in front, closely followed by his engine. From each wing a slender boom reached aft, to be joined by the tail which was above, and just clear of, the jet efflux. Equipped with 20 mm guns as an interceptor, it could also carry bombs and rockets for ground attack work. During those early fifties the Vampire was in action in Malaya and Kenya and formed the backbone of the 2nd Tactical Air Force in Germany. Although nearing the end of its career as a first-line fighter with the RAF, it was to remain in service with many overseas air forces for years to come.

Our first flight in the two-seater had shown us that things happened "a bit quick" in the circuit and you couldn't afford to get them wrong. The ground school housed a cockpit in which we practised the circuit drills over and over again. We were also lectured on the aerodynamic, navigational, air traffic, meteorological and physiological implications of flying at higher altitude, airspeed and Mach number. Before taking the plunge we were given further dual, for which the Vampire T.11 had recently replaced the unit's Meteor T.7s. True it hadn't yet got ejector seats but neither had the fighter version which we would then strap ourselves into. Instead of bone domes we still wore the same snug leather flying helmets we'd used from the start on Tiger Moths, except now the masks were connected to oxygen.

Without ejector seats our planned escape was roughly as follows. 1: slow down. 2: goggles down. 3: lower seat. 4: jettison cockpit canopy. 5: disconnect aircraft oxygen and R/T cable. 6: roll aircraft onto back. 7: release seat harness. 8: fall clear complete with parachute, emergency oxygen and dinghy. 9: when you guess you're below 10,000 feet pull the ripcord!

Wearing a somewhat wistful expression at Merryfield was Plt. Off. Ripon, who'd been a couple of courses ahead of us at Feltwell. In climbing his Vampire through 20,000 feet he'd radioed that the cockpit had filled with acrid smoke, but he'd first opened the canopy by sliding it aft in the normal way. When it all got too hot he lowered the seat and disconnected his plumbing, but when he tried to roll upside down as per the book he found that the controls were slack, burned through by the engine fire. He undid his straps and kicked himself half out of the cockpit, whereupon the airflow flattened him across the top of the opened canopy while his parachute and dinghy, strapped to his backside, were firmly wedged inside the canopy's leading edge. He was lucky to fight himself free while the aircraft plummeted earthwards.

The man who took me into the jet age was Flg. Off. Barnden, an affable young army pilot who had transferred into the RAF for "the real thing." Barnden took me through the Vampire's general handling and gave me ample practice going around the circuit. The Vampire's stalling speed was much higher than we were used to, which meant there was no such thing as touching down slowly. Forced-landing practice now omitted the time-honoured phrase "pick your field." Only a supreme optimist would pick a stretch of landscape and in practice we now *had* to find an aerodrome. Having said this, the 100 knots "over the hedge" which initially took our breath away must seem like child's play to the modern operational pilot, only the Harrier offering any dramatic relief from this relentless upward trend. When he thought I was ready, Barnden suggested I had a go on my own. He'd rehearsed me well but I still considered the prospect for a moment. We both surveyed the sunny late autumn sky with only broken cloud and he added gently: "It's a good day for it." He was right. Nearly forty-five flying years later it remains one of my most pleasurable memories.

Once strapped into the snug single-seater cockpit everything seemed nicely to hand. Positioned right up in the nose, ahead of the engine, one's view is superb. Accompanied by the smooth hum of the Goblin I taxied out until I reached the holding point for take-off, the nose nodding gently on the forward leg of the new-style tricycle undercarriage. I went through the vital actions carefully and lined her up on the runway. Opening up, the feeling of acceleration was enhanced by the low-slung little fuselage, one's eyes being a mere 2 metres (less than 7 feet) above the runway racing beneath. Raise the nosewheel and by 120 knots she's well airborne with the end of the runway dropping below rapidly. Brakes on and off, undercarriage up and locked by 175 knots – the Harvard's flat-out level speed! Keep climbing and climbing, easing the stick back to hold the speed down to 260 knots. Leaving the broken cloud behind I levelled out in the sunshine at about 10,000 feet. It looked good, it felt good, and I settled down to manoeuvre the craft, the horizon banking and swinging steadily in ready response to my touch on the stick. Nothing feels more like an airborne extension of oneself than a responsive single-seater and shortly I was happily 'making like bird.' All too soon I would be expected back and after 30 minutes I made the first of many happy landings in that little fighter.

Consolidation training followed, both dual and solo, as we explored the aircraft's capabilities and our own. This included aerobatics, spin recoveries, flying with external fuel tanks, high Mach number dives and lots of solo formation flying, led by an instructor. This last was chummy and we trained to take off together in close vee "vic" formation and climb to 30,000 feet or more where we could see the contrails forming behind each other's jet pipes. Changing formation backwards and forwards to echelon first on one side, then the other and then back again to "vic," we would descend in line astern, opening up to chase our leader all over the sky, manoeuvring to stay tenaciously on the next man's tail. This was like a game of follow-my-leader on a massive scale, diving and soaring through thousands of feet, grunting and sighing with the effort of pulling to the edge of blackout as we strove to cut corners in sweating, exasperated glee. During this strenuous exercise we would fly just by instinct with all the hot-blooded yet calculating competition of dog-fighting but without its tears – surely the most exhilarating sport anywhere on earth or above it.

Sadly there was a tragic price to pay for all this excitement. On my first arrival at RAF Merryfield I was greeted by the sight of a party of young officers in "best blue" and black armbands. On following them into the Mess I learned that they had just formed a funeral party for one of their number. It did not seem to be an isolated incident: a short time later two AFS students diverting to us from Weston Zoyland were both killed attempting to land their Meteors on a foggy night after one of their course had already crash-landed on their own runway. During my 19 weeks jet conversion we had two more fatal accidents and so had Weston Zoyland. At our sister Vampire school at Valley (No.202 AFS) it was a similar story. One day I had a particularly hairy ride in a two-seater, spinning with Flt. Lt. Horrocks DFC, during which the aircraft flicked from one direction to the other and back again in its seemingly unstoppable autorotation earthwards. To my great relief Horrocks managed to rescue the situation. When we taxied in we were greeted with the news that an experienced instructor and his student had baled out too late from their spinning Vampire at Valley and all intentional Vampire spinning was now *verboten* until further notice! I didn't know it at the time but it was Algy over at Valley who had had the luckless responsibility of being the first officer at the scene.

To get the flying stakes for those early jets in perspective it has to be remembered that their greatly increased performance had been accompanied by some demanding new characteristics which had to be contended with until later refinements in safety measures and technical systems caught up to restore the balance of risks. Firstly, fuel consumption was very much faster and fuel reserves minimal. We routinely flew 45-minute sorties out of what would certainly amount to less than an hour's fuel. If you couldn't see where you were going to land at the end of your sortie you hadn't got much time to find out. Obviously we needed a means of high-speed navigation. Instead, we still had to grope around the countryside clutching a map like grandfather in his Sopwith. Our lifeline was the new CRDF (Cathode Ray Direction Finding) then coming into service, which enabled the duty controller to quote us a bearing from his screen over the R/T without waiting for our hitherto prolonged VHF/DF transmission. This we used for homings and to help us let down through cloud. But Merryfield had no talk-you-in approach aid such as GCA or ILS – they were for the "All-Weather Boys" –and airborne avionic navaids, let alone GPS, still belonged to the future.

Secondly, gas turbine engine acceleration was much slower than a piston engine's, too slow to haul you out of last-minute trouble near the ground, and if you were tempted to push the throttle open at more than a gradual rate all acceleration ceased while the compressor stalled. You then had to ease the throttle *back* to unstall it! In consequence one's powers of anticipation increased by leaps and bounds. Thirdly, there was the destabilising effect of compressibility which, without power-assisted flying controls, we were at the mercy of as we approached what in those days was popularly called the "sound barrier." This caused both the Vampire and the Meteor to be flung about in a violent and uncontrollable way as shock waves interrupted normal airflow, until one could slow down using airbrakes to regain control, all of which was quite character-building after the friendly old Harvard!

The aeronautically initiated will know better than to condemn any aeroplane except by the standards of its day, and by those the DH Vampire was a world-beater. It held the World Altitude Record (the Gloster Meteor winning the World Speed Record) and had been the first jet aircraft in the world to cross the Atlantic and to land on an aircraft carrier. Looking back, I think we just had to accept the problems I've described as an unexpectedly challenging part of the game we'd chosen to be in. Solutions would be found but aircraft like the Hawker Hunter were still just a gleam in their test pilots' eyes, none having yet reached RAF squadrons. Years later I was to read that the casualty rate was officially recognised as having been "appalling for peacetime" and I believe that the Fleet Air Arm fared no better during this period. All this was despite everyone's best efforts, including the diligent maintenance teams – it was good to belong to *their* air force too! True, there were some lucky escapes, but not enough of them. Even so, I suspect that this was not a unique situation on conversion to operational types; discussing this in the crew room, Vincent recalled that while he had been converting to heavy piston-engined fighters, young pilots were "dropping out of the sky all over the place," often as a result of inadvertent spinning.

Anxiety in these circumstances is inevitable and it was probably the strain that resulted in two of our number, one instructor and one student, quietly leaving the Unit. Fortunately they departed from sight before either had hurt themselves. Little was said by the rest of us but there was a measure of understanding that would not have existed at flying school. We had now developed an unspoken allegiance, a sense of belonging which somehow left the rest of the world behind. Even so, our individual fears were seldom articulated and so remained to be dealt with privately. The relish with which I opened up for take-off began to be tempered with a grim determination that it would "not be my turn today," and when I caught myself nervously checking my cockpit vital actions twice over I realised just how 'windy' I had grown. Fortunately it was a passing phase but while it lasted it provided some tiny insight into what aircrews must endure and conquer in time of war. When one of our chums was dropped from further training our little course closed ranks. Brian Longworth, a natural leader if ever there was one, introduced his "45 Course anthem" which he led to the tune of the Eton Boating Song whenever spirits flagged.

> *"Forty Five forever, all together we sing,*
> *Forty Five forever, our motto 'The end is the thing.'*
> *Our Crest an immovable finger,*
> *Our aim to successfully skive,*
> *And we don't give a damn what you call us*
> *Just as long as we stay alive!"*

Sadly, the accidents did not stop with the Vampire and Brian himself would be killed within a year flying an F-86 Sabre. He was a very nice chap indeed, and of all my fellow travellers the one most likely to have made Air Marshal; I trust our paths might yet cross again beyond this life, who knows? But for the time being the six of us carried on, and then one morning Jock nearly 'bought it.' With a hitherto unblemished record, he felt unwell returning from a sortie, despite selecting 100% oxygen. He was so groggy on touchdown that he was unable to keep straight and his fighter swung off the runway and hurtled across the grass towards the control tower. For once even the resilient Jock was not smiling; he not only frightened himself but also 'the management,' who arranged for him to finish his national service flying Chipmunks in his native Scotland – an enviable outcome.

After Jock had packed his bags the room I had shared with him seemed very empty, but at least he was still alive. Along with Algy Allington we'd kept together from the beginning. I was glad to catch up with Algy shortly afterwards when I had a particularly enjoyable flight up the scenic Welsh coast to Valley and back. Here they seemed to be living in Nissen huts but otherwise life was progressing in a similar fashion. Like Jock, Algy had also narrowly escaped hitting a ground-level obstruction, but in his case it was the airfield crash-wagon hell-bent on rescuing him from a seemingly doomed arrival through the undershoot area after they had seen him lift his Vampire, complete with underwing drop tanks, over the roof of an unexpected train!

Algy and I were both in the process of completing various aspects of the course including low- and high-level cross-country exercises. Our low-level sorties were along carefully authorised tracks which managed to avoid too many chimney pots en route. Although this fighter would comfortably exceed 450 knots (well over 500 mph), I think we flew these exercises at no more than 400 knots which, from a couple of hundred feet up, still gave a powerful impression of speed and probably allowed us to complete the course without running out of fuel! Navigating at low level by the silhouettes on a fast-moving skyline is fascinatingly different, and having to fly and read the carefully-folded map at this speed and height could be pretty riveting! Anticipation and reflexes are at a premium and one of Algy's contemporaries whose Vampire just touched the sea off Anglesey became a short-lived legend when he escaped from the cockpit after his aircraft had stalled and settled in 30 feet of water. At his second attempt a week or so later his luck finally ran out when what he hit was a dry stone wall.

The high-level cross-country was a different matter altogether. At 30,000 feet the sky took on a deeper blue and the featureless white carpet far below crept by at an imperceptible pace. The military radio was mostly silent and, with nothing within sight or sound, the little condensation-covered cockpit became an unbelievably lonely capsule. While aviators therefore need a fair measure of self-reliance, their essential attribute must surely be judgement. Not just the easier judgement of hand and eye but that more intangible judgement which can differentiate between "press on hard" and "don't even try." Just as *joie de vivre* needs tempering with caution, so a disciplined confidence is needed if fear is not to get the upper hand. Such balanced judgement can take time to acquire – hence the oft-quoted scarcity of "old bold pilots" – but it is not uncommon to frighten oneself (or worse) on the way, and I was to be no exception.

In the course of assessing my instrument flying, never my favourite occupation, my White Card "beginners" instrument rating was duly validated for jets. A few days later I set off to revise my aerobatics above cloud. They were by now familiar fun and I practised large lazy figures taking up a thousand feet or more at around 250-350 knots, much easier than at higher airspeed when the manual controls have stiffened up. At the top of a loop I could catch a glimpse of the Lyme Bay coastline 20,000 feet above my head, peeping through a cloud gap. It was all a great pursuit but in due course I called RAF Dunkeswell for a "QDM" course to steer. When halfway through their homing exercise I was instructed instead to return to Merryfield. This I acknowledged but it had been a cheerful morning so far and I was in no hurry to come in from play. I dawdled like a reluctant child, probably performing a few insolent slow rolls on the way.

When I did call Merryfield the controller confirmed the recall with a note of insistence in his voice. I dutifully transmitted for CRDF bearings, noting on the way that the cloud below was now reaching up to my altitude in an unbroken mass. Unappreciated by me, the winter weather had closed in and solo flying was being called off for the day. I prepared for a controlled let-down through cloud and, when lack of bearings indicated I was overhead Merryfield, turned onto the runway's reciprocal heading, put the airbrakes out and plunged earthwards through the enveloping cloud. Scanning the instrument panel intently, I endeavoured to hold everything steady, speed 250 knots, down, down, down, concentrating on the dials every inch of the way. Lose concentration and, disorientated, you are last seen emerging from a cloud in a terminal dive!

As the height wound off my altimeter I held my speed, direction and rate of descent as steady as I could. As 3,000 feet appeared on the altimeter I carefully steered through 180 degrees to head blindly for the invisible airfield somewhere ahead, then airbrakes out again, reducing speed to low safe cruising. It was still solid cloud outside – *concentrate* – height, direction, airspeed, rate of descent. Passing 1,500 feet I was getting steady bearings from the controller in response to my transmissions and I reduced the rate of descent as trained. But the lower I got the darker it grew and the more my self-confidence ebbed. At 1,200 feet we had usually broken out of cloud and I glanced up in the hope of seeing something discernible ahead. Instead, I was met with the chilling sight of snow, solidly packed against the windscreen and blanketing any forward view! I glanced anxiously sideways. Outside the canopy it was still dense 'clag.' *Concentrate.* Seconds later 1,000 feet came and went on the altimeter. I pressed on, increasingly alarmed about what might now lie ahead and how I was going to cope with it. *Concentrate, or it will be your turn today.*

Old hands may smile indulgently but there's a first time for everything and this felt like mine. At that moment I was more determined (than certain) that it wouldn't also be my last. Then, when my heart was heading for my boots a flash of darkness swept past the edge of my vision, to be repeated by another a moment later. None too soon the dark images of ground below became more frequent and, as heavy rain now washed away the snow, I could make out the wet runway through the murk. I ran in over the top of it, clinging now to a few visually recognisable features below, relieved to be freed from the tyranny of the blind-flying panel. Turning tightly in low circuits over the rain-lashed airfield I got down at the second attempt, feeling absolutely shattered.

"Airtrap 115," I called, "clear and complete." There came the routine acknowledgement over the radio. We always called "clear and complete" at the end of a sortie, so I must have done. I must have taxied back to dispersal, switched off everything and climbed out of my FB.5. I must have closed my cockpit canopy and sprinted across the rainswept tarmac to the shelter of the single-storey "flights" building which flanked the hangar. I must have done, but I have no recollection of it at all. My mind was still in turmoil, still reliving the last ten minutes of the flight I'd just completed. I had done it, I was down, thank God sincerely.

The first thing I actually registered consciously doing was walking into the crew room. At this point I had rejoined the human race. They were all there, my young friends lounging and reading unconcernedly, just as I had left them an hour or so ago. The routine friendly nod: "OK, Ali?"

"Fine," I said and slumped into an easy chair. Oh! that wonderful old battered standard-issue crew-room chair! I sat there, silently sensing *terra firma*. I ran the palms of my clammy hands along its wooden arms, a simple gesture but incredibly necessary and reassuring as the bottled-up fright drained out of my body. Gradually I put the ingredients of that sortie into perspective – complacency, the elements and mounting under-confidence held in check by discipline. The cryptic entry in my flying log simply reads: *"Vampire FB.5, No.WA288. Aerobatics and Controlled Descent, 45 mins solo, 10 mins in cloud,"* but I had learned much that day, and next time I was a whole lot better!

*   *   *

If you are still alongside, gentle reader, then judge our youthful story, if you will, in the context of its era for, like our ancient steeds, it belongs to a bygone flying age. The Royal Air Force had given us the adventure of our young lives and had brought us safely through it. As a little leaving present there was promotion to Flying Officer in the VR but the Service had also wrought changes in us which would be of lasting personal benefit. Happily, the three of us survived to tell our tale and now that tale is told, albeit a mere snapshot of non-combatant and little-chronicled Service life in the early fifties.

Afterwards, Jock and I returned to industry to become chartered engineers and Algy and I stayed with aircraft in our different ways, he joining BOAC and ending up a senior Check Captain. Our luck has extended to an active retirement and, somehow, the mothers of our children still choose to live beside us! As for my friend Norman Cuddeford, the national serviceman who commanded an RAF station, if you tune in to Wimbledon you can hear his tennis commentaries which will, I trust, continue to entertain us for many seasons to come.

CHAPTER 19

A JOB WITH A COMPANY AEROPLANE

(MORE OR LESS)

by

Arthur W.J.G. Ord-Hume

[NOTES ON THE AUTHOR: Arthur Ord-Hume 'cut his aeronautical teeth' with the restoration of two Aeronca monoplanes and then built and flew several Luton Minors. Later he formed Phoenix Aircraft Ltd and was responsible for the design of the Luton LA.4A Minor and the Luton LA.5A Major. He acquired the rights to the French-designed Minicab and re-designed it to meet British home-built aircraft requirements. One of the earliest members of the Ultra Light Aircraft Association (later to become the Popular Flying Association), he was instrumental in the revival of the home-built aircraft movement after the war but first had to convince the then Ministry of Civil Aviation that amateur aircraft were safe. His exploits in trying to build an aeroplane while fighting red tape and officialdom are related in his book "On Home-Made Wings" published in 1997 by GMS Enterprises. Part of the following is extracted from his new book "Flight on Frail Wings" due out at the end of 1998. His untiring work for the amateur aviation cause earned him honorary membership of the Experimental Aircraft Association in America in 1956 and the Resseau du Sport de l'Air in France in 1957. He was awarded the first EAA Trophy for Outstanding Contribution to the Development of Home-Built Aircraft.]

Plans and events often pan out in a peculiar way. Five years in the Royal Air Force convinced me that I was not cut out for Service life. The alternative was a job in 'civvy street.' There were plenty of jobs available and the airlines were perfectly happy to take suitable candidates without Commercial Pilots' Licences and bang them through the course at Air Service Training at Hamble – and pay them a (small) salary into the bargain.

Set on the idea of becoming an aerial bus-driver, I had already approached British European Airways clutching a glowing reference (which had taken me hours to draft) and a mostly empty Flying Log Book.

Yes, they said, as soon as you are out of the RAF, come and see us again and we'll talk about training to CPL.

Naïvely, I took them at their word, not recognising the polite version of a well-known expression alluding to sex and travel. Once free of the King's Blue I found that there was a glut of highly-qualified ex-RAF pilots, most of whom were out of work, and the training scheme no longer existed.

The need to earn money inspired scrutiny of those depressing job ads where they want somebody with slightly different abilities than those you think you have. Having built my own aeroplane, driven a designer's drawing board for some years in my spare time and being both resourceful and a good liar, I responded to an advertisement for a junior line-drawer at Handley Page's factory in Cricklewood, North London. It would do as an interim job while I sought out something more aero in the aeronautical line.

The job was fine and undemanding and my weekly pay packet jingled nicely. Only more senior staff aspired to those silent pay-packets which contained paper money. Anyway, I was earning and this meant that I might be able to plan to have another aeroplane – I had just sold my home-built Luton Minor, G-AFIR, to Frank Parker of the Popular Flying Association.

This temporary if steady state of things came to a sudden and unexpected end from an unsuspected source. Feeling in need for a break from London where I was living with my father at Evelyn Drive, in Hatch End near Pinner, I decided to fly down to the Isle of Wight to see family and friends.

On March 17th 1956 I went to Elstree Flying Club and hired the Chipmunk G-AOSY. This was one of the very first machines to be 'civilianised' for club flying and it was a great delight to fly.

My destination was Bembridge Airport. I had been told that the flying club had just been closed and there was nobody there, but that John Britten and Desmond Norman, who had built the BN-1F and whom I knew quite well, would be at the airport. I flew down and made a full precautionary landing. The grass had not been mown for a very long time.

As promised, John and Desmond were there to meet me. Almost as soon as I got there, John Britten asked me what I was doing and whether I might be looking for a job. I said "not a lot" and "yes." However, my relatives were champing at the bit: it was time to get home for lunch. I promised to get back early for a chat with them both.

Mid-afternoon I made it back to Bembridge and resumed talking with John and Desmond.

For some while the small business operated by these two chaps – Britten-Norman Ltd – had been building a Druine Turbi which was sponsored by a commercial TV programme called "*This Week*" The programme, fronted by the legless pilot Colin Hodgkinson, was a sort of news and current affairs thing and once every few weeks they came down with a camera to film Colin Hodgkinson 'building his aeroplane,' or pretending to. The B-N workshop was in Ryde behind the Commodore Cinema which happened to be part of a small chain of cinemas owned by John Britten's father, Colonel Britten, who was also the island's magistrate and senior judge.

Anyway, there turned out to be problems. Their tiny work-force was also involved in the bread-and-butter work of converting Tiger Moths for crop-spraying and they had a second company called Crop Culture (Aerial) Ltd which was run by a broad Australian duster pilot called Jim McMahon, who spent most of his time abroad battering the living daylights out of crop pests by Tiger Moth, usually, I suspect, with the wheels. The result was that they were stretched to the limit and the Turbi project was getting further and further behind, while at the same time the television people were getting more and more up-tight.

"Was it," Desmond asked, "the sort of project I could take over and manage to completion?"

Naturally I said: "Yes."

Very decently Desmond produced a 50-gallon drum of petrol from which he and John Britten decanted a sufficiency to replenish the Chipmunk's tanks for the return flight. This, thoughtfully, they provided free, for which I was grateful.

I warmed to the two men for we were all about the same age and with similar interests. We left matters on the table with no definite offer, let alone decision.

I resumed pencil-pushing at Handley Page. You have to remember that in those days very few people except extremely senior managers had access to an outside telephone at work. There wasn't even a public coin-operated phone anywhere on site. And when, as frequently happened, people had wives (not all of them I recall were actually wives) who were having babies, nascent fathers had to wait until lunchtime and then dash down Claremont Avenue outside to a red phone-box on the corner. Since there were usually forty or fifty others with the same intent, the high-speed sprint down the road was a common occurrence. One learned not to stand in the way of burly men, each clutching fourpence in pennies and Rugby-tackling each other on the dash past the Express Dairies from whose semi-subterranean, eye-level-with-pavement office windows nervous girls working strange typewriters built to type details into huge leather-bound ledgers would look up, a fan of fingers across an aghast mouth.

So when a telegram arrived at Evelyn Drive, my father wondered how he could get a message to me. Dad, never one to beat about the bush, telephoned Sir Frederick in person! He said he did so because he thought

An evocative shot of Vampire T.11s of No.5 FTS, Oakington, spring 1955.
Photo: via Clive Elton.

UPPER: Clive Elton takes off in 139 Sqn. Canberra B.6 WT369 from Luqa, Malta, May 1957.
CENTRE: BEA DC-3 ("Pionair"-class) G-ALPN at Jersey, March 1959.
LOWER: Jackaroo G-ANZT after its precautionary landing on the Kent County Cricket Ground on September 6th 1958.
Photos: via Clive Elton.

UPPER Sqn. Ldr. A. Murray-Preston with 'friend' before the outbreak of WW II.
LOWER: Provosts lined up in the early morning sun at at RAF Ternhill, 1956.
Photos: Anthony Preston.

UPPER: Charles Cooper's Miles Hawk Major G-ADAB outside the family garage c.1936.

CENTRE: Charles Cooper's Flying Flea G-AEEI, with son John practising the "Armstrong" method.

LOWER: John seen with his appropriately-registered Tripacer G-ARAG at Fair Oaks c.1962.

Photos: via John Cooper.

UPPER: Halifax G-AHZM after its port undercarriage collapse at Elstree in September 1946.
CENTRE: A.R. "Tiny" Pilgrim's Beech D.17S Staggerwing at Elstree c.1948.
LOWER: The late E.J. Riding about to take off in Piper L-4 Cub G-AKAA, probably from Eaton Bray in Bedfordshire, in 1949.
Photos: Richard Riding.

UPPER: Derby Aviation's Anson 1 G-AMDA (with London School of Flying insignia), seen at Elstree in 1962.

CENTRE: Uncompleted Aerovan G-AMYA, snapped on the day it was taken out of the hangar at Elstree to be moved to Stapleford Tawney c.1959.

LOWER: Elstree Flying Club's Autocrat G-AGXT, used for aerial photography by both Eddie and Richard Riding in the '40s & '50s.

Photos: Richard Riding.

the general office number was likely to fend him off. He was right. But, when Sir Fred's secretary answered, Dad said "Ord-Hume here. Put me through to Sir Frederick at once, will you, there's a good girl."

And she did! I can only imagine the conversation but, whatever was said, my old man and the maverick aviation pioneer seemed to get on pretty well. The next thing was that my Section Leader took a phone call – and immediately stood up!

"Yes, Sir Frederick! Certainly, Sir Frederick! At once, Sir Frederick!"

He sat down, looking wan and flustered.

"You are to telephone your father at once," he said to me, adding almost incredulously: "on *this* phone!"

He was clearly shattered that while even *he* wasn't allowed to use the Company Telephone, here was me, a lowly-paid pencil-pushing runner, being instructed from the Highest Authority to have free use of the Company's Telephone machine!

The laugh was that when I called home, rather in a state of fear for it sounded as though it might be bad news, the message was that Desmond had sent me a wire reading: "If interested come immediately stop will pay £700 yearly stop Desmond."

I hung the Company Telephone back on its rest, turned to my still-shocked immediate boss, and said: "I'm leaving!"

My arrival at Britten-Norman was heralded by a thunderstorm which marked finis to a long and hitherto unbroken spell of hot weather. I reported to the place marked Labour Committee Rooms in Star Street, Ryde, and the first thing I encountered on arriving was the sight of a Tiger Moth fuselage being carried out through the narrow doors into the road, where it was loaded into a Lacey's removal van and taken off to Bembridge Airport. The locals seemed quite accustomed to this sort of business and nobody batted an eyelid.

With the Tiger no longer blocking the entrance I went in for a formal meeting with my new employers. Office accommodation in the former Labour Rooms which formed the Britten-Norman headquarters and works was rather limited. One shinned up a rickety open wooden stair with two small rooms at the top. There was also a sort of landing from which one could gain access to the circle of the cinema itself. It was thus possible, with some difficulty, to open the emergency exit and watch the film being shown in the cinema. I was warmly welcomed and told I had a free hand to do whatever was necessary to get the Turbi completed. I asked about the engine and found that Desmond had agreed to use the 50 hp Coventry-Victor Flying Neptune air-cooled flat-four which was currently being evaluated in a Piper Cub. That, I thought, would be both interesting and a challenge.

I was also told that the abandoned Bembridge Aerodrome, deserted and unlicensed since the previous summer when the former Bembridge

Flying Club had suddenly shut up shop and vanished when tipped off that police and Customs & Excise were interested in coming to see the place, would shortly be taken over by the company. And, I was told, I would have personal use of my very own company aeroplane!

"Wow!" I thought. Most people get cars — I was going to get an aeroplane! And it would be an Auster as well! This was very exciting because I knew there would have to be some trips back to Elstree to collect my bits and pieces. And, of course, I didn't own a car.

Downstairs from the eyrie that formed the more or less communal offices was the workshop. The airframe of the Turbi, rather incomplete, formed the barely-recognisable contents of one corner while a Tiger Moth, which had rather incongruously been inserted through the ordinary double doors of the building, took up the rest of the space.

The B-N workforce was very small and had to spend most of its time on the crop-spraying side of things making and assembling rotary atomisers and converting Tiger Moths. The Turbi was, therefore, rather a low priority. Anyway, here I was going to be paid to do the job I loved — building an aeroplane!

Desmond said it was time to collect my own personal company aeroplane! It is as well to point out here and now that in due course I found out that it never was actually my own nor was it my personal one, but that was the way it was presented to me. For now though I was getting a brand, spanking-new Company Aeroplane! The wise and the cynical will see that delusion has existed in my family for a long while . . . The aircraft was at Croydon Aerodrome and all I had to do was go and collect it.

Feeling pretty chuffed about the whole deal, I set off enthusiastically for Croydon by train and bus. I walked in through the aerodrome gates. Funnily enough this was the first time I had done this since those heady pre-war days when I had gone to Croydon with my father. All my visits since had been by air. Entering via the gates, therefore, was a rare experience. There ahead was all the bustle and tussle of a busy private and charter aerodrome. There were smart, stylish Tiger Moths, clean and dazzling Austers, sparkling Rapides and immaculate Proctors. A gleaming Nighthawk, a spanking-new paint-job on a Hornet Moth almost too new to touch yet, a dazzling Gemini and a brilliant Moth Minor. Ah! Yes, this was the place to be. And one of these dazzling, brilliant aeroplanes was going to be in my charge! Ah! It was a lovely day!

I reported to Rollasons and sorted out the chap I'd been told to ask for. Somewhat aloof, as all youthful private owners of executive company aeroplanes should be, I announced my name, said that I was from Britten-Norman and that I had come to collect my aeroplane.

The fellow looked at me, thought for a moment and said: "Oh, yes! This way, mate!"

I didn't like being called "mate," especially as I was here to collect my executive aeroplane. In any case, I really expected him to bring it to me, rather than me have to go to *it*. I visualised a team of white-coated mechanics polishing a gleaming Auster whose engine ticked over sweetly with a disc of dazzling light reflected by the prop before it. I could smell the sweet smell of new leather upholstery, petrol and rubber tyres, dope and brand new paint which new aeroplanes exude. Now I was being led by this chap in rather grubby overalls out of the hangar.

We walked past several pristine planes, one of which, a Rearsby Rooster, I was certain was mine. But no, we kept going. We passed a few rather run-down club aeroplanes and proceeded on towards the far end of the buildings. Here were one or two rather derelict aircraft, sad one-time sky warriors whose owners had abandoned them to a life of being picketed down in the open. Denied the comfort of a hangar, they were now well weathered and in need of a pretty good overhaul before ever dancing in the skies again.

We carried on walking until in the distance I spotted the scrap-heap. Every aerodrome has a scrap-heap. It is the place where empty dope cans see out their days and old pieces of cloth rendered forever rigid by cellulose soakage rest, frozen in that scrunched-up shape which was imparted immediately prior to their being discarded. It is the place where those parts of aircraft which have fallen victim to careless contact with a hangar door while being pushed out in a hurry are removed and consigned to oblivion. It is the place where the tortured frames of those mangled one-time flyers that have come into forcible and irreparable contact with *terra firma* are tossed to await the ultimate if slow dissolving effect of corrosion.

It was also the place where somebody had abandoned a clapped-out old Auster. I looked at this aeroplane with mild disinterest, a thought flitting through my mind that wasn't it a pity that a one-time nice aeroplane had fallen on such hard times. I carried on walking, only to find that my mechanic escort had stopped.

"Here it is, mate!" he said. He pointed to the fairy on top of the rubbish-dump. I stopped and my jaw dropped. My legs went slightly free at their down-locks.

"That?"

"Yup! I'll help you push it out and start it up."

I questioned whether it was likely to be pushable, let alone start-upable. As for flying, well, it didn't look as if it had seen a critical eye for a few years.

"It's OK, mate. When we heard you were coming for it we gave it the once-over and it's had an engine run. The chief engineer's signed it out and it's all fuelled up and ready to go."

G-ANHW looked pretty tatty. Because normal aircraft are always known by their 'last two' (unlike my Luton Minor G-AFIR which earned either its name in full or the soubriquet 'Gaffa'), this aeroplane became *"Horrible Willie"* from that moment forth. We heaved the thing clear of the rubbish dump and he found a pair of chocks for the wheels. On my insistence, he opened the cowlings and let me look at the engine. Most of it seemed to be there. I climbed in and tried the controls. The stick banged from side to side with the ailerons like they do in all Austers. The flap-lever worked although the 'up' notch was so worn that even when 'up' the flaps were down a bit. He gave me a swing and the engine started with less protestation that I had somehow imagined. All the revs were there, too. What's more, nobody had fitted a mag-drop, so all was pretty good.

I said I would stop and notify the Control Tower of my impending departure.

"Don't bother, mate!" said Overalls. "You take your time taxying out and I'll phone the tower for you and they'll give you a green."

Sounded fair to me, so I kept the engine running, bid my mechanic an overly-formal "good day" and shut the door. There was a pervading aroma of mustiness. Not the smell you get in a library, but the one you get in a once-flooded unventilated bedding store. I looked around the cockpit as my mechanic disappeared into the distant building.

Cautiously I let off the handbrake and taxied slowly towards the hangar. As I approached, my mechanic appeared and gave me a thumbs-up sign. Ready to go! I taxied out past the tower and to the corner of the field where I turned crosswind and faced the tower, watching for a green. Nothing happened. I looked around the sky. It was deserted. I opened the throttle and taxied round in a wide circle back to where I had been before. I watched the glazed windows of the tower. Nothing. Again I looked at the sky. Apart from a disorientated starling, nothing. Once again I ran the circle, gunning the engine in short bursts in the hope that it could be heard above the sound of whatever it was the bods in the Tower were listening to on the radio.

It dawned on me that perhaps the green I was waiting for wouldn't come from the tower, but from somewhere else along the line of buildings. I scanned the skyline. Nothing. I had been running for ten minutes using valuable petrol and nobody seemed to notice me. I reckoned that if I had been in one of the smart private-owner jobs I'd have had people flashing pleasing messages at me all the while, but because I was in *"Horrible Willie"* there was some sort of "don't notice it and maybe it'll go away" scheme afoot.

I decided something had to be done. No lights was a bad thing. Even a white light would have told me that somebody had detected my presence out there on the lonely grass. I felt unloved and unwanted. Above all I couldn't wait all day and I couldn't see any reason for my not being cleared for take-off. Once more I did a circle, watching the sky very closely. It was deserted. I gunned the throttle, hoped *"Horrible Willie"* was willing to remain in one piece, and roared off along Croydon's famous turf.

The flight to the Isle of Wight would not be long and it was a fine, lovely day with the sun dead ahead. But suddenly I was aware that I had an awful pain in the head. Just above my left temple. It was a very sharp and unending pain. What on earth had happened? What had I done to get a spontaneous attack of the headaches? It is not funny to be taken ill in the air when you are alone and happen to be the pilot-in-charge. I got worried. I moved my head from side to side and the pain seemed to stop. As soon as I concentrated on the view ahead, back came this piercing pain like a knitting needle being pushed through my skull.

Mystified and approaching panic, I put my hand up to rub over the affected spot. As I did so, the pain transferred in an instant to the back of my hand. This was getting peculiar. With my hand in front of my face, it felt like somebody was boring a hole in my hand. Take my hand away, and the hole was being bored into my head.

It gradually dawned upon me that there might be some external cause. Less than ten miles later I had identified the culprit. There was a small hole in the windscreen and the prop-wash was being concentrated through this as if it was a lens. The upshot was that I was receiving a high-speed air-jet whose tip was no more than around an eighth of an inch in diameter. And it was right level with my forehead!

Relieved the reason had been found and that it was not my head that was about to go wrong, I completed the flight sitting slightly askew. I approached the still-deserted Bembridge Airport, landed short in the very long grass and then had a full-throttle taxy towards the closed and deserted hangar. I stopped close to the doors, tied the stick back with the harness and roped the lift-struts to some close-by concrete anchor blocks. I then took the bus into Ryde and told Desmond I'd collected the aeroplane and explained about the hole in the windscreen.

"Dab of chewing gum'll fix that" was the best he could offer. Since neither of us indulged in ruminating, it seemed a more than pointless comment to make.

The next day, with a length of rubber band pushed into the hole with a wire to act as a temporary closure, I flew to Elstree and got back to Evelyn Drive to collect bits for the Turbi. Over the weeks which followed I did the journey several times. To ease the bit of the journey from Elstree to Hatch End, I kept my old bike at Elstree.

Finally, I reckoned it was time to take the bike down to Bembridge. Simple, I reckoned. I would fly it down in the back of *"Horrible Willie."* Have you ever tried to get an ordinary large bike into an Auster? I can tell you it ain't easy! Shoving a fully-grown, uncooperative Indian elephant into a Sainsbury's plastic carrier-bag is probably easier. I tried front wheel first, then back wheel first, and so on. The main problem seemed to be the handlebars and even if I took one or both wheels off, I seemed likely to be little better off. Another problem was that I had built a large, tailor-made wooden pannier which slotted over the back wheel and into which I could stuff enough in the way of luggage to mount a ten-day expedition to the Chilterns. This box was not easy to remove which is why I tried to leave it in place.

After spending far too long trying every way to get the Raleigh into the back of the aircraft I came to the inevitable conclusion that there was indeed only one way to get the bike airborne with me and that was to tie it on outside the aircraft. In fact, rope it to the lift-struts. The Auster having V-shaped struts, I would have to tie the bike up against the underside of the wing at the top of the struts. With the aid of some wire and a few bits of thick string, the bike was secured under the starboard wing. The job was soon done and, engine started, off I went at an altitude of about 2,500 feet for Bembridge.

The drag of the big wooden pannier seemed more significant than that of the rest of the bike frame and to fly straight required constant left rudder and a lot of starboard aileron. Each few minutes I would cast a glance out the window to see that the bike was still there. I could imagine the headlines in the papers should it fall off. Manna from Heaven, maybe, but a bike! Bloody heck! I was concerned that I had left the pump clipped to the frame instead of taking it off and putting it into the wooden pannier at the back and was left hoping it would stay on for the duration. It did.

Other than the trim problem, the presence of the Raleigh Roadster under the wing did not seem to have any effect on the handling of the Auster and the cruising speed seemed about the same. I thought it unwise to chuck the machine around as a test on the strength of the string. In due course, when Bembridge hove into sight, I did my usual low fly-past to alert people in the hangar that I was back. This time, there was a large knot of people watching curiously as I came in on my final approach. The presence of the bike, clearly visible from the ground, had apparently raised some questions in the minds of the many.

I reminded people that in the twenties the RAF biplanes used to trundle around with a spare wheel and a spare propeller hitched on to the outside, so what was wrong with a bike?! And soon afterwards, Boeing used to fly a spare engine for its 707 airliners mounted in a pod under the wing. On second thoughts, perhaps they got the idea from me and my bike!

April 24th found the TV people filming the application of fabric to the wings. The scenario was that we kept the workers out of the picture and the impression was that Colin Hodgkinson was building the aeroplane and Desmond and I were supposed to be his assistants! Hodgkinson was a terribly nice fellow. Unlike Douglas Bader with whom I had had several brushes (one, unfortunately, in front of television cameras at Denham), this man was self-effacing, polite, quietly-spoken – and humorous. Now the ITV people wanted to get the machine flying as quickly as possible. They said "next week." We all laughed politely. They were serious. We explained it would be next to impossible.

Great interest was being generated by the Turbi project. The Popular Flying Association, through my continued presence on its executive committee, maintained a close watching-brief on the project. It was, of course, being televised and therefore was providing excellent publicity for the Association. It had to *be* right – and *go* right! PFA Engineering Committee would ensure that the paperwork went through as smoothly as possible. I was already a licensed PFA inspector for wooden aircraft and we had a ground engineer on the company payroll, so there would be no hold-up on the inspection side.

With a nod to the right person in the right department, we secured an out-of-sequence registration, G-APFA, for the Turbi. While this procedure is common practice now, in those days it was very hard unless the letters you wanted happened to be fairly close to where the strictly sequential allocation of alphabetical registration letters had reached.

I soon discovered that the construction team I had was in name only, and that most of the time there was other work to be done like building, fitting and testing Britten-Norman's patent rotary atomisers for Crop Culture's Tiger Moths. This meant that sometimes I would have a team, though mostly I was on my own.

By dint of long hours and hard work, the aircraft approached completion. Painting, spraying, masking out for the registration letters, fitting the engine, trying to make the cowlings fit – it was seemingly an endless task.

As it was, the TV crew did not turn up on the Thursday. They probably got wind of the fact that we were just not ready. However, after tea that day, I fitted the propeller and prepared to run the engine for the first time. It burbled into life reasonably happily – and then settled down to running on only three pots. More fiddling around until finally we got all four cylinders going merrily. The engine sounded very nice and it had a smoothness of running which, funnily enough, you did not always find with a Lycoming or a Continental.

Desmond, who had put himself down to make the first flight, decided that his moment was nigh and jumped in and taxied out to the end of the grass runway. The machine sounded delightful and Desmond was out to enjoy it! He opened the throttle and after a hundred feet or so of ungainly bouncing on its rather spidery undercarriage, the little blue monoplane cleared the ground and flew the length of the runway. It disappeared over the top of the hill – and was gone!

Suspecting that a Turbi out of sight over a hill and also a silence broken only by birdsong didn't augur well for aeronautical well-being, I ran the length of the runway, arriving breathless to find the Turbi bogged down in a muddy area just short of the drop into the woods at the Brading end. Desmond was doing his best to lift the machine out, turn it round and, it being a windless evening, fly back to the starting point. However, I spotted that the coaming in front of the windscreen was distorted and split around the fuel filler.

A quick look inside showed that the fuel tank rear attachment bracket had split away, allowing the whole weight of the tank and its fuel – a total of 115 lb – to hang from the ply deck and rest on the fuel cock! Desmond, flying from the rear cockpit, hadn't noticed the disaster unfolding in the front cockpit and was all for making another flight. The consequences would have been appalling, for the tank would certainly have fallen out and probably burst or been torn open.

We drained off all the 14 gallons of petrol into empty dope cans and then set about pushing the aircraft more than half a mile back to the hangar across the grass. At the end of that lot, and with mixed feelings – after all, the thing had actually flown – we repaired to the bar, had a suitable quantity of alcoholic refreshment, then went home to our respective beds.

Early next morning, having slept on the problem, I reckoned I could salvage the top coaming by carefully easing the tank filler-neck out of the hole, which could then be repaired with a stiffening ring of plywood around the inside. However, brilliant though this was in practice, the tank would not come out from the inside. The coaming had to be cut away, spoiling the brand new paint scheme.

The reason for the failure was easy to see. The sweated-on bracket had just peeled off the tank because it was not properly fitted in the first place. The tank had been made at Cowes by Saunders Roe. I hoped their bloody flying boats were made of sterner stuff. I washed out the petrol and, because the dangers of hot carbon tetrachloride had not then been discovered, filled the tank with carbon-tet, swilled it around – and then applied a blow-lamp to the outside to refit the bracket.

That job took about an hour all-told. Refitting the tank took rather less. Cutting, shaping, fitting, fabric-covering, taping, doping, filling, rubbing-down and then spraying the new plywood deck took three days.

On May 13th, Harold Best-Devereux came down representing both the Air Registration Board and the Popular Flying Association and flew the Turbi officially for the first time. He didn't seem terribly secure in the thing and it appeared to porpoise around the sky rather. He explained afterwards that it flew like a Turbulent with a very sensitive elevator which took some getting used to. But at least the engine seemed to work

224

OK. Desmond then flew a circuit and again it seemed to be highly sensitive fore and aft.

The TV people finally came and filmed Colin Hodgkinson climbing into the Turbi with his tin legs and being strapped in and then the engine being started. Then they filmed him getting out after which Desmond got in and they filmed a take-off and landing. When edited, it looked as though Hodgkinson had done all the flying!

There remained much to do on the machine with all sorts of bits and pieces to attend to which had not been completed earlier. Now the pressure was off and the TV people had finally departed for good, there was much more time. Desmond, who had made the preliminary test flights, was now preoccupied with other matters so I had to do both the flying and the mechanics, which suited me fine.

Now I found out for myself about the elevator sensitivity and also discovered that the aircraft was alarmingly nose-heavy. With the 50 horsepower Coventry-Victor motor, the machine was more than 50 lb above its anticipated empty weight. Tests with ballast in the front cockpit quickly proved what I had feared all along, namely that the aircraft would be underpowered and overweight with two up and that it should only be flown solo. The controls had to be re-rigged and a small ballast weight put in the tail. After that it flew much better.

A recurring problem to sort out was the engine cooling. After running for a short while, the engine would begin to run rough and start missing on its rear cylinders. I borrowed a set of thermocouples from Saunders Roe and connected their terminal washers under the sparking plugs in place of the usual copper washers. With these in place it was clear that the rear cylinders were heating up twice as fast as the front ones.

I experimented with a number of different shapes of baffles until it dawned on me that it was not so much the rear cylinders as the front ones which needed attention so that the airflow front to back was able to be accelerated and properly vented.

I spent many hours fiddling with different shaped bits of bent aluminium. The theoretically-designed ones worked no better than the ones we eyeballed. I fitted deflectors in the air inlets in the nose cowl, I fitted scoops between the cylinders – I tried everything. And, between each experiment, the job of making detailed notes and sketches and then doing an air test had to be completed.

During this difficult period of experimentation, we took delivery of a brand new Auster Alpha, 'we' being Britten-Norman and the aeroplane being G-APAR. Ultimately this would be converted for crop-spraying but in the meanwhile it became my runabout since *"Horrible Willie"* had gone terminally u/s and had been part-exchanged (by Desmond) for an aeroplane. My first flight in *"Arthur's Runabout"* ('AR, as 'HW, was known by its 'last two' and one of the girls in the office called it this one

225

day and it stuck) was to get some air-to-air pictures of Harold Best-Devereux in the Turbi. Then it was used at weekends to fly to Hatch End to see my father.

All fliers can tell embarrassing stories. The best of them, though, they prefer to keep quiet about because they are just too cringeingly embarrassing. Since I never had minor events happen to me, most of my escapades hit the latter category. So it was with the story of the Hirtenberg and Jack Cosmelli.

Jack was co-owner of the Hirtenberg HS.9A, a really magnificent German open-cockpit two-seater dating from 1937. Registered G-AGAK, the aircraft was a frequent visitor to Bembridge and, knowing my love for this highly individual machine with its Gipsy Major 120 hp engine, Jack would allow me to fly it. Never solo, mind you. He treated it like a jealous husband looks after his wife, and like all jealous husbands, he never trusted anybody else up alone in her. He would sit happily while I flew, but would draw the line at P1 solo. Fair enough, it didn't worry me.

On this particular day, Jack arrived clutching a brand new Super 8 cine camera. Would I fly him out over Sandown Bay so he could take some pictures of the esplanade? Fine.

Only one problem, he said. I would have to fly from the front seat since this cockpit was right under the wing with no camera visibility while the rear cockpit (technically the P1 spot in this dual-control tandem aircraft) was superior for filming, having an unrestricted field of vision.

Now this was fine except for two technical details. There was no working intercom. Neither Gosport tubes nor headset were fitted. The other problem was that because of the width of the fuselage and the depth of the cockpit, the view over the shoulder from the front cockpit was on the par with a brick wall at two inches.

"No problem," enthused Jack, demonstrating a familiarity with such situations; "I'll signal to you by waggling the stick!"

We worked out the routine. He would take off and fly to where he wanted to film. Then he'd waggle the stick for me to take control and I would signal with my right hand up. When he wanted control again, once more he would waggle the stick and I would signal with both hands up. Simple! Foolproof and reliable . . . so we thought.

I climbed into the front seat and got myself sorted out. Plenty of space, just not much in the way of view. Jack got in the rear cockpit almost four feet behind me. We taxied out and Jack took off, heading for Sandown Zoo the other side of the hill. We were at five hundred feet about four hundred yards offshore and flying west parallel with the water-line. The stick gave a positive left-right-left. Clearly this was where Jack was going to start filming. I took the stick with my left hand, raised my right and at the same time gave the rudder bar a little kick just for good measure. I craned my neck and tried to see round the edge of the seat-back. Yes, in my peripheral vision I could just see the lens of the camera pointing out. I continued flying holding course (a curve round the bay) and altitude – 500 feet.

Suddenly the stick went left-right-left. The 'Jack-was-back-in-control' signal! I let go and raised both hands. As I did so, the rudder bar kicked slightly. Good, Jack had cottoned on to my little extra signal. I kept both hands up for at least ten seconds. Gradually the Hirtenberg's nose began to turn to port. Well, I reckoned, he knew what he was doing.

We turned further away from the beach and, without any increase in power or altitude, set out for the vast open spaces of the sea in a wide circle. I was a bit worried because Jack was a sensible sort of fellow and that wasn't really on the agenda. In any case there was b***** all to film out here. As I thought that to myself, a small steamer hove into view. Ah! I thought. That's what he's after! And settled back to wait, arms folded and feet drawn up clear of the rudder bar.

The circle took several very long minutes during which I wasn't really at ease. I don't like water when it is below an aeroplane that's flying low. At long last, the beach came back into view and once more the stick wobbled and shook and the rudder twitched. I grabbed control and held up my right hand. Did he want me to continue along the beach towards Ventnor or return the way we had come? I decided to continue as we were. When we got to Dunnose Point beyond Shanklin pier, the stick gave a good triple wobble and the throttle lever opened in my palm. Jack was in control. I let go and raised both hands. We climbed under power, turned over the cliff at Luccombe Village and returned to Bembridge where Jack made a good landing.

We taxied in, stopped the engine and unstrapped ourselves.

"Did you get what you wanted?" I asked cheerily.

"Yes, I think so," replied Jack a little thoughtfully. "But why did you turn out over the water like that? Were you trying to show me something? All I saw was an old boat."

Well, gradually we realised what had happened. Jack, busy with his camera, was shuffling about in his cockpit trying to get a good squint through the viewfinder and must have knocked the stick with his knees. Of course he did not see me put a hand up, or two hands come to that. With nobody flying it, the Hirtenberg had quietly made a large circle and come back to where it had started while both of us sat there like lemons. The second kick was him trying to get the beach into his viewfinder again! We had a harsh moment of realisation, and then a hollow laugh. Yes, he said. Left to its own devices, the aircraft did tend to turn slowly to port . . .

Meanwhile my flights in the Turbi were anything but routine. There were countless problems. The tachometer drive broke in flight, the engine mounting cracked, the instruments under-read or over-read: it was a major hassle. Right through it all, though, the engine ran very sweetly and was quite free of vibration. The old problems with overheating, though, were not entirely cured and on very hot days the engine would start misfiring after ten or fifteen minutes. The technique was to close the throttle and let the machine glide for as long as possible to cool off a bit before opening the tap again. Since there was no carburettor heat control, this was a process which was a little risky but proved to be the only solution pending a more thorough investigation of the cooling problem and a permanent solution.

Then came the day when I was ready to undertake an endurance flight. I would keep the Turbi airborne for two hours minimum to see that all was well. I should have known better, but there it is. I had agreed with the PFA to do such a trip as part of the certification programme, so there was nothing for it but to get on and do it. The Flying Neptune burbled into life and, with the sweet sound of a well-oiled sewing machine, G-APFA and I climbed (slowly) into the blue skies. It was a nice clear day and once I was airborne with a few hundred feet on the clock I could clearly see the white chalk rocks of the Needles at the far end of the island.

My plan was to fly to Yarmouth and back and then fly two complete circuits of the island and see how much time was left. But first an 'out and back' to Yarmouth, as much as anything else to try to calibrate the airspeed indicator. There was virtually no wind so it was a good day to work a stopwatch and watch the instruments.

All was going smoothly and I had got myself lulled into a false sense of security when suddenly this huge storm came up. At least, I thought it was a storm because within a moment my vision was obscured and my face and helmet running with liquid. At this point I couldn't help noticing that the windscreen, hitherto clean clear polished Perspex, had turned a sickly yellow colour and was tending towards the opaque. What had I flown into? A hand up to my opaque goggles soon revealed the problem. I was covered in warm engine oil as was the windscreen and most of the rest of the fuselage, as later confirmed.

As lubricant-storms had not been forecast for the West Wight that morning, I looked at the oil pressure gauge. It was doing what barometers often do before a storm, gently falling. Still the oil flowed in a fine spray through the narrow gap between fuselage and cowling. Broken up to a particle size which would do credit to a Britten-Norman rotary atomiser, I marvelled at the even dispersal of the spray about my person.

However, years of experience with things mechanical and possessed of a finely-honed inquisitive mind made me suspect that all might not be well in the engine department, a supposition now confirmed by the oil pressure gauge which had now come to a rest just a gnat's cock short of 5 lb. Beneath me was the straight stretch of the Military Road which runs from Niton to the west of the Wight. I was at 5,000 feet and Bembridge

Airport was still clearly in view. I reckoned that by throttling right back, the Turbi's reasonably good gliding angle of slightly better than one in two was worth experimenting with in the hope that we might get back to base before either hitting the ground or welding the moving parts of the motor into a solid mass.

The sun was well up by now and I found to my surprise that I was travelling east with the motor quietly ticking over without losing appreciable height. Surely I couldn't be soaring in an aeroplane with an aspect ratio which sounded like a poor mark in a pop-music contest! As we came over Shanklin, however, the machine suddenly began to increase its rate of descent and Bembridge began to look a very long way away. It would have to be Sandown Airport.

No sooner had I altered course slightly for Sandown's flat grass field than the aircraft got another dose of what felt like 'green ball' – and carried on floating. Five minutes later I was over Bembridge with three hundred feet to spare. Gingerly I felt the throttle. The Flying Neptune responded as eagerly as ever. This motor clearly ran just as well without oil as *with* the stuff! Anyway, I didn't chance my luck but landed quickly and opted not to risk taxying in. I stopped the engine where I was and waited for somebody to come out and help push.

Once in the hangar the problem was obvious: the oil feed pipe had fractured and sprayed the contents of the tank over everything. I wondered how many washing-lines I had inadvertently polluted, although I suspect that from that height nobody would ever have noticed! Rectification was a long long job. I remembered the old joke about the mechanic's bill: "To hitting lump of metal: 6d. To knowing where to hit: £6." The oil pipe was fixed in half an hour and it took a whole day and more to get the oil off the aircraft and me.

Shortly after this, Crop Culture acquired a really gorgeous Tiger Moth, G-ANFT. A one-time RAF machine and newly-civilianised, she was a delight for two reasons. First, she had the sweetest Gipsy engine imaginable, and second, she was perfectly rigged and would fly effortlessly hands and feet off. I grew very fond of this machine and during 1957 did many hours in her with countless trips across the water to Portsmouth Airport to collect urgent materials, to Rearsby to see Austers, to Croydon, Bognor (to land on Lec Refrigeration's funny little landing strip by the river: the only place I know with a runway that looks like a footpath and which has a 30 degree dog-leg in it!), to Ipswich, Cardiff (Rhoose) and so on.

I had a laugh one day when I telephoned Croydon for permission to arrive in 'FT and to post an ETA.

A rather snooty female at the other end said: "Have you got a radio?"

I answered: "No, but not to worry as I've got a jolly good book."

229

I never did find out who the lady was but she didn't stop me from putting 'FT on Croydon's daisies.

G-ANFT never gave any trouble, always started first time, flew like a dream and, as I soon discovered, when it was foggy she always knew her way home. She brought me back through some pretty foul weather at times. When I heard she was to be converted to crop-spraying duties and was going out to the Middle East I felt really really sad. My feeling then was that once a machine has been converted for spraying or dusting duties, that's it. It's damned hard to convert it back again, always assuming that it both survives and isn't corroded to blazes.

It was around this time, on a date which even now I dare not specify, that I did something more than usually stupid. Everybody at Elstree was advised to renew, maintain or acquire an instrument rating, the exact procedure depending on whether or not they already had one. I had not flown on instruments since leaving the Royal Air Force. Elstree Flying Club had installed one of the Link Trainers from the store of derelict ones in the lower hangar.

Based on previous experiences, Link Trainers and me never quite gelled. I had been told, in the dim distant past, that one either flew Link Trainers or aeroplanes and often the person who could handle the one could not handle the other. In my case it was a case of not being able to handle the Link.

For those of such tender years that they may not directly recall the Link Trainer, allow me to refresh your memory. This was a synthetic flying machine made in America by the Link Piano Company Inc of Binghampton, New York State. Founder Edwin Link was a maker of coin-operated pneumatically-played musical instruments, in particular player-pianos. Link's instruments during the 1920s were renowned as being among the best in the business. Link was a remarkable man and I actually had the pleasure of meeting him in America in the 1960s. Besides player pianos, he also developed manned miniature submarines for undersea exploration, a skill which came into its own during the 1950s and 1960s. But here the story concerns Link, the amateur flyer.

Back in 1926, Ed Link realised there was a need for a synthetic aircraft trainer. His skill at pneumatically-controlled mechanisms naturally led him along the path to an air-operated mechanism and his machines were actually built using the regulator parts from player-pianos.

Link also built a player-piano-type mechanism into an aircraft, the perforated paper rolls of the player controlling light bulbs under the aircraft wings. Power to drive the paper roll across the tracker-bar of light-switch-control openings and suction power for the operating mechanism was generated by an airflow turbine. This displayed advertising messages from the air such as "Spaulding Bread" and "Enna Jettick Shoes." Three Ford Trimotors were converted and flown by Ed

Link's company as one of the first businesses to go in for aerial advertising using moving light signs. That was in 1930.

However, the Link Trainer for aircraft instruction was so successful that it was supplied in thousands to the American Air Force, the Royal Air Force and to flying schools the world over.

The little Link Trainer was a pedestal containing a complex assembly of electrical components and pneumatic valves and motors. On top was mounted a blue-painted plywood box with a little stylised plywood tailplane and rudder and two little wings. The 'pilot' climbed inside and closed the hood which was quite opaque. The instructor sat at a table on which was a large map upon which sat a little movable 'vehicle' termed 'the crab.' This was linked by umbilical cord to the trainer. The instructor could talk to the pupil pilot through a microphone and earphones.

To fly the trainer, you climbed in and switched on the vacuum pump. As it powered up, your instructor undid two steel straps which prevented the thing from falling over against its movement-limiting stops. The instructor gave you flight information which you did your best to follow and as you proceeded, the 'crab' moved slowly across the chart on the instructor's table. You as 'pilot' had a special set of instruments which produced readings comparable with what you would expect from those of a real aeroplane.

In theory, it was easy. In practice it was better to fly a real aeroplane 'blind.' I was no good at the Link. My sessions with Elstree instructor Bill Bailey were poor. I was rated 'below average.' This worried me and I couldn't understand why because, when I flew Elstree's Miles Magister with the blind-flying hood up, I was rated 'very good.' Bill made me fly the "Maggie" regularly and I always did well. But when the same instructor shoved me into the Link I was all over the place. As a Link Trainer pilot, I think I suffered more terminal crashes than most!

I wondered what it would be like to fly G-AFIR 'blind,' meaning using instruments only. The problem was that I couldn't really shove a hood over the cockpit. What I needed to do was to practice self-discipline and only look downwards and not, under any circumstances, look out! A cardboard visor tucked under the front of my helmet and sticking out over my goggles would help.

I had taken G-AFIR out to the compass circle and checked the compass carefully. The corrections were made using the corrector box and I was satisfied that it was accurate. Meanwhile, I noticed I was having a little bother with the slow-running jet of the carburettor which needed careful adjustment. I carried a 5/16"-1/4" King Dick spanner in my pocket so that I could make the minute adjustments needed until I got it just right.

And finally came the day when I thought I would practise some 'head-down' blind flying in G-AFIR. I decided to do a short flight to Stapleford

Tawney and back. I would fly at 3,000 feet which was above local traffic level so I would not hit anything. It was a perfectly clear day with a blue sky and no wind. Just right, I thought.

I took off, spiralled slowly up to altitude and flew over the runway to line up with Stapleford. Flight time 20 minutes. Then I put my head down and watched airspeed indicator, compass – and stopwatch. At the end of the appointed time, I straightened up and looked out the side. Stapleford was immediately below me!

Filled with confidence, I landed to have a cup of coffee and see ground engineer Eric Thurston and pass the time of day. As I taxied in, I noticed the slow-running was just a wee bit fast. I got out and adjusted it. Something distracted me and I completed the job quickly while talking to a bystander.

Coffee done, now for the return leg. Same procedure: take off, climb to 3,000 feet, fly over the airfield and set course for Elstree – then head down and cardboard visor as blinkers. I concentrated on instruments and stopwatch for about fifteen minutes when I began to get a very strange feeling that all was not well. For a start, the shadow of the sun, apparent to me as I flew head-down, didn't seem to be where it ought to be. But the compass said I was dead on course for Elstree. It had worked correctly on the way out, so it must work the same on the way back.

But I was still uneasy. Finally I decided that I would break my self-imposed discipline and actually take a look. What I saw gave me the shock of my life for ahead there was nothing but mud and water! Beneath me were two vast high-tension pylons. I knew exactly where they were – they were the biggest pylons in the National Grid and were situated at Dagenham to take the cables across the Thames. And somewhere up ahead in what was now hazy would be the Ford car factory! And yet the compass still showed that I was heading west while my eyes showed that I was going pretty well due south. I turned starboard quickly and flew up the Thames. The sun on my left showed I was flying west: the compass pointed nearly north.

I passed nervously over Hackney Wick stadium – I know because it said so in big white letters on the roof – and ahead lay all of London. Thanking my lucky stars that it was a Sunday (although what difference that made I was not quite sure), I followed the chain of open spaces. Keeping an eye on Regent's Park and Primrose Hill to my left, I made first for Hampstead Heath, then Hendon Aerodrome and finally back to Elstree. The compass told me that I was now flying north-east when I knew it was west of north.

I landed very puzzled as to why the compass had suddenly gone haywire. As I taxied in, I noted the slow-running was a little bit too slow. I must have over-corrected it at Stapleford. I reached into my pocket to get my special spanner out – and found it wasn't there. I soon found it: it was on the little shelf behind the instrument panel and just next to the compass ...

Yes, I managed to learn a few lessons from my mistakes, and to be sure they were learned the hard way. It proves, though, that flying training is largely down to experience and hands-on struggle. We didn't have sophisticated navigational aids, satellite position-indicators and lightweight radio transceivers. We didn't have very good maps, but we were taught how to read them, read the ground and watch out for other aircraft. And navigation was achieved with old-fashioned mathematics and not a calculator in sight!

Some of that raw fun of flying, though, is lost forever. There's no room for the sort of flying we did half a century ago in today's formalised and crowded skies. Pity, really.

CHAPTER 20

NO SKYLARK

by

Chris Dearden

Think of the golden era of private flying. Think of a grass aerodrome. Think of the daisies, the buttercups. Think of a skylark singing. Think of a bright dawn, or the haunting indolence of a summer's evening, a light haze lingering, a small aeroplane on the approach, pottering home to roost. Think of all this. Then think again! It was part of a dream we once lived.

For me the dream ended on the 23rd of October 1961 at Redhill aerodrome. Redhill! Scene of my first fumbling attempts at flying an aeroplane when I'd joined the Club there in August 1947. But the place became much more than that to me. It became almost a second home.

In the spring of 1953 I'd gone to work in a drawing office there and stayed about eight and a half years. I came to know the 'drome in all its moods through the seasons. I felt I knew almost every blade of grass there. Ah! Redhill! Scene variously of high-jinks and low spirits – alas, the enchanting Boo-Boo loved another! However, life went on.

When the Flying Club rates became a bit too heavy for my meagre wages to bear I found to my delight that the Chelsea College (which had an outpost there) would hire me their Tiger Moth, 'MNN, for little more than the cost of the fuel per hour.

Lunchtime flights with colleagues became an established if irregular feature. It was all so easy; we were there, the 'drome was there, the Tiger was there. Maybe best of all was that period when the aerodrome was officially closed. The College had 'flying rights' in the terms of its lease, so we had the place to ourselves give or take the odd 'Prior Permission' arrivals and the very odd arrivals who claimed to be lost. Peace reigned supreme over that lovely expanse of grass. But I can look anyone in the eye and say that I continued to observe the procedures and disciplines taught me by the Redhill Flying Club. No cutting corners just because there was nothing else about. This was a thing which baffled me later on. What did I do wrong?

Naturally, as a Private Pilot, I was not allowed by law to seek any financial reward from my passengers, though they usually donated a few shillings to my pocket-money. I mention this because it recalls that happy episode with Sid the maintenance man, a lumbering soul with a heart of gold and the face of a clown.

I'd taken him for a lunchtime flight and afterwards asked him what he'd thought of it.

"Bit like ridin' on top of a bus," he said blandly.

That was all. There was no mention of anything else.

Top of a bus, eh? Had my flying been all that jerky? No matter.

The following morning Sid came loping in to the drawing office, plonked a packet of twenty cigarettes on my board and said simply: "Fanks fer yesterday," turned as pink as a blancmange and loped away without another word.

That simple act of sincerity meant more to me than all the blustering: "Wizard prang! Share expenses, old boy!" Bless you, Sid, wherever you are! I remember you for that fleeting moment of joy.

So life had a more-or-less ordered pattern. It was "Summertime and the flyin' was easy." Yet all good things come to an end (as the dog said when he bit his own tail). Drawing office work was getting scrappy, the old brigade had largely dispersed, the mood was changing. I felt the need to move on. It was 1961 and "Summertime" had given way to "September Song."

Well-intentioned but ultimately bad advice took me to a small firm in Redhill itself. Here I met up again with Lol, who'd previously been at the 'drome, had flown with me several times and who was a bit irritatingly persistent with his cry of: "Come on! Get the old Tiger out!" He said it again on the morning of the 23rd October 1961.

"Why not?" I replied (for want of anything useful to say). "If I phone the College they'll have it out ready for us. And if we get away from here a bit smartish at lunchtime . . . Yes, why not?"

We knew perfectly well there was no way we could get over to the 'drome, have any sort of worthwhile flight and be back at the factory within the hour. But all and sundry agreed we could play that one on the fiddle.

It felt strange to be back on the 'drome again, even after only so few weeks away. 'MNN was indeed out and ready for us, but otherwise there was little sign of life about the place. Spooky!

A spook with substance, though. Unknown to me – or anyone else I've subsequently met – the Royal Navy had established a small outfit at Redhill, something to do with helicopters, I believe. Of course, I should have known . . . It's the pilot's responsibility etc. etc. . . . . But I didn't.

So the flight in 'MNN was a pleasantly predictable affair: a couple of wide circles over the factory, a circle over Lol's house (again!). Then back to the 'drome for a regulation circuit, as umpteen times before and a tolerable landing (as not so often before). All nicely to the book.

But what was this? As I taxied in I noticed a little chap on the apron, apparently waiting for me. More than that, he seemed to be leaping up and down in a high state of excitement. Marvellous, I thought! He must have some stupendously good news for me – Mafeking's been relieved, or maybe someone has invented the phonograph.

Not a bit of it! As soon as I'd cut the switches and before I could even think of getting out of the aeroplane, "Mr Shorthouse" came leaping over to me.

"Cor blimey!" he yelped in a rather thin voice, "I wouldn't wanna be in your shoes! You ain't 'arf for it! They wanna see you in the tower!"

"The tower?" I questioned in some alarm, "of London?"

"No, no, the flyinge control tower."

"Oh, *that* tower. But there hasn't been anyone up there for yonks."

He gave a rather nasty little laugh.

"Well, there is nah, Mate. An' they wanna see yer. You'd best git up there a bit quick, like. Cor, you ain't 'arf gonna cop it!"

With that, he turned his back on me and wandered off, still leaping a little and muttering on about not wanting to be in my shoes. Come to that, I didn't much care for the look of *his* shoes, but I wasn't beefing about it.

I checked 'MNN back into the College, asked Lol to wait for me (but not longer than five years) and got up the tower a bit quick, like.

And there was this gorgeous Naval Personage (I can call him nothing less), heavily-decked with gold braid and a full set of whiskers. The works! He didn't actually have a parrot on his shoulder, though I felt he should have had.

He looked me up and down a time or two with evident distaste and then said: "Wah wah wah, haw, haw, haw, wah wah wah?" (Which, as any student of the subject could tell you, is Naval-Officer-Speak for: "Are you the fellow who was flyin' that little Moth thingy?")

I confirmed that I was he.

"Captain Hogwash" then weighed in to give me a severe talking-to. Coming from a Naval family, as I do, I knew the form. So I suitably grovelled and swore on my dear grey-haired old grandmother's grave – wherever that might be – that I'd never do such a thing again. Happily the interview ended in smiles and handshakes. There was no further aggro.

But the stupid part is that to this very day I don't know what it was I'd done wrong. Had I unwittingly taxied across the Quarter Deck? Failed to dip my ensign to the Admiral's Barge? Shivered my timbers when I should have spliced the mainbrace? Or simply been ignorant of their 'flyinge control' system?

Whatever it was, "Captain Hogwash" didn't tell me and I didn't like to ask. After he'd just expended so much effort in telling me off, I felt it would have seemed ungracious if I'd turned round and asked: "What the hell have you been talking about?"

That way could lie only further conflict and I knew I was out-gunned. I settled for going quietly on my way with a brass-bound flea in my ear, if not a parrot on my shoulder.

There was something else, though; something deeper, sadder. I had a feeling in my gut that this was the end of an era. When I couldn't go to Redhill – of all places – and have a harmless dabble in the Tiger without being hauled before authority, then the writing was on the wall. When I could be guilty of breaking rules I didn't even know existed, it was time to take stock.

And that's how it worked out. Although I didn't realise it at the time, that proved to be the very last occasion on which I flew as a licensed pilot. The party was over. Only the debris remained. It wasn't as any direct result of the 'Naval' incident, it just worked out that way. Maybe it was a fitting end to my fumbling efforts to be an aviator.

No skylark would ever again sing for me at Redhill.

EPILOGUE

So that was the end of the line for me, but not for 'MNN. Others flew her from time to time until June '64 when an ace lost it completely on take-off from Redhill and left the old girl in a very second-hand state. ("There but for the Grace of God," I thought when I heard of it). It looked a bit like the end of the line for 'MNN too.

Return, for a moment, to the spring of '61 and my lunchtime flights. On 19th April that year it happened to be the turn of one Dorothy Collins to come for a ride (it was to lead to a very happy and enduring marriage). By pure coincidence my drawing office colleague, Pete Sullivan, was going off to do some air-to-ground photography in his own Turbulent, G-APBZ.

"Keep the Tiger throttled well back," he said, "and I'll snook alongside and take an air-to-air of you, if you like."

And so it was. Some years later I gave a copy of the picture to the Chelsea College, at a time when the future of 'MNN seemed to be sulking under a cloud of mystery.

As is well known, the College students at Shoreham have recently done a magnificent restoration job on her and the 'first flight' was featured on Meridian TV. Dorothy and I gazed starry-eyed. Suddenly the picture cut to that black-and-white still.

"Good heavens!" we squealed (almost) together, "That's us!"

Next day I phoned the College to express my pleasure and they suggested I might like to go over to look at the Tiger again. I was treated like visiting Royalty and invited to sit in it and "take my time."

Without shame I admit I was hard-put not to shed a nostalgic tear as I sat in that cockpit again. Time had slipped away . . . Was that a skylark I heard singing? No, it was only a ghost. Yet another ghost haunted me as I struggled with the simple tasks of getting in and out of the aeroplane. Did I really once leap in and out of it with the ease and grace of a gazelle? If I ever did it must have been in a previous incarnation. No chance now!

Afterwards they presented me with the old strip of fabric from the rudder, bearing the magic letters G-AMNN. Also, they gave me the original VNE plate from the dashboard: *"This aircraft must not be flown at ASI readings in excess of 160 mph (139 knots)."*

I note it well! To ignore that rule in life would be to take a short cut to the great 'Flyinge Control Tower' in the sky . . . "Hold it, Hogwash, I'm on my way!"

Meanwhile, the sun shines again on 'MNN. And, on reflection, it shines on me as well.

CHAPTER 21

FLYING FREEDOM IN THE FUN-SOAKED FIFTIES

by

Clive Elton

One of the many changes to have taken place over the last forty or fifty years has been the curtailment of flying freedom, simply because of the nature and intensity of aviation today, whether it be commercial, military or GA.

The fifties represented a wonderful period, as we put the war well and truly behind us and recaptured some of the aviation delights of the thirties. Later, restrictions and controls took some, but not all, of the happy-go-lucky carefree atmosphere away.

Of mid-thirties vintage, I was born on the 25th March 1935; when 1950 arrived, I was fifteen years old and had never flown at all! I admired all things flying, there being plenty to admire and thrill to, living as I did in Sanderstead, with Croydon, Kenley and Biggin Hill all within a few miles. As a five-year-old I had watched from our back lawn as the Battle of Britain took place in the skies above. I had become skilled at recognising both allied and German aircraft by sight and sound. We survived the bombing until July 1944 when a V1 'doodlebug,' which fell at the end of the garden, finally forced us temporarily out of the area.

It was whilst at Whitgift School in Croydon that the opportunity came to participate in this flying game: the RAF section of the Combined Cadet Force, April 1950, as a very junior cadet on a one-week camp at Cranwell. The back seat of a Prentice was not the most exciting initiation but little did I anticipate what the decade was to bring me. Nine years later I was again very junior, but this time as a co-pilot in British European Airways flying Dakotas, or *"Pionairs"* as BEA called them.

What happened to me between April 1950 and April 1959 and indeed on into the sixties could fill a book; this after all can only be an overview but I am sure that my contemporaries would agree that it was a time of great opportunity. The Royal Air Force was huge by comparison with today, the airlines were expanding (as they are once more, following a lean period) and sport flying was establishing itself.

After that back seat ride in a Prentice there followed flights in a Harvard, low-flying over the Lincolnshire countryside, and more in the Prentice, with my first experience of handling the controls. So this was flying, and I wanted more. Back at school we learnt of the communications flight at RAF Kenley which operated Ansons to various airfields in southern England. A call to the unit, ostensibly from our CO, with the information that there were two cadets keen to fly, and we were on our bikes, clad in cadet uniform, and ready to sample the delights of Martlesham Heath, Cambridge, Swinderby and Hornchurch, amongst others. The passenger seats of the Anson may not be everyone's idea of exciting flying, but it was a start. A landing at Newton near Nottingham did produce some mild drama, when, having noticed something fly past the window after touchdown on a fairly soft grass airfield, it all went a bit quiet; then the pilot, Master Aircrew at that, rushed past us and left the aircraft by the port door. The two of us followed slowly to find the aircraft closer to the ground than usual. Damage from this wheels-up landing appeared minimal; the problem was, how we were going to get home?

Then in the glorious summer of 1951 there was a week's gliding course at Detling in Kent. The T.21B Sedbergh, T.31 Tutor, Prefect and Grunau Baby would perhaps be laughed at by today's gliding fraternity, but for me it was great to fly solo over the pleasant Kent countryside and feel a long way from school studies and the pending 'O' level results. Two years later while awaiting 'A' level results I was back at Detling doing the more advanced course. 1951 was also the year of the Festival of Britain, and 1953 was Coronation year, so there were other distractions from exams, which may have partly accounted for rather moderate results!

The main distraction from 'A' level studies came in 1952 with the award of an RAF flying scholarship, which in those days was worth a full PPL course. The month of August was spent in the company of other cadets at the old Redhill Flying Club. The CFI was Alan Sproxton, ably supported by Peter Chinn, "Tiny" Marshall and Glyn Ward with a fleet of three Miles Magisters. When Redhill closed in April 1954 the club moved to Croydon and became the Surrey Flying Club, only to have to move again in September 1959 to Biggin Hill as the Surrey and Kent Flying Club. That as they say is another story.

Open cockpits, Sutton harnesses and Gosport tubes, it was the real thing. Not too easy to understand what was being said at times, probably just as well, as instructional technique has improved considerably since then. In fairness it was mostly the CFI who resorted to strong language, but in spite of that we all survived and passed the course. One feature of the inter-cockpit communication was the mouthpiece, which was situated just below the coaming on the right-hand side. A tell-tale dirty mark around one's mouth, especially after a rather intense dual flight, was most noticeable, rather more so on the instructor than the pupil perhaps.

First solos were celebrated at the local pub, the Station Hotel in South Nutfield; as none of us had cars in those days this involved a rather pleasant walk across the fields. Maybe sometimes we behaved like a bunch of schoolboys, but then we *were* a bunch of schoolboys. I think we appreciated how very lucky we were and we certainly did appreciate the dear old "Maggie." Our favourite, registered G-ALFE, was needless to say affectionately known as "Alfie." There were also a couple of Auster Autocrats which later proved ideal for flying one's friends and family in. One friend I took up was a keen photographer and he took some splendid pictures of our school. Copies of these were subsequently sold to schoolfriends, the proceeds more than adequately covering the cost of the flying – my first venture into commercial aviation.

Back at school in September, having not quite completed the course, three weekend visits to Redhill were required to do the cross-country flying and the Royal Aero Club test, as it was called in those days. The triangular cross-country was to Southend, Shoreham and back. A week after the dual trip I set off to do it solo but turned back halfway to Southend because of poor visibility. The first airmanship decision of my career had been taken but I was most uncertain how my early return would be greeted by the CFI. His reaction was to send me straight off to Shoreham and back, before dispatching me once more to Southend later in the day when the conditions were better. This time I was successful and then flew the long leg to Shoreham before returning once more to Redhill. Nothing really remarkable about all that, except that to me it had been a very exciting day, and bear in mind there was no radio, just a map and a compass. I seem to remember I was on a bit of a 'high' returning to school on the Monday.

Armed with a shiny new PPL and with a year to go before I could join the Royal Air Force, the problem was how to finance more flying. It seemed to me that the answer was to find where I could be paid to fly without having a commercial licence. Then I heard of the RAFVR. At the Volunteer Reserve Headquarters in London I was duly enrolled as 2614630 Cadet Pilot, to be attached to No.15 Reserve Flying School at, of all places, Redhill!

So for ten glorious months I flew Chipmunks, with the occasional flight in an Oxford. Travel to and fro from my home was by public transport, with the last part on foot across fields of cows, avoiding the longer route round the lanes. The only sound was usually that of aircraft, as I neared the airfield with that great feeling of expectation. As if all this was not enough, each month I received a pay cheque for around £10, a small fortune to a sixth-former in those days. It was this business of still being at school which threatened to curtail my flying, so I decided to add Wednesdays to my weekend visits to the RFS.

The inevitable happened when I was invited to the Headmaster's study to explain my absence from school on three successive Wednesdays. Maybe I wore a slightly hurt expression when I just said: "Oh! Wednesday is the day I go flying."

After a short hesitation he just said: "Well, that's alright then."

Dual instruction on the Chipmunk now involved aerobatics and instrument flying, with an introduction to formation flying. It was all tremendous fun, with just a touch of military discipline, but mostly like a glorified flying club. Low-flying was one exercise we could not get enough of. One chap got himself into a little trouble by unofficially low-flying over his girl friend's house in a Sussex village. Nothing new about that, but he incurred the wrath of the village bobby, who telephoned Redhill to report that one pass would have been acceptable, but as could be heard when he held the telephone receiver outside the call-box, the unmistakable sound of a low-flying Gipsy Major was clearly causing a *prolonged* disturbance.

The school holidays at Easter provided an opportunity for 15 days continuous training, and by now my confidence as a pilot was high. However I was warned of what was then called the 30-300-3,000 syndrome. After 30 hours you think you know all about flying, after 300 hours you are sure you know all about flying and after 3,000 hours you are quite certain you will never know all about flying. Over-confidence has claimed many lives over the years and I was fortunate to have some wise old pilots to advise me. Great days, but there was just not time to study for 'A' levels, fly *and* pursue my other sport of cricket. It was not exactly over-confidence which was responsible for my failure in the exams!

1953, with the coronation of Queen Elizabeth, also featured the Queen's review of the Royal Navy at Spithead and the Royal Air Force at Odiham. Two of us hitch-hiked to Portsmouth for the RN review, having slipped out early from an 'A' level paper one beautiful summer morning. It was well worth it, being a most memorable occasion, lasting late into the evening when the fleet was famously all lit up.

No hitch-hiking was necessary for the RAF review; for some extraordinary reason my CO at the school cadet force put my name forward and I was selected to fly as a passenger in the Home Command formation of 16 Chipmunks in the flypast. That turned out to be something of an honour as it transpired that there was one cadet representing Scotland, me from England and various other representatives including Cliff Michelmore who did a BBC radio commentary from the formation. We flew from Booker, following a single Sycamore helicopter which led the flypast. After us came formations of all the types then operational in the RAF. On the ground at Odiham there were lines of aircraft with their crews formed up in front, the Queen inspecting them as she drove by in her Land Rover. For the flypast she stood on a dais and, whilst my pilot concentrated hard on formating in quite turbulent conditions, I was able to glimpse Her Majesty, clad as I remember in a blue coat.

In later years I met several pilots who had flown in that flypast and I learnt of the tremendous organisation involved, and of all the rehearsals which went into making it such a spectacular occasion. The numerical strength of the RAF in those days compared with today was quite staggering.

My pilot on that memorable day was a Group Captain and by some strange quirk a mere twelve days later I was being flown by another Group Captain; this time it was the station commander at Ternhill in Shropshire where we spent our cadet summer camp. The aircraft was a Harvard of No.6 FTS and it seemed to be a very appropriate way of rounding off my flying as a cadet, having flown in a Harvard on that first camp almost three and half years before. I was later to return to No.6 FTS, but by then it would have re-equipped with Provosts. There was another gliding course at Detling before my final farewell to the cadets. It had all been a wonderful experience and if there was one lesson to pass on, it was to recognise opportunities and not be afraid to take them.

National Service was still in existence in 1953, so having been granted deferment whilst at school, I volunteered for the Royal Air Force before actually being called up. This proved to be a very civilised method of joining up as I could even choose the date upon which I was to report to RAF Cardington, which was then the Reception Unit. I signed up for an eight-year short-service commission as a general duties officer, which was to be followed by four years on the reserve. Although it did not seem strange at the time, I was given a new service number, 4137586.

After four days at Cardington, where we were kitted out with uniform and various other items of equipment which were going to require considerable attention over the coming weeks, there was a short stay at the aircrew transit unit at Cranwell. This period included an introduction to 'squarebashing' and 'bulling,' at which we would later be expected to be very skilled. Then it was off to No.1 Initial Training School at Kirton in Lindsey for twelve weeks. We were not going to get anywhere near an aeroplane but we were going to enjoy, along with the hardships, the comradeship and fellowship of like-minded young men, which in the parlance of today would be referred to as the development of inter-personal skills.

As Officer Cadets we were paid 42/- (£2.10) per week. Halfway through the course some records must have arrived from the Air Ministry and it was discovered that I was entitled to an extra 6d (2½p) per day because of my service in the RAFVR. There was also a clue here as to why I had two service numbers. However what was much more important was that I had all that back pay to splash out in the NAAFI one evening!

We endured and to a degree enjoyed all the standard military pleasures associated with this type of training: kit inspections, ablution duty and the rest. There was classroom work and outdoor exercises, all the time with the knowledge that success at this stage would lead on to flying in the new year.

For some years pilot training in the RAF had been on the Prentice and Harvard. In 1953 the new concept was to award "wings" only after qualifying on jets. The piston-Provost and the Vampire were to be standard until the arrival of the Jet Provost some years later. For us Ternhill and Oakington would be our training bases, 6 FTS and 5 FTS respectively. Following a wintry time in Lincolnshire there were the first signs of spring in the lovely Shropshire countryside, although it was still mid-February when the course began. The relative comforts of the Officers' Mess (for now we were Acting Pilot Officers) and the freedom to explore the local beauty spots and pubs provided a very pleasant way of life. The Alvis Leonides-powered Provost with its side-by-side seating turned out to be an excellent training machine. Although not a difficult aircraft to fly, it could be quite testing, especially in performing a really accurate slow roll.

Spring and then summer, sunshine and flying, along with some cricket for the station team, for whom a willingness to turn out rather than any particular talent was all that was expected. This delightful existence had to have a down side: this was known as "the chop." There were two types of termination, "the chop" and "the big chop." The failure rate in RAF training in those days was quite high and it was always sad to see someone taken off the course. Far worse, and tragically too often, were the fatal accidents. With six courses of student pilots operating as six different flights, there would have been between 150 and 200 trainees based there at any one time. That can add up to a considerable amount of flying and, despite all the discipline, a collision on final approach between one Provost overshooting ("going around" in modern parlance) in response to a signal from the runway caravan, and another Provost who was close behind and did not see the aircraft in front pull up so sharply, resulted in the deaths of two students and an instructor. The sight of the blazing wreckage on the airfield was my first experience of the horrific side of aviation. Despite this and other tragedies it was predominantly a very happy time leading up to the graduation parade in mid-August of 1954. The standard of instruction had been very good, as it was to be at Oakington for the jet phase of the training.

The Vampire to us at that time was a revelation; this was something quite new, flying in the stratosphere and experiencing buffet as we learnt the importance of compressibility Mach numbers. I will never forget that first high-speed run across England on a fine clear day and the realisation of how small this country of ours is. There was a bit of glamour attached to jet flying in those days, even in the rather underpowered Vampire with its DH Goblin engine providing only about 3,500lb of thrust.

Dual training was on the side-by-side-seat Vampire T.11 but the single seat FB.5 was another first-time experience. There is something about flying a single-seat aircraft which is more exciting than flying solo in a two-seater. Perhaps we are all fighter pilots at heart, although as things turned out, I was to be a bomber pilot.

Sadly there were more fatal accidents, far too many, but none of them were caused by the high-spirited activities for which most of us would have been strongly condemned if the authorities had become aware. Unofficial formation flying and low flying, aerobatics over London at night, and then there was the time two of us joined the circuit at Croydon and made an approach to land, much to the consternation of the controllers who fired red Very lights at us.

Since the closure of Redhill in the spring of 1954, Croydon had become the airfield from which I did my private flying, mostly with the Surrey Flying Club. Instead of the Magister and the Auster it was now the Tiger Moth and the Hornet Moth, amongst others. It was a privilege to fly from the historic Croydon turf, and particularly memorable was approaching Runway 24 alongside the famous control tower – whether it be by Tiger Moth or Vampire!

Oakington was a typical RAF airfield with a 6,000 ft runway and a dispersal area backed by standard military hangars. The surrounding countryside, though flat, had a definite charm as it stretched out towards Cambridge and the Fens, with the famous twin canals providing a most helpful landmark. The University town was a great attraction with its splendid selection of pubs, and with contemporaries from school days amongst the undergraduate population there was access to some of the colleges and the social life which went with them. Punting on the Cam was also a pleasant diversion, such a complete contrast to the more demanding activities of mastering high-level formation flying and aerobatics.

Wings Day in June 1955, with Mums and Dads and girl friends attending the parade and the lunch which followed, was a most memorable occasion. Air Chief Marshal Sir George Mills, the then AOC in C. of Bomber Command, was the reviewing officer who pinned the wings on us. The sun shone, the band played and we got that end-of-term feeling as thoughts turned to what lay ahead. A group of us selected for Canberras were to wait seven months before we finally got to the Operational Conversion Unit.

Due to a number of reasons, not fully explained, there was a backlog of trainees for bombers so the Air Ministry, in its wisdom, sent some of us to Dishforth in Yorkshire to do a second pilot's course on the Transport Command Hastings. This turned out to be a wonderful experience, flying

245

that famous old four-engine tail-dragger. It was the duty of the flight engineers to set the power as requested by the handling pilot; clearly they thought they knew better than these upstart young pilots, resulting from time to time in a shout of "Plus Eight" (boost) to correct a rather low approach.

August in Yorkshire was followed by September in Norfolk. For no doubt very good reasons we were sent to Feltwell to do a refresher course on the Provost. More fun flying in another lovely part of England, before it was back to jets, at Worksop in Nottinghamshire.

We were now on what was called a dispersed camp, laid out either side of a long road which ran from the guardroom to the airfield, living quarters, offices and messes all being hutted. On arrival we were all issued with bicycles, which inevitably led to some incidents with the odd echelon starboard ending up in the ditch as someone in the middle wobbled. On reflection, formation flying in aeroplanes was safer and certainly better briefed and more professionally led!

The Meteor is on my short list of favourite aircraft I have flown. A spate of accidents gave it a bad name but this was a reflection of the number in service, along with the way it was flown, rather than the aircraft itself. The asymmetric exercise was notoriously demanding though, such that a detail evaluating your critical speed left you with a leg like jelly. From the tandem-seat T.7 we graduated to the single-seat F.8 which really was a great thrill to fly. Strange how one remembers relatively small and unimportant details – the novelty of having an electric hood operated by a button has left an impression, childish perhaps, but it was fun having the canopy slide forward into position. With two Rolls Royce Derwents the power was sufficient to loop from the climbing attitude; in those days that was quite something.

It so happened that my instructor on the Meteor lived near Bromley, so at weekends he would borrow an aircraft and fly to Biggin Hill, leaving it with station flight after first making a small donation. As I lived near Croydon, I was able to join him, and thus enjoyed the high-speed commute at low level on a direct route, which nowadays would be out of the question.

Light aeroplane flying had not featured highly in 1955, but 1956 was to be quite a vintage year for me, both service and private. The year began with a pilots' bombing course at Lindholme near Doncaster. Flying from the right-hand seat of a Varsity T.1 we learned the patter associated with a visual or Gee-H bombing run. There was a lot of "Left, left – steady," and "Right – steady." The word "left" was always repeated to avoid confusion in what could be a very noisy environment. The Varsity was the tricycle-undercarriage version of the Valetta, which in turn was the military version of the Viking which saw service with BEA. The generic term "Pig" was often used because of the rather short fat appearance. However the

Varsity was good fun, though it achieved some notoriety because sometimes it was known for personnel to lie in the bomb-aimer's position in the nose on landing for a bit of a cheap thrill. A tragic accident put paid to that.

At long last on 16th February 1956 I had my first flight in a Canberra. Bassingbourn near Royston was the home of 231 OCU, where owing to shortage of space in the officers' mess many of us were accommodated in caravans. More tragedy, for within two weeks the Canberra was grounded following an unexplained fatal accident. There had been previous accidents which had been attributed to inexperience or over-exuberance, but this one involved an instructor and there were indications that control had been lost. Suspicion fell on the tail-trim actuator which subsequently was found to have run away nose-down. A modification was fitted in due course in the form of a slow-speed actuator. In the meantime a speed restriction was imposed, and after three weeks we were flying again.

Despite this serious electrical fault, the aircraft was without doubt one of the finest ever built, remaining in service for nearly half a century. It looked right, it flew right and it was outstandingly versatile. Designed by Petter for English Electric and powered by Rolls Royce Avons, it was capable of surprisingly long range flights, as was shown by its performance in setting a number of records, including (although not non-stop, of course) London to Christchurch, New Zealand, in under 24 hours in October 1953. High altitude manoeuvrability was too much for the fighters of the day; above 40,000 feet it was in a class of its own. Many of us in due course were to fly well above 50,000 feet, which was above the limiting altitude for the oxygen pressure demand system with which we were fitted. A world record of over 70,000 feet was set in August 1958.

One object of the course was to get used to the idea of flying as a crew and we pilots were duly paired off with navigators. Training together at the OCU the crews would continue on joining the squadron, where a second navigator would join them. This relationship between pilot and navigator/plotter and later with a navigator/observer was vital to efficient and accurate bombing. Familiarity with slight inflections in verbal communication during a bombing run could make all the difference.

For me as a twenty-one-year-old bachelor it was quite a responsibility to be crewed with a married Flight Sergeant who had two small children. Mike Heather and I made a pretty successful team over the next two and a half years, with most of the credit due to his diligence and application, coupled with considerable experience going back to the Wellington. In due course he became a Master Navigator, a much deserved promotion in recognition of long service in the Royal Air Force (and putting up with me!).

The furthest Canberra base from my home was Binbrook in Lincolnshire. Needless to say that is where we were posted: the airfield on the hill amongst the undulating wolds. Despite my first impressions, I soon became very attached to the area, with the contrasting attractions of Grimsby, Cleethorpes, Louth and the many charming villages. With five squadrons it was a busy station, a little friendly rivalry and a very good spirit in the mess. We found ourselves on 139 (Jamaica) Squadron which was then the only specialist marker squadron in the RAF. Target marking, made famous by the Pathfinders in WW II, was a new skill to acquire and, as it turned out, one of the most rewarding experiences of my flying career.

The object of target marking is first to find the target and then to leave some clear indication to the main bomber force where they are to bomb. In daylight it was normally straightforward enough, but at night it demanded very accurate navigation and instrument flying. The planning stage was crucial, involving the selection of a suitable feature which could be found reasonably easily, from which point the specific heading, speed and time had to be calculated in order to arrive over the target area. Illumination of the target was by parachute flares, dropped on time from a suitable height, usually around 8,000 ft. Then, with the target in sight, dive bombing with 500 lb target indicators would leave a spread of bright red or green flaming chemicals for the incoming main force of bombers to aim at.

We operated on exercises and operations as a four-aircraft team, all carrying flares and with just the lead two aircraft with target indicators (TIs). First in would be the leader, known as Marker 1, the others arriving at two-minute intervals were Marker 2, Flare 1 and Flare 2. The leader issued instructions as required over the radio to his team and to the main force. By far the most exciting part was the dive-bombing, which we would practice regularly using 25 lb practice bombs on the ranges. It was called shallow-dive bombing, but even at 30 to 40 degrees it seemed pretty steep.

The technique was to position the target beneath and slightly to the left, commencing the dive from 4,000 ft. Roll and push, positioning the target just above the coaming; with no gun sight it was a somewhat inexact science, yet with practice and a little bit of luck errors of less than 25 yards were quite normal. The navigator called the height out every 100 ft, his voice rising to quite a pitch as the 1,200 ft mark was reached; this was the release height and the minimum considered safe for the pull-out; below that there was a danger of really hitting the target, as one unfortunate crew did at the El Adam range in eastern Libya.

The pilot controlled the bomb doors, bomb safety switch and the bomb release button, which was on the control column and was not to be confused with the radio transmit button. On one exercise where we were doing a night mark of Filfla, an islet off Malta used by the Royal Navy as well as the RAF as a range, our leader, the Squadron Commander, having dropped his first TI, pulled up and whilst turning over the Maltese coast 'transmitted' on his bomb release button. The outcome was that the famous blue grotto temporarily became the red grotto.

I reckoned that the navigator's role must have been quite frightening, sitting at the back, unable to see what was happening. However he was spared the sight of the parachute flares as we dived through them, sometimes too close for comfort.

High-level bombing was also on the agenda and we as a crew had to be proficient in Gee-H and visual as well as shallow dive-bombing before we were granted our combat rating. This we did in time for the Suez campaign in which our squadron was to play a prominent role. Putting all that training into practice, even in that rather controversial war, was another remarkable experience.

We were an 'Alacrity' squadron which meant that we had to be ready to fly off on detachment at very short notice. Having arrived back at Binbrook by Hastings on the 18th October following a three-week detachment to Malta, I was about to go on leave when I was informed that we were to be airborne at 07.00 the next morning bound for Nicosia. The whole squadron was on the move again, but for me as a junior pilot, instead of travelling on the transport aircraft, I was to fly the first Canberra B.6 to depart. As one of the early arrivals in Nicosia we had the pick of the accommodation; as the mess was already full of operations and administrative staff, we were to sleep three to a tin hut, whilst later arrivals were under canvas.

As a rule pilots do not join the Royal Air Force in peacetime with the idea of going to war. They join for the flying and all that goes with it on the ground as well as in the air; it is the camaraderie and being part of a team. So it came as a bit of a surprise to find ourselves at the sharp end of a political conflict where military action was being opposed by both the Labour party and the United States. Our allies, it turned out, were the French and the Israelis, our 'enemy' the Egyptians. We, in the best traditions of the British armed services, did as we were told. Being ignorant of the full significance of the operation, we entered into it all with some enthusiasm: never had the spirit on the squadron been better.

At first we marked targets by night, and then, when so little opposition was encountered, by day too. This enabled us to carry three 1,000 lb bombs in addition to target indicators, so once the target was marked we could dive-bomb with high explosives. The targets were entirely military, such as parked aircraft, runways and radio stations. A warning was issued to the Egyptians to keep away from certain facilities well in advance to minimise loss of life. Thus we could find out the target before attending briefing simply by listening to the BBC World Service.

Being unarmed ourselves and with no fighter escort (the targets were mostly beyond the range of the Hunters and Venoms), there was a somewhat lonely feeling at low level over hostile territory. However we did not meet much to alarm us except on one raid, and never was it in the same league as subsequent operations in the Falklands and the Gulf, which took place long after I had left the service. The more senior pilots on the squadron had WW II experience; it was noticeable how easily they slipped back into the ways of operational duties.

We all got home in time for Christmas, just. It had been quite a year; the post-Suez period being spent in Cyprus very pleasantly, with a mix of training flights and touring the island, avoiding Eoka terrorists as far as possible. One flight back to the UK in that time was ostensibly to collect diplomatic mail which, it turned out, was the Sunday newspapers for the staff officers at HQ.

During the summer of 1956 I had enjoyed some most delightful flying from Croydon, adding the Leopard Moth and the Messenger, amongst others, to types I had flown. The big event in light aircraft operation though was the founding of the Tiger Club, which was to become the leading sport flying club in the country, if not the world. It was also to figure prominently in my flying activities over the succeeding years; happily in 1998 I am still an active flying member. Those of us who have benefitted from this unique club have a great deal to thank Norman Jones for. It was his benevolence and his enthusiasm which provided the opportunity for hundreds of pilots to enjoy a wide variety of flying activities which otherwise might have been denied to them. However in 1956 I had only *heard* about the club: it all seemed way out of reach for pilots of my experience and ability.

The contrast of flying Canberras with the RAF and flying Tiger Moths and similar splendid pre-war aircraft from Croydon was to continue until I left the service in November 1958 at the end of a two-and-a-half-year tour on the squadron. It was then that the defence cuts initiated by the Minister, Mr Duncan Sandys, forced me and many others to make a very critical decision. However it so happened that the two national carriers of the day, BOAC and BEA, were in need of pilots and were recruiting direct from the services.

As it turned out we were very fortunate to have this opportunity, the only proviso being that we were in the last three years of contracted service. My choice of British European Airways was based on my preference for short sectors, and plenty of them: less glamour than long-hauling around the world but, I reckoned, a lot more fun.

Post-Suez flying at Binbrook had continued to be based on the three disciplines of bombing, in which all three members of the crew had their opportunity to get in on the act. The navigator plotter was responsible for the Gee-H bombing which used a radio facility dependent on ground stations. Accurate positioning was possible, information being read off a screen. Subsequently I was to use the civilian version, Gee, for

250

navigational purposes and found it to be a very useful aid. The navigator/observer was responsible for visual bombing using the bomb sight in the nose, and of course the pilot had his turn carrying out the shallow dive-bombing.

All training flights had to last at least three hours in order that the squadron target of 1,000 hours a month could be met. The squadron commander was insistent about this, such that even a minute under time prompted an interview with him. Inevitably this led to what one might call recreational flying to fill in the time after the main training element had been completed. This could be something fairly productive like a visit to another airfield to shoot a GCA (Ground Controlled Approach), or it could involve a scenic tour, weather permitting.

On one occasion we chose the Highlands of Scotland on an idyllic summer's day. The tour, at a level from which we could more easily admire the beauty of the countryside, ended with a run down the Firth of Forth. Evidently a rather diligent controller at Turnhouse (Edinburgh) saw a Canberra as it passed over the Forth railway bridge and reported it. No doubt a signal was sent to HQ Bomber Command who in turn informed all stations operating Canberras. After landing back at Binbrook I was met by a member of the service police complete with clipboard who requested to know where I had been. Fortunately, with unusual presence of mind, I muttered something about Cornwall. No more was heard.

There was always a Canberra squadron kept in the Mediterranean, this duty rotating amongst the various UK-based units, it being appropriately known as a "Sunspot" detachment. Our three-week tours came up in the spring and autumn which was ideal, effectively adding some warm weather at each end of the English summer. Luqa in Malta and Idris (Tripoli) in Libya were the two most common locations. In between times we would fly lone rangers to RAF stations in Germany and also to Gibraltar for long weekends. This was really a perk, but it did provide some useful training en route, as well as some very useful time off in different locations.

One of my extra duties on the squadron was entertainments officer and it was my job to organise the parties. It was whilst on a Malta detachment that it was agreed that I should fly to Gibraltar to collect some duty-free spirits from Saccone & Speed, so keeping the cost down and at the same time providing us with a training flight. It was planned as an "out and back" one Saturday morning; in the event we finally returned to Malta on the Tuesday.

Two aircraft were dispatched with a total of six crew, but before reaching Gibraltar we were informed of a weather deterioration and ordered to divert to Oran in Algeria. A second attempt later that morning also failed so we decided on a night stop in the French transit mess at Oran. That afternoon we travelled into town in search of the British

Consul; we needed local currency and he seemed our only source. His office was shut, and at his home we were informed that he was aboard a British merchant ship in the harbour. The 10,000-ton *"Hesperides"* was anchored some distance from the quay and we had to persuade a friendly Arab to row us out to it. Once on board we found our way to the Captain's cabin where the Captain was entertaining the local agent of the shipping line and the Consul. Judging by the number of empty bottles, they had been there for a while which may have accounted for their generosity, for after being made very welcome suitable sums of local money were passed over, enabling us to have a most enjoyable evening in town.

For a number of reasons, not the least of which was a problem with fuel, it was Monday before we reached Gibraltar. A night stop at the officers mess, North Front, was then necessary due to not all the members of the party being fully fit to fly; it was assumed that something in the food had been largely responsible! Although the outcome of the operation was entirely successful in that we delivered a full consignment of liquor to the squadron, I found that as leader of the expedition I was expected to write a report explaining our actions which had led to the squadron being deprived of two aircraft for three days.

Back at Croydon Aerodrome in June 1957 I happily took the opportunity to fly a Tiger Moth via Deauville to Flers for the annual rally. Whilst there, two of us did an impromptu formation duo which seemed to go down quite well with our French hosts. Within a few days of our return to England I received a letter from C. A. Nepean Bishop, known to everyone as "Bish," in which to my astonishment he invited me to become a member of the Tiger Club. Bish was CFI of the club and he too had been in Flers, so the trip had an even happier bonus.

A whole new world of flying was opened up to me for 30/- (£1.50) an hour, which even in those days was cheap, subsidised as it was by Norman Jones. I was able to practise and take part in air displays and races (including the King's Cup), improve my aerobatic and formation flying, and to participate in numerous stunts and demonstration flights.

Glider-towing and parachute-dropping were other skills to acquire and ultimately gain the requisite qualification for; it was all huge fun and added further to the breadth of experience. By 1958 we had formed the tied-together trio, where three Tiger Moths were linked by nylon cord attached to the picketing points. Those days were unforgettable as we tried to re-enact the old barnstorming era with a fleet of Tiger Moths and, later, Turbulents. The pilots were a most enthusiastic bunch, and it was a great privilege to fly with them. There was a freedom in the skies which cannot possibly exist today. For example it was regarded as quite acceptable to fly the direct route from Croydon to Elstree across London: no radio, no clearance, VMC and the Mk.1 eyeball!

252

However that freedom did not stretch to us being able to practise for displays at Croydon. Sunday mornings would see a mass exodus as the fleet departed in formation for Stapleford Tawney or Fair Oaks for the day. Bish always insisted on RAF-type discipline in the way we flew. Arriving overhead in an echelon, from which we would break to a stream landing, after which we would park tidily in line abreast, not switching off engines until receiving the signal from Bish, bringing about a simultaneous shut-down.

The final phase of that incredible decade for me was the move into airline flying. From being a pilot in command of a twin jet I was to become a second officer on a Dakota. Not the first and certainly not the last culture shock of my career, it required a major readjustment, but one which turned out yet again to lead on to a most rewarding time. BEA posted half the new entry of eighteen pilots to Manchester and the other half to Renfrew Airport, Glasgow. Needless to say I found myself in Scotland, though not entirely by choice. Clearly however it was ordained as that is where I met Moira, who was to become my wife two years later.

Two years flying the Dakota around the Highlands and Islands of Scotland provides as good a school as you could wish for: the performance of the aeroplane, the terrain, the navigational aids (or perhaps the lack of them) and, above all, the weather, which made getting into some of those delightful airfields very demanding at times.

The weather in Scotland can change fast and it can also show marked variations over relatively short distances. Simultaneous fog in Glasgow and a limiting cross-wind in Stornoway is not that uncommon. Whilst the conditions could be violent, it could also be so beautiful that it would take your breath away. The sight of the Highlands on a perfect summer's day was matched by the sight of the Highlands on a perfect winter's day. With snow on the ground, the runways around the North were not swept, they were dye-marked with a purple dye down each side enabling you to land on virgin white snow.

From flying at Mach 0.8 at 48,000 feet in a Canberra I was now flying at 140 knots at 7,000 feet, and much lower. Concern that my days of low flying were over was soon proved wrong. Flying off the west coast of the Outer Hebrides from Benbecula to Stornoway with one of the old hands, I swear I could see the prop-wash on the surface of the sea. Another occasion and with another Captain, down over Loch Ness en route from Inverness to Glasgow – he did say he used to be on flying-boats! We climbed up after passing Fort William in order to fly along the length of Glencoe and then down again over Loch Lomond. The passengers appeared to be quite unconcerned; it must have been that they were used to it.

The RAF, BEA and the Tiger Club all provided flying in the fifties for me. This meant visiting many different airfields and flying a wide variety of different types. The RAF and BEA paid me to fly, which was splendid as this enabled me to pay for my flying with the Tiger Club. Participation in displays and races, sometimes in front of huge crowds, was always exciting, but some of the most memorable flights were when returning to base. A gaggle of Tiger Club aircraft, like so many school children heading home from school, would be sometimes hurrying, sometimes scurrying around the woods and hedgerows, sometimes together, sometimes apart, flying over the glorious English countryside in the calm air and fading light of a summer's evening.

Another flight to remember was in a Jackaroo, the four-seat cabin version of the Tiger Moth. In September 1958 I flew three friends to Belgium to visit the Brussels World Exposition. My crew consisted of a fellow pilot (RAF), a navigator (RAF), and an accountant (who failed to control our finances). We flew from Croydon to Knokke de Zoute on the Belgian coast and thence by train to Brussels. Having spent nearly all our money at the exhibition and funfair, where today only the Atomium remains to be seen, we were unable to stay at a hotel. So after playing cards with some locals in a pub until closing time, it was then time for a little sleep at the railway station before catching the first train back to de Zoute. It was therefore an early departure for our return to England, having first checked the weather and filed a flight plan.

All went well until halfway across the Channel when low stratus forced us down below 500 feet. This had not been forecast. With no radio and only a 'P'-type compass to steer by, I was relieved to eventually see the blurred coastline of what proved to be Folkestone. Our first stop was to be Lympne for customs clearance, so no problem, just follow the railway line from the harbour and it would lead us to it. As we flew over the town I noted a green open space and thought that if the worst came to the worst we could always land there. Seconds later I turned back as the cloud was meeting the rising ground ahead.

We duly landed at the Kent County Cricket Ground at what was still a relatively early hour, and parked in front of the giant score board. Fortunately we were able to gain access to the pavilion to make some appropriate telephone calls. In due course, customs, immigration, police and press arrived and, having satisfied all their requirements, the friendly constables drove us into town with a promise to return us to the cricket ground as soon as the weather had improved.

By early afternoon there was blue sky and warm sunshine; the police, as good as their word, drove us back to collect our Jackaroo. One problem: it was Saturday and so not unreasonably they were playing cricket – not a county game, but the local club. Nice chaps, cricketers; after a chat with the respective captains and umpires, stumps were drawn so that we could take off, being very careful to avoid the square. After refuelling at Lympne, it was back to Croydon to find that we were in the evening papers.

A year later Croydon Airport was closed, so the Tiger Club moved to Redhill, reopening that airfield after five and a half years of closure. For me, I was back where I had begun and there the Tiger Club remained for the next thirty years.

This has been a brief overview of one pilot's decade, which formed a firm foundation for my career which followed. It most certainly had been fun flying in the fifties, combined with a freedom which no longer exists.

CHAPTER 22

TWO UNREQUITED LOVE AFFAIRS WITH THE ROYAL AIR FORCE

by

Anthony Preston

[NOTES ON THE AUTHOR: Anthony Preston has held a pilot's licence uninterrupted for over forty years and has been an instructor for many of them. First trained on Austers and Tiger Moths at Ipswich, he later flew piston-Provosts and Vampires in the RAF from 1956-8.

With the family engineering firm of George Kent he moved to Central Africa in the early sixties, instructing at Mount Hampden (now Charles Prince) on Cub, Tripacer, Colt, Mooney Super 21 and Tiger Moth; he also provided the crazy-flying spot for their Air Days. At Ndola Airport he instructed on Cherokee 140 and Cessna 182. He demonstrated the first Mooney in Kenya, and flew himself regularly on business trips in the Rhodesias, Nyasaland, Tanganyika, Kenya and Uganda.

As a qualified flying instructor he has also instructed on Chipmunk and Citabria and for a time joined Mile Riley to give aerobatic instruction on Stampe and CAP-10 at Booker for Tony Bianchi's Personal Plane Services. He produced the first issues of the British Aerobatic Association's newsletter when the committee included Neil Williams, Manx Kelly, James Black and John Blake, and was an occasional competitor in a Stampe at Intermediate Level. He also flew Zlin 526s and Stampes in aerobatic displays and competitions in France and Italy.

He gained his Commercial Flying Licence over in the USA in 1977 and then joined a Norfolk-based crop-spraying company, flying Cessna 206s and Grumman Ag-Cats in Egypt and Sudan.

His flying training experience was extended when he joined Singer Link-Miles in 1983 and worked with flight simulators and part task trainers for aircrew.

He has been a regular contributor to "CIVIL AVIATION TRAINING" and "MILITARY TRAINING & SIMULATION" magazines, and has provided voice-overs for CBT (Computer Based Training) pilot training courses for the BAe Flying College at Prestwick.

He is married to a university lecturer and writer and they have two sons and a daughter. In 1994 he was appointed general manager of the Popular Flying Association at Shoreham Airport.]

It was as if a cadaver that I first clearly recollect my father – a walking, talking cadaver. He'd served in the Royal Air Force during the Second World War, in Burma and India, where he'd been struck down by a near-fatal case of polio. Sqn. Ldr. Alec Murray Preston, RAF – he loved the Squadron Leader bit – had been robbed by the disease not only of a career but of the jaw muscles that pad out the skull to make a living face. Sunken hollows replaced the flesh between each eye and its neighbouring ear, exaggerating the size of the ears. The skull-like effect was accentuated by the taut, sun-mottled skin which gave a polished wood appearance to high cheekbones.

To chew meat my father rested chin on thumb of right hand, lifting and lowering his head with the muscles of the neck. This enforced mannerism, you might call it, was at first an embarrassment to us children in company, but he managed to make a charming idiosyncrasy of it, posing like a gaunt version of Rodin's '*Thinker,*' without too much of the thinking. It always seemed to be accompanied by a half-smile, but that was a result perhaps of the forefinger of that same right hand making a letter 'L' with the thumb, giving support to the right cheek-bone.

His best friend was a 6ft 4in tall, boyishly handsome Canadian, Mike Nesbit. He too had contracted polio in India and sailed back to England in the same hospital ship. Mike's polio was of the more conventional sort, depriving him of the use of his legs. He'd been an immensely powerful swimmer, reportedly covering 100 yards in around the 51 seconds which was at the time Johnny Weismuller's best. The muscles of Mike's legs had atrophied so badly that they were nothing but skin on bone and a few ligaments. As a child I often wondered why those thin, pink legs didn't just fall apart. He would swing himself to the edge of the pool, those absurdly broad shoulders further widened by the lifting of the body on elbow crutches, of the athletic, aluminium sort, where the hands and forearms take the weight, not those wooden, crippling contraptions with horsehair pads under the armpits. From sitting on the edge Mike would flop into the water and then prove that the legs had little to do with propulsion by ploughing from one end to the other with effortless style and speed, big bow wave and little splash, all the power in the arms and shoulders, legs trailing, inert.

One day Mike was visiting my father on the farm in Suffolk. They'd been for a stroll around the farm buildings, my father controlling his pace to match his friend's powerful dot-and-carry rolling motion, first crutches jabbed forward together, then legs as one following like a child's swing between them. I met them in the muddy yard on my return from school.

They were so relaxed with each other; a lonely child, I guess I might have been a bit envious.

"Look what I learnt at school today, Dad," I said, and without warning gave him a hard blow to the solar plexus. Don't ask me why.

Certainly I had no idea of the impact. With a gasp he crumpled to the ground. Quicker than the blink of an eye, Mike tossed his right crutch in the air and, grabbing its foot with his right hand, took an almighty swing at my head. Fortunately I saw it coming, ducked and ran for my life. At least he couldn't chase after me.

His violent reaction symbolised for me the unique sense of camaraderie, *esprit de corps*, whatever you like to call it, that came out of the Royal Air Force; of shared experiences, achievements, dangers, youthful vitality and sudden adversity, particularly powerful as products of war. Prior to moving to the country my father had been Secretary for SSAFA (1945-48) at Queen Anne's Gate and, no surprise, it was a job Mike himself took on some years later.

My recollection of my father before the war is vague; I was, after all, only two; but photos show him as being square-jawed, handsome in a Douglas Bader kind of way. What I do remember only too clearly is his return to our home in Radlett in 1945, on sticks, thin as a skeleton, jaw hanging open, ravaged by the disease. The stories he told his initially frightened children – who was this skeletal stranger with a stick and a crooked smile? – fitted in with the horror of his looks and his physical shape, but perhaps they helped us to come to terms. One paradoxical theme carried through everything he told us and that was his abiding love of the Royal Air Force.

And it was this very same Royal Air Force, just ten years later, that I was preparing to join as an Officer Cadet on a short-service commission. Could it possibly live up to those high expectations? There was no war, nor one imminent. Would the same loyalties and affections be developed? Would the flying be as good? Would I get my hands on a Spitfire?

In 1955 potential aircrew were assessed at RAF Hornchurch. Arcade games and other physical co-ordination tests were a doddle for someone who had grown up driving tractors, shooting rabbits and swinging through the trees in the woods being Tarzan, but officer qualities are not nurtured in communion with tractors, rabbits and fantasies among the boughs. I knew I wasn't doing well when, having remained speechless through several questions on current affairs, I felt obliged to have a stab and, in response to "What does 'NATO' stand for?", got no further than "Er, National . . . something something something"; I saw all three pairs of interrogators' eyes roll up to heaven. They kind of gave up at that point and, with sinking heart, even if rather pleased at getting the 'National' bit, so did I.

It came as a pleasant surprise to find a couple of weeks later that I'd been invited by Her Majesty to attend Cardington for induction into Her service. At a brief interview with the AOC Flying Training Command, AVM Graham, at a rather low point some time later in my short career in the Royal Air Force, I learnt that I'd been accepted as 'a calculated risk.'

I soon got to know what NATO stood for. Another valuable piece of information gathered at about this time was that you *never* referred to the 'raff,' preferably not to the R-A-F, but always, in all its glory, to the ROYAL AIR FORCE. The same semantic acknowledgement was due a cloud, so we were informed by a meteorological instructor at RAF Worksop. Never, he whined, refer to a 'cu-nim'; always show it the respect it deserves by calling it by its full thundering name – 'cumulo-nimbus.' He was right, of course, but I shouldn't be at all surprised if he didn't refer to the service we young men loved as the 'raff.' It's hard today to understand just how much the red, white and blue roundel meant to us then, especially if painted on an aeroplane's fuselage or wing.

Kitted out at Cardington, issued with an Officer Cadet's uniform and given a very short haircut, we immediately took our peaked hats, flat as mortarboards, and crushed them into the kind of shape better suited to our new images as fighter aces – an illusion soon to be painfully shattered at the end of the train journey from RAF Cardington to RAF Kirton in Lindsey in Lincolnshire. Nothing had prepared us, not even the brutal haircuts, for the reception by the fire-breathing Lance Corporal strutting up and down the station platform. It was as if the platform had been transformed into a parade ground. The fact that every shrieked command, full of new swear words, was suffixed with a "Sir" just added to the awful horror of it. How had "Sir" suddenly become a contemptible expletive? That diminutive Lance Corporal, no more than 5ft 6in tall, did a grand job cutting those cadet pilots down to size, at the same time managing somehow not to diminish the proper hierarchical order of things in the Royal Air Force. A far cry, I thought, from Squadron Leader A. Murray Preston with his grey stallion "*Samson*," his syce and sepoys, or whatever they were called, in Poona and Delhi during those final years of the Raj.

Kirton was officer-training. I managed to carry off the deception not by exhibiting any of the so-called officer qualities but by a dramatic *tour de force* during the end-of-term athletics contest, crossing the finishing line in front, for both the mile and half-mile events, with a face so hideously contorted with pain, collapsing doubled-up in agony on the ground immediately after breaking the tape, that I was instantly attributed with that valuable commodity – guts. It served me well.

It was whilst at Kirton that our first acquaintance with a real aeroplane, one in which we might be doing our initial training, took place. We were in the classroom learning the fine art of 'Service Letter Writing' when there was the most gorgeous blast of sound from the airfield. A

Pratt & Whitney Wasp was making it known that a Harvard was in the vicinity. How the goose-pimples rose and our hearts fluttered with anticipation and delight! I'd already got my PPL on Tiger Moth and Auster and I loved them both dearly but the sight and sound of a real man's aeroplane, and an American one at that, was overwhelming.

It was also at Kirton that we would be told whether we would be going on to Canada to learn on T-6 Harvard/Texan and T-33 Shooting Star or on Percival Provost and DH Vampire at home in Britain. That brief visit certainly made most of us wish for the North American option but at that time we had yet to meet the beefy Provost and develop a love affair with that most British of hunky flying machines.

From Kirton we were posted to RAF Ternhill in Shropshire. Ternhill. It sounded good, the right place for the intrepid birdmen of Flying Training Command's Course No.129. It was a significant move. Gone was the square bashing, dormitory and lowly cadet label. In their stead were Officers' Mess with four-star hotel food, a bedroom in light green to oneself, a batman to bring a morning cup of tea, make the bed and call one "Sir" with ostensible conviction, an ante-room with all the trappings and most of the atmosphere of a wartime fighter station – at least for those of us with a bit of Walter Mitty – and, above all, there were the Flights and Ground School and *flying*.

I remember my introduction to the Provost as if it were yesterday. Above all I was deeply grateful for the privilege. We had admired the beasts as they stood in dispersal, silent, glinting in the early morning sun, lined up like their pilots on parade in a precisely-dressed rank. There on the apron, some spilling onto the peri-track, they looked, with their tails to the hangars and noses tilted up over the smooth green of a well-tended grass aerodrome, as ready for the sky as we were. It wasn't until you got up close that you realised how much bigger they were than the DH Chipmunk, to which they bore some superficial resemblance.

If one had doubts about so beefy a machine being capable of getting airborne, they were dispelled by the sight of the radial engine whose name alone might seem enough to provide the power – the Alvis "Leonides." Compare for a start Pratt & Whitney "Wasp" with Alvis "Leonides" – no contest! Unlike the Harvard, the Provost had a three-bladed propeller. Both engines gave out about the same power. Fully rated the Leonides was supposed to produce 550 bhp at 3,000 rpm and Plus 8 boost. We were told that pots had blown at these settings which explained why aircraft at Ternhill were governed to around 2,700 rpm and the throttle gate wired to limit boost to 6 psi maximum.

My instructor, Paddy Mulholland, was tall and thin with a pale, lugubrious face. He had a musician's long, delicate fingers with which he held the burly control column as if it were a cello's bow. Climbing into the cockpit was easy for him and me, but little Tony Bostock – 5ft 4in in shoes – must have had some difficulty.

It was a shoe that caused Tony a little concern, his mentors on the ground rather more, on a solo circuit later during the course at Ternhill. What do you, as an air traffic controller, say to a student pilot flying solo who calls up on the downwind leg: "Ternhill Tower, this is Charlie Bravo, I've got a shoe stuck under one of the rudder pedals!"?

Then there was Geoff McLean who drove his MG TC like a lunatic along the narrow Shropshire lanes, but called up one day on the circuit: "Ternhill Tower, this is Charlie Juliet, I do not feel competent to land this aeroplane." Gulp.

Each had a happy ending but nerves in the control tower were put to the test. You could perhaps understand Geoff's problem. Some of us had gone solo in 5 or 6 hours. To reflect suddenly on the enormity of what you were doing might shatter an imaginative character. Hornchurch was supposed to have filtered them out.

Having almost got over the excitement of putting on pale blue inner helmet, bone-dome with tinted visor, flying overalls and oxygen mask for the walk out to the waiting Provost, the adrenalin again surged as you swung into the cockpit, did up the parachute harness, then the seat harness and sat and surveyed the scene. Predictably, I remember the number of instruments and switches, doubting the possibility of learning what each was for. I was much taken by the control column, a solid binnacle-like extension from the floor for fore and aft elevator control, with a hinged top portion for lateral aileron control. Compared to the flimsy twig with which I'd attempted to control Auster and Tiger this was indeed a man's joystick for a man's aeroplane. Robust manoeuvres only perhaps? Yet those fingers of Paddy Mulholland . . .

The Provost felt solid. You knew it wouldn't break easily. Plus 6 g we were allowed to pull and, although pushing was strictly prohibited, minus 4 g was there if you couldn't resist the bunt or even a modest Derry Turn. Bunts were not permitted, nor were flicks or tail chases, but a Porteous loop, today called an avalanche, was a favourite of the CFS trappers and I remember being impressed when shown a loop decorated with a flick at its apogee.

The smell inside the cockpit was a sexy combination of sweat, aviation fuel, wire looms, Leonides oil, the remnants of thin air, high clouds and oxygen, and something uniquely military; it was the smell of *flying*. Our ancient instructors – they must have been all of 30 at the most – looked with amused disdain at the dazzled students as they sat beside them evidently overcome by the dignity and power of this heady machine.

Between seats of pilot and instructor was an ominous lever hinged at the rear and painted bright red. It was a kind of legacy of the Hornchurch phase: a test of the nervous student's ability to avoid blinking and react without getting flustered. The aptly named Koffman cartridge starter-unit was fired by pulling up on this lever and detonating a cartridge about the size for a twelve-bore. The expanding gases spun the engine and the trick was to catch enough responding cylinders to keep it rotating until all nine were gloriously burning. As we all started up our engines at about the same time, there was a great deal of pleasure to be gained by watching fellow students grappling with fuel booster pump, primer (the button was on the tip of the red lever), throttle and an engine that was determined to humiliate, determined to prolong its coughing and wheezing, its sudden exuberant blast of full song followed inexplicably by another spate of coughs and gasps as the inexperienced student over-primed and flooded.

Each instructor had his own secret. The best method seemed to be that of Flight Lieutenant Thomas, a compact little man with a neat non-handlebar moustache. He it was who introduced me to the dangers of over-priming. Select fuel 'on'; bring up fuel pressure on the gauge by easing the booster pump forward; shut off the booster pump; pull up on the lever; bang goes the cartridge (if you were lucky – it quite often merely hissed at you and filled the cockpit with blinding and acrid white smoke); keep the engine turning over using the primer until all nine caught. The advantage was that it maintained the impulse, or was it inertia, to the sparking plugs and gave you a better electrical chance even if at the expense of a fuel one.

Taxying the Provost was an enjoyable experience. The brakes were pneumatic. Differential braking was achieved by application of the rudder and judicious squeezes on a lever, like a bicycle's hand control, mounted vertically in front of the control column's contoured hand-grip. It was contoured for a manly, spatulate hand; so what about those thin spidery fingers of Paddy Mulholland? Each squeeze was accompanied by an angry hiss. Compressed air also operated the windscreen wipers but, unlike those on cars operated by inlet manifold vacuum, which obligingly slowed down or stopped as you accelerated, these smote back and forth with aggressive and undiminished gusto, bashing out a rhythm to accompany the accelerated beat of the pilot's stimulated heart.

On that first acquaintance, seated a little dumbfounded in the rugged cockpit environment, it was the prevailing black, matt black, extending even to the top of the engine cowling that I remember most. The flash of yellow stripes, red handles, light blue harness, khaki parachute and amber screens stood out against the dull blackness. The windscreen with its lattice of sturdy frames made stingy concession to visibility, although the deceptively narrow tube of the engine allowed a better-than-expected view ahead, even with the tail on the ground.

The Provost was, of course, an absolute joy to fly. Like the vulture strutting awkwardly on the ground, or the ungainly pelican, once airborne the contrast was complete. Compared to the Harvard the Provost was a thoroughbred. Everything from the pilot's position to the crispness of the controls spelt aerobatics. It didn't take long before the keen pilot could begin to believe that the aeroplane was an extension of himself – an essential ingredient of true aviating. How the pilot of the Harvard, seated on a kind of framework stretched above the underbelly of the aircraft's fuselage, could have been expected to become one with his machine escapes me. Those artistic fingers of Paddy Mulholland would have been wasted on the crude control column of the T-6.

Most of our circuit work – 12 & 13 in the log book – was carried out at Ternhill but, with several courses at once bashing the single runway, we were sometimes transferred to the subsidiary of Chetwynd. This roughly circular expanse of lush green grass richly deserved its romantic name.

Before dawn the black and white chequered van would make its way from Ternhill to Chetwynd. On board were tea-brewing facilities and the rudiments of air traffic control. The van would park itself somewhere in the middle and, after a cup or two of tea, the crew would gauge the wind and mark out the runway direction with large white 'Toblerones,' ready for the arrival of the fledglings.

It was on about my second or third solo flight – it had taken me just over five and a half hours to solo the Provost – and I was practising 'touch-and-gos' at Chetwynd. There came about a change of wind. The controller instructed those airborne to orbit. At the time the word 'orbit' hadn't entered my orbit. I experienced that marshalling of the sweat glands that invariably accompanies the frequent moments when I find myself at a loss. What, for God's sake, did 'orbit' mean? We certainly hadn't covered that in ground school. Panic stricken, I searched my imagination and, for some reason, managed to associate the word 'orbit' with 'going round.' With some pride and a calming of the sweat glands I recalled the NATO question but knew this time I'd got it right – well, almost right. I got the general drift of orbit but managed, in the heat of the moment, to get its orientation wrong.

The loops went extraordinarily well but even better were the rapid rolls off the top. Airspeed for each manoeuvre was pretty much guess-work. After all, I'd only done circuits and landings, and the speed on the approach to land was no reliable guide to entry speed for aerobatics.

Another teaser was working out the best direction for the stall turn. Being a British aircraft the Provost needs left rudder to offset yaw on take-off, so left rudder progressively goes on in the vertical climb. It works well in a Tiger or a Chipmunk. It works better in the Provost because the lovely Leonides with its fuel injection system keeps on churning out the horses, even when the over-zealous pilot goes over the vertical, where normally-aspirated Gipsies with float chambers begin to gasp. For a good stall turn you need as much rudder movement as you can get. You also need propeller slipstream over it. These two factors easily override the adverse effect of engine-induced yaw when the throttle is closed. Stall turns to the right were a joy. But it was, as I said, the rolls off the top with which I was most proud.

In the Tiger I used to find myself at the top of the loop, inverted, with insufficient speed to achieve anything better than a graceless wallow with full top rudder and a return to straight and level accompanied by boot-loads of unwanted yaw. In the Hunting Percival Provost there was not only buckets of power in the climb but it kept on delivering upside down. This meant you could exit at the top still flying. Forward pressure on the stick overcame the need for excess of top rudder. That, as I learned later, was how it was done. It wasn't exactly how I was doing it. Having only some brief experience of aerobatics in a Tiger at Nacton Airport, Ipswich, under the inimitable instruction of Stanley Ward, I had been applying the same procedure to the Provost.

Eventually the new runway direction was marked out and we were instructed to land. As I wound the cockpit canopy back I was surprised to find a fuming Mulholland, delicate white fingers groping at my throat. Apparently it wasn't so much the unscheduled aerobatics themselves but the way in which they were being executed that had enraged this otherwise placid Irishman. From the lawn-like expanse of Chetwynd a group of experienced aviators had instinctively grouped together to look up at one of their prized Provosts being abused in incompetent hands. What Preston – Charlie Mike – had been calling rolls off the top had appeared to the experienced eye as inadvertent flick rolls from which they had been anxiously awaiting the spin and *pat-a-poum* into the treasured grass of Chetwynd. Oh, the unsightly brown stain!

Hauled from the safety of the cockpit I crouched in the kind of deferential bow that goes with plucking at the forelock (which forelock was tucked inaccessibly inside the RAF-issue bone-dome) and it wasn't so much deference as the nearest one could get to upright wearing a parachute pack designed for a seated position. I was subjected to the kind of abuse known only to the Irish and to the criminally insane.

"Now," says the towering figure of Mulholland to the bent and trembling figure beneath him, "you horrible little maggot, you'll run round the airfield . . . twice."

I went to hit the disk to release the parachute harness.

"No, *no*, you miserable object, that stays on."

Sitting in the pilot's seat in the harness was uncomfortable enough, the crotch straps and certain private parts never seemed to accommodate each other. Standing was hell, but *running* . . . I used to claim my feelings for the opposite sex took a dive after the event but that could have been due to other things.

Mulholland stopped me with a grin after a few dozen yards. That grin said an awful lot.

It should be explained that in the mid-fifties there still lingered a covert regard for the fighter pilot spirit. Overtly it was Bunny Bramson-style contempt for the reckless, the bold, but Bader, Tuck and Malan were still, unashamedly, our real heroes then. Books like Brickhill's biography of Douglas Bader, *"Reach for the Sky"* and Forrester's of Bob Stanford Tuck, *"Fly for your Life"* were not only the bibles of the students but of the instructors too, many of whom had flown in combat.

I'd been born in 1937 and, if Freud is to be believed, spent my most formative years under the influence of war. My father away in India, it was my mother, with her demonstrative adoration of the Spitfire, Hurricane and Lightning pilots, who dictated how we thought and felt. I remember vividly the thrill transmitted to us when a P-38 Lightning flew over Radlett on some mission to the south (we seemed to see more Lightnings than British warplanes). It was as powerful as the fear when the siren wailed and I was hurried from my bedroom upstairs to sleep under the dining-room table, often to hear the clatter of a 'doodlebug' clearing the rooftops.

Fighter pilots like Bader, Tuck and "Sailor" Malan were lionised and we were willingly led to believe they were the saviours of our nation, even of our generation. We were deeply moved by the mighty words of Winston Churchill. I remember seeing him in Westerham in an open coach and pair and believing that I was looking on a god. The Few had won the War – that's how it seemed to me as a child; they were our heroes.

Was it then so odd that just a decade later we thought of ourselves as Baders, Tucks, Malans? The nuclear war had not in our minds replaced the concept of conventional airborne battle, and the dogfight above the fields of Kent was still a viable notion.

It didn't appear to me as behaving in an unacceptable way when flying over the abandoned airfield of Tilstock; nearby there was reputed to be a nudist camp well worth a visit from the air. The main runway was a busy road. Lorry drivers would pull onto the intersecting runway for a snooze. Ternhill students could think of nothing more amusing than flying as close to the front of the lorry as they dare and, with a burst of power, startle the driver out of his skin.

My own variation on the theme was, to my mind, Bader-like; I only did it once. Having blasted past the lorry at 180 knots or so, I decided the proper thing to do was a slow roll. I knew the routine well enough at altitude by then. Why was it the second half of the roll had to go so wrong the one time it really mattered? Pitch up; just a bit more than usual because we're close to the ground; roll left, it always feels more natural that way; everything fine so far, nose has stayed well above the horizon as we get fully inverted, still plenty on the ASI; forward on the stick to keep it there, remembering opposite rudder at this point to overcome adverse aileron drag; hold the nose on the selected ground feature. Which selected ground feature? It wasn't, I guess, that I'd forgotten, but this low there was nothing to select. Never mind; through 180 degrees of roll; top rudder (from right to left) as the nose begins to drop . . . and drop.

Why is it that with almost full top rudder the nose is so determined to drop? I got away with it but didn't deserve to. The right wingtip clipped the top of a hedge. I can see it as a photo in my mind to this day. Sheepishly back to the security of *terra firma* at Ternhill where I was quiet for a couple of days.

The impulse to fly low was hard to resist – it ended me up in court in civvy street – especially given the covert encouragement of our instructors. Take Flt. Lt. McMinn as an example of the prevailing playfulness. He got his fun at night.

Picture the nervous student pilot (Charlie Juliet for instance) completing his first solo night cross-country, peering anxiously through the dark to pick out the ident. and runway lights of Ternhill. Unknown to him, a little above and between himself and his destination lurks the Provost of McMinn with its own nervous student on board. Why, the latter might be asking himself, has the respected instructor turned off all the aircraft's lights? You can guess.

Losing height and levelling off at precisely the same altitude as the eager night navigator, McMinn's aircraft, black as the night surrounding it, flies the same flight path, only in the opposing direction. When impact seems inevitable McMinn switches on all the lamps the Provost possesses: navigation, taxi and landing lights, causing heaven-knows-what reaction in the other machine, much mirth in his own. An improvement, you might agree, over lorry-driver-teasing at Tilstock. I've often wondered how he knew which way to go when making the last split-second evasive manoeuvre. Both think the same way and *pat-a-poum*.

Another night-time prank, to which the air traffic controllers under the aptly named Sqn. Ldr. Moon turned a blind eye, involved taxying. Everyone listening out on the same circuit frequency would hear: "Charlie Mike, clear port," indicating that I had completed my landing roll and had exited the upwind end of the duty runway to the left. At this point I would switch off nav. and taxi lights and belt round the peri. track between the glimmering blue lamps as fast as I possibly could, aiming for the shortest duration between "CM, clear port," and "CM, ready for take-off," carefully timed by fellow students dotted about the night sky and their instructors and, one has to believe, by Sqn. Ldr. Moon and his men in the tower.

Fast taxying and low flying sometimes came close to being the same thing. Barry Stott and his instructor, on the course ahead of ours, may have wondered which of the two they were doing when they struck a signal on the railway line they'd been following. Perhaps the smoke from the train got in their eyes. They came to a rapid halt. The only physical injury was to the instructor who twisted his ankle on a sleeper whilst looking for help. We didn't hear much more about that incident, maybe because there was an instructor involved. "Black Saturday," as it came to be called, was something quite different.

Roger Korner showed no greater daring than the others on his course at Ternhill until that famous Saturday. It was the day of his low-level cross-country exercise solo, but so low? Two hundred and fifty feet agl (above ground level) was stipulated, but such stipulations were anathema to hot-blooded pilots with a passion for daisies viewed from as close as possible from above and, if Freud is to be believed, from below.

The little bit of sanity that survived the assaults on reason inflicted by the lust for danger persuaded the exuberant Korner to remain above daisy-top height, but only just. Acting Pilot Officer Korner was no doubt brushing the dainty petals of the daisies with the wheels of the Provost and joyously skipping over hazards such as hedge and hog when his attention was momentarily distracted. Perhaps a pretty dairy maid winked at him. Few believed that it was his map, as he claimed, which robbed him of a split second of time.

Korner's Provost ploughed through the top of an indignant tree. The fixed undercarriage encouraged in the aircraft a pitch-down moment. On bursting from the foliage the machine was decidedly nose-down. Contact with the ground was made in an almost straight and level attitude, accounted for by a frantic Korner, both feet against the instrument panel, heaving back on the stick with all his might. Several knots had been lost as a result of the brief acquaintance with the tree and were now being further dissipated by the wheels churning through mud.

When they arrived at the ditch there was still sufficient speed to snap each undercarriage leg from the wings without throwing the aircraft onto its back. The Provost sank on its belly, which soon absorbed the remaining knots, and APO Roger Korner found himself, when the noise had stopped and he dared open his eyes, piloting a very stationary RAF trainer.

He climbed from the cockpit, surveyed the scene without much enthusiasm, and trudged miserably to the nearest farmhouse to phone friendly RAF Ternhill. His account of the events fell on unresponsive ears. The commanding officer, Group Captain Carter, seemed unmoved by Roger's fortunate escape.

The lack of sympathy may be better understood in the knowledge of a telephone conversation that had taken place a few moments earlier. Carter had received a call from a wing commander, an old acquaintance. The conversation ran somewhat as follows:

"That you, Carter old boy?"

"Yes, speaking. How are you? What can I do for you?"

267

"Well, it's rather interesting. Was in me bathroom this morning, shavin' at the mirror – happened to glance out of the window when damn me if I don't see there below me one of your bloody little Provosts, registration Mike Alpha Kilo. Thought that a bit much, you know – nearly nicked meself."

Roger's map-reading explanation seemed less plausible in the face of the indignant Wingco's call. One could understand the Group Captain's wrath.

Unfortunately there was, on that same Saturday, another episode which contrived to add fire to his ire. Preston (Charlie Mike), in a continuing effort to live up to his call-sign, persistently and despite repeated instructions to desist, tried to judge each approach to land with a fineness up to which his finesse was evidently not. Coming in on a short landing attempt over the road (where the temptation to brush the wheels ever so gently over the helmets of passing motorcyclists was hard to resist) he made it just too short and collected a moderate ribbon of decorative barbed wire around the undercarriage legs. In a desperate last moment effort to rectify the situation he had applied full power and avoided contact with the ground.

During climb-out CM's glowing ears were subjected to cool comments concerning the condition of the aeroplane and instructions to fly past the tower for closer inspection. As a result he was instructed to land. The landing was uneventful and unaffected by a punctured tailwheel tyre.

An upright pole of the fence had gouged an incision along the underside of the fuselage and the prop was found to have a serrated leading edge. About fifty feet of barbed wire had to be unravelled from the left leg whilst an anxious Charlie Mike prepared himself to meet his Carter. The latter was unhappy about this further blemish on the good flying record of RAF Ternhill.

Amongst a barrage of high ranking abuse was to be heard: "Preston, on no account shall I tolerate your presence on this station any longer than I have to and, irrespective of what the AOC Flying Training Command has to say, you will be posted elsewhere."

Thinking of nothing better to say than a polite "Thank you," I took my leave to await further instructions.

Less than a week later Roger Korner, Preston and a dapper Carter climbed aboard an ancient Anson and set wing for Training Command HQ where, we were informed, we would meet the grim Air Vice Marshal Graham.

A sad tale attaches itself to this worthy AVM who no doubt did many a brave thing during the war. All this had been forgotten or rather overshadowed by a recent incident at Whipsnade Zoo. Graham had apparently witnessed a child being mauled by a lion and had done nothing in the way of interceding, reasoning perhaps that a little boy plus an AVM in the jaws of the lion was twice as bad as one little boy with no heroic record and a runny nose in the same plight. *Sic transit gloria.*

Preston was relying on this fortuitous carnivore for moral support through the threatened ordeal. He had prepared a rather muddled statement embracing very local earthquakes causing a sudden upward shift of ground level at the runway threshold, a sudden twitch of the rotational velocity of the earth causing the threshold to leap out of reach, and other equally convincing phenomena to account for what might, on the face of it, have seemed like an error of judgement.

Roger Korner was first to be invited to enter the presence. We all knew, Roger included, that his was a most heinous crime and he was due for the chop. It was therefore with disbelief that Roger announced, reeling from the AVM's door a very short while later, that he had been reprimanded and invited to refrain from doing the same sort of thing again. The Preston interview was almost as bizarre. No opportunity was given for the reciting of the rehearsed speech. All I actually had the chance to do was mouth a tremulous "Thank you, Sir," which probably remained unheard above the clatter of knee bones dancing together.

"Preston, your CO and I," (Graham speaks, Carter stands in the corner, glowering,) "we have decided that you should continue with your flying training. Don't let it happen again."

AVM Graham's eyes were of a particularly startling shade of light blue. I could have told him, had we met before the Whipsnade adventure, that he'd have had nothing to fear from the lion; not with eyes like those.

We flew back to Ternhill in the Anson without our CO who understandably took exception to his fellow passengers and, so far as I know, covered the couple of hundred miles by foot.

Korner continued his aviating career, flying around tall trees and past houses owned by retired Wing Commanders on the side away from the bathroom. I continued to land as close to the threshold as possible, firm in the belief that some natural phenomenon, of which only the supernatural, blue-eyed AOC Flying Training Command was aware, had accounted for the misadventure.

A couple of days later I learned that the Provost that had let me down had been suffering from a flat spot caused by a faulty injector system, explaining why it hadn't responded more promptly to the throttle. During the pre-flight run-up I'd failed to spot the problem, nor had I noticed another symptom of incorrect fuel supply, demonstrated by the mechanic, which was that the Alvis engine was hunting at idle. Unfortunately it wasn't the only time I wrapped decorations around undercarriage legs. I managed to do it again in a Cub in Southern Rhodesia, but that's another story.

"Black Saturday" should have reminded us gently of the perils attached to machines that fly in the air and the unforgiving nature of unintentional contact with the ground. We may have enjoyed our flying too much but above all we wanted to be skilled, professional and masters of our machines. Sudden death was something of which we were aware but when it happened to one of us it still came as a shock. It seemed unfair that it was not as a result of the kind of irresponsible act which accompanied our flying. It seemed unfair that it should happen to the most professional Royal Air Force officer among us and the only one to be a father.

Others may have been more conscious of the risks than we were ourselves. One morning I discovered I'd got a new batman. No explanation at the time but it turned out a swap had been agreed. John had persuaded his predecessor to make the change as he wanted to be known as the batman of the late APO Preston. Chances were taken but they were always carefully considered. Having this much fun, any death wish would need to be ridiculously strong to prevail. Punishment for misdemeanours was usually grounding; our instructors knew how painful that was.

Most times one didn't get caught. It was bad luck that on a low level cross-country exercise the transmissions between CM and another student from Course 128 who had joined me were intercepted by an instructor. He was leading a formation. Transmissions on the chosen frequency went something like:

"Hedgehog leader to hedgehog formation, starboard, starboard, go."
"Mind that cow!"
"Hedgehog, hedgehog, echelon starboard, echelon starboard, go."
"Hedgehog one."
"Hedgehog two."
"Look out for the wires, two o'clock."
"Hedgehog ... *screech* ... " and so on.

On that particular flight I remember with great clarity cresting the brow of a hill and finding myself charging down a street of terraced houses in Coalville.

Being confined to the ground was especially cruel to me on one occasion as I'd been caught tail-chasing with Charlie Lima and was grounded during the end-of-course aerobatic contest which I'd been determined to win.

Why tail-chasing, the equivalent of the dogfight, should have been prohibited was a puzzle. The Provost was equipped with an accelerometer with tell-tales that couldn't be cancelled in the air. Being professionals, we would keep to the permitted 'plus 6 – minus 4' limits. Charlie Lima (Mike Porter) had heard a couple of bangs during our Battle of Britain re-enactment but decided to continue. When he landed, the 'g'-meter showed no more than 'plus 7' but the top surfaces of both mainplanes had developed corrugations. The authorities were not pleased.

UPPER: The 'orchestra' in action inside Herald G-APWA during its flight from Nice to London on December 2nd 1959.
LOWER: Herald G-APWA landing at Rio (Santos Dumont) Airport, April 1960.
Photos: John de Uphaugh.

TWO ATMOSPHERIC SHOTS OF HERALD G-APWA DURING THE 1960
SOUTH AMERICAN SALES TOUR.
UPPER: G-APWA frames a wonderful selection of Brazilian-registered classic
propliners.
LOWER: A night-time shot of G-APWA.
Photos: John de Uphaugh.

UPPER LEFT: M.O. F/O Brian Burne examines the health of a Meteor T.7 at Shallufa, Egypt, March 26th 1953.
UPPER RIGHT: Another Meteor-scape.
LOWER: AOC's inspection at RAF Coltishall, May 25th 1956. AVM "Paddy" Crisham takes the salute (he died in 1997); Flt. Lt. Dennis Bird (ADC) is on far left.
Photos: via Dennis Bird.

Sir W. Sefton Brancker, seen at the 1923 Grosvenor Cup Race.

Sir Alan Cobham in a DH Moth.

Photos: via "AEROPLANE MONTHLY."

TWO MORE "TOP MEN."
UPPER: Henri Mignet in an early HM.14 Flying Flea.
Photo: via "AEROPLANE MONTHLY."
LOWER: Gp. Cpt. Edward Mole in the front cockpit of a BAC VII glider, with
(it is thought) designer Lowe Wylde behind. Barbara Cartland sponsored this
attempt on the first cross-channel glider flight, in 1931, for which the "DAILY
MAIL" had put up a £1,000 prize. Unfortunately they did not win!
Photo: via Liz Mole.

TWO MORE
"TOP MEN."

David Faulkner-Bryant
(centre), with Trudi
Benjamin and Phil Irish,
at Cranfield 1997.
Photo: Lewis Benjamin.

Norman Jones, founder
and hands-on leader of
the Tiger Club.
Photo: via Ann Jones.

As mentioned earlier, in addition to the tail-chase, flick rolls and outside manoeuvres were prohibited. On Course 129 there were two diametrically opposed approaches to aerobatics: the Grzybowski versus the MacDonald. Grzybowski, our Flight Commander, was a little pugnacious man whose shoulders were reportedly constructed of tin as a result of a number of contacts with the earth when giving low level aerobatic displays. His manoeuvres were uncomfortable in the extreme: bootfuls of rudder in inexplicable places, violent application of controls, lots of 'g.' Sergeant Mac was smoothness epitomised. Grzyb's theory was that all the violence made for a better display as viewed from the ground. Mac was in favour of precision and co-ordination. A neat, tidy man, he flew neatly and tidily. It all kind of symbolised the difference between flying a piston and flying a jet. Sgt. Mac went on to be a display pilot with the Red Pelicans in Jet Provosts.

Flying Officer Derek Brett was a neat, tidy officer. He was a little older than the rest of us, having transferred to Flying Training Command from another GD branch. His mess dress was different and immaculate: jacket cut up at the back like a waistcoat, numerous small brass buttons festooning sleeves and the front. He even boasted some ribbons, not perhaps the AFC but neither, as the uncharitable hinted, awarded for excellence in storekeeping. Derek's posture was in marked contrast to the affected slouch of the conscripts, the National Servicemen. At the bar in the mess he would stand stiffly upright with pint mug (pewter) held down by his right trouser leg, thumb accurately aligned with the seam. He looked equally impressive in his flying suit, everything in place where it ought to be.

The flying suit was provided with integral knee pad, pencil holders, numerous pockets and a sheath on arm or leg into which a small knife was inserted. This was not for use in the event of capture by the enemy but had a more immediate purpose.

From RAF Ternhill we were posted to RAF Worksop, a 'temporary' airfield of Nissen huts constructed rapidly during the war. Here we were introduced to the nifty little DH Vampire. Well, the FB.5s and FB.9s were nifty, the two seat T.11 more of a lump.

Worksop didn't have quite the same ring to it as Ternhill, nor Gamston, its subsidiary, to Chetwynd. That might have been seen as some kind of omen. The station was split in two halves: Vampires and Meteors. Neil Williams was stationed there at the same time, converting from T-33 to Meteor and making a very fine job of it.

The Vampire was quite a change from the Provost. For me it presented a peculiar problem. In the Provost we rarely flew above 10,000 ft. In the Vampire it was not uncommon to hit 33,000 ft and down again in as little as 10 minutes. My ears wouldn't take the coming down and, after repeated haemorrhages and burst eardrums, I was sent to Ad Astra House for interview with the otorhinolaryngologist. The diagnosis was narrow eustachian tubes causing otitic baratrauma. It seemed like the end of the world, but of course it wasn't; not as Derek Brett's was.

I got to fly the single seat Fighter Bomber (FB).9 a few times. It was truly a delight. The pilot sat snugly in an extremely narrow cockpit way ahead of the wings; the space within the bubble canopy was just adequate for the bone-dome, shoulders lining up with the canopy runners. There was nothing to restrict your view. You put on the Vampire FB.9 like the proverbial glove, in marked contrast to the Harvard and even the T.11 version.

Underneath the rearmost tip of each fuselage boom was a skid which they painted white. On your first solo you were shoehorned into the cockpit and given a pre-flight briefing which included demonstration of the pitch angle for landing. Instructor and fellow students – our Flight Commander, with dashing handlebar moustache, was appropriately named Flt. Lt. Skidmore – weighed down on the tail. Up went the nose with you in it.

"This," says Skidmore, "is your landing attitude."

Imperceptible movement: "This is the skids touching the runway."

The white paint was inspected after every flight. Signs of abrasion were not taken kindly to.

A fellow student, Charlie Hotel (Mike Jolley), managed to remove not only the white paint but the skids and some of the underbelly too. Retracting the undergear with the alacrity of the fighter ace was cool. It wasn't so cool to retract it even quicker.

The speed of the Vampire meant that, if wished, you could soon be flying over water. As a result one sat on both parachute pack and dinghy.

In 1958 ejector seats were not yet fitted to all military aircraft but they were coming in. A critical dimension measured on fighter pilots was from hip to knee. Beyond a certain length both kneecaps would be neatly removed by the instrument panel if the ejector seat was fired. Having long femurs, I was relieved to be flying non-ejector equipped aircraft.

The parachute was inflated by pulling the D-ring, the dinghy by opening the valve on the CO_2 bottle. The latter had been known to discharge itself inadvertently. It was for this reason that we carried the knife on the flying overall.

Fg. Off. Derek Brett was on a QGH with his instructor in a T.11 when the worst happened. The dinghy pack suddenly inflated under Derek's seat. The mass of billowing yellow squeezed out and applied force to the control column, pitching the aircraft violently forward. They were at about 6,000 ft agl. Ever the professional, Derek knew exactly where to find his knife and managed to puncture the dinghy; this much we found out later. But before they could pull out of the dive the aircraft struck a slag heap in Sheffield. As some kind of rite we were formally shown Derek's bone-dome, surprisingly unscathed.

The funeral at the cemetery in Worksop was a small and dismal affair. Suddenly we felt uncomfortable about the flippancy of our ways, looking surreptitiously at the parents, the wife and the very small son at the grave.

This was *peacetime*. My father had come back from the war a damaged man but he'd come back alive.

CHAPTER 23

ON A SUMMER'S DAY

(THIRTY YEARS AGO)

by

Lewis Benjamin

[When I was offered this article to include in a book about the fifties (it had originally appeared in Air-BP's house magazine in 1968), how could I refuse?! Whether a Tiger Club display such as is described here took place in the late fifties or sometime in the sixties, the atmosphere was always very similar, full of nostalgia and (one might almost say) enchantment; many of us doubtless remember it as well as if it were yesterday – Ed.]

Tiny Turbulents were tipping their wings, slaloming in and out of posts like demented butterflies, their gay colours reflecting the sun at every turn, bewitching the spectator and putting the wind up the Display Director. He stood to one side of the commentator, watching closely. Behind him lay the weeks of rehearsal, the paralysing hours spent on the phone, the diplomacy, the arm-twisting and all the follow-up, the final result of which was this, a real live air display in the year of relative Grace 1968.

The audience, a living thing of several thousand souls, almost breathes as one. The commentator, nearer than the pilots to the exciting atmosphere, plays upon their credulity like some olde-tyme master of ceremonies. He alone can urge their hearts to stop beating, their hands to clap and, in the same breath, command little boys to get back behind the ropes. The year '68. The year of the Concorde and of variable-geometry wings; of VTOL, bus jets and the 50th anniversary of the RAF. Yet in the middle of it all is an anachronism as much a part of the scene as the 1930 Bonnie and Clyde in a mini-maxi-skirted London – an old-fashioned, down-to-earth air display. No jets, little noise, and propellers that will top 3,000 revs only if someone pushes too hard. The pilots look like you and me in sports jackets and sweaters. There are helmets with Gosport tubes dangling, and ½-million maps stuffed behind the odd tube in the fuselage. There are cushions and birds, and grass beneath your feet, and a hand-swung engine-start routine you'd never thought to see again.

Come with me and I'll lead you to a light aeroplane revival that's growing year by year here in Britain, right under our very noses. Overhead, the coloured airways, through which an elite of radio-controlled pilots direct gleaming airliners, their mien not unlike that of an office executive: but beneath them . . . that's where the sporting pilots draw breath, and that's where a lot of those airline boys *fly* in their time off. To feel again a responsive machine under your hands. To enjoy the deep satisfaction of a lushed three-pointer after a day of communion with the wind and the sweet fresh air. Contrary to general belief, a club display pilot is invariably a professional; some are active RAF, others airline or test pilots, and the few – the skilled amateurs. There is only one club in the world that trains and regularly exhibits its pilots' skill in air displays throughout the country, and that's the Tiger Club of Redhill, down in Surrey.

The Turbs have gone, leaving behind them a spattering of burst balloons, their wrinkled skins fluttering atop a cardboard post, mute testament to a pilot's prowess – and the odd upended posts with their intact balloons kissing the grass, tributes to a near miss. Then, one by one, the little single-seaters slip in to land, using up no more field than a cricket length or two.

It's a two-hour show of slick timing. The commentator now has control as firmly as if he were leading the crowd by the hand. "Over to your left," he says, and 20,000 expectant eyes swivel together. From out of the blue a flamboyant yellow and red biplane cavorts in a display of aerobatics that's as far removed from the classical style as the mind can conceive. To make a point: in theory a flick manoeuvre must, by definition, be an uncontrolled one; yet we see flicks positioned to every point of the compass – and, worse for the blood pressure, from the inverted to the inverted. For here the Tiger Club draws upon the country's greatest aerobatic exponents.

Without question, the cult of light flying is growing in Britain, but it is a case of self-determination, with the powers-that-be firmly shutting their eyes in case the growing child will present a problem. Eventually it will. Already in the USA there are so many private aviators that if they were to ground themselves for a week the authorities would leave no stone unturned to get them airborne again. To think that such a state of affairs could one day exist over here is wishful thinking, but it would be nice to know where we are being led. It isn't that the administrating authorities in this country are 'anti'; they aren't. Too many of them have been flying men themselves, but they lack a firm policy. So, in passing, I eliminate government assistance. Self-determination it has always been: we are used to it. For ten years now the Tiger Club displays have toured the country promoting airmindedness; from appearances at Farnborough to a week-long trip to Caithness, with every conceivable stop in between, and doing it successfully.

A colourful formation of nine aircraft roars overhead, a nostalgic mixture of old biplanes and wee single-seat monoplanes. The four Turbulents that bring up the rear now carefully ease themselves out of the diamond and then, well tucked in, return for a dazzling display of formation flying. (None of the "now you see us, now you don't" stuff about *this* act. Each pilot's head and shoulders can clearly be seen. The spectator almost flies with him in the cockpit and wiggles his feet and flexes his fingers in sympathy.) The Turbulents move up-stage with a superbly-timed turn that in the plan view reveals a tight formation that would not discredit a services jet team. Which isn't surprising, since some of the pilots are past members of such teams; they remark only: "It's easier in jets."

The pilots have names and personalities, and the commentary tells you all about them. There is a lot of the 'tween-wars garden party atmosphere in this – an intimate familiarity that never pales, no matter how often the show revisits a place. The bevy of Rollason Turbulents, bouncing around behind the staid biplanes, are firm favourites with the crowds that flock to the displays in increasing numbers. It is easy to associate a dream with them. "After all," the commentator says, "they can be built at home." Add a reliable VW engine and tell them the mpg is 40 and they'll assess it along with the family car. This the man in the street can understand. The jets above are distant, expensive. He is as likely to fly one of those as fly to the moon.

"Now from the west come the five biplanes." There's something unreal about a biplane these days. Five together is almost history come alive, a scene to remember. With a growing roar they're upon us. A change of formation and two have shot straight up into a paired stall-turn to begin an exciting display of *duo aeros*. From the sandwich, which is a one-up/one-down combination with a thin layer of air in between, to a mirror act that includes an inverted circuit for one and a very close piece of formation for the other. Six feet between fins is the norm. And then, with a spirited show of flying, in exacting, non-radio unison, they scream away in a breathtaking finale that belies the pilots's airline background. A few years ago these old aircraft were fairly commonplace, but now they are becoming scarce. Especially the Tiger. Even as little as two years ago a Tiger Moth could be picked up for £300 to £400 – occasionally one popped up for as little as £100. But not now. The cheapest seem to come in at £800, and £1,000 is nearer the mark.

From tight-formation discipline to an even tougher discipline, for crazy-flying. There can be no easier act with which to come to grief. The higher the safer – the antithesis can never be better than second best. It takes great ability to succeed consistently at this game. But it is a favourite with the public, and no air display would be complete without this time-honoured act. Invariably the pilot is hidden among the crowd and is called out for a "free trip." He climbs clumsily into the cockpit, inadvertently opens the throttle before his pilot can get in, and proceeds to scatter everyone in a hilarious take-off. His subsequent slides, slips and flat turns are guaranteed to tie up any viewing pilot with apprehension. The crowd is dying to help, to shout advice to the panicking pilot, and in no time – in response to the commentator's appeal – everyone is yelling "close the throttle" at all the right moments.

The pilots enjoy display work. It follows, because they're not paid for it. Professional amateurs, that's what they are. In any four-plane formation you can find a commonplace 12,000 hours of flying experience. And it isn't *any* pilot who can cope. Regardless of hours. The best must have a flashing exhibitionism about him that *shows*. He has to be the complete showman and there aren't many.

Overhead the Turbs, this time in echelon, are preparing a surprise. Even from 1,200 feet below, one can see the arm of each pilot extended, and then suddenly the sky is filled with streaming paper, and the boys are in line astern, playing follow-my-leader, seeing how many streamers they can intercept before the paper embraces the ground. A rip-roaring descending kaleidoscope, ending with an immaculate series of passes under a hoop.

In an age of unsurpassed third-party concern, safety is a top feature. If a growing public awareness is to be promoted it won't be helped by accidents. The Display Director does a great deal to reduce the untoward incident to nothing more than a calculated risk. The briefing on the day is thorough but no more than a programme run-through with the constant reminder: "Never fly towards or over the crowds." Real safety begins months before, with careful pilot selection and training, followed by practice and more practice. One cast-iron rule has been proved beyond question: *no last-minute changes.*

"GIRL ON WING," the posters shout. And, sure enough, there she is, perched high on a Tiger. Sometimes there are two brave damsels and the aerial twosome work each end of the crowd, waving and blowing kisses to the populace. It is an act with a strong human element and, like the ever-popular parachuting, is applauded with great feeling.

Too soon the two hours are up. There has been the vintage fly-past, balloon bursting, flour-bombing, and the noisy and exciting race – fourteen or more aircraft bent on making this finale a memorable one for the spectators to go home on. The PA system, no longer an animated friend, plays exit music and long lines of patient cars trace their ways to countless homes. The pilots refuel, and keep a tolerant eye on the enthusiastic Mums and Dads and their families who flock around the aircraft to see and to touch and to question. Like modest heroes, our pilots wave goodbye, to join up overhead into a last salute before setting course for home. At long last the ringmaster unwinds. His charges have left and only he remains on a now quiet field. If I know my ringmaster he'll shrug imperceptibly and move off to find a cup of tea.

CHAPTER 24

OF CARS AND 'CRATES'

by

John Cooper

(as told to Peter Campbell)

Both cars and aeroplanes were very much a part of my family for as long as I can remember. My father, Charles Cooper, was an apprentice at Napiers, and worked on S.F. Edge's cars, and later on Kaye Don's cars. I was born in 1923, and as a child I used to go to Brooklands with him; that's when I knew a young Donald Campbell, who was quite important even in those days, having such a famous father.

In 1934 or thereabouts my father built me a little car with a lawn mower engine, and also he built himself a Flying Flea aeroplane. I remember him making the wings out of spruce, and my mother sewing up the fabric and doping it. He put an Austin Seven engine in the plane, which was highly tuned but underpowered and a bit overweight, being water-cooled. I can remember him suspending the whole thing by a bungee cord round a girder in the garage and testing the effects of different props. Anyway the aircraft was a bit dicey; it did just get off the ground, but it was obviously potentially dangerous because it was too heavy and underpowered. So then he got hold of a Henderson four-cylinder in-line air-cooled engine from an American Henderson motor-bike, took the Austin Seven engine out, and put the Henderson engine in. Then it did fly, without a doubt; he learned to fly it down at Redhill. Mind you, like all Flying Fleas it could not bank: it just turned left or right, or went up and down, and you had to be very careful where you positioned the front wing, it could be very dicey.

He then built me an Austin Seven Special (I was about twelve then) using this lovely high-powered Austin Seven engine. This was in fact my second car, and it is still running today, having been completely rebuilt recently. At a later date, probably towards the end of the war, he bought a Miles Hawk Major, G-ADAB.

I was trained as an engineering draughtsman and designer, and went into the Air Force towards the end of the war. I wanted to be a pilot but finished up as a toolmaker; I was only in the forces for just over a year.

At the end of the war we started building racing cars based on the 500 cc formula; they were really four-wheeled motor-bikes, with a motor-cycle engine and gearbox. We went to 1,100 cc and then to the Cooper-Bristol, which was a front-engined car, and then went to Climax-engined cars and eventually we won the World Championship in 1959 & 1960 with Jack Brabham.

In those days we were at Surbiton, and I knew a lot of the Hawker people very well, such as Sir Sidney Camm and Tommy Sopwith, who had several of my cars, including Cooper-Jaguars and bob-tailed sports cars. I remember that he wanted to put a Turboméca jet engine in a Jaguar, and we went up to Blackburn's, who had the licence for the engines, to see one, but in the event it was never finished in time and the car had a Jaguar engine fitted in it.

There was someone called Stanley who worked with Sir Sidney Camm, and he was very helpful to us. We had built a streamlined record car for breaking 500 cc and 1,000 cc records, and in 1955 when we were building the bob-tailed sports car, the one with the sawn-off back, it was Stanley's idea to test it in the Hawker wind-tunnel. He was sure that this design would give it more stability as a road car and that there wouldn't be any loss in performance. A lot of other manufacturers started to do the same thing, and it became known as the 'Kamm-tail' (after a German aerodynamicist), but really it was the 'Camm-tail' (after Sir Sidney Camm). I still have the wind-tunnel model in our garage showroom. Stanley later went to Rolls Royce and helped to design the cars that we know today. Motor racing and, I suppose the motor industry in general, was much more of a family affair in those days.

In about 1959 several of us in the motor racing profession decided to learn to fly, which we did at Fair Oaks under Wing Commander Arthur. Colin Chapman had a Comanche, and Jack Brabham initially had a Cessna, a 170 I think, although he had a 310 later. I then bought a Tripacer, which funnily enough belonged to a chap called Eddie Portman, who is now one of the richest men in England! I'm sure he has a title now. He had an interest in racing cars as well, and I think we did a deal with him and I took over his Tripacer. The registration was G-ARAG, and until very recently I hadn't appreciated the significance of the letters as 'personalized' marks: they were purely a coincidence!

Although I learned to fly at Fair Oaks, I never did aspire to an instrument rating. Apart from Wing Commander Arthur, who oversaw all my basic instruction in a Chipmunk, "Sport" Martin, a Dan-Air pilot, also taught me quite a lot, and I did all my stalls and spins with him in one of the Club's Tiger Moths. I thought at the time that it was like flying a ping-pong ball on top of a water squirt!

When we'd finished he said: "Now I'll show you what flying is all about," and threw the Tiger all over the sky; that was quite something! He became a good friend of mine.

We used to go to race meetings in the Tripacer. I remember coming back from Goodwood once with Jack Brabham; when we got over the South Downs the weather was terrible, and Jack said to me: "Don't you wish you were down there in the traffic jam?", to which I replied: "Not 'arf!"

I did a lot of flying with Colin Chapman in his Comanche. On one occasion we went to the German Grand Prix at the Nürburgring. The race was on a Sunday, and then on the following day, which was Easter Monday, there was another race at Brands Hatch. I was intending to fly back by scheduled airline, but Colin said after the race: "No, you come back with me."

There were four of us altogether, including Jim Clark and Innes Ireland. Colin's Comanche was at a military aerodrome not far from the Nürburgring, and when we got there the weather was really terrible. The authorities told us that we were on no account to take off from there, so apparently that was that. I must admit that I was rather relieved, and told Colin that I would revert to my original plan and fly back from Cologne, even if it meant missing Brands Hatch.

At this Colin said: "Oh! Don't worry about that, we'll be all right!" and in fact we did eventually take off. Jim and Innes were half-asleep in the back seat and so didn't have any worries. Colin climbed through all this muck up to about six thousand feet and then he said: "You fly the plane now, I've got a few things to sort out."

When we got to the Belgian border, we had to get permission to cross the Channel, and were told to descend to two thousand feet. I said to Colin: "They must be joking!" but he said: "No they're not!"

So we had to go down to two thousand feet and then we couldn't see even the end of the wingtip: I was scared stiff, I don't mind telling you! I should mention that Colin was a great 'kidder,' by the way, but a great flyer, a good pilot. Somewhere over the Channel the engine started to run a bit rough and I voiced my concerns to him that there must be something wrong with it, to which he replied with an all-knowing look: "Yes, I know." He was playing me up actually; anyway he altered the pitch on the prop and did various other things, but the problem was actually due to carburettor icing. He frightened the life out of me anyway, I thought the thing was going to blow up! Anyway, we did eventually manage to land safely at an aerodrome not far from Brands Hatch, so everything turned out all right in the end.

I also used to fly quite a lot with Jack Brabham. He used to take along spares in his Cessna, gearboxes and things like that. I remember that once he got permission from Mrs Topham to land on the back straight at Aintree Race Course; this was an almost unheard-of thing at the time.

While I was learning to fly, another student at the same time was Dick Emery, the comedian and actor. Of course he was a real 'character' and turned out to be a very good pilot eventually. I did my qualifying cross-country flight to Luton in the Tripacer without incident, and when it came to Dick's first cross-country, off he went in a Tiger Moth. He managed either to get lost or to get short of fuel, or both, and he made an emergency landing at RAE Farnborough. I ask you, Farnborough in a Tiger Moth! They went mad, of course; they rushed out to him and said that the plane would have to be taken apart as soon as possible and moved out on a lorry. Then they realised who he was, filled the plane up with fuel, and told him in no uncertain terms to clear off!

There was another chap at Fair Oaks, whose name I can't remember (perhaps it's just as well), who was an absolute nutter. We all told him that one day he'd have a serious accident or, worse still, kill himself.

Well, one evening he came into the bar with a support collar on his neck, so of course we all said: "Uhuh! You've done it now, haven't you?"

"No, really!"

"Come on, tell us the truth!"

"You won't believe me if I tell you."

"Come on, what have you done?"

"Well, I was lying on the floor watching television with my head on the fire fender, and one of my children jumped on my chest and damaged my neck."

One tragedy which happened fairly locally was the death of Mike Hawthorn, who used to drive for me, of course. He was also a pilot, and he and his father had owned two aircraft at Fair Oaks, a Fairchild Argus and then a Percival Vega Gull. One evening he was driving a Jaguar on the Guildford bypass and 'lost it' completely. It was damp weather; he had just passed Rob Walker's Mercedes, and he went across the central reservation and hit a lorry. The irony of it was that he had recently given up motor racing because he thought it was getting too dangerous.

Ron Flockhart also flew from Fair Oaks; he had an Auster and then a Bellanca. When Jack Brabham sold his first Cessna, Ron and Eoin Young flew it back to New Zealand, I believe.

On Sunday April 8th 1962 we had a meeting at Fair Oaks where a photographer from "FLIGHT" magazine was going to take some air-to-air shots of racing drivers who were also pilots. It was a windy day with quite a bit of cross-wind on the usual runway. I hadn't had my pilot's licence for that long, and my father was with me and was concerned about my flying the plane in those conditions. So I went to Wing Commander Arthur, and he suggested that I took along with me "Sport" Martin, the Dan-Air pilot I mentioned earlier. Colin Chapman also came along, and he sat in the back with my father, while I sat in the pilot's seat with "Sport" alongside me. Arranging it that way gave me confidence that if anything was to look a bit dodgy "Sport" could look after things. We did our air-to-air session with the "FLIGHT" Gemini, and then I asked "Sport" if he would land the Tripacer. Well, he came in too steeply, the nosewheel snapped off, and the plane finished up on its back! It didn't catch fire, fortunately. Jack Brabham landed his Cessna 310 right alongside, and ran over to see if we needed any help, but we all got out safely. The Tripacer was dismantled and returned to MacAlpine's at Luton for repairs.

While I was flying back from MacAlpines after the damage had been put right, with a friend whose name escapes me, I must have got myself a bit lost; I used to do things like following the river Thames while I was chatting, rather than keeping a close lookout on exactly where we were.

At one point he looked down and said: "That's a bloody great house down there!"

I peered over the side and realised that it was Windsor Castle! So we quickly came down to about two hundred feet and flew back to Fair Oaks. It goes without saying that I thought I would be in deep trouble. Anyway a few phone calls were made and we were let off. At least at two hundred feet we wouldn't have hit any airliners from Heathrow.

When we got back to Fair Oaks, we found there was an air display on somewhere fairly near, so I decided to go, and took a passenger with me. When I went to get in the plane as we were leaving to come home, my passenger reminded me that I had better carry out the usual pre-flight inspection; when I did so, I found that the tail was all bent. Somebody had run into it on the ground (and did admit to it later) and as we couldn't fly it in that condition, back it would have to go to MacAlpines once again for repairs. We phoned up Fair Oaks to ask them if they could send someone to collect us, which they did, although he managed to get lost on the way back!

I had actually gone to Fair Oaks that day in a twin-engined Mini, an experimental car with one engine at the front and one at the back. That night I was due to have dinner with Roy Salvadori and Jack Brabham. On my way I had a bad accident; I went end-over-end and must have nearly killed myself. When I came round I couldn't remember anything about the accident at all, but I did remember the flying bit earlier and thought I must have been in an aeroplane crash. Well, to cut a long story short, for various reasons I decided to sell the Tripacer after it was repaired, and that was really the end of my flying career.

Back in 1961 I had been to Indianapolis with Jack Brabham. We had the first British rear-engined car to go there, and we were treated like lords. They knew we weren't going to win because the car was a bit underpowered, but they really looked after us well. We happened to mention to somebody that we both flew aeroplanes, and they brought us one to try out. We were scared to death, but they encouraged us to have a go anyway.

There's an interesting story about the sponsorship we got in the States. In 1959 we won both the American Grand Prix and the World Championship; there was a chap there called Roger Ward who had won the Indy that year, and he was running a meeting car that he thought would blow us all off the track. Anyway he said that we must come to Indianapolis with our car. When we took it there, we realised that it was quite quick, but we couldn't afford to enter it for the next race. At that time there was a Professor of paediatrics, Dr Frank Faulkner, who was a great racing enthusiast, and he came to all the Grands Prix and gave lectures, without any payment, at a local hospital in each country while he was there. Amongst other responsibilities he was an adviser to the American Government on children's health, and he was in the process of testing the new disposable nappies ('diapers') made of paper. The manufacturer of the nappies was Kleenex, which was owned by Bill Kimberley. He finished up sponsoring the car, which was called the Kimberley-Cooper! We were racing in various places at the time, and he used to fly us either in his own plane or pay for us to go by scheduled services.

While in the States in the early sixties I also met Howard Hughes. He had a factory at Santa Monica, where he was building aircraft, including helicopters; when he came to the American Grand Prix in about 1963, he found out I was there and said that he wanted to talk to me, so we had a meeting in his air-conditioned limousine. He suggested that we build a rear-engined sports car in America using an Oldsmobile engine (which, incidentally, was later purchased lock, stock and barrel by Rover). However the project never took off, but I *can* say that I have met Howard Hughes!

To finish, a bit about the history of the Mini-Cooper! I had first met Alex Issigonis in 1946 when we were both at the Brighton Speed Trials, and we became friends. We used to see each other at various race meetings and at the Steering Wheel Club in London. I knew him when he made the Morris Minor, and in the late fifties there was a racing formula introduced called Formula Junior, in which the cars had to be fitted with production engines, so we used the Morris Minor engine. At the time he was developing the Mini, and I took a pre-production one over to Italy, where Roy Salvadori drove it. The chief engineers of Fiat and Ferrari also drove it and pronounced it the car of the future, with an east-west engine, front-wheel drive and so on. When it came out, Salvadori, Brabham and myself put Formula Junior 1,100 cc engines in them (they were originally only available with 850 cc). They couldn't stop, but they were quick!

In 1960 I went to see Issigonis and suggested that we ought to build some of these 'for the boys,' but he was not too keen on the idea. But we went to see the 'Headmaster,' Sir George Harriman, and he told us to take one away and do it. So I went to Lockheeds, who were experimenting with disc brakes in a Mini wheel, and eventually I came back with a Mini with disc brakes and a Formula Junior engine. I said that we would have to make a thousand of them to get the type homologated, so that we could use it for competitions, but Harriman reckoned that they would never sell that many. I expressed the opinion that I thought they would, and of course they ended up selling 150,000 of them before Stokes stopped it.

Originally the Mini-Cooper had a 1,000 cc engine, but when we realised how good it was as a competition car (the handling, the feel and so on), we then built a Homologation Special, which was the 'S'; this had a Formula Junior engine, bigger brakes, radial-ply tyres, wider rims and so on – we really had a go. That came out in 1963 and Paddy Hopkirk won the Monte Carlo Rally in it in 1964. After that it won the event again on several occasions. Then we built the 1,275 cc version, which won the Tulip Rally, the RAC Rally, the Touring Car Championship and so on. Then in 1970 Stokes decided to stop it; we didn't go to the same school or something – we just didn't get on. He closed the Competition Department so that was that. But it was reborn in 1990 when Graham Day was in charge, since when another 75,000 have been sold, and the new Mini for the year 2000 will also be manufactured in a Cooper version!

CHAPTER 25
SNAPSHOTS OF ELSTREE
by

Richard Riding

Aviation has been part of my life as far back as I can remember, and even before: I was born during an air raid in March 1942! My earliest memories are of V1s passing over our house at Hendon, and one that didn't pass overhead one day blew in all our doors and windows. Recognising the spine-chilling sound of their pulsating motors, I often used to run out into the garden while everyone else in the street was rushing for cover, and yell out: "Look, Mummy, another ruddy 'doodlebug'!"

My father was E.J. "Eddie" Riding, the aviation photographer, writer, journalist and aeromodeller, and our house was always full of flying scale models built for "AEROMODELLER" magazine. Our garage was occupied not by the family Ford car but by the mortal remains of Comper Swift G-ABPE, of which more later. After serving an apprenticeship with A.V. Roe my father worked during the war as an Aeronautical Inspection Directorate inspector, first on Albacores with Fairey Aviation at Hayes and then with London Aircraft Production at Leavesden on Halifaxes, later moving across the aerodrome to de Havilland to sign out Mosquitoes.

His aeromodelling for the magazine, and the accompanying articles illustrated with his own photographs and drawings, took up much of his spare time. Invariably the models were the subject of C. Rupert Moore's cover artwork and I still have four of these original paintings hanging up at home. In addition my father produced three-view drawings featuring a variety of full-size aircraft, for his regular feature 'Aircraft Described.' He had a drawing board at home and I always had a preview of what was going to appear in the next issue.

His office was at the Eaton Bray Sportsdrome, a purpose-built aeromodellers' paradise built by the late D.A. Russell in a field in the middle of nowhere near Leighton Buzzard, Bedfordshire. I was taken to work with my father on countless occasions. There, in addition to "AEROMODELLER," the classic series "AIRCRAFT OF THE FIGHTING

POWERS" was produced. My father prepared all the masterly three-view drawings for the final volume in this series, which he co-authored with the late Owen Thetford. There was a photographic darkroom at Eaton Bray and I recall spending countless hours watching my father print photographs. Never tiring of watching ghostly images appear magically from nothing, I would excitedly shout out the aircraft types as soon as they became recognisable.

During the same period I also had contact with full-size aircraft. My father used to take me flying from Elstree in Piper Cub G-AKAA; this was then owned by Wing Commander "Titch" Holmes and it is still flying today. By the age of seven I could recognise almost every aircraft just by its sound. My father and I even had a kind of 'double act' at Elstree: he used to blindfold me, stand me on the bonnet of his Ford car and, much to the amusement of incredulous bystanders, I would correctly name every aircraft type that came within earshot. They of course thought it was some kind of elaborate trick and that my father and I communicated via some kind of code.

During the late 1940s Elstree played host to a wide variety of aircraft. A.R. "Tiny" Pilgrim hangared Beech 17 G-AJJJ there, and early in 1950 he bought the sole surviving Heston Phoenix G-AESV, keeping it at Elstree also until he crashed it in the French Alps in April 1952. In time I was able to recognise all these locally-based types just by the sound of their engines, the easiest of all being the Hercules engines of the largest and most distinctive of all Elstree residents before or since, the blue Halifaxes of London Motor Services (LAMS). These came in to Elstree from time to time for servicing, work that was later carried out at nearby Stansted. On one occasion one of these Halifaxes appeared overhead while I was doing my party piece atop the Ford. Asked to identify the aircraft, my shrill "It's a Halif****r" was greeted, much to my innocent surprise, with roars of appreciative laughter from those gathered around. One Halifax, G-AHZM, suffered an undercarriage collapse while taxying out for an air test and was left to languish behind the main hangar for many years, well into the 1950s.

In addition to flying G-AKAA (on which he learnt to fly and soloed on March 15th 1949), my father used the two Elstree-based Autocrats, G-AGXJ and the infamous G-AGXT, for air-to-air photography. The latter had earlier featured in a particularly gruesome murder, having been used to drop the dismembered body of one Stanley Tillingham Setty on the Essex marshes in October 1949. Air-to-air subjects were usually light aircraft, including Chilton G-AFGH, Comper Swift G-ABUS (then doped silver overall) and Chrislea Super Ace G-AKVF. Many of his photographs appeared in "THE AEROPLANE," "AEROMODELLER" and "THE LIGHT PLANE," a short-lived monthly that catered for private and club pilots for two or three years in the late 1940s. Life for me at this time was never-ending aeroplanes and I remember wishing it could last for ever. Then, one day, it all stopped.

On April 6th 1950 my father set off for Rearsby in G-AKAA, with aviation artist and former Air Transport Auxiliary pilot Stanley Orton Bradshaw (SOB) as passenger, to collect Auster Autocar G-AJYM. This was the second J/5B to be built and was owned by the Mitchell Engineering Company at Peterborough. The plan was to take the Autocar back to Elstree and then fly it the following morning up to Boston in Lincolnshire to cover the opening of the Boston Aero Club for "THE AEROPLANE." The two flew back in formation from Rearsby that evening, arriving back at Elstree at 6.30 pm. Dad's logbook entry for that flight reads: "*6.4.50 Piper Cub G-AKAA Rearsby - Elstree 1 hr 15 min. In formation all way with SOB in Autocar 'JYM. Shot up Eaton Bray. Low flying at 2-300 ft all way.*" It was the final entry in the logbook, but not his last flight.

The following day my father, together with Bradshaw, Norman Stoneham of the Redhill Flying Club and a youngster by the name of Peter Newberry, took off from Elstree and arrived at Boston, where the weather was reasonable but very windy. During the afternoon Peter bumped into another Elstree pilot who had flown up alone, and knowing the Autocar was somewhat intimate with four up, he offered Peter a lift home. A little later the Autocar took off for the return trip to Elstree. It is thought that Bradshaw, the pilot, decided before heading for home to take advantage of the strong wind to demonstrate the Autocar's slow-flying ability, for it was seen to fly extremely slowly with full flap into the strong gusting wind. And then something went terribly wrong: at about 700 ft the Autocar flicked into a spin. Although it recovered at very low altitude it flew slap bang into a 40 ft-high dyke that bordered one side of the grass airfield. The three occupants were killed instantly. From that moment my contact with aviation ceased, and it was to be another eight years before I was able to get sufficiently close to touch another aeroplane.

*   *   *

One day during the Easter school holidays in April 1958, George Cull, who had succeeded my father at the "AEROMODELLER," asked if I would like to visit Elstree aerodrome. Having not set foot there since Easter 1950 I accepted with somewhat mixed emotions.

Elstree looked very much as I had remembered it. The first thing I noticed was old G-AGXT standing outside the top hangar; it was no longer resplendent in its original pristine colour scheme of cream overall, but was doped in the lurid light-blue scheme of the Elstree Flying Club. In the same livery were the Derby Aviation Chipmunks G-AOSN & G-AOSY and Miles Hawk Trainers G-AHYL & G-AKPG. Messengers G-AKBN & G-ALAE were on the tarmac with Proctor G-ALES and visiting Chrislea

Super Ace G-AKVB. Aerodrome leasee John Houlder's Gemini G-ALCS and Hunting Aerosurveys' Autocar G-AOFM were residents. Marshall's Rapide G-AKNN called in, as did Aiglet Trainer G-AOEZ.

Poking my head into the top hangar I recognised immediately the bereted horizontal form of John "Tubby" Simpson, grappling beneath a Gipsy engine cascading oil. During the war Tubby had flown as a flight engineer in London Aircraft Production-assembled Halifaxes, many of which were signed out by my father, who always flew on the first flights of those for which he was responsible. After the war Tubby was involved with LAMS' Halifaxes, and shortly after that he started up Simpson Aero Services at Elstree. As a young child I knew him well, but would he remember me, eight years older, six feet tall and wafer-thin? His obvious pleasure at seeing the son of his old friend immediately set me at ease and we got on well, so much so that that he promised me a summer job after I had left school, an offer that was accepted with alacrity!

July 1958 found me on the point of leaving school. Though still deeply interested in aviation, I had decided that I wanted to be an archaeologist. My headmistress had inspired my interest in history, but when I told her what I intended to do she surprised me by trying to dissuade me from this course. I was told that unless I became another Mortimer Wheeler (a prominent archaeologist and TV pundit of the day) there would be little money in such a career. Her tone of voice and the pat on the head suggested that this was unlikely! Somewhat disillusioned, I returned home to Hendon to await my GCE 'O' Level results; miraculously I scraped through in five subjects. In the meantime I had decided that I wanted to be an aircraft designer! I applied for an interview with Handley Page at Cricklewood, but having failed miserably in maths and science I didn't stand an earthly. Somewhat dispirited my thoughts harped back to April, my visit to Elstree and Tubby Simpson's invitation.

So it was that one September day I pedalled my trusty Raleigh Trent Sports bicycle the seven miles to Elstree. Tubby Simpson was true to his word, and I started my holiday job the following week.

September and October of that year were weeks of sheer heaven. Within a few days of starting I was removing fabric inspection panels and doping new patches onto the wings of an Auster V in for C. of A. renewal. By the end of September I was helping out with header tank modification kits on a couple of former RAF Chipmunks in for civil conversion.

The real high point occurred on September 27th, when Tubby persuaded local private owner George Moore to take me up in the all-red two-seat Auster J/4 G-APJM. Registered to the North Middlesex Flying Club, this was the last J/4 built, and was made up of parts of the J/2 G-AJPU; it had first flown earlier that year. My last flight had been in G-AKAA with my father in April 1st 1950, exactly a week before he was killed. The joy of being back in the exciting world of light aviation far outweighed the trepidation I felt during that ten-minute local flight. On returning safely to *terra firma* I knew that though I had no particular ambition to be a pilot, I was certain that somehow aeroplanes would play a prominent part in my life. Incidentally G-APJM ended up in the English Channel near the Varne lightship when my friend John Duer ditched it following engine trouble on May 27th 1961.

Meanwhile the holiday job continued. On October 9th I was given a ruddy great axe and told to dispose of a Proctor that had been languishing behind the main hangar for some considerable time. This was before the days of aircraft preservation, and I set about my task in youthful exuberance and with no qualms whatsoever. Still in its RAF silver scheme, the Proctor had been allocated the registration G-AIZA, but had never been converted. It takes quite a while to dispose of a Proctor, I can tell you. Eventually the wooden airframe was reduced to manageable chunks, and was removed piece by piece to the dump at the eastern end of Elstree's main runway, where it probably met its maker one November 5th.

Shortly afterwards Tubby Simpson gave me a Fairchild Argus! The only snag was that I had to take it away pronto – not an easy task with only a push-bike at one's disposal! Moreover, there was nowhere at home to put it, the garage, as I have already mentioned, being occupied by bits of Comper Swift G-ABPE which my father had brought home one day in April 1947, after the owner had pranged it at St. Albans shortly after its C. of A. renewal at Heston. Thus the Argus fuselage was left to languish in Tubby Simpson's garden for many years.

One luchtime towards the end of October, I was in the hangar eating my sandwiches inside the fuselage of Miles Aerovan G-AMYA (assembled but not completed by Handley Page [Reading] Ltd.), when I saw a chap emerge from an office on the other side of the hangar carrying a large aerial camera. I gobbled my sandwich, followed him outside and watched as he climbed into the sideways-facing back seat of Auster G-AGXT. The pilot got in after him and, as someone swung the prop, the photographer removed the little triangular window in front of him. Seeing me watching, he playfully aimed the F.24 camera at me and, with a wink, pretended to take a photograph. A burst of throttle and the Auster taxyed away, to take off a few moments later; I watched it until it was a mere speck in the sky. An hour or so later I heard the Auster taxy back and stop at the mouth of the hangar, and I watched the photographer climb out and gather his camera and maps from the back of the aircraft. I intercepted him on the way back to the office and we got talking; his name was Michael White, and he worked for Derby Aerosurveys, an offshoot of Derby-based Air Schools, an organisation that ran PPL & CPL courses at Elstree.

The grand-sounding Derby Aerosurveys actually consisted of just two people, Michael White and his boss, 70-year-old Lt. Col. H.C. Butcher

DSO, who had started an aerial photographic company called Photoflight shortly after the war. In 1957 Photoflight was taken over by Air Schools/Derby Aviation and renamed Derby Aerosurveys. The company had the use of the two school Austers G-AGTP & G-AGXT, and school instructors took turns to fly photographic trips. I asked if I could have a look round, and 'watched' in the darkroom as Michael processed the film he had just exposed. After the film had been developed and dried, contact prints were made and once more I found myself watching images appear from nothing, not of aircraft but aerial views of a sewage works! Memories of my happy hours in the darkroom at Eaton Bray flooded back and I realised that this was what I wanted to do, and intimated this to Michael. It just so happened that Col. Butcher was looking for someone he could take on as a kind of apprentice. A moment later I was ushered into the adjoining office where, under a cloud of cigarette smoke and perched behind an enormous and ancient Underwood typewriter, sat the fearsome figure. He was thin, frail and pale, but though he was disabled he drove himself in to Elstree each day at breakneck speed from nearby Oxhey in one of those awful blue, plastic-looking invalid cars that were common in the fifties and sixties. But he was charm itself, and many questions and several cigarettes later he offered me a job, there and then. It was arranged that I should start the following Monday. My starting salary was £1-15s a week; I could hardly believe my luck!

I took to darkroom work very quickly. My printing was excellent and I loved every moment of it. Soon I was entrusted to developing aerial film. Wrestling with 25 ft lengths of film some five inches wide, and loading them onto developing spirals in total darkness, was not an easy task at first but I soon got the hang of it.

As time went by I badgered the old colonel to let me go off in one of the Austers and try my hand with an F.24. On the evening of April 10th 1959 he finally relented. The pilot was CFI Eddie Wild and the aircraft was G-AGTP. There followed a 30-minute low-level local trip during which I photographed everything furiously. Returning to Elstree I locked myself in the darkroom and remained there until midnight. The end result was a stack of 40 beautiful 12 in x 10 in photographs, which I left prominently on the colonel's desk so that he could not fail to see them on his arrival the next morning. I pedalled home to Hendon that night the happiest person alive.

Next morning I arrived at work to find my prints spread out all over the floor beneath a 10/10ths cloud of cigarette smoke. The old boy's face broke into a smile as I entered.

"Did you take these, Richard?" he asked.

I nodded assent.

Obviously impressed, he asked: "How would you like to go off on a *real* sortie?"

I was like a dog with two tails, but it was not until May 15th 1959 that I strapped myself into the back of Auster G-AGTP behind Ginger Bedggood, one of the school instructors, and set off to photograph a factory in St. Albans. On June 18th I flew with Janet Furgusen to photograph another sewage works at Tottenham, with Michael White keeping an eye on me from the right-hand seat. The photographic aircraft on this occasion was G-AGXT, the aircraft my father had used for aerial photography a decade earlier. After that Michael and I alternated photographic sorties until he left the company later that year to work for Meridian Air Maps at Shoreham, where his home was.

There followed three glorious years of regular flying, always in either G-AGTP or G-AGXT. The Austers were originally Cirrus-powered and at the end of the day's work we would often be weary both from the noise and the tediously slow progress. In 1960/61 G-AGXT was re-engined with a Gipsy Major 1C, as was G-AGTP a year or so afterwards – what a difference in performance *that* made.

Subjects included new towns (including Stevenage, Bracknell, Hemel Hempstead, Basildon and Harlow), dozens of sewage works, power stations for the Central Electricity Generating Board, the new Severn and Forth road bridges and countless new roads and bridges all over the British Isles. Memorable trips include 7½ hours flying in one day in G-AGTP, photographing CEGB sites in the north of England with Mike Buxton, on August 8th 1962.

In 1962 the company was once asked to carry out some aerial survey work, something it had never undertaken before. All our commissions had been oblique photography, carried out with a hand-held F.24. The company's Anson 1, G-AMDA, already equipped with an Eagle 9 for aerial mapping, was flown down from its Burnaston base at Derby, and for several weeks I acted as camera operator on a number of survey flights.

My first trip in the Anson took place on May 4th 1962; I shall never forget walking up to the aircraft while the pilot was running up the Cheetahs almost to full bore and seeing the way that the tailplane, seemingly inches from the grass, flapped violently in the slipstream. The pilot for the Anson trips was John Schooling and on this first sortie we flew 3 hr 15 min, carrying out work for British Railways and calling in at Hamble for fuel. Other flights followed, mostly photographing Basingstoke and Swindon, then quite small towns that were destined for expansion, the survey photographs being taken to determine where the expansion was going to take place. The "cloth bomber," as we dubbed the Anson, was also used by CPL students for twin-engine training and this wonderful machine was kept very busy. On long photographic trips the other crewman and I played cards at the navigator's table. Having spent a few years with the Skyfame outfit at Staverton, when it was invariably flown by John Schooling, old G-AMDA is currently at Duxford, but sadly it will never fly again.

In September 1962 Derby Aerosurveys went bust, but Lady Luck was just around the corner. One of Elstree's private owners was Keith Ewart, who owned a TV commercial advertising studio in Chelsea. He also owned Aiglet Trainer G-AMMS, which had previously been owned by Jimmy Edwards. He was keen to run the aircraft on the company, and I was asked if I would like to carry on with my aerial photography, using his aircraft and the darkroom facilities in Chelsea. Would I?!

There then began a long and happy association with Ewart Studios. Former Elstree CFI Bill Bailey (his christian name *was* William) always did the flying, and life went on much as before. Compared with the Autocrat the Aiglet Trainer was a lively little machine. Its bigger engine and shorter-span wings gave it a more sprightly performance, particularly in the climb. One job was for the Stevenage Development Corporation, who wanted to monitor the use of some new car parks, and we were asked to take aerial photographs every two hours throughout one particular Saturday, April 13th 1963. We flew a total of four hours and had become pretty fed-up with Stevenage by the end of the day!

In 1964 Keith decided to change the Aiglet Trainer. Wanting to buy British he fancied the recently-introduced Beagle Airedale and was at first interested in buying the bronze prototype G-ARKE, probably because the last two letters of the registration bore his initials. But this never materialised, and in May 1964 he purchased Airedale G-ASAH. Although old 'MMS is flying to this day, most of the 40-odd Airedales built have disappeared. All one can say about the Airedale is that, like the proverbial brick outhouse, it was well-built and strong. We used to fly it with the door off, but it was not much of an improvement over the Aiglet Trainer. Keith kept it for five years; its replacement proved to be far more exciting, *and* it had a personalised registration. Cessna 337 G-AWKE was our camera aircraft from 1969 until I stopped flying in 1971 to take a job with "FLIGHT INTERNATIONAL."

CHAPTER 26

HERALD FUN AT HANDLEY PAGE

by

John de Uphaugh

[NOTES ON THE AUTHOR: John de Uphaugh joined the de Havilland Aeronautical Technical School at Astwick Manor, Hatfield, in 1951, subsequently transferring to the Airspeed Division at Christchurch where he spent four happy years doing his best to ruin the production of Ambassadors, Vampires and Sea Venoms, as well as working on jig design for the Sea Vixen and enjoying duty as flight test observer from time to time with George Errington in the Ambassador.

There he learnt to fly at Tommy Marshall's Christchurch Aero Club, instructed by John Pothecary, Jack Elphick and Ron Hayter, and soloing in Taylorcraft Plus D G-AHUM, pictured in the previous volume with its nose in a hedge. Subsequently he worked at Handley Page in the sales and publicity department (hence the words which follow) until that company's sad demise, which prompted a departure to non-aviation pastures.

Today he owns a piece of the ex-Irish Air Corps Provost based at Shoreham and is much involved with the de Havilland Moth Club's Mainwaring Volunteer Force – and if you don't know about that group of stalwarts, it's about time you did! They need you to help run events like Woburn, without which no vintage flying year would be complete.]

I was lucky enough to do a fair amount of flying in the three first Dart Heralds, namely G-AODE, G-AODF and the venerable G-APWA, recently restored by the enthusiastic Herald Society team at Woodley.

That was in the late fifties and early sixties. Happily the timing coincided with the early sales tours and, as a youngster fresh from the de Havilland Aeronautical Technical School and National Service, I found myself working for that amiable and much respected Head of Publicity at Handley Page's Cricklewood headquarters, Hugh Scuffham.

Naturally no time was lost in volunteering for any travel assignments. These usually involved being responsible for making movies, taking photos, organising the local publicity effort and being general dogsbody. That included, on a tour to West Africa and South America, the duties of purser, which meant handing out the daily cash allowance everyone was due and settling the hotel bills. No mean feat in the days before credit cards and when inflation in Brazil was so rapid that room rates changed weekly, and sometimes daily. This was in the spring of 1960.

My other tasks included taking the fuel consumption readings during the staging trips. To do that, one stood between and behind the pilots during take-off and approach & landing. All very exhilarating, but hardly up to CAA approved safety standards.

I will make no attempt to document those sales trips and the route-proving exercise on BEA's Highland and Islands network, since that has been done in Cowell's excellent book on the Herald ("*Handley Page Herald,*" Jane's, 1980). However some more personal memories may amuse.

I first flew in a Herald (G-AODE) on 16 June 1958 with Hazelden in control on a demonstration flight to Ansett Airlines, but the first time I flew in Whiskey Alpha was on 2 December 1959. We were detailed to give a demonstration flight to Onassis in his role as owner of Olympic Airways. It being near Christmas, and he being tucked away in Monte Carlo, his request was to be flown to London for a little shopping.

The message was that he would bring some friends and "an orchestra."

We positioned at Nice (overflying the sobering sight of the devastation created by the Frejus Dam which had burst its wall with much loss of life in storms two nights previously) and awaited events. The friends turned out to be Prince Rainier of Monaco and Princess Grace. They carried their own bags to the aircraft which impressed us no end.

What impressed us even more was the orchestra. This comprised various black-tied gentlemen from the Sporting Club de Monaco, bearing violins, an accordion and other musical impedimenta (this was mid-afternoon).

Off we went with John Allam at the helm. The distinguished passengers seated themselves in the tail (luckily as events turned out), demanded that a couple of rows of seats be removed for dancing, and called for music and refreshment. Some bright person back at Cricklewood had had the foresight to ensure we had an air hostess on board, I think from British Air Ferries, and a rare party developed.

All was well for the first hour. Then the cockpit filled with smoke. With thoughts of the engine fire which had written off the first prototype on its way to Farnborough, there was a rush to examine the exterior of the Darts with torches pointed through the darkness from the cabin windows – discreetly of course. The presence on board of a potential customer with a bigger bank balance than Crœsus made us all bob a bit.

The smoke got worse; indeed it was so bad that the crew had to don oxygen masks. The order went to the valiant hostess to keep the champagne flowing, which she did, bottle in one hand and air freshener in the other. Luckily the distinguished guests in the rear remained unaware of the panic. Equally luckily the source of the smoke was identified as an electrical fire in the instrument wiring and was extinguished.

Blissfully ignorant of the fracas, our VIPs were decanted (probably the appropriate word after the doses of champagne and air freshener) at Gatwick, to the pop of countless flashbulbs.

Those photographers were nearly my personal undoing. Being determined to get some pictures of my own for the HP archives, I nipped out of the back door and headed towards the front, from which our guests were emerging. Blinded by the flashbulbs, I forgot the spinning prop which blocked my way. Luckily the mechanic positioning the chock reacted quickly, kicking my feet from under me. Measuring my length on the tarmac I felt foolish, but at least I was still in one piece.

HP got a lot of press coverage the next morning, but as we know Onassis never unbuttoned his wallet. And I never discovered how the "orchestra" got home.

Despite that experience, the Herald proved to be a remarkably trouble-free aircraft, especially when operating with little support under difficult conditions on its tours. The only other incidents I recall were a broken trailing link on an undercarriage main leg which caused some violent shimmy on landing at Radlett one day, and a variety of burst hydraulic pipes, one of which meant we had to use the emergency back-up compressed air to lower flaps and undercarriage when returning to Rio de Janeiro one night.

It is a pity the reliability failed to get the venerable Sir Frederick airborne very often. I got quite used to VIP potential customers like King Hussein being delivered to the steps of the aircraft with a cheery "See you when you get down." I never saw "HP" fly. Can anyone shed light on this apparent aversion? Quite unlike his chief research man, that extraordinary pioneer Gustav Lachmann, with duelling scars on his face from student days at Göttingen University, who used to sit in his eyrie at Cricklewood dreaming of laminar flow wings and telling any young visitor like me in his thick German accent about "ven I had my famous spin." He always claimed, probably correctly, to have been the first-ever pilot (in around 1910) to survive this early killer of pioneer aviators. Others say the Englishman, Lieutenant Parke, had this dubious privilege. But I tended to believe Doctor Lachmann, if only because he was always honest enough to say that the only reason he discovered the secret of recovery was because he was so scared that, as a last resort, he reversed all the controls.

Days on the so-called "Two Continents Sales Tour" in West Africa and South America provided more than their fair share of amusement and excitement. Our pilot for that period was Rex Shilton who, whilst arguably not quite as able as Hazelden at flying the Herald close to, or outside, the performance envelope, nevertheless put on some sterling performances into and out of tiny and appalling airfields, particularly in Brazil. At most of these the Dart Herald was the first ever turbine-powered visitor and huge crowds used to collect. Persuading them to disperse before take-off was always a problem, Brazilians not being noted as having a high regard for danger.

Shilton invariably cut an engine on take-off, sometimes before we were airborne, and this never failed to impress the spectators and the guests on board because, as one Cruziero Captain remarked: "In these circumstances in a DC-3, engine failure on take-off must be presumed not to be a possibility." That was because most of the strips were too short to hold that aircraft down until reaching the 85 knots below which you can do nothing if an engine fails. A DC-3, well loaded, will happily fly itself off at much lower speeds (and indeed had to in these conditions) leaving a significant time on initial climb-out sweating until the 90-plus single-engine speed is attained. No wonder the pilots used to mutter: "Trust in God and Pratt & Whitney."

Several times I sat in the right-hand seat with Panair pilots and marvelled at the way they operated a DC-3 on a single-pilot basis. Just managing the engine controls on take-off seemed (and usually is today) a full-time job for a P2. And the obvious control misharmonisation and pure brute strength needed was awe-inspiring. Those huge, low-geared but ineffective ailerons were most of the problem. When a wing dropped the large control wheel – large to give the pilot leverage – often needed to be rotated through over a hundred degrees, crossing arms in the process, before the wing reluctantly decided to pick itself up. Interesting to reflect that in Brazil not only was there nothing between the mule and the DC-3 but that thirty-five years later the DC-3s are still happily flying in outlandish places and the Heralds which were to replace them are mostly long since grounded.

Those Brazilian airfields were of poor quality, short and rough dirt strips covered with loose stones, often with hills all round and severe adverse gradients. Others rejoiced in long unmown wet grass. All normal stuff for the DC-3s and Curtiss Commandos which rumbled in and out overloaded with people and livestock, but a sharp test for the Herald. Also, the fields were often difficult to find – the maps were somewhat erratic. When found, there was usually no indication of runway length. The guest pilots from Varig, Cruziero, Panair etc. had little idea either. They knew that Dakotas got in and out and usually chose the worst field on the network to see how this new 'feederliner' would cope.

Shilton developed a method of overflying the field at 50 feet at a set speed whilst one of us wielded a stopwatch to time the strip length. This gave a figure which was either within limits or not. One day we tried this trick at Cabofrio. The result was marginal, so we decided to try the best of three just to be sure. It proved to be just outside limits so we diverted to nearby Saquerema, an airfield on the coast with sufficient length and a spectacular approach past a beautiful little church on a steep hill just off the threshold. This was the long wet grass variety and, as we slithered to a halt, I saw from my window alongside the main leg a prone body.

Our nosewheel had passed one side of him, the main leg the other. We taxied to the terminal hut, suggested that airfield employees should be discouraged from taking siestas on the field and tried to instigate a square search in the long grass to find the unfortunate fellow and rouse him from his slumbers. This was met by firm refusal. The field was crawling with snakes. Anyone dumb enough to walk there was bound to be bitten, as in all probability our supine friend had been. Eventually a tractor was produced and a recovery party set off, including yours truly who can hardly be called a snake-lover. However I was the only person with any idea of the man's whereabouts. We did find him; he was in a bad way, though whether from snake bite or the local snake oil, I never did discover.

Snakes seemed an unfortunate feature of that tour. At the very beginning I arrived at the Ikeja Arms at Lagos Airport, tin-hutted home to countless West African travellers at that time. Heading gratefully to the swimming pool in the heat I found the pool boy fishing out, as well as the usual drowning geckos, a large and active snake. I settled for a shower instead. (Years later, an ex-BOAC Hostess who regularly stayed at the Ikeja Arms said that reading this story reminded her that on one visit she did not bother to unpack and put her kit in the chest of drawers, which was just as well because the roomboy told her on the next visit that a green mamba had been kipping in one of them.)

On recounting my swimming pool encounter to WAAC's about-to-retire Chief Engineer, he told me I was unlucky. In all his years in Africa he had only once seen a snake and that was very dead. It happened that he climbed into his car one morning and pressed the starter button, only to be greeted by the slow grinding noise which indicates a flat battery. It was a cold morning, so that seemed reasonable. On opening the bonnet to check said battery he found that a long, and obviously cold, fellow had wrapped himself round cylinder block and fan belt for a warm night's kip. Activating the starter had turned the fan into a bacon slicer and ended his peaceful night's rest.

Apart from snakes, my main memories of Nigeria, Ghana and Senegal are the excitement of the 'smell' of Africa so often remarked on by travellers (once experienced never forgotten), and the ever present 'ju-ju.' At Jos Airport a tree stood sternly and dangerously on the runway threshold. It could not be cut down because it was good 'ju-ju.' Peculiarly, native Nigerian pilots then beginning to make their appearance as second officers on WAAC's DC-3s were bad 'ju-ju,' possibly a local rationalisation of downright incompetence. The magical art of flying was, to the locals, best left to Brits. In those days of tail-wheel aircraft, passengers boarded first. Then the pilots entered the same back (and only) door, clambered past their flock up the steeply-sloping floor to the cockpit, being careful to wear pristine white shirts to disguise the hangovers which many flying men seemed to suffer from permanently in that part of the world, and nodding left and right to increase the impression of confidence since this would be their only contact with passengers on what would probably be a very turbulent flight.

If, as I saw one day embarked for Jos, a pilot was Nigerian, all his fellow countrymen instantly got up, muttered something like: "I'm not flying with *that* fellow," and clambered in reverse out of the back door, leaving the few Europeans to stoically sweat it out, greatly aided by a couple of Catholic nuns telling their rosaries. Probably unfairly, black piloting skill was directly equated with their demonstrable inability to conduct a bus or lorry along the road safely. And in Accra the British flying community used to happily gather in the Airport bar in the evening to watch the antics of the Ghanaians being trained on Chipmunks. To be fair it seemed their bounces and general incompetence were no worse than at any *ab initio* training school and certainly no worse than mine.

But back to South America. My diary and logbook show that a wide variety of local airline and military pilots flew the Herald, including the then head of the Brazilian Air Force, General F.A.C. de Mello. One of the things which greatly impressed those who piloted Whiskey Alpha out of Rio's domestic airport, Santos Dumont, was the fact that though the runway pointed directly towards the city's famous 1,430-foot-high Sugarloaf mountain, just two and a quarter miles away, the Herald could achieve what the assembled Dakotas, Constellations, Scandias and Commandos could not, namely plough straight over the top, Darts whining happily, whilst the local machinery executed a sharp turn to port down Guanabura Bay.

Indeed this party trick attracted photos in the Rio papers and small crowds were known to gather to watch. Perhaps they were also prompted by a less fortunate exhibition by a US Army Globemaster at that time. Fully laden it headed down the runway, its pilot having forgotten to lower take-off flap. Its tracks crossed the fence at the runway's end and continued down the beach before entering the sea. I recall that those on board had a lucky escape, which is more than could be said for the US Marine Corps band who were flying in for a visit by the then American president and who all lost their lives in a mid-air collision over the Bay in bad weather.

Weather was a great problem over Guanabura with its two airports with almost overlapping circuits and, for those days, very high traffic densities without the benefit of radar or real ATC. It was found that when things got crowded in bad visibility, the only answer was for the pilots to talk to each other and sort themselves out. Needless to say things could get very noisy and excitable. Never more so than in the couple of days surrounding the official opening of Brasilia as the country's new capital, which coincided with our visit. Aided by the good offices of our Ambassador in Rio, Sir Gerald Wallinger, the Herald was roped in to provide transport up to Brasilia for the British Embassy party and the Ambassadors or representatives of Ceylon, Canada, Australia and South Africa, accompanied by Peter Hogg from the "DAILY MAIL" and some-one, whose name my diary does not record, from "Auntie BBC." The date was 20th April 1960.

Sir Gerald carried on board a very impressive old Locks' hat box, which indicated to me that at least one member of the party would be correctly dressed for the ceremonies. Not a bit! He revealed the contents to be a Primus stove, a tin of baked beans and other assorted essentials for survival in this new capital city.

He was wise. His hotel was splendid, built on stilts over the lake which is a feature of Brasilia. The electricity failed that evening and it transpired that there were no stairs, only lifts. Sir Gerald and Lady Wallinger were the only people who got supper and the story was that the whole diplomatic contingent had to be retrieved the next morning for the ceremonies by the Fire Brigade ladder.

What is certainly not legend is that a Grand Prix was a feature of the celebrations, contested by all the best Ferrari and Maserati drivers of the day. It was to be run up and down the huge dual carriageway linking the new airport with the city centre and round the roundabouts at either end. Problem number one was that the race was to be run clockwise around the circuit, that is to say in the opposite direction to the normal traffic flow. Problem number two was that nobody closed this main traffic artery for the afternoon practice session, which coincided with our drive in from the airport. Contraflow Ferraris at full chat make an exciting spectator sport, much in the Brazilian mould!

On our return to Rio on April 22nd with our distinguished passengers, we did our best to contribute to the general celebrations with a wonderful beat-up of crowded Copacabana Beach which is indelibly etched in my memory. The ever-present excuse to monitor the fuel meant a grandstand view from the cockpit. The other, and infinitely more memorable, beat-up was at the waterfalls at Foz do Iguaçu, which form the meeting point of Brazil, Argentina and Uruguay and which lay claim to a greater water flow in flood than any other.

We navigated there with difficulty in very bad weather and found the airfield eventually in driving rain. Then, unlike today when the falls are on every tourist and film-maker's itinerary, the field at Foz was the short, long-wet-grass variety, though the snakes were confined to spectacularly long Anaconda skins forming a frieze around the arrivals hut. It was a twenty-mile journey on a dirt track in a jeep to the falls, though today I believe there is a two-lane highway. Oh! the joys of unspoilt pioneering travel.

A main feature of the falls is a mile-long winding valley in which the river runs below the falls. This leads in a long funnel up to the Devil's Mouth – the main falls themselves. It was decided that this gorge was well wide enough for the Herald and we flew up it below the level of the surrounding plateau, and pulling over the top, enjoying ourselves so much that Shilton did it twice more, once up the gorge again and once over the top the other way, when the feeling of vertigo going over the falls was distinctly disturbing. I tried my best to photograph this excitement but it was in the days before shutter cocking and film wind were interconnected. Hence most are at least double-exposed.

After that we went on to Argentina and Paraguay, but my diary records little worth recalling, except the note that I had to pick up "orchids for Volkert" in São Paulo. You have to get the priorities right: Chief Designers matter, even when they wear gardening hats.

Also, as I discovered later, we were departing Buenos Aires' Ezeiza airport at precisely the moment when the Israelis were smuggling out the kidnapped Eichmann. Finally, after refitting the long-range tanks and loading fuel drums into the Herald at Recife, strapped like sleeping gourmands to the seats to be flown to Fernando do Norona in the Atlantic to provide staging fuel on the haul home to Dakar against the current winds, those of us not essential to the aircraft's operation flew on a Panair do Brasil DC7-C, PP-PDO, to Dakar, there to meet Whiskey Alpha for the journey home to Woodley by way of Las Palmas and Gibraltar.

If these notes seem a little light-hearted and lacking in technical detail it is simply because these trips were enormous fun, and probably very hard work as well. But you forget the bad and boring bits and rejoice in the privilege of being part of a never-to-be-repeated experience.

CHAPTER 27

A PENGUIN IN THE EYRIE

by

Dennis Bird

[NOTES ON THE AUTHOR: Born in 1930, Dennis Bird grew up with the RAF in his own home. From 1940 to 1946, airmen and officers of No. 277 Air Sea Rescue Squadron at Shoreham were billeted on his family. As a result, he chose the RAF for his National Service in 1949. He liked the life so much that he took a permanent commission and served until 1968, retiring as a Squadron Leader. He had postings to Egypt and Germany, was several times a Station Adjutant, and twice served as PA or ADC to air vice-marshals.

He then joined the Home Office as the most junior of mandarins, and was on a team getting a Bill through Parliament with Merlyn Rees, MP (also ex-RAF). For seventeen years he was on the staff of the Civil Service College, latterly as senior lecturer in Parliament and Government.

From 1959 to 1978 he was also part-time skating correspondent of "THE TIMES," covering many international championships and four Winter Olympics, including 1976 when John Curry won a gold medal for Britain. He is now the official historian of the National Ice Skating Association of Great Britain.

He has also competed in TV and radio quiz shows, from "Double Your Money" (1963) to "Mastermind" (1975) and "Brain of Britain" (1995). He has written several books, and with Tim Webb co-authored "Shoreham Airport, Sussex," published in 1996.]

Whenever I say I was in the Royal Air Force for almost twenty years, I am always asked: "What did you fly?" My reply is that I flew a desk, for I was in the Secretarial Branch. As a wingless Bird, I was a penguin in the eagles' nest. However, in those two decades I managed to accumulate some 120 hours of flying time as a passenger.

The thrill of one's first flight is never forgotten. I was posted to RAF Felixstowe, which then housed the Marine Aircraft Experimental Establishment (MAEE), and on 6th July 1950 I took to the air for the first time

302

– not from any mundane airfield, but from the waters of Harwich Harbour. A launch took me and the crew out to a Short Seaford, a development of the wartime Sunderland. Flight Lieutenant Doug Butler was the pilot, and I was allowed on the flight deck as we raced across the water until we were 'on the step' and took off. We flew over Walton-on-the-Naze, and I had my first sight of those mysterious islands nearby which the Swallows and Amazons surveyed in Arthur Ransome's *"Secret Water."*

The sensations of flying were much as I had expected. Always an avid reader of aviation literature, I had anticipated the build-up of speed and then the great surge of power as Doug pushed the four throttles forward and we rose up from the waves. The only queasy moment was when we banked over Felixstowe; I looked inwards and downwards, to see the myriad houses and the moving dots that were cars and people – and for an instant the Seaford's wing seemed almost to move backwards as we did a tight turn and headed off to Walton.

Felixstowe was a fascinating station, and one of my happiest postings. The CO of MAEE was a much-decorated officer, Squadron Leader Frank Squire, DSO, DFC – generally known as "Squib." He could look quite intimidating, with a searching gaze and with odd outcrops of hair on his cheekbones. They must have been hereditary, for they can be seen on his son – now Air Marshal Sir Peter Squire. But, belying his appearance, Squib was a most kindly man and at the same time a fine pilot and leader.

His unit had a remarkable diversity of aircraft – Short Seaford and Solent flying-boats, and Seagull and Sealand amphibians. We also had the Saro SR.A/1, the single-seat jet fighter flying-boat designed for use against the Japanese but never needed. I believe only three were built. One (TG267) crashed in tragic circumstances when Squib's predecessor, Squadron Leader Ken Major, was killed while practising for a Battle of Britain air display in September 1949. One (TG263) still survives in the Imperial War Museum's collection at Duxford, and I do not know the fate of the third. *[According to the historian Bernard Martin, TG271 hit an object while alighting off Cowes in August 1949; the hull holed and the aircraft sank in the Solent. Presumably the remains could be salvaged if some intrepid divers would like to try! – Ed.]*

The RAF unit was only a part of MAEE; as its name implies, it was a research institution, with a large complement of civilian scientists and aeronautical engineers. By this time, the RAF's interest in marine aircraft was waning, but there was still a good deal of flying to be done, and frequent liaison with various manufacturers. Geoffrey Tyson, Saro's chief test pilot, was a frequent visitor.

Felixstowe had a number of lodger units. There was No.1103 Marine Craft Unit based in Felixstowe Dock, and a small contingent of the RAF Regiment. We also parented the most famous station in the history of radar: RAF Bawdsey, a few miles up the coast. But by far the most important unit was the Metropolitan Sector Operations Centre at RAF Trimley Heath, which was responsible for the air defence of the whole Greater London area.

This *pot-pourri* of units could have degenerated into wrangling factions, but in practice it worked quite well. We lived in a friendly atmosphere of give-and-take, and we all knew who was boss: the formidable Station Commander. He was a red-headed Welsh navigator, Wing Commander Dilwyn Henry Thomas DSO, DFM. His fierce ginger eyebrows and moustache gave his brick-red face a daunting aspect, reinforced by his clipped speech and strict sense of discipline. He was a martinet, but a fair one, with strong views on morality, politics, and life in general. It did not surprise me to learn that in retirement he stood for Parliament. What did amaze me was that he stood as a Liberal.

I was sorry to leave Felixstowe in the summer of 1951, and did not much enjoy my next posting as P3 Officer (in charge of airmen's personnel records) at RAF Oakington, near Cambridge. This was a flying training station – No.206 Advanced Flying School, with Gloster Meteor 7s. Fortunately my time there was short, for in February 1952 I heard I was on "P.W.R." – that is, my name was on the Preliminary Warning Roll for an overseas posting within the next few months. When my posting to the Middle East came through, it had obviously been sent by someone at the Air Ministry with a sense of humour. There were three names on the same signal: Flying Officer D.L. Bird, Flying Officer R.D. Catt, and Flying Officer N.A. Fish. I was to meet Roy Catt briefly during my overseas tour.

On a Saturday in mid-June 1952 I was off on my big adventure: two and a half years in Egypt. I left RAF Lyneham just before 18.00 in a big comfortable Handley Page Hastings TG607. In forty minutes we were over Cherbourg; we flew over France in fading light, and so I did not then get a first sight of the Mediterranean. We landed at Luqa, Malta, just before midnight for a two-hour stop – and there I had a shock. As I emerged from the aircraft into a velvet-black night, I seemed to be engulfed by a tidal wave of suffocating heat. How ever was I going to survive 30 months of this?

Fortunately, I never experienced anything quite so bad again. The Egyptian climate is hot, but it is a dry heat, not humid, and one soon becomes accustomed to it. I remember once seeing the thermometer at 110°F but it seemed not much more than a very hot day in England.

We took off from Luqa at 02.00 and landed at Fayid in the Suez Canal Zone at 07.30 local time. I was taken by coach to my temporary base, RAF El Hamra near the Great Bitter Lake, where I was to spend three nights under canvas, in a tent with a brick-built base. Here I met a very old friend. Len Healey DFC, DFM, was something of a boyhood hero of mine when he lived with us for the best part of a year in 1943-44; now a Flight

Lieutenant, he commanded his own unit at El Hamra. Later in my tour, Len and I were to serve together under the same squadron leader.

This was not a good time to be coming to Egypt. Britain's relations with that ancient country were far from friendly. In October 1951 the Egyptians had abrogated the 1936 treaty which gave us the right to station our Forces there; they wanted us out of their country, and we were not going to leave. Guerrilla warfare broke out in the Canal Zone. Attempts were constantly made to blow up British military installations. Vehicles were likely to be ambushed. Telephone cables were dug up and cut (sometimes this was rather to be welcomed: nagging voices from HQ were temporarily silenced at the remoter stations).

Everyone was in a heightened state of readiness. Camps were surrounded by high barbed-wire fences; perimeters were constantly patrolled. To travel anywhere by road, there had to be at least two vehicles and four armed guards.

The political situation became even more confused five weeks after my arrival when King Farouk was overthrown by a military coup. The nominal leader of the revolution was General Mohammed Neguib, who became Egypt's first President, but the real instigator was a much younger man – Lieutenant-Colonel Gamal Abdel Nasser. The world was soon to hear more of him.

My first posting in the Middle East Air Force (MEAF) was to RAF Shallufa about six miles north of Suez. Like Felixstowe, it was a station of lodger units; its main flying function was to provide facilities for "Sunray." This was an exercise codeword. Squadrons of Avro Lincoln heavy bombers flew out to us from England for month-long detachments, during which they practised bombing on the desert ranges. No one told me the details of this, and on my first Saturday night at Shallufa I was alarmed to hear loud explosions which were clearly only a few miles away. Was World War III about to begin?

I soon learned the reassuring truth, and settled down to a happy posting as Station Adjutant. I even managed a little flying. We had no aircraft of our own, and the Lincolns were too busy to offer joyrides, but the Station Commander was sometimes able to borrow from the HQ MEAF Communications Flight at Ismailia. Thus I had a couple of hours as passenger in early 1953, in a Proctor and then an Anson. Both times my pilot was my CO – Wing Commander David Lumsden, the finest man I ever served with, who became a lifelong friend; he had earned a DFC on D-Day pressing home attacks on enemy warships which were trying to hamper the invasion fleet.

My time at Shallufa was sadly cut short. The unwitting cause of my departure was the CO's wife, Rhoda. She was the hostess at a cocktail party in our Mess, to whom various VIP guests were invited from

Command HQ. She asked me to look after the Senior Air Staff Officer (SASO) and his wife for the evening. So I did.

Some months later, in March 1953, I was unexpectedly summoned to HQ MEAF. What terrible crime had I committed, I wondered, as I was driven the 40 miles or so up the Canal road to Ismailia. I was interviewed by the SASO himself, and it turned out he was looking for a new Personal Assistant. Previously he had had *pilots* as PA – men of action who were unfamiliar with the administrative demands of the SASO's office. When offered yet another aircrew officer, he had exploded in a manner with which I was to become all too familiar, and had said: "I want a Secretarial officer who can keep the (expletive deleted) files straight – like that adjutant at Shallufa." He had remembered me from the party.

That was how I came to be secretary, valet, and general factotum to Air Vice-Marshal G.R.C. "Cocky" Spencer. I was never able to decide whether or not I welcomed this turn of events, and Rhoda certainly felt some remorse when I recounted to her and David some of the more extreme eccentricities of Spencerean behaviour. He was an impossible man to work with – or so I at any rate found. He was a real heavyweight, tall and burly, with a grizzled moustache and little eyes that frequently popped with anger. He had an unusual command of invective; his favourite epithets to those he despised are just not printable here! When angry he went purple in the face, jigged up and down in his chair, and smashed his fist on the table.

And yet, through him, I had a unique insight into some of the political and military problems of the Middle East – particularly concerning the negotiations with the Egyptian Government over a new agreement about the use of the Suez Canal base. As the man in day-to-day command of MEAF's air operations, he was closely concerned with getting the best deal possible for the future. He also had to cope with problems over Israel, Jordan, Cyprus, Syria, the Persian Gulf, and the Buraimi Oasis. Foreign Office telegrams flowed across his desk and mine, and we had to be in constant touch with the British Middle East Office and with our Army and Navy colleagues. As a junior Flying Officer, I found all this high-level work somewhat awesome, but thoroughly fascinating.

There were also opportunities to get airborne. Egypt's virtual blockade of the Canal Zone meant that many desirable goods were scarce, so every so often SASO would present me with his wife's shopping list and say: "Take an Anson from the Comm. Flight and go over to Cyprus." So off I would go to buy eggs, fruit, consumer goods, and other desirable items in Nicosia. Sometimes I would cadge a lift with the Commander-in-Chief (Air Chief Marshal Sir Arthur Sanders); sometimes the Comm. Flight would lay on a special navigation exercise to cover the trip.

Once AVM Spencer piloted me himself – an experience not to be repeated. We were flying in a DH Devon to my old haunt – Shallufa – on an official visit. The air marshal had a gammy leg, and suddenly it seized up on him, provoking a rich outburst of colourful language. Fortunately it settled down again, and we landed in one piece.

In January 1954 I managed to escape from SASO for a few weeks home leave. There were three Vickers Valettas going home almost empty, and I managed to get on one of them as 'supernumerary crew.' The standard route was known as the 'milk run,' from Fayid to Malta via El Adem (Tobruk), Benina (Benghazi), and Castel Benito (Tripoli) – and every time, on landing, which was roughly at three-hour intervals, the crews would receive the standard Transport Command meal of fried eggs and bacon.

We had an unexpected experience on the leg to Luqa, flying over the bright blue Mediterranean. Suddenly there was the most almighty bang, and looking out of a porthole I saw flashing lights dancing up and down the starboard wing. "Whatever was that?" I asked a passing crew member. "Oh! we've just been struck by lightning," he said nonchalantly. "Doesn't matter – we're not earthed."

We reached Malta mid-afternoon, and I spent the night at Luqa's Air Movements Hotel – or part of the night, for we took off again at 04.45. We landed fifteen minutes later – faulty plugs. (Transport Command's motto: "If you've time to spare, go by air.") We finally got off at 08.00, landing after 4½ hours at Istres, near Marseilles. Here I saw some interesting and unfamiliar French aircraft: the four-engined Languedoc airliners, the experimental supersonic Leduc 010, Dassault Mystère fighters, and a Lioré et Olivier LeO 45 bomber. Another four hours later we landed at Lyneham in Wiltshire, at 17.00 GMT.

I had flown home on what the RAF called an 'indulgence' passage. No convenient return flight from England was available, so I decided to pay my own fare to Malta a few days before my leave expired, and then sit there in the hope of another free flight. Accordingly, on 13th February 1954 I left Heathrow in BEA's Airspeed Ambassador G-ALZT *"Sir John Hawkins"* and flew via Nice to Ciampino (Rome). There I changed flights, and whom should I meet but an old friend from Felixstowe days, Flight Lieutenant Athol McGrath – a New Zealand Pathfinder who had earned a DFC in Bomber Command. We flew together in a Malta Airways Vickers Viking, G-AIVD, and he invited me to spend a day with him and his wife in their flat in Qui-si-sana, Sliema – right beside Valletta Harbour. That passed my time in Malta very pleasantly, and early next morning I was lucky enough to catch a Transport Command Valetta flight to El Adem and Fayid. (Curiously, the town of Valletta is spelt with two 'l's but the aircraft with only one.)

Back at Ismailia, AVM Spencer and I mutually decided that the time had come to part company – much to my relief. My last months were spent in HQ MEAF's Organisation 1 branch, working as Deputy to the Squadron Leader to whom my El Hamra friend Len Healey reported.

I was able to do a little more local flying, in Proctors, Devons, and once in a Percival Prentice. And on 22nd July 1954 I had two of the most enjoyable flights of my life – brief trips in an Auster. You really felt you were part of this little three-seater, which responded to every puff of wind like a sailing dinghy.

My two and a half years in Egypt ended in November 1954. By then the new Anglo-Egyptian agreement had been signed by Colonel Nasser and the British Foreign Secretary, Anthony Eden, under which British forces were to withdraw from the Suez Canal Zone with a right to return at times of international crisis. My last few weeks were mainly concerned with the move of HQ MEAF; they went to Cyprus, and I returned to England. But not quite at once: taking off from Fayid at 06.30, our Handley Page Hastings had to turn back after half an hour in need of an engine change. That gave me a few extra days at El Hamra to see old friends. Finally I got off in a Skyways Avro York, and after a two-hour stopover in Malta arrived at Stansted, Essex, at 18.00. So ended my tour of duty in Egypt: a chequer-board of good and bad, but generally to be recollected with pleasure.

My next posting was as Adjutant to a small CHEL Type 52 radar station at Hopton, near Lowestoft in Suffolk. This was one of the most tedious postings of my career, and I determined to get myself out of it as soon as possible. The CO teased me by saying I would probably do the usual 2½-year tour, but when he went on leave, events moved swiftly. A signal came from HQ No.12 Group at Newton, Nottinghamshire, calling for volunteers for the post of ADC to the Air Officer Commanding. I put my name forward, was accepted, and was able to tell my CO that he would be getting a new Adjutant.

Just promoted to Flight Lieutenant, I left for RAF Newton on 6th February 1956. 12 Group, Fighter Command, was responsible for the air defence of the middle part of England, from Wales to Great Yarmouth. The AOC's main task was to ensure the operational readiness of the fighter squadrons in our group and the effectiveness of the C and R (Control and Reporting) radar system. At that time most of our squadrons flew the reliable Gloster Meteor, but No.56 Squadron at Waterbeach had recently converted to the new Hawker Hunter. It was a splendid aeroplane, but there were serviceability problems in those early days which caused the AOC much concern.

Any ADC or PA job depends almost entirely on the personality of the air marshal whom one is serving. I could not have wished for better than Air Vice-Marshal William "Paddy" Crisham. In only one respect was he like "Cocky" Spencer: both had quick tempers. But Paddy's occasional rages came and went in a single explosion; next minute he would take you by the arm and say: "Let's have a drink in the Mess."

He was a Southern Irishman from Galway, with all the Irish warmth, charm, and generosity. He was passionately fond of horse racing. One day I mentioned how broad-minded he was to allow the Communist "DAILY WORKER" to be among the newspapers available in his HQ. "Communism be damned," he said: "they've got the best tipster in the business!"

The other memorable character at HQ No.12 Group was Johnny Kent, one of the leading participants in the Battle of Britain. Group Captain John Alexander Kent, DFC and bar, AFC, Virtuti Militari (Poland) was a tall, upstanding, well-tailored man whose impeccable Oxford accent disguised his Canadian nationality. Before the war he earned his AFC as a test pilot – he had over 200 types in his logbook – and in the Battle of Britain he shot down 13 enemy aircraft and commanded the Polish wing based at Northolt. At Newton, he was our SOA (Senior Officer in charge of Administration), a not-very-demanding job which he regarded as a comedown. As ADC, I had a lot to do with him without in any way being under his command. He was not an easy man to work with. Supremely competent himself, he had no time for fools or knaves – or those who disagreed with him.

He was always very kind to me, and as he often had little to do, he would come into my office for a chat. He had a fund of good stories, which he told with humour and a neat sense of timing. One of the grimmer ones concerned a young Pilot Officer who had served with him before the war in No.19 Squadron. His name was Neville Heath, and he ended on the gallows in 1946; he was the notorious Bournemouth Chines murderer.

I accompanied the AOC on all his formal inspections of the stations in the Group. Johnny Kent often came too. We went by road if the station was near, but more often we flew. On the day we went to RAF Ringway (now Manchester International Airport), the AOC flew himself in a Meteor, while Johnny piloted me in the Anson. As we cruised over the Derbyshire hills, Johnny gave an exclamation of alarm. "Oh! God!"

"What's happened?" I asked.

"The AOC's had a flame-out."

He was in radio contact with the AVM, who could be in serious trouble. The Meteor's two powerful Derwent turbines gave it a cruising speed of over 400 mph; if one of the engines went out, its asymmetric flying characteristics were not easy to handle. But Paddy Crisham, although in a desk job at the time, had kept his hand in as a pilot, and he was somehow able to re-light the dead engine. It was with some relief that we greeted him at Ringway; he was as cheerful as though nothing had happened.

On these AOC's inspections, naturally each station was expected to be at its best. Usually they were, and Paddy – although strict – was always glad if he could give a unit a good report. He was not one to find fault for form's sake, so long as he was satisfied that everything was operationally 'on top line.'

However, one of our visits became so like an Ealing comedy film that it sticks in my mind to this day. The Station Commander had been a much-decorated war hero, but his grasp of administration was slight. His station seemed to take its tone from him; if ever deadlines were missed or some organisational mix-up occurred, it was usually that station that defaulted.

It was Friday the 13th when we carried out the AOC's inspection, and things went badly from the start. Criticisms could be made – and were – of the turnout and drill on parade, and the subsequent inspection of the camp left a lot to be desired. The AOC drew me aside.

"Go and set off a fire alarm," he said, "and let's see what happens."

What a pantomime! Alarm bells and sirens went off; and airmen hurried here and there. The fire picket turned out and dashed into action. The driver climbed into his seat in the fire engine and pulled the self-starter. The knob came away in his hand, followed by a long piece of wire.

Undaunted, the airmen seized a hose and fitted it to a hydrant near the supposed fire. It happened to be a two-headed hydrant and the hose was on the wrong head. Nothing came out of the nozzle; the water just gushed straight into the ground from the other head. However, hose and hydrant were at last properly connected – and we all had to dodge as AOC, SOA, ADC, Station Commander and others were all generously sprayed before the water-jet was properly aimed.

After Newton, my postings included a spell at RAF Bicester as an accountant officer (not at all the sort of work I found congenial) and then as a works services officer at HQ Bomber Command, High Wycombe. Then came another thoroughly enjoyable overseas tour as Station Adjutant at RAF Butzweilerhof in Germany. Butzweilerhof was the original civil airport for Cologne, and it was where Neville Chamberlain landed in 1938 on his way to meet Adolf Hitler at Bad Godesberg. I was by now married and with a baby daughter, so was entitled to a married quarter – and I have seen a photograph of our house in Ikarostrasse with Neville Chamberlain driving past, in a Mercedes decorated with swastika flags.

I flew out on 4th January 1961 from RAF Manston, in a Silver City aircraft – the Handley Page Hermes G-ALDU *"City of Gloucester."* We landed at Wildenrath, near Mönchen Gladbach, and a car took me to "Butz." This was another of those lodger unit stations, like Felixstowe and Shallufa, and again proved a good posting. The airfield was not ours; under NATO arrangements it was run by the Belgian Air Force. We were responsible for a number of non-flying units, the most important of which was No.5 Signals Wing – an important "Sigint" (Signals Intelligence) Unit.

The Station Commander, to whom I was Adjutant and Personal Assistant, was a most colourful character. He was Wing Commander Clive Beadon, a bomber pilot in the war who had earned a DFC by bringing home his crippled Liberator in extraordinarily difficult circumstances and thereby saving the lives of his cew. He looked exactly like the film actor Cecil Parker (*"The Lady Vanishes," "Captain Boycott"* etc.); he was clearly a public-school product with an upper-crust accent and the air of one born to command. He was inclined to form instant judgements, and I often had to restrain him. When hearing charges against airmen, he was apt to make up his mind before hearing the evidence; and he once wanted to write to a High Court judge to tell him what his decision should be in a court case. I had to point out that this might be contempt of court.

He was a most entertaining man to work for. One never knew what he would do next. He bred chinchillas – a delicate species of animal sold for its fur – and his German secretary Ingrid Lasser spent much of her time arranging meetings with fellow enthusiasts. He was also an enthusiastic sub-aqua diver, and later in life he developed a talent for water-dowsing.

Sunday 13th August 1961 was one of the most dramatic days in the history of post-war Europe. It began innocuously enough. The RAF Butzweilerhof Motor Club had organised a rally, and Wing Commander Beadon decided to take part in his large and stately Armstrong Siddeley Sapphire saloon. I was pressed into service as his navigator, and his young son John came too.

There was a radio in the car, and soon it was disseminating highly disturbing news. The Communist Government of East Germany, scared by the constant drain of their citizens escaping to the West through the four-power city of Berlin, had overnight erected a high concrete wall around East Berlin, to imprison their people. The Cold War had suddenly taken a new and sinister turn. Was this the prelude to more provocative Russian action against the NATO powers? Would Nikita Krushchev order an assault on the Allied zones of West Germany?

Wing Commander Beadon reacted like Sir Francis Drake at Plymouth. Even if a Russian attack was imminent, he would finish his car rally. We had an uneasy lunch at Herchen, drove on to Much and the autobahn to Cologne, and returned to Butzweilerhof at teatime. We finished 12th out of 23 – and the Russians did not come. But the Wall stayed until 1989.

Early in 1963 the AOC RAF Germany sent a signal to all stations, urging all personnel to take part in a special *"Double Your Money"* TV quiz which Hughie Green (an RCAF pilot in WW II) was running in West Berlin. I volunteered, and with others was selected to compete.

On 2nd April 1963 we took off from RAF Wildenrath in Percival Pembroke XF799 of HQ 2nd Tactical Air Force communications squadron, and flew up the Berlin corridor a little behind Mr Green's Cessna 310. Then our pilot, Flight Lieutenant Roger Streeton, received disturbing news over the radio: Hughie had been shot at by a MiG 15. Would we meet the same fate? It was a dicey half-hour before we landed intact at RAF Gatow at 16.35. Fortunately, our flight plan had been properly cleared with all the authorities concerned, including the Russians. Hughie's – through no fault of his own – had not. Consequently the Russians had sent up fighters to investigate, and had fired warning shots. Later, in the Officers' Mess bar at Gatow, Hughie gave us a vivid account of his adventurous flight.

Hughie died in May 1997, and among the obituaries and tributes were two letters in the "DAILY TELEGRAPH" which amplified this incident. David Miller (7th May) wrote: "He entered the Berlin air corridor and within minutes was being buzzed by two Soviet fighters, which flew across his flightpath, rocked their wings, and raised and lowered their undercarriages as a signal for him to land. When he had ignored all these, they fired seven bursts of cannon fire close to his aircraft. Green flew steadily on and landed according to plan at RAF Gatow. It was generally recognised at the time that he had shown a considerable degree of *sang froid* in very hazardous circumstances. But although the Allies lodged strong complaints, the sole Soviet response was that they had 'no objections to the aircraft's *return* flight.'"

In the next day's issue a BEA First Officer, A.C. McLauchlan, added that Hughie had called up the USAF air traffic controller "in considerable alarm at being intercepted, saying: 'They're shooting at me!' The pragmatic American inquired: 'Are they hitting you?' 'Negative!' The controller said, 'Then in that case they are not shooting *at* you.'"

I doubt if Hughie appreciated the difference. He was certainly – and justifiably – angry when he told the story in the Gatow mess bar.

He was a complex personality, as the obituaries recounted. On television he came across as a maudlin sentimentalist ("I mean that most sincerely, folks," he would say, wringing his hands). But as I remember him, he was shrewd, forceful and incisive.

In *"Double Your Money,"* if you had got through as far as winning £500, you either risked everything by going for the £1,000, or you chickened out. That's what I did. Hughie later told me what the questions for £1,000 were – and I would have failed!

So I have only happy memories of him. After all, I took £500 off him!

CHAPTER 28

EITHER SIDE OF FIFTY

(NAMING THE TOP SIX MEN THIS CENTURY)

by

Lewis Benjamin

Now that the millennium fever is upon us, expect a rash of look-backs. Already a brave fool in the States has come up with a fiercely disputed list of the world's top leaders this last one thousand years. Mostly generals, no mention of Ollie North. In the shorter term there will soon be a rush to produce a line-up of the best him or her during this last century. Already Collins have published their *"Words that Define the Modern Age,"* a word a year for the last hundred. Who'd have guessed 'Aspirin' represented 1897 and 1900 saw 'Labour Party'? Latin for toil; Olde English for pain and grief. The things one learns.

So if ever there was a moment to assess our sort of top personalities it is now, especially since flying itself is approaching its own 100th anniversary.

Well, no accredited historian me, no serious books, no professorship, no nothing, but I don't see why I should be left out since I've been around for half of that period and all of it at the sharp end. So let's set the ball rolling with a modest and strictly hedged-about list of those who have stood out for *us, the ordinary bunch to whom the very sport of flying means so much.* And the collective noun means just that, those of us marooned on these islands. Some will argue that the selected few deserve a wider stage; could be. But for the sake of simplicity let's keep it home-grown. Another hedging precludes the heavy metal, the commercials have a different song to sing. No, our field embraces men who were not just leaders but men fired by a genuine belief. Men – sorry, no ladies just yet – whose driving force made them dedicate so much to our movement: who gave us light aviation this century.

My parameters too tight? I think not. The men I have in mind often headed up organisations to further their word and often with never a sniff of profit in sight, although presumably it wouldn't have been sniffed at if it *had* reared its head. Profit was never the object. Enlightenment was. So before I move into the realm of aviation consider the movements that

313

have stayed the course in similar vein and in so doing inspired others to venture out. You see, I believe that with one important exception – this briefly with aviation in mind – no real contender for our top men ever succeeded without an organisation to promote their direction.

Baden-Powell, of beloved memory – at least to an ex-patrol leader – led the field at the turn of the century with the Scout movement. And a particular favourite of mine, William Booth of the Salvation Army. Favourite? Well as a young airman away from home in wartime, the "Sally Ann" was everywhere dishing out cups of tea, bars of precious chocolate and friendship. There's a debt I could never repay. It's OK, I'm not really meandering from my point, but just pausing long enough for you to appreciate the founding concepts that perhaps encouraged the flying movement in those early days. For along with the men whose names became aviation legend there often dwelt within them a touch of evangelism – shades of Booth and "B-P" – towards their particular flag, and this conviction carried their followers forward with a fervent enthusiasm.

I will offer up two lists, each of three men. The first trio covers the period 1900-1939. The war that started in '39 then in effect divided the century. The second takes us post-war in 1946 to the century's end. True, there's a couple of years to go yet, but I'm acting on the fair assumption no one is going to get in on the act at this late stage.

The first half of course was never such. Flying began in 1903, was strictly in the experimental stage and stayed that way until the eruption of WW I, which got flying going with a vengeance in the following four years, although private flying didn't actually begin till 1925. Arguably it started when a Dr Reid of Canterbury bought an SE.5A in that year for his own private use. True, there were light aeroplane trials in 1923/24, but it wasn't until Capt. Geoffrey de Havilland built the incomparable Moth in '25, the first *practical* light plane, that things literally took off.

There followed a spell of pure magic. Fourteen years into which so much was crammed before another war interrupted, fourteen golden years of accelerating achievements. My selection therefore has something of the chicken and the egg about it. For instance, was the seed of interest sown whilst attending one of Alan Cobham's Air Circuses that toured the length and breath of the Kingdom in the mid-thirties, or was it the well-publicised opening of airfields from 1925 onwards, the direct result of the Director of Civil Aviation's hands-on policy? The Director, AVM Sir Sefton Brancker, was one of the country's most charismatic personalities with his declared intent of opening an aerodrome in every town in Britain for light aircraft. Both men shared an enormous pioneering spirit. They are both contenders.

Then, outside of my original criteria, looms the unforgettable figure of Henri Mignet, yet how can anyone ignore his influence on our embryonic

314

movement? I did mention an exception. He and his Flying Flea almost single-handedly introduced home-building to this country. He was also the exception in that he founded no national organisation to further his ideals, yet his belief in his tiny aeroplanes carried the nation into raptures of emulation. It was as if every man could fly and, better still, build his own aerial mount right there in his home: and how they tried. An unprecedented excitement took hold, aided and abetted by the "DAILY EXPRESS"; there were at times scenes of near-national hysteria that predated the Beatles and Spice Girls. It was in the end to prove a flash in the pan of time, but even more seeds were sown.

Whatever came first, the idealism of these men saw a widespread surge of interest. Airfields, courtesy of Sefton Brancker who, poor fellow, was to die in the R101 tragedy in 1930, laid the ground work.

It was he who also thought through the idea of a Civil Air Guard, a trained reserve of pilots in case of another war. Their training took place alongside and with the flying clubs, offering training to the 'A' licence, the forerunner of today's PPL. Their very being owed everything to Brancker.

Certainly the would-be pre-war pilot didn't lack for choice in his training. Thanks to a subsidy (Brancker again), a licence with the CAG cost £25, with the conventional clubs around £40. At one stage in 1938 you could get a licence for £14 providing you learnt on what was then called an ultralight – a BA Drone for instance. Ah! sweet memory. Go on, say it, what do you know? But, believe it or not, the same requirements for the 'A' licence were current in the early post-war years, and mine in 1946 cost – I think – a princely £1. No test was asked since I was RAF-trained, and the one question I was asked I got wrong – well, some of it. Ask and thou shalt get. I got.

In parallel with power-flying there grew the sport of gliding. Here Latimer-Needham, who founded the London Gliding Club, which in effect saw the start of the national gliding movement, must surely be considered. And what of Geoffrey de Havilland who gave us the Moth? Perhaps he didn't lead and personally inspire to the same degree, yet his brilliance was instrumental in much of our movement's history.

Names spring to mind to be considered and reluctantly rejected. Claude Graham White, C.G. Grey, even Moore Brabazon, and what of the record breakers, Amy Johnson, Jean Batten and Jim Mollison? We cheered, we loved, but none in my opinion approach that incomparable trio who made it all happen.

In the case of AVM Sir Sefton Brancker, Director of Aviation, that champion of civil flying, his star shone brightly for a brief but unforgettable dozen years. That short, jaunty, dapper and relentless striver for our cause must be a finalist.

Sir Alan Cobham. Now there's a name to conjure with. What a full active life he led. A brilliant pilot, a pioneer surveyor of early air routes –

proof of his exceptional airmanship – but above all it was his national recognition as the man who brought light flying into the public domain with his touring air shows that earns him his place. If he alone of the three sought a profit – after all he had wages to find – I doubt he ever made one. And if he did it probably only lasted till the next washed-out air show.

Last but not least, that irrepressible little man Henri Mignet. True, he wasn't from the UK, but his influence over here was such that he became a household name with his highly different Flying Fleas. Without any doubt he was the founding father of all the home-builders. While his aeroplane was never the success it might have been, the enthusiasm he engendered was the catalyst for so much to follow. He's right up there in the top three. For followers of this brief, hilarious and sometimes tragic chapter of history do read Clouston's *"The Dangerous Skies."* His chapter on Flea-flying is a classic of its kind.

To Brancker, Cobham and Mignet then, those great pioneers, a belated and hearty vote of thanks. The second half though isn't so easy. If hindsight helped me with the first three, it won't with the second. Ah! well, in for a penny, in for a pound.

*   *   *

It's not easy to sit back at my ease fifty years on and remain completely dispassionate as I report on the past. Too many friends, too many memories must be put to one side to ensure a reasonably sound judgement. Lovely word that – "reasonably." I fear a touch of bias lies in every heart. Never mind. Then I've used the word "movement" to describe our sport. It's a clumsy word and doesn't begin to convey the essence of what it's all about. On one hand it embraces all the flying clubs. Yet again it's called upon to cover the almost unseen legions of home-builders, every one of whom fires up the adventure of DIY. Include too the countless supporters who so often do no more than read magazines and follow air shows, but they all count, all united by a love of flying. It soars above the mundaneness of our earthly world. Escape if you like. And still I haven't covered what "movement" means. Gliding, microlights, hang-gliders, there's a wealth of expression out there to compress into a word, no matter how inadequate.

Over the years each of these disciplines has gathered to itself a "movement" – I'm beginning to regret even starting with the word: it's a long list. The Royal Aero Club has gathered under its wing twenty-five associations and clubs. Big, small, they all cater to a different following, yet it's essential in this quest for the best to get down to the nub, to establish which did the most to encourage this ever-growing movement.

Notice I no longer say "who" at this stage. In the first half of this century it was the few individuals that attracted a following. Characters who led the way in a community of flying that was small enough to be considered "family." Everyone seemed to know of everyone else, almost literally, for in spite of the growth of interest in the thirties we are still looking at something of a closed shop. The explosive growth occurred in the second half. I fumble for realistic statistics. By 1939 a total of some 22,000 licences had been issued since the year dot. But of that number how many were still flying in 1946? 7,000? And today? Well, guessing that some 3,000 PPLs were issued each year, that gives a total of roughly 150,000, of which say half are still valid. 75,000. It's a big ten-fold gain.

That's it. No more guesstimates, because that's what they are. The only reason I drag them in is to illustrate a growth from the fairly close-knit to the present growing horde of followers for whom it is no longer a person's name that registers but the name of an association or club.

If I've made a case it is that the second half of the list comprises followers of an *organisation* rather than a character recognised by a helmet-clad figure on the front page of a newspaper. Where are the famous names of today? With the exception of the early space-walkers and the ever-young Chuck Yeager few are household. Pity, but true. Yet these great leaders do exist to lead us forward. They take some identifying but they are the ones I seek.

Let's narrow the field. Two organisations stand above all in the formative years of the forties and fifties. They were there at the start, are still with us, and both were – in my opinion – the top sowers of interest in light aviation after the war.

And one of them is not the Royal Air Force. Although the RAF trained tens of thousands of pilots, relatively few stayed to fly light aircraft. Some became instructors and even they petered out with age and as their well-worn flying jackets became obsolete with the coming of enclosed machines.

Nor was the Royal Aero Club the other. Popular leadership and inspiration was never their scene. For many they were too elitist, instead they represented, and still do, a useful umbrella. If I were to pinpoint RAeC personalities in this second half it would be Bev Snook, a vibrant Chairman, who also saw the RAeC into its bicentenary in 1985, and the irrepressible John Blake, *the* air show commentator. But an umbrella organisation, with no aircraft and no airfield of its own, is seldom suffcently hands-on at the sharp end, in spite of arranging our national air races.

Discount too officialdom. No leader has emerged from the busy HQ of CAA bureaucracy to equal a real civil *servant* such as Sir Sefton Brancker, who so actively encouraged our sport. The cheerful lot at the Civil Aviation Authority (and individually they *are* a cheerful lot) are too entangled in an empire-building web of regulations. Personal initiative has long fled. Heaven knows how many faceless ones are needed these days to control each and every hapless pilot. Tears stain my log book for what might have been, or the leadership they might have shown. It's a tough old world, isn't it?

Once upon a time there was a fiery editor who thundered his opinions in "THE AEROPLANE." His sharp voice was heard and heeded in the land, but then aviation in the thirties was smaller and the few carried more weight. C.G. Grey's memory has been kept alive, for his equal, and there is one, has in turn fought against foolish legislation for over twenty years, his pen an illuminating probe; but bureaucracy, frequently his target, is too strong, too self-supporting to listen to a near-lone voice. Yet the editor of "PILOT" magazine will not be subdued. Long may James Gilbert continue to see the wood for the trees.

The two organisations that remain when all is said and done are the Popular Flying Association and the Tiger Club, and thanks to these two outstanding outfits the gloom that might well have settled on sport aviation post-war has been banished. The more I delve into the past the more fascinating becomes the task I've set myself; so many facets, for the many channels that flow ever outwards and ever stronger have original links that tie one to the other to the common good.

The Popular Flying Association, founded in 1946, was the first. Four men got together in London to encourage ultralight flying under the banner of the Ultra Light Aircraft Association. The concept was of course a continuation of the thirties thinking, i.e. the lighter the aircraft, the cheaper to fly, the better to gain the hours for a licence and so encourage ordinary folk to get airborne. The cheaper the better was still the thinking in the middle forties. Come to think of it, it still is.

After some months of exploratory meetings one man took control. His was a natural selection. The saying "the right man at the right time and in the right place" comes to mind. In 1946 Group Captain Edward Mole was in his prime, just forty, still with the RAF and with a sound career behind him, one that had started at Farnborough in 1928 as a Scientific Officer. A natural progression from observer in oft-dangerous flying experiments, he entered the RAF to become a pilot. The war years eventually took this gifted pilot and engineer to an offer of an overseas posting with the rank of Air Commodore. He turned it down to be seconded to BOAC to become manager of their new Flight Development branch at Hurn. Now here was a pilot with 148 different types to his credit who had never forgotten the joy of simple flight; who better to put his skills to a new movement?

There has always been a common denominator between those great men of pre-war years and those that followed. All shared a lifelong belief in the future of light flying. Not only was Edward a founder member of a gliding movement – British Certificate No.6 – but he was in his own right one of the country's leading glider pilots. (Who else but a believer would have established a world record of 147 consecutive loops in a glider whilst on service in Egypt in 1938?) If it wasn't gliding it was powered flight. In 1930 he started with a Parnall Pixie for which he paid £52-10s. It was the first of many.

No way am I trying to write a potted history, more a lightly sketched background to the man who by his natural command and drive firmly established what was to become the finest flying association in Europe.

There were perhaps two keystones of the PFA's subsequent growth. The first was the agreement of the authorities to allow ultralights to operate without the expense and complication of first obtaining a Certificate of Airworthiness. It was here that Edward's authority and standing stood the youthful ULAA to great effect. With the issue of the simpler Permit to Fly awarded on the Association's recommendation, the first great step forward had been taken.

The second, and the one that was to prove so far-reaching, was the permission to accept home-building, with the final inspection by a voluntary band of ULAA-licensed inspectors. A bonus to help the builders along was a supply of 24 pre-war JAP engines of 36 hp arranged by Edward with a loan from the Kemsley Trust.

It was all so long ago, yet these sound decisions by an unassuming man driven by a vision (sadly Edward Mole died in 1997 aged 90) was to set the PFA (it became that circa 1952 when the Association embraced co-ownership flying groups and was able to persuade the authorities to allow them to operate as private owners rather than as proprietary clubs) on solid ground to be developed in the fullness of time by the second man of the trio: "D.F.B."

No man can do it all. It needed many fine friends and supporters to contribute to that vital development period of the Popular Flying Association: that and the good fortune to find a second man of Edward's calibre. David Faulkner Bryant – ever after known as "D.F.B." – was to rally the troops for no less than seventeen years as Chairman. Essential years. When "D.F.B." took over, the membership stood at 1,000. There was no money in the kitty, no HQ. When David stood down the membership had grown to around 7,000, there was a third of a million pounds in the bank, they had a fine HQ at Shoreham Airport with ten permanent staff and the largest annual Air Rally in Europe.

Bare statistics. But what of the man and what of those intervening years? It was DFB who originated the Strut system of PFA branches throughout the country, building-blocks for so much to follow. From the Struts came the new membership and the volunteers who set up the big rallies, who ran fly-ins and local events. Then DFB promoted home-building, for he was a home-builder himself. Most of the construction of his beloved Currie Wot was his. He was a pilot who flew all over Europe in his tiny single-seater representing the PFA. There were those unsung hours on endless committees, always fighting for the freedom of the air.

All was, as ever, a voluntary service that brought success to the PFA at the expense of family, business and pocket. Figuratively I guess he shrugged: it had all been so much fun. Today he is a cattle farmer on Skye, still flying, still organising. Sadly he is the only one of the post-war trio still alive. Long may his shadow never grow less.

Before I offer my last finalist I must first doff my cap to one other, who, because he became absolutely besotted with 'Moth-ery' (alright then, all things DH and little else), failed to collect sufficient points to reach the top three.

Mention Stuart McKay, and the de Havilland Moth Club pops to mind. He and the Club have become inseparable. With a late start in the mid-seventies the Club, its world-wide membership with their colourful mounts, is today perhaps as strong as it will ever be. Never question their enthusiasm, just that the ravages of time must eventually reduce the number of irreplaceable Moths of every kind. Brief words, but they recognise widespread support for this *crème de la crème* of vintage clubs.

And the last name? Ah! the last. There is where my heart betrays me because I've saved the strongest of the three till last. And his name was Norman Jones.

There used to be a regular feature in Readers Digest, *"The Most Remarkable Character I Ever Met."* Real characters are few, indeed it's not easy to define them, but they exist, believe me, and when you've met one you know it. Norman Jones was one such. Like Edward Mole, Norman started flying in the twenties. He raced his own aeroplanes and was a member of 601 RAF Auxiliary Squadron so his grounding in flying was sound. A move to yachting around 1931, then the RORC and offshore racing eventually led to the RNVR in 1940. At the war's end he was a Lt. Commander leading a mine-sweeper flotilla. In 1954 he resumed flying and two years later formed the Tiger Club.

In the confines of a chapter, and that in someone else's book, nothing I have charted does much for the reality, but a peek into the past so often reveals the future and helps prepare you for Norman's bold un-encumbered assurance that anything was possible. I suspect he bought Rollason's Aircraft and Engines Ltd in 1956 as a sudden whim when Group Captain Rollason died, and then found himself busy renovating Tiger Moths for the civilian market. Saddled, happily, with a base at Croydon Airport and lots of Tigers he founded the Tiger Club, whose pilots used the surplus aircraft and occupied the upstairs of the big hangar. It all fell together like a dream. Foreseeing the time that the supply of RAF surplus Tigers would dry up, Norman set up a production line for the two-seater Condor and went ahead and made 50 of them.

There was a lovely story going the rounds in 1966.

"But the question is, Norman, will you ever make money out of the Condor?"

"Oh! yes, I've got it all worked out; I've only got to make them twice as fast and spend half as much on materials and I'll do it."

He also built thirty Turbulents. He was in fact a serious manufacturer. Norman used to say that whatever field of business you were in, sooner or later you would come up against a competitor backed by public funds. Doubtless he had in mind Beagle, into which the Labour government of the day poured millions. Rollason's products carried the proud slogan *"No Taxpayers' Money."*

When Croydon closed late in 1959 the Club moved to Redhill but by then the ideals were already taking shape, to foster greater public interest in light flying, and the first of the famous full displays were already being seen. But Norman Jones' fertile drive was already embracing other causes. He wished to see Britain successful in international aerobatics and designed the Super Tiger for our team and introduced the Stampe. No one did more *for*, or *to*, the DH Tiger Moth. His variants were never dull; he put one on floats and donated it to the Seaplane Club; made a cabin four-seater of another; adapted several to glider-towing; and the best one of all, his Tiger designed to place a man (or woman) on top.

It is now possible to begin to grasp what a huge contribution Norman Jones made to air awareness. The 'Standing on the Wing' act alone made the headlines. On its first outing at Panshanger in 1963 over 16,000 turned up to watch; the popular BBC outside broadcast *"Tonight"* caught the public imagination. Then later headlines: "GIRL FLIES CHANNEL ON WING." These were all grist to the mill, to the surge of interest in light aviation after years of post-war austerity. It still pulls 'em.

Norman sought further fields. The Dawn to Dusk Competition he started in 1962 is still contested annually. His early interest in air racing was resurrected when he invited Tiger Club members to enter for the National Air Races each year with a fleet of aircraft. No wonder half and more entrants were regularly Tiger Club, after all Norman had placed twenty-plus aircraft at the members' disposal. They couldn't be let to go to waste, could they? They weren't.

The design contest he offered for the best midget racer saw the winning design built by Rollasons (this in 1964); in fact Rollasons built three or four of the speedy Beta and their presence hastened the introduction of Formula 1 racing, again under the Tiger Club banner. It was all go.

Little underlining realities of Norman's enlightened outlook existed that can't accurately be quantified. Consider the upwards of 2,000 Tiger Club pilots over the years who were exposed to a form of flying that today can only exist in one's dreams. Put simply: take it; use it as if it were yours; land where you like; go where you like; no questions asked. One was merely on one's honour not to let the side down. It sounds unreal, yet it happened. Heaven knows what this liberalisation had on subsequent thinking. To have sampled such freedom, was one not honour-bound to spread the word, if not the deed? I said this one aspect couldn't be quantified.

Was there ever such a public-spirited adventurer? His horizons knew no bounds. And he *was* public-spirited you know, given to lend aircraft freely to clubs on their uppers, and on the odd occasion to make a donation of one in a good cause. For instance the British Women Pilots' Association had grateful reason to thank him for a Condor.

In 1972 he dipped briefly into editorship when he bought an ailing flying magazine called "PILOT." He ran it for a few years before the present editor took it on and developed it into the most successful magazine of its kind in the country.

If our memory of Norman Jones is to linger (he died in 1991 aged 86) it will surely be with the image of one of his Tiger Club's full airshows that broadened everyone's enjoyment of *real* light flying and introduced so many to our sport. These two-hour carefully timed non-radio shows always opened with an exciting bang when something like a Cosmic Wind whistled in unexpectedly. On order eyes switched to a stately Balbo, a tableau often of sixteen aircraft. What followed was a kaleidoscope of colourful formations, aerobatics, crazy-flying, races, balloon-bursting and girls-on-wing, every act totally within the airfield boundaries, the better to entertain and entice the spectators to feel part of the circus.

No one ever went home unhappy: the total commitment of the very real amateur professionalism of the pilots ensured that, pilots who were proud to offer the finest airshows seen in Europe. What better tribute to the man who made it all happen? I can think of none.

Perhaps Mandelson's Millennium Dome to the future will one day reveal another half-dozen, if so let's touch wood they prove as sound as Alan Cobham, Sefton Brancker, Henri Mignet, Edward Mole, David Faulkner Bryant and Norman Jones.

I sigh. Finished, but my pen stays in my hand, and I linger at my desk, unwilling to abandon my thoughts just yet. Effortlessly they escape, as they are wont to do of late, to tranquil Surrey skies. It's a late summer's evening, the air is sweet and warm, and somehow I find myself on Box Hill with the sun leaving lengthening shadows around, and I listen. An echoey pulse of aero engines grows. I wait patiently for now I know where they are. Suddenly a straggly gaggle of aeroplanes pops out from behind the Hill, out from the oh! so familiar Dorking Gap, and dance before me in the sunlight.

I gaze in delight, in wonderment. Their leader is in an Avro 504K; he flies very precisely, a little nose-high as if reproving his smaller companions for not keeping up. There's a Flying Flea out of position on his left going flat out, and on the other side is a Parnell Pixie which, whilst in nice and tight, is slowly losing ground. Behind them and a little below are three more, two much younger than their leader, a wartime relic, a SE.5A whose pilot is overcorrecting as he strives to curb his impatience to be away. His companion to port in a bright blue Turbulent is already edging away easterly as he senses home. The third is a Currie Wot, steadily dropping back but hanging in there for company's sake. The pilot, a friendly sort, waves and I wave back.

They are going home, drifting down the still sky. Imperceptably they gather speed and ease a little more to the east as Redhill's lush green field beckons. My heart is with them.

The wind is in my face and in my hair. I am once again flying the Arrow Active. A Bücker Jungmeister formates inverted beside me. The pilot grins and thrusts his arm out. I laugh and the sky around fills with an endless gathering of friends in every conceivable kind of aircraft.

The main actors have left the stage, we the audience cluster together, content in each other's company. Been there, done that. Well, haven't you?

Other aviation books published by Cirrus Associates (and available directly by mail order as well as through bookshops) include:

TAILS OF THE FIFTIES (the first volume in this series)
AN ANTHOLOGY OF AVIATION MEMORIES
compiled and edited by Peter G. Campbell, published in 1997
(ISBN 0951559834)
Price: £11.95 (plus £1.50 p/p if ordered by mail)

SHOREHAM AIRPORT, SUSSEX:
THE STORY OF BRITAIN'S OLDEST LICENSED AIRFIELD
by T.M.A. Webb & D. Bird, published in 1996
(ISBN 0951559826)
Price: £14.95 (plus £1.50 p/p if ordered by mail)

CAN ANYONE SEE BERMUDA?
MEMORIES OF AN AIRLINE PILOT
by Archie Jackson, published in 1996
(ISBN 0951559850)
Price: £7.95 (plus £1.00 if ordered by mail)

THE FIFTIES REVISITED
AN AEROBIOGRAPHY
by Peter G. Campbell, published in 1994
(ISBN 0951559818)
Price: £5.95 (plus £1.00 p/p if ordered by mail)

SHOREHAM AIRPORT: RECORD OF VISITING AIRCRAFT 1946-1970
Compiled and edited by Peter G. Campbell, first published in 1996, revised in 1998
Price: £5.95 (plus £1.50 p/p if ordered by mail)

FAIR OAKS AERODROME: RECORD OF VISITING AIRCRAFT 1952-1970
Compiled and edited by Peter G. Campbell, first published 1995
Price: £2.50 (plus £0.50 p/p if ordered by mail)

WISLEY AIRFIELD: RECORD OF AIRCRAFT MOVEMENTS 1954-1969
Compiled and edited by Peter G. Campbell, first published 1995
Price: £1.50 (plus £0.50 p/p if ordered by mail)

HAVE YOU WRITTEN A BOOK ABOUT AVIATION THAT YOU WOULD LIKE TO HAVE PUBLISHED? IT IS POSSIBLE THAT WE COULD ARRANGE TO DO THIS FOR YOU AT MINIMAL COST (PRINT RUNS FROM 100 COPIES UPWARDS). PLEASE CONTACT US EITHER AT THE ADDRESS SHOWN AT THE FRONT OF THE BOOK OR ON TEL/FAX 01747 838165.